HUMAN RESOURCES LIBRARY
FROM WILEY LAW PUBLICATIONS

SEXUAL HARASSMENT IN THE WORKPLACE
MANAGING CORPORATE POLICY

SUBSCRIPTION NOTICE

This Wiley product is updated on a periodic basis with supplements to reflect important changes in the subject matter. If you purchased this product directly from John Wiley & Sons, Inc., we have already recorded your subscription for this update service.

If, however, you purchased this product from a bookstore and wish to receive (1) the current update at no additional charge, and (2) future updates and revised or related volumes billed separately with a 30-day examination review, please send your name, company name (if applicable), address and the title of the product to:

Supplement Department
John Wiley & Sons, Inc.
One Wiley Drive
Somerset, NJ 08875
1-800-225-5945

For customers outside the United States, please contact the Wiley office nearest you:

Professional and Reference
    Division
John Wiley & Sons Canada, Ltd.
22 Worcester Road
Rexdale, Ontario M9W 1L1
CANADA
(416) 236-3580
Phone: 1-800-263-1590
Fax: 1-800-675-6599

John Wiley & Sons, Ltd.
Baffins Lane
Chichester
West Sussex, P019 1UD
UNITED KINGDOM
Phone: (44) (243) 779777

Jacaranda Wiley Ltd.
PRT Division
P.O. Box 174
North Ryde, NSW 2113
AUSTRALIA
Phone: (02) 805-1100
Fax: (02) 805-1597

John Wiley & Sons (SEA) Pte.
    Ltd.
37 Jalan Pemimpin
Block B ♯ 05-04
Union Industrial Building
SINGAPORE 2057
Phone: (65) 258-1157

SEXUAL HARASSMENT IN THE WORKPLACE
MANAGING
CORPORATE POLICY

JULIE M. TAMMINEN
Prudential Securities Inc.
New York, New York

Wiley Law Publications
JOHN WILEY & SONS, INC.
New York • Chichester • Brisbane • Toronto • Singapore

Library of Congress Cataloging-in-Publication Data

ISBN 0-471-58640-4

Printed in the United States of America

10 9 8 7 6 5 4 3 2 1

PREFACE

This book is designed to offer technical and strategic guidance on developing and implementing a preventive approach to dealing with sexual harassment—a prevalent and costly problem for employers. It will help employers to develop policies and practices that protect employees and the organization from the destructive impact of sexual harassment. As the law of sexual harassment is continuously evolving, and reasonable men and women can differ on what sexual harassment is, the only sound approach for organizations is to become educated on preventing sexual harassment and well-prepared in dealing with it.

The media have provided more extensive coverage of sexual harassment complaints than ever since the 1991 Clarence Thomas United States Supreme Court confirmation hearings, and the E.E.O.C. reported a surge in the number of sexual harassment charges filed from under 6,000 in 1987 to over 10,000 in 1992, a trend continuing to-date. In fiscal 1993, over 7,000 charges were filed.

In a 1992 poll conducted by the National Association of Female Executives (NAFE) of 1,300 members, 53 percent said they or someone they knew had been sexually harassed in the workplace. In a New York Times/ CBS poll reported in 1991, 40 percent of women responding said they encountered sexual harassment at work and 50 percent of the men responding said that at some point while on the job they had said or done something that would have been construed by a female colleague as harassment.

This book is designed to address the needs of a diverse group: human resource professionals with employers of all sizes and in a variety of employment settings; government workers and officials; educators; employment lawyers, unions, and labor relations consultants; advocacy and public interest groups; and institutions of all kinds. Every reader brings unique circumstances, needs, organizational realities, goals, and resources to the problem of sexual harassment—and each will use this book differently. Whether you are interested in developing a sexual harassment policy, investigating a complaint, training employees and managers, or familiarizing yourself with the law, this book offers practical solutions to meet your needs.

Several approaches are covered in each chapter: select the strategies and techniques that have the greatest likelihood of succeeding in *your* organization. There is no one formula for success, and as your organization's needs and culture evolve, different strategies and techniques discussed in the book may become relevant.

Each chapter covers useful action steps, a detailed treatment of each topic, and illustrations of difficult situations and suggestions on how to resolve them. Where appropriate, model language for policies, sample programs and survey instruments, checklists and other aids are included to help get you started on handling sexual harassment more effectively. The book will be supplemented to ensure that readers continue to benefit from a state-of-the-art resource.

The views, policies, and procedures recommended and discussed herein do not necessarily reflect those of my present employer. Nor does publication of the views, policies, and procedures discussed herein imply endorsement by my present employer in any way.

New York, New York   JULIE M. TAMMINEN
March 1994

ACKNOWLEDGMENTS

This book is dedicated to all of the men and women who are courageously trying to find a solution to the problem of sexual harassment, some of whom are listed below. While it is not always easy, I hope that the practices described in this book will be implemented in the following spirit articulated by Rosabeth Moss Kanter of Harvard: "Distancing men and women as though they were different species undercuts the move to find common ground."

I wish to thank the following individuals for their support and/or inspiration:

Professor Terry Bethel, Indiana University School of Law, who got me hooked on labor and employment law in the first place

Susan Brecher, Director of EEO Studies for Cornell, New York City

Professor Louise Fitzgerald, University of Illinois, Champaign

Professor Barbara Gutek, California Institute of Technology

Robert Hamilton, Human Resources, DuPont Corporation

Steven Hickok, Senior Executive Administrator, Bonneville Power Administration

Freada Klein, Consultant, Klein Associates, Cambridge, Mass.

Steven Landis, Research Associate

Jane Lang, Esq., Sprenger & Lang, Washington, D.C.

Marena McPherson, ABA Commission on Women in the Profession

Kathy A. Osborn, Senior Editor, Wiley Law Publications

Mary Rowe, Administration, Massachusetts Institute of Technology

Tom Sigerson, Esq., and Jack Sjoholm, Esq., Law Department, Northern States Power Corporation

Vicky H. Speck, Managing Editor, Wiley Law Publications

Paul Sprenger, Esq., Sprenger & Lang, Washington, D.C.

Beata Sykes, Human Resources, AT&T

Patricia Towner, Director, California Commission on the Status of Women

Ann-Marie Van Bockstaele, French professor and friend extraordinaire

William White, Director of Training & Consultation, Lighthouse Training Institute, Chestnut Health Systems

Thank you to my husband for giving up all of the weeknights, weekends, and vacations, and for sharing my belief in the importance of this project.

I invite those who have developed solutions to the problems of sexual harassment in their work setting to allow me to showcase their achievements in upcoming supplements. I am grateful to all of those who allowed me to do so in this first edition.

ABOUT THE AUTHOR

Julie M. Tamminen is Employee Relations Manager and Associate Vice President for Prudential Securities Inc., New York, handling employee relations issues for the firm's nearly 300 offices. Previously, Ms. Tamminen served as Employee Relations Officer at the Chase Manhattan Bank. She received her J.D. from Indiana University in 1987, and is a master's degree candidate in Industrial and Labor Relations at Cornell University. Ms. Tamminen has served as co-author or editor of numerous publications and has worked as a practicing attorney with special emphasis in discrimination law. She is a member of the Society for Human Resource Management, the American Bar Association, Minnesota State Bar, and the New York State Bar Association.

SUMMARY CONTENTS

DETAILED CONTENTS

CHAPTER 1

MANAGERIAL AND LEGAL CHALLENGES IN PREVENTING SEXUAL HARASSMENT

§ 1.1   Sexual Harassment: A Management Challenge

This chapter gives managers, administrators, and human resource professionals practical guidance on the managerial and legal issues which sexual harassment raises. While the aim is not to give legal advice or make lawyers out of nonlawyers, those in management positions in most organizations can greatly benefit from some basic knowledge regarding the law. This is an important component of the prevention strategy.

§ 1.2   Sexual Harassment Prevention: Where Law and Management Meet

It is useful to define sexual harassment, and even discuss some of its causes. However, managers should keep in mind that they are not expected, nor are they trained, to diagnose, psychoanalyze, cure, heal, or perform any other miracles on harassers or victims. In most cases, managers can only effectively approach the problem of sexual harassment on an organizational level, by adopting and enforcing policy, and on an individual level, by prohibiting disrespectful behavior. Appropriate referrals to other professionals with specialized expertise can always be made to assist individuals, as is discussed in **Chapter 4.** Managing sexual harassment is really about prevention built through a system that promotes respectful behavior and discourages abuse.

Once sexual harassment occurs, it is too late: careers are derailed, individuals are emotionally distressed, reputations are damaged (harassers are labeled criminals and victims are speculated to be "sluts" and emotional invalids), entire work groups are disrupted, productivity and morale decline, and the financial impact increases as the organization suffers turnover and lawsuits, negotiates severance packages, and fires managers.

While it is useful to understand some of the complexities that give rise to sexual harassment and the most effective way to resolve complaints, there is no substitute for observing the following preventive steps:

Seven Steps of Sexual Harassment Prevention

1. Encourage victims to come forward by empowering them with a strongly-stated, widely-communicated and well-supported policy and procedure. Communication of the policy should be repeated periodically in order to maintain a high level of awareness.

2. Communicate and enforce the nonretaliation policy covering complainants and witnesses in an investigation.

3. Conduct prompt, consistent, and thorough investigations with due regard for confidentiality.

4. Discipline perpetrators, up to expulsion from the organization, consistently with the nature and seriousness of their violations.

5. Keep informal channels of communication open so that members of the organization have a full range of approaches to complaint resolution, including informal and formal complaint procedures.

6. Educate and train employees at all levels on sexual harassment prevention, recognizing that nonmanagement employees, first-line supervisors, and high-level managers have different training needs.

7. Persist. Get the message out from the top down and the bottom up: sexual harassment is unacceptable—there is zero tolerance.

Each of these steps is covered in upcoming chapters.

§ 1.3   Definitions of Sexual Harassment

It is helpful to try to lend some definition to the concept of sexual harassment, as being able to identify harassment is an important preventive tool. Sexual harassment is most commonly defined legally or behaviorally.

Sexual Harassment as a Legal Concept

Sexual harassment evolved out of the law of sex discrimination. In the 1986 case of *Meritor Savings Bank v. Vinson,*[1] the United States Supreme Court recognized sexual harassment as a form of unlawful sex discrimination under the federal civil rights law, Title VII of the Civil Rights Act of 1964. It is a form of differential treatment based on sex that operates to deny individuals equal employment opportunity and poses a barrier to their career advancement. As such, sexual harassment is a major contributor to the phenomenon referred to as "glass ceiling," by impeding the upward mobility of its victims.[2] Sexual harassment impacts men and women, as was evidenced in 1993 when a male subordinate in California was awarded more than $1 million against his female former supervisor. In that case Sabino Gutierrez was sexually harassed by his supervisor, a female officer of Cal-Spas, a hot tub manufacturer, over a period of six years, including unwelcome sexual advances and requests for sex. Sexual harassment has been defined in terms of three legal theories that continue to be refined, or confounded as the case may be, through judicial interpretation.

Sexual bribery, referred to as *quid pro quo,* or this for that, involves situations where an individual's employment is conditioned, explicitly or implicitly, upon acquiescence to unwelcome sexual requests or treatment of a sexual nature. Compliance with requests bears rewards. *Example:* "this job would be a great move for you, and if you want it, you have to be prepared to cater to a customer's every desire . . . if you know what I mean. I trust an occasional night out entertaining won't be a problem, at the company's expense of course?"

Sexual blackmail whereby individual's submission to or rejection of unwelcome sexual advances, or a willingness to submit to unwelcome conduct of a sexual nature, whether verbal or physical, is used in decisions regarding an individual's advancement or other terms or conditions of employment. Failure to submit brings punishment. *Example:* "You know,

---

[1] 477 U.S. 57 (1986).

[2] In her work entitled Sexual Shakedown: The Sexual Harassment of Women on the Job, Lynn Farley states that "it is not uncommon to find working women who have left two, three, and even five or more jobs over their working career because of sexual harassment."

I'm starting to think you don't like me, and I really need someone in the new project leader spot who will be responsive. I have asked you three times to dinner, and you're still playing hard to get. And what's this brushing my hand off your shoulder when all I'm trying to do is help you loosen up a little. I'm beginning to think you're not the right candidate for the promotion."

Unwelcome conduct of a sexual nature or advances that have the purpose or effect of making it unreasonably uncomfortable or difficult for an individual to function in his or her job *or* of creating a hostile work environment. *Example:* "I can't stand the way the men in this office leer at me. I have asked them to stop, but it's not making any difference. They leave dirty jokes or cartoons on my desk almost every week, and everyone walks by, reads it, and snickers. It's demeaning, and I can't concentrate on my work anymore. Even my boss thinks it's funny and that I should just lighten up."[3] This form of harassment, often more subtle and covert than the others, has become more common and makes prevention difficult. This is because victims of more subtle harassment may be more reluctant to report it, particularly when it is "his word against hers," as is often the case. It is also more difficult for managers to address this type of harassment as they may not notice it until it is too late and escalates into a complaint or charge.

Sexual favoritism, the practice of promoting or otherwise benefitting those with whom one is intimately involved, to the detriment of those with whom one has no romantic involvement, may also constitute sexual harassment. As with all theories of sexual harassment, the reader is cautioned that the U.S. Supreme Court has thus far only reviewed one case, *Meritor Savings Bank v. Vinson,*[4] in 1986, which defined hostile work environment discrimination. State and federal court decisions are not always consistent. Sexual favoritism is a case in point, as the following examples illustrate.[5]

The theory of sexual favoritism holds that employees who are more deserving of advancement or rewards, but routinely lose opportunities to others who are rewarded because of their involvement with the boss, may have a cause of action for sexual harassment. One well-known case is *Broderick v. SEC.*[6] Catherine Broderick alleged that her office had an environment of pervasive harassment whereby female subordinates engaged in sexual relations with senior male officers, and derived benefits,

---

[3] See E.E.O.C. Guidelines on Discrimination Because of Sex, 29 C.F.R. § 1604.11 (1988).

[4] 477 U.S. 57 (1986).

[5] The U.S. Supreme Court has also reviewed the case of Harris v. Forklift Systems 114 S. Ct. 367 (1993) which poses the question of whether someone claiming a hostile and offensive work environment form of sexual harassment must prove "severe psychological injury" in order to prevail. The court answered in the negative.

[6] 685 F.Supp. 1296 (D.D.C. 1988).

including at least one promotion, because of their office romances. The court held that consensual relationships created a sexually hostile work environment when other employees who engage in the relationships receive job benefits related to those sexual relationships. This echoes the "EEOC Guidelines on Discrimination Because of Sex"[7] which provide that:

> [W]here employment opportunities or benefits are granted because of an individual's submission to the employer's sexual advances or requests for sexual favors, the employer may be held liable for unlawful sex discrimination against other persons who were qualified for but denied that employment opportunity or benefit.

However, in another case, *Mundy v. Palmetto Ford,*[8] decided by the Fourth Circuit Court of Appeals in July 1993, a terminated male employee failed to state a cause of action for sexual harassment where his boss and his female co-worker were intimately involved. The court refused to define "sex . . . so broadly as to include an ongoing, voluntary, romantic engagement."[9]

The outcome of this analysis suggests that absent a pattern of extending preferential treatment to employees who engage in sexual relations with those who are in a position to grant or withhold job opportunities, an employer may not be liable for favoritism. (See **Chapter 2** for a discussion of the related topic of office romance policies.)

While sexual bribery and blackmail may result in liability after only one occurrence, generally hostile work environment and sexual favoritism require the demonstration of an ongoing and/or pervasive practice pattern of harassment to be actionable. There are, however, instances when a single act of sexual harassment, although carrying no reward or punishment for the victim, may be serious enough to create liability, such as when an individual exposes him or herself, grabs someone's body part or gestures with his or her own body part, or seriously threatens an individual in writing or orally.[10]

The Greater Social Context of Sexual Harassment

There are countless examples of conduct of a sexual nature that are demonstrated in workplaces everyday. Society is preoccupied with sex, constantly bombarding us with sexual messages, and by nature we are curious

---

[7] 29 C.F.R. § 1604.11(g) (1988).

[8] 988 F.2d 1010 (4th Cir. 1993).

[9] *Id.*

[10] See E.E.O.C. Policy Guidance on Current Issues of Sexual Harassment, reprinted in Fair Empl. Prac. Man. (BNA) 405:6681, 6690–91.

about and interested in people's sexuality. *The Janus Report on Sexual Behavior,*[11] based on a survey of 2,765 men and women across the United States, released in 1993, presents the following findings:

- 35 percent of married men and 26 percent of married women reported having at least one affair
- 10 percent of men and 4 percent of women reported having sex with more than 100 partners
- 31 percent of those who consider themselves "very religious" have had an affair
- 26 percent of women who consider themselves politically "ultraconservative" have had an abortion
- 22 percent of men and 17 percent of women reported having at least one homosexual experience
- 45 percent of women and 19 percent of men said they have been sexually harassed at work.

Such data begs the question: how can we expect sexual behavior to not play itself out in the workplace? The challenge is to regulate it, that is, create reasonable boundaries for, the healthy and noncoercive expression of sexuality in the work environment. However, the workplace presents opportunities for abuse of power unparalleled in purely social, and consensual, settings that compels us to limit sexual interaction in work settings. While a supervisor may enjoy a sexual liaison with a subordinate, this carries with it enormous responsibility that does not exist outside of the work setting and greater risk for the subordinate, the supervisor, and the organization. Conduct that is "welcome" is not unlawful whereas conduct that is "unwelcome" is unlawful. This means that as long as the subordinate freely wishes to be involved in the relationship and there are no coercive undertones to it, the organization would not be liable, in theory. However, once the relationship is no longer welcome by the subordinate, it must cease or subject the employer, and potentially the manager individually, to liability for sexual harassment.

The legal intricacies discussed above often leave managers unable to identify what constitutes sexual harassment. The following section covers behaviors that have been found to constitute sexual harassment and briefly discusses some of their potential causes. These behaviors can be recognized, and hence monitored and controlled, by well-trained managers. They can be used in raising awareness of sexual harassment in conjunction

---

[11] The Janus Report, John Wiley & Sons, Inc. (1993).

with an organization's training efforts. (See **Chapter 6** for a discussion of training programs.)

Behavioral Definition of Sexual Harassment

Sexual harassment is often defined in terms of specific types of behavior. As will be discussed further below, defining sexual harassment in terms of specific behaviors can oversimplify matters since whether an action is sexual harassment depends on how the action is delivered, in what context, and how it is subjectively perceived by the recipient, that is, "the totality of the circumstances."[12] For example, Jim says to Linda "great blouse!" Some of the considerations surrounding this action are:

- Was Jim looking at Linda's face or leering at her breasts when making the comment?
- Has Jim made it a habit of commenting on Linda's and/or other women's appearance and body or is this an isolated incident?
- Does Jim have any real or perceived power over Linda?
- Would a reasonable person under the circumstances have been offended or intimidated by Jim's behavior?
- Is Linda offended or intimidated by Jim's behavior?

Despite the limitations of identifying behavior that can constitute sexual harassment, it is an essential part of the prevention strategy, as it offers standards against which other behavior observed on a day-to-day basis can be compared. In addition, as one commentator has noted, "[d]efinitions . . . are important because they can educate the community and promote discussion and conscientious evaluation of behavior and experience."[13]

The following is an excerpt from Ball State University's sexual harassment awareness materials, and illustrates the usefulness of behavioral definitions that apply to most employment settings.

---

[12] This standard, a combination of objective and subjective standards, was recently affirmed by the U.S. Supreme Court in Harris v. Forklift Systems, stating that "[t]his standard requires an objectively hostile or abusive environment—one that a reasonable person would find hostile or abusive—as well as the victim's subjective perception that the environment in abusive."

[13] P.L. Crocker, *Signs,* An Analysis of University Definitions of Sexual Harassment, *Signs,* 697 (1983).

Sexual Harassment: What Is It?[14]

The National Advisory Council on Women's Educational Programs has developed the following working definition of sexual harassment of students:

> Academic sexual harassment is the use of authority to emphasize the sexuality or sexual identity of a student in a manner that prevents or impairs that student's full enjoyment of educational benefits, climate, or opportunities.

Five types of activity were described by the Council as sexual harassment:

- generalized sexist remarks or behavior
- inappropriate and offensive but essentially sanction-free sexual advances
- solicitation of sexual activity or other sex-linked behavior by promise of rewards
- coercion of sexual activity by threat of punishment
- sexual assaults.

Each case of sexual harassment is unique. Although the activities listed above are arranged from least to most serious, there are no real lines between them. In fact, many cases involve several categories. For example, a student may be promised something, such as a higher grade, in exchange for sexual favors. At the same time the student may be threatened with punishment if he or she does not cooperate.

In addition, some victims may feel that some forms of harassment are more serious than others. A punishment-free sexual advance accompanied by touching might seem more threatening or harmful to some students than an offhand offer to improve a grade in return for a sexual encounter. Whatever the incident, however, any act of sexual harassment is a serious offense.

Sexual harassment can happen to anyone—male or female. And either males or females can be guilty of sexual harassment. Harassment can also take place between employees of the same sex.

Common elements in harassment cases are:

- distortion of a formal, sex-neutral relationship (e.g., teacher-student, counselor-client) by an unwelcome, nonreciprocal emphasis on the sexuality or sexual identity of the victim
- infliction of mental or physical harm on the victim

---

[14] Reprinted with permission of Ball State University.

Level of Harassment	Behavior
Sexual coercion	Unwanted physical relations
	Refusal to hire or promote; granting or denying certain privileges because of acceptance or rejection of sexual advances
	Promise of a work-related benefit or a grade in return for sexual favors
Physical harassment that contributes to a hostile environment	Unwanted touching of a person's clothing, hair or body. Examples: hugging, kissing, patting, stroking, pinching, grabbing, massaging neck or shoulders, standing close or brushing up against a person
Verbal harassment that contributes to a hostile environment	Referring to an adult as babe, girl, honey, etc.
	Turning work discussions to sexual topics
	Telling sexual jokes or stories
	Asking personal questions of a sexual nature
	Making sexual comments about a person's clothing, anatomy, or looks
	Asking someone repeatedly for dates and refusing to take "no" for an answer
	Making kissing sounds, smacking lips
Nonverbal harassment that contributes to a hostile environment	Looking a person up and down
	Prolonged staring at someone
	Giving personal gifts
	Winking, throwing kisses or licking lips
	Making sexual gestures with hands or through body movements
	Posting suggestive cartoons or calendars
	Posting nude centerfolds

When using behavioral definitions, the organization should emphasize that harassment is very much based on the specific circumstances surrounding an occurrence and that the behaviors described are only illustrative and not a complete list.

Why People Harass and How It Is Manifested

It is also useful for managers to have some insight into why people harass. While managers should not play the role of psychologist, it is helpful to have an enhanced understanding when developing training and awareness approaches.

There are several theories as to why people harass and how harassment is manifested by these individuals in the workplace.

The first theory is that harassment is a manifestation of a negative self-image or psychological insecurity, or an emotional illness that causes individuals to act out their intimate feelings and needs in inappropriate, deviant, or illegal ways, including unwelcome threats to touch (assault) and unwelcome touching of another person (battery). The situation often involves someone in a position of trust who violates the accepted limits of that trust. Examples include the male judge who constantly ogles and propositions his female clerk and women who appear before him in court; the clergyman who fondles young male parishioners; the female high school teacher who invites male teenage students to have sex with her; or the male lab technician who rubs his body up against his female co-workers', simulating sex acts.

A second theory is that sexist behavior, insensitivity, or seductive conduct has the effect of greatly disturbing another. This conduct may not involve actual touching, but may be experienced by recipients as hostile and intimidating, and disrupt their abilities to function at work. Examples include the computer programmer who transmits depictions of nude women in demeaning positions via electronic mail to women co-workers; the male executive who routinely organizes customer outings to topless bars despite the presence of a female account executive; the female boss who refers to her male secretary as "loverboy" and tells him that he looks good enough to eat and makes other lewd remarks.

A third theory is that group behavior results from an organizational tolerance of sexually-oriented or sexist behavior. William White, Director of Training and Consultation for the Lighthouse Training Institute Chestnut Health Systems in Bloomington, Illinois, advances a Systems Model of sexual harassment based upon four basic premises:

1. Sexual harassment or sexual exploitation can best be viewed as a process rather than an event.

2. The process of sexual exploitation and the sexual exploitation event that emerges from this process are ecologically nested within professional, organizational, community and cultural environments. These elements of influence can serve to promote or inhibit boundary violations in [work] relationships.

3. Strategies and programs to address sexual exploitation must reflect an in-depth understanding of dynamics through which organizations resist and experience change over time.

4. A change in one part of a system produces accommodating changes in all other parts of the system, raising the potential for unforeseen problems created by any attempt at problem resolution.

White's hypothesis is that sexual harassment is a manifestation of an organizational/systemic problem which must be abated at the organizational level, not just the individual level. He states that "it is much easier to extrude one sexual predator than to confront an entire organizational culture that has lost its service focus or has become toxic and abusive."

Manifestations of the Systems Model of sexual harassment include ritual gatherings where it is "traditional" to engage in sexually promiscuous and degrading behavior with or toward women (such as can occur at office parties, fraternities, and "Tailhook"-type conventions); manufacturing plants where posters of centerfolds, cartoons with sexual content, and other explicit materials plaster the walls, language regularly used is obscene, and sexual advances and acts on the premises are not uncommon; or a male-dominated office where women are not expected to ever advance to the professional ranks, are regularly hired based on their appearance and their perceived "easy" disposition, and are offered pay increases based on their extracurricular sexual favors, not their performance on the job. Organizations may be able to use some of the diagnostic tools described in **Chapter 5** to help gauge how sexual harassment-friendly their culture is.

The Shades of Gray Continuum

Behavior that can constitute sexual harassment may be identified in terms of a continuum. Kathleen Ryan, author of *Driving Fear Out of the Workplace,* developed a useful model, the Shades of Gray Continuum[15] to capture the range of behavior that can constitute sexual harassment. This model is used in training of managerial and nonmanagerial employees of the City of Bellevue, Washington. (The complete training program is reprinted in **Chapter 6.**)

Light Gray	Medium Gray		Dark Gray
Decorations	Comments/Jeers	Touches	Assault
Stares/Leers	Jokes	Propositions	Rape

[15] © Kathleen Ryan. Reprinted with permission of Kathleen Ryan and the City of Bellevue.

This continuum is a useful starting point for identifying harassment, but should be interpreted, as the courts remind us, from the perspective of a reasonable person of the same sex as the victim.[16] That is, if the victim is a woman, leers and jokes of a sexual nature may be sufficient to create a hostile work environment, whereas a male target may not find such actions sufficiently offensive to interfere with his ability to work. A study conducted by researchers on perceptions of sexual harassment made the following findings:[17]

Survey Items Used as Dependent Variable, Perceptions of Sexual Harassment

Survey Items	% Agreeing	
	Men	Women
Is sexual harassment . . .		
Being asked to have sexual relations with the understanding that it would hurt your job situation if you refused or help if you accepted?	94.5	98.0
Being asked to go out with someone with the understanding that it would hurt your job situation if you refused or help if you accepted?	91.1	95.8
Touching at work that was meant to be sexual?	58.6	84.3
Touching at work that was not meant to be sexual?	6.6	7.3
Looks or gestures of a sexual nature that were meant to be complimentary?	18.9	28.9
Comments of a sexual nature that were meant to be insulting?	70.3	85.5
Comments of a sexual nature that were meant to be complimentary?	21.9	33.5

The discrepancies in the perception of men and women as to which behavior constitutes sexual harassment signal a need to devise a more universal standard for behavior in work settings: respectful behavior.

One Standard: Respectful Behavior

The cover memorandum to the sexual harassment policy of the Bonneville Power Administration is reprinted in Appendix H in order to illustrate

---

[16] Ellison v. Brady, 924 F.2d 872 (9th Cir. 1991).

[17] B. Gutek and A. Conrad, *Impact of Work Experiences on Attitudes Toward Sexual Harassment*, Administrative Science Quarterly 31 (1986).

how the "reasonable person" standard can be effectively tied into a "respectful workplace" approach to dealing with sexual harassment. (The complete BPA policy is reproduced in **Chapter 2.**) Since sexual harassment is essentially in the eye of the beholder, managers must be more resourceful in trying to recognize it and in knowing their people. Other factors which help managers determine whether certain behavior is sexual harassment can include:

- the relationship of the victim and the perpetrator
- the specific nature of the acts
- the number of incidents involved (one joke or ongoing off-color jokes, for example)
- the impact on the victim (is the victim widely known to be sensitive to the particular conduct, or to be particularly vulnerable due to personal circumstances, and so forth).

Sexual harassment is often referred to as a "gray area" where there are no bright lines, no definitive answers. As the shade of gray darkens, the answer gets easier and it is likelier that the conduct is sexual harassment. This approach is discussed further in **Chapter 6** in the context of training programs.

Identifying and Preventing Harassment

No matter how it is defined, sexual harassment is a highly complex phenomenon. Individuals bring their unique desires and needs—some conscious, many not—into places of work, study, and worship everyday. Trying to predict who will harass, who will be a target of harassment, and who will bring a complaint is impossible, as:

1. Victims of harassment may not decide to bring a complaint until much time has passed. While Anita Hill's is an extreme example of this, complainants may wait a full year (commonly the time limit set by statute to make a complaint) because of the difficulty of the decision involved or other events in their life, such as transitioning into a new job if they quit the last one.
2. Over time harassers have become subtler, and it may be difficult to identify someone's inclination to harass until something of a more blatant—and serious—nature occurs.

What administrators, first-line supervisors, managers, and Human Resources professionals need to be concerned about is not so much why people harass (as it is difficult to change beliefs and attitudes), but how to keep *behavior* in the workplace respectful (as employers can legitimately regulate conduct in the workplace). While it may be difficult at times to define what sexual harassment is, respectful behavior is easier to identify and relate to. One should ask oneself: "Is this the kind of conduct that I would like to be seen engaged in on the evening news? In front of my family? Or defending on Court TV?" If the answer is "no," then it probably is not respectful behavior and should be avoided.

A standard of respectful behavior should be adopted by organizations, as new federal legislation may be introduced that will prohibit harassment against individuals on the basis of *any* protected characteristic, including race, religion, gender, disability, national origin, and so forth. (The proposed legislation is reproduced at Appendix B.) Promoting respectful behavior is also consistent with the workplace diversity initiatives of many organizations. Managing a diverse group of employees demands a greater awareness of and sensitivity to individual differences—with a concommitant increase in the number and types of behavior that can be perceived as offensive or discriminatory.

According to sexual harassment law, the impact of behavior on victims is what counts, not the motivation behind the acts. (EEOC guidelines contain language prohibiting conduct that has "the purpose or effect" of creating a hostile or intimidating work environment.) The only motivation that is relevant is whether the victim "welcomed" the behavior. Unlike other forms of discrimination against individuals which focus on the intent of the perpetrator, sexual harassment is chiefly concerned with the impact of behavior: is it offensive to the reasonable woman or to the reasonable man, under the particular circumstances?

This victim-oriented standard makes sexual harassment more challenging to manage: many perpetrators believe that it is a defense that they did not MEAN to intimidate or disturb another. However, this defense implies that the PERPETRATOR's standard for what is offensive conduct is what counts. Legally, and therefore practically speaking, the perpetrator's standard is irrelevant: what organizations and individuals must learn first and foremost about sexual harassment is that ignorance of the law is no excuse and even well-intentioned actions can give rise to liability. The legislature in crafting this law, and the courts, in intererpreting it, demand that employers be educated and educate their employees on what sexual harassment is and that it is prohibited. An example of this are the increasing number of states that have passed legislation requiring employers to train their supervisors in sexual harassment prevention and post notices regarding sexual harassment laws.[18] An increasingly important part of managers' responsibility is learning and teaching others to be more aware

---

[18] States include: Alaska, California, Connecticut, Maine, and Vermont. Further, legislation has been introduced at the Federal level that would require all employers to provide

of acceptable standards of behavior. More managers' performance reviews should include an assessment of their achievement in maintaining a harassment-free, that is, respectful, work environment.

§ 1.4 Sexual Harassment and Power

The most common, and perhaps most pragmatic way to define sexual harassment is as an abuse of power by a person in a position of authority over someone in a subordinate position. While peers do harass each other, and sometimes exercise informal or perceived power over one another, the most prevalent form of sexual harassment is that committed by individuals with *formal* workplace power—supervisors, managers, administrators, professors, and so forth. It is noteworthy, however, that power does not only emanate from official authority, but also from the greater social context. For example, a female manager of a convenience store was awarded damages under Title VII of the Civil Rights Act because the male assistant manager, her subordinate, harassed her by making advances and verbally abused her. The court explained that sexual harassment in the form of a hostile work environment can be "the product of a supervisor harassing a subordinate, a subordinate harassing a supervisor, or of harassment between two equal co-employees."[19] Therefore, building limiting processes such as "upward reviews" and "open door" complaint processes that "check" abuse of power may be effective tools in preventing harassment.

Most people work out of economic necessity and cannot afford to lose their jobs. With managers possessing the authority to hire and fire, with professors possessing the power over academic progress, with administrators possessing the power to ease the way or make the going rough, those in a subordinate position are truly vulnerable. This power relationship is critical to understanding sexual harassment dynamics.

One such dynamic involves the complaint process. Victims of harassment have no obligation to make a complaint. It is not uncommon for an organization to first learn of an incident of harassment when it is filed as a union grievance, an agency charge, or described in a lawsuit. While failure to make a complaint is one of the factors considered by adjudicators

---

sexual harassment training and education. In addition, Illinois, like many other states, requires that state contractors (those firms doing business with the state) have an affirmative action plan and a sexual harassment policy which includes training of supervisory employees. Federal legislation, H.R. 2829, "Sexual Harassment Prevention Act of 1993," has been introduced that would require all employers to post notices regarding the prohibition of sexual harassment and to educate employees on sexual harassment prevention.

[19] Cronin v. United Service Stations, 92-T-604-N (M.D. Ala. 1991).

in evaluating the credibility of a claim, or whether the alleged harassment was "welcome," it is not dispositive of a finding of liability for sexual harassment.

However, the more widely disseminated and accessible a complaint process, the more likely it is that people will come forward and the less plausible it is that employees did not know about a complaint process or did not know how to use it. (See **Chapter 3** for a discussion of how to develop an effective preventive complaint process).

Finally, there is a dynamic that many managers do not anticipate: reversal of power. What managers often do not realize until it's too late is that they also in many instances give up the power to manage based on legitimate job-related criteria and make themselves vulnerable by engaging in sexual harassment. If a manager engages in sexual harassment against subordinates and then tries to discipline them, warn them, or terminate them for poor performance, the first thing the employees will do is allege that they are being terminated because of failure to comply with sexual requests or because the relationship fell through and the manager is retaliating against them.

Many managers are unaware of the fact that in many jurisdictions, an employee need only demonstrate that discrimination was a "determining" factor in the adverse employment action—so-called "mixed motive" cases. In these cases, if the employee can show that an employment decision was motivated in substantial part by unlawful considerations, even if the employer can show that the employee's performance was poor, the employee may still prevail and be awarded damages. This means that even where there is cause to terminate if he or she can prove that sexual harassment played a substantial part, the employee can prevail.

Sexual Harassment in Academia

Sexual harassment in universities receiving any form of public funds (almost all) is prohibited by federal law under Title IX of the Education Amendments. The principal difference between Title IX and Title VII is that Title IX mandates the implementation of a grievance or complaint procedure for faculty, staff, and students, while Title VII has been interpreted as recommending a complaint procedure, as through the EEOC Guidelines or the *Meritor* case.

According to a 1988 sexual harassment study of over 2,000 participating male and female undergraduate and graduate students from two major universities, conducted by Professor Louise Fitzgerald, University of Illinois-Champaign, and other researchers, commissioned by the National Education Association:

- Approximately 50 percent of the women at one university, and nearly 76 percent of the women at the other, answered at least one of the questions in the affirmative direction, indicating that they had experienced some form of harassing behavior during their college careers.

- Five percent of female respondents indicated that they had dropped a course to avoid such situations; nearly 20 percent noted that they had avoided taking a course for this reason.

- Only 3 percent of the women attempted to report the harassing situation. Many of the students who had been harassed indicated that they felt that they would not be believed, or that they had not wanted to cause trouble and/or be labeled a troublemaker.

A similar study by the same researcher involving female faculty members and administrators found that over 50 percent of female faculty and 75 percent of female administrators had experienced some form of gender harassment in the workplace. In particular, behavior reported included "being the object of unwanted sexual advances, of suggestive stories and offensive jokes, crudely sexual remarks, seductive comments, nonverbal harassment such as staring, leering or ogling, the use or distribution of sexist material or pornography, a pattern of sexist remarks about women, and-most frequently-being treated less well because they were women."

Sexual harassment in academia is increasingly being recognized as an impediment to a successful academic experience, and many of the best antiharassment initiatives are coming from academia. A sample university sexual harassment is provided in **Chapter 2.**

An Illustration of the Reversal of Power from the Workplace

One of the most damaging impacts of sexual harassment, which managers often do not recognize until it is too late, is the way it robs them of their ability to make legitimate business decisions. The following is an illustration of this phenomenon from the workplace.

A female employee's performance begins to deteriorate. She's coming in late with no good excuse, she's demonstrating a "poor attitude," that is, lack of interest, initiative, responsiveness, and she is forgetting to follow up on important tasks, thereby exposing the organization to potential losses. She used to be a good performer, has a file with three years' worth of "fully satisfactory" performance appraisals, and used to show commitment, working more than just the "9 to 5."

The department manager wants to terminate her and is prepared to do so when he learns that she had been sleeping with her supervisor and that she recently broke the relationship off, finding it too difficult to work for and be sexually involved with the same person. The manager learns that the supervisor has since started up a sexual relationship with another employee in the office. The manager weighs the facts of the female employee's declining performance against the fact that he may have to face a sexual harassment lawsuit that the organization might lose if he fires her. He is trapped: he should be able to terminate her for documented poor performance, but what if she claims that her performance is suffering because of retaliatory treatment by her supervisor after she broke the relationship off—and what if it is substantiated.

The manager will have to undertake an investigation of the matter, either on his own or with the assistance of the "big guns," a time-consuming and disruptive process. He may have to terminate or discipline the supervisor, someone he was counting on to be an important player in the department's future, and/or he may have to find a way to separate the supervisor and the female employee by transferring one of them out to a different office. Given the female employee's negative feelings toward the organization, he may have to negotiate her out of the organization entirely with an expensive separation package and a signed release of liability.

Supervisors should be educated on the risks of becoming sexually involved with a subordinate. They should be held accountable for their actions, professionally and financially. Supervisors who sexually harass may be on top while they are involved with their subordinate, but they can end up on the bottom themselves, when they are at the receiving end of a sexual harassment lawsuit, or graver still, a criminal charge for assault or rape. Many careers have been destroyed by such charges.

Section 1.5 will discuss in greater detail some of the legal considerations that managers need to know to be well-prepared to manage and prevent sexual harassment in their organization.

§ 1.5 What Managers Need to Know about Sexual Harassment Law

It is difficult to effectively manage or prevent sexual harassment without having a basic understanding of some key legal concepts. Depending on the setting of your organization, private vs. public sector or union vs. non-union, some of the applicable laws may differ. The differences lie mainly in the impact of remedies available to complainants and procedural matters. However, the concepts are all similar.

The laws governing sexual harassment include federal, state, and local laws, including: Executive Order 11246, Title IX of the Education Amendments, Title VII of the Civil Rights Act of 1964, and Civil Rights Act of 1991, Section 1983 Protection. See Appendix I for a listing of laws.

In addition, there is a vast body of common law, based on the state courts' interpretations of the law, that help to define sexual harassment and offer insights into how to prevent sexual harassment and avoid liability.

There are several legal issues that can arise in conjunction with a sexual harassment claim, including for assault, infliction of emotional distress, wrongful termination, negligent retention, and defamation of character. These are referred to as common law claims, law developed through the state's judicial process, and are thereby distinguished from statutory claims which originate from legislation. The state law claims are explored further in § **1.6.**

Equal Employlment Opportunity Commission (EEOC) Guidelines

The EEOC is the federal regulatory agency charged with enforcing the federal civil rights laws, including Title VII of the Civil Rights Act. According to the EEOC Guidelines,

> prevention is the best tool for the elimination of sexual harassment. An employer should take all steps necessary to prevent sexual harassment from occurring, such as affirmatively raising the subject, expressing strong disapproval, developing appropriate sanctions, informing employees of their right to raise and how to raise the issue of harassment under Title VII, and developing methods to sensitize all concerned.[20]

Although the EEOC Guidelines are advisory in nature and do not require employers to adopt a sexual harassment policy, most employers recognize the utility of a policy, training, and a user-friendly complaint procedure in preventing sexual harassment and in reducing the organization's potential exposure to liability.

In pertinent part, the EEOC Guidelines make the following points with respect to determinations of liability for sexual harassment:

- Employers, employment agencies, joint apprenticeship committees, or labor organizations are responsible for their acts and those of their agents and supervisory employees with respect to sexual harassment regardless of whether the specific behaviors complained were authorized or even forbidden by the employer and regardless of whether the employer knew or should have known of their occurrence.
- With respect to conduct between fellow employees, an employer is responsible for acts of sexual harassment in the workplace where the employer (or its agents or supervisory employees) knows or should have

---

[20] Equal Employment Opportunity Commission, Guidelines on Discrimination Because of Sex (29 C.F.R. § 1604.1 *et seq.,* 1990).

known of the conduct AND FAILS TO TAKE IMMEDIATE AND APPRO-
PRIATE CORRECTIVE ACTION (emphasis added).

- An employer may also be responsible for the acts of nonemployees with respect to sexual harassment of employees in the workplace, where the employer (or its agents or supervisory employees) knows or should have known of the conduct and fails to take immediate and appropriate corrective action. In reviewing these cases, the Commission will consider the extent of the employer's control and any other legal responsibility which the employer may have with respect to the conduct of such non-employees.

The Guidelines have been widely accepted by the courts, administrative agencies, and arbitrators for use as the standard by which to determine liability. Given that employers are stricly liable for the acts of their supervisors and are potentially liable for the unlawful acts of non-supervisors and nonemployees, developing a strong anti-harassment program makes good business sense.

The Guidelines include the following definition of sexual harassment:

Harassment on the basis of sex is a violation of Title VII of the Civil Rights Act of 1964. Unwelcome sexual advances, requests for sexual favors, and other verbal or physical conduct of a sexual nature constitute sexual harassment when:

(1) submission to such conduct is made either explicitly or implicitly a term or condition of an individual's employment,

(2) submission to or rejection of such conduct by an individual is used as the basis for employment decisions affecting such individual, or

(3) such conduct has the purpose or effect of unreasonably interfering with an individual's work performance or creating an intimidating, hostile, or offensive working environment. Numbers (1) and (2) are often referred to as "quid pro quo" sexual harassment. Number (3) is often referred to as hostile work environment sexual harassment.

In simplified or "plain English" language, conditioning job opportunities on the granting of unwelcome sexual favors (sexual blackmail) or creating a work environment that would intimidate or offend a reasonable person constitutes sexual harassment.

Hostile Work Environment

While the bribery and blackmail forms of sexual harassment are relatively easy to recognize and deal with, the more subtle hostile work environment form of sexual harassment can be more troublesome. Under civil rights law, a hostile work environment is a form of unlawful sexual harassment and sex discrimination. A hostile environment is assessed in the totality of the circumstances. Each incident cannot be evaluated in a vacuum.[21] In one case, the Eighth Circuit directed that the district court should not "carve the work environment into a series of discrete incidents and then measure the harm occurring in each episode."

Instead, the trier of fact was instructed to keep in mind that "each successive episode has its predecessors, that the impact of the separate incidents may accumulate, and that the work environment created may exceed the sum of the individual episodes."[22] This "totality of the circumstances" view is important because "A play cannot be understood on the basis of some of its scenes but only on its entire performance, and similarly, a discrimination analysis must concentrate not on individual incidents but on the overall scenario."[23]

A hostile environment, once established, can last a long time and ensnare many people, both as perpetrators and victims. Particularly in environments that are traditionally male-dominated, when the few women working in the environment witness or share the experiences of the others, every incident of harassment affects each woman, whether she is the direct target of the harassment or not.

Indeed, since the environment is the focus, "even a woman who was never herself the object of harassment might have a claim if she were forced to work in an atmosphere where such harassment was pervasive."[24]

To prevail on a claim of hostile environment, claimants must show:

- That they belong to a protected group
- That they were subjected to unwelcome sexual harassment that was based on their sex
- That the harassment was so pervasive that it altered the conditions of their employment
- That the employer knew or should have known of the harassment and failed to take proper remedial action.[25]

Behavior is tested against a reasonable person in like circumstances standard. The behaviors must also meet the second element of a hostile environment claim of being "unwelcome." The threshold for determining

---

[21] Burns v. Mcgregor, 955 F.2d 559 (8th Cir. 1992).

[22] *Id.* quoting from Robinson v. Jacksonville Shipyards, Inc., 760 F. Supp. 1486 (M.D. Fla. 1991).

[23] Andrew v. City of Philadelphia, 895 F.2d 1469 (3d Cir. 1990).

[24] Vinson v. Taylor, 753 F.2d 141 (D.C. Cir. 1985), *aff'd in part and rev'd in part,* 477 U.S. 57 (1986).

[25] Burns v. Mcgregor, 955 F.2d 559 (8th Cir. 1992).

that sexually harassing conduct is unwelcome is "that the employee did not solicit or incite it, and . . . that the employee regarded the conduct as undesirable or offensive."[26]

Evidence that conduct was unwelcome can include overt acts such as rejecting advances, tearing down offensive pictures, crying out or otherwise protesting verbally or non-verbally, complaining to co-workers or directly to the harasser orally or by letter, and so forth. Often as a price of survival in the hostile environment, women do not openly fight the harassment, but that cannot in any way be inferred as welcoming the behavior. Victims have no legal obligation to openly protest against harassment, however, a failure to demonstrate any kind of protest or rejection, no matter how subtle, such as through body language indicating resistance, is generally considered when "welcomeness" is assessed. As the court stated in the landmark *Robinson v. Jacksonville Shipyards*[27] case, "that some women do not complain does not alter objective offensiveness of the environment."

The sexual nature of most sexual harassment raises the inference that it is directed at women because of their sex.[28] Moreover, harassment that is not overtly sexual in content, but is directed at men or women and motivated by animus against men or women, also meets this element.[29]

In most cases, in addition to targeted harassment, the pervasive presence of pornographic pictures, magazines and graffiti, and the use of vulgar language can contribute to and cause a hostile work environment. Vulgar pictures and graffiti create a barrier to women seeking to enter and advance in work places because they convey the message to women that "they do not belong, that they are welcome . . . only if they will subvert their identities to the sexual stereotypes prevalent in that environment." "[A]ny reasonable person would have to regard these (sexually explicit) cartoons as highly offensive to a woman who seeks to deal with her fellow employees

---

[26] Henson v. City of Dundee, 682 F.2d 897 (11th Cir. 1982).

[27] 760 F. Supp. 1486 (M.D. Fla. 1991).

[28] *See* Burns v. Mcgregor, 955 F.2d 559 (8th Cir. 1992) and Robinson v. Jacksonville Shipyards Inc. 760 F.Supp. 1486 (M.D. Fla. 1991) in which the courts had no trouble making the inference discussed.

[29] Andrew v. City of Philadelphia, 895 F.2d 1469 (3d Cir. 1990); Lipsett v. University of Puerto Rico, 864 F.2d 881 (1st Cir. 1988); *See also* Hall v. Gus Constr. Co., 842 F.2d 1010 (8th Cir. 1988). The view that workplace harassment is prohibited when directed at any individual because of his or her protected status Under Title VII was supported by the U.S. Supreme Court in the October Term of 1993 in the case of Harris v. Forklift Systems, Inc., 114 S. Ct. 367 (1993).The court stated "the very fact that the discriminatory conduct was so severe or pervasive that it created a work environment abusive to employees because of their race, gender, religion, or national origin offends Title VII's broad rule of workplace equality."

... with professional dignity and without the barrier of sexual differentiation and abuse."[30]

Most recently in *Harris v. Forklift Systems,* the U.S. Supreme Court reaffirmed the emphasis on looking at all the circumstances surrounding a complaint of harassment. Looking at all the circumstances demonstrates why one should use behavioral illustrations in isolation with caution in training employees, as it may be misleading.

Employer's Duty to Remedy the Work Environment

An employer has a duty to remedy or prevent a hostile or offensive work environment of which management level employees knew or, in the exercise of reasonable care, should have known.[31]

It is often argued that management knew or should have known of the hostile environment by virtue of its pervasiveness, even if no one complains to management. At times, it appears to the victims that management condones the harassing atmosphere, or even specific acts of harassment, and they therefore do not come forward to complain.[32]

However, an employer cannot excuse its inaction by blaming the victims for not using the grievance procedure. While failure to have an effective grievance procedure can create liability for an employer, the mere existence of a grievance procedure and policy against discrimination coupled with the plaintiffs' failure to invoke the procedure does not insulate an employer from liability.[33] Employers cannot escape liability by blaming the victims; Title VII imposes an *affirmative duty* to seek out and eradicate a hostile work environment. As stated by the court in *Robinson v. Jacksonville Shipyards,* "[a] duty to conduct further investigations arises when a report or reports of sexual harassment to management suggests that the work place may be charged in a sexually hostile manner."[34] The employer does not discharge this duty by burying its head in the sand instead of trying to learn more about the environment in which its female employees work.

---

[30] Bennett v. Corroon & Black Corp., 845 F.2d at 106.

[31] Hall v. Gus Constr. Co., 842 F.2d 1010, 1015–16 (8th Cir. 1988). Smolsky v. Consolidated Rail Corp., 780 F. Supp. 283, 293 (E.D. Pa. 1991)(quoting Hirshfield v. New Mexico Corrections Dept., 916 F.2d 572, 577 (10th Cir. 1990)).

[32] See Hall v. Gus, 842 F.2d 1010, 1016 (18th Cir. 1988); Lipsett v. University of Puerto Rico, 864 F.2d at 906 (atmosphere so blatant that it put the defendants on notice).

[33] Meritor Savings Bank, FSB v. Vinson, 477 U.S. 57, 72 (1986).

[34] 760 F. Supp. 1486 (M.D. Fla. 1991).

To avoid liability, an employer must act immediately upon notice of harassment,[35] and it must do more than merely request that the perpetrators refrain from discriminatory conduct.[36] It can be insufficient for managers to simply talk to or even orally "warn" a harasser against whom a claim was substantiated. The court in one case found that just talking is not enough, noting that employers send the wrong message when they do not impose discipline for sexual harassment. The employer in that case at least had posted and reaffirmed its EEO policy and held sensitivity training at the plant, but the court still called these responses "long on words and short on action."[37]

Individual Liability

An issue of great concern to managers and employees with supervisory responsibility is that of individual liability. Under Title VII of the Civil Rights Act, employers are liable for sexual harassment, and some courts have imputed such liability to supervisors who exceeded their authority or acted outside the scope of their duties when harassment occurred. However, the direction of the courts appears to be shifting gradually away from liability of individual employees to holding employers responsible for the harassing behavior of supervisory employees. In the case of *Henry v. E.G. & G. Missouri Metals Shaping Co.*,[38] the district court for the Eastern District of Missouri dismissed an employee's claim of sexual harassment against her manager. Rather than rely on cases from the Fourth and Sixth Circuits finding supervisors individually liable, the court followed a Ninth Circuit ruling that supervisor cannot be held personally liable under Title VII.[39] Thus the circuits remain divided on the issue of personal liability of supervisors for sexual harassment. Employers should assume they will be held liable and continue to educate supervisors in awareness and prevention.

Unions' Duty of Fair Representation

Unions also have a duty to protect their members from sexual harassment, and to represent grievants fairly. In the case of sexual harassment, grievants are often the disciplined harassers seeking to overturn the employer's disciplinary action not just those who are complaining of harassment.

---

[35] Davis v. Tri-State Mack Distributors, Inc., 60 E.P.D. 41,920 (8th Cir. 1992).

[36] *Id.;* Ellison v. Brady, 924 F.2d 872, 882 (9th Cir. 1991).

[37] Hansel v. Public Service Co. of Colo., 778 F. Supp. 1126 1132 (D. Colo. 1991).

[38] 93CV12065NL (E.D. Mo. Nov. 19, 1993).

[39] *See* Miller v. Maxwell's International, 991 F.2d 583 (9th Cir. 1993).

Unions must seek to balance the responsibility of representing those harassed against the need to also represent members in the disciplinary process. Unions' challenge is to find ways of addressing these conflicting interests, often divided along gender lines, if they are to remain a viable force, particularly as more women join the ranks of unionized workplaces, traditionally men's domain. One way of accomplishing this might be to designate certain individuals, without making the decision based on the sex of the union representative, to represent the interests of the victim and others to represent the disciplined harasser. Unions, just like employers, can be sued for discrimination, including sexual harassment, under Title VII.

Unions should work proactively along with management to institute an effective policy against sexual harassment, to hold training classes for employees, to take effective steps to prevent recurrence of harassment, and to curb hostile work environments.

Class Actions

An employer should be aware that entire groups of employees may be able to bring a class action against it where a hostile environment is allowed to persist. The United States Supreme Court has stated that "[o]ne can readily envision working environments so heavily polluted with discrimination as to destroy completely the emotional and psychological stability of [the] workers."[40] Such an environment would surely give rise to a class-wide cause of action. Moreover, the Eighth Circuit has recognized that a small group of women workers can bring a hostile environment claim using evidence of the entire abusive environment as proof.[41]

Firms cannot rest comfortably just because they have not received any sexual harassment complaints. They should still initiate steps to prevent harassment as described throughout this book. All it takes to begin a class action is one brave soul who has decided she will not "take it anymore." Usually others will follow suit.

Link Between Sex Discrimination and Sexual Harassment

The discriminatory attitude toward women which can be found in a hostile environment also can be found to affect women's opportunities to be hired, trained, promoted, retained, and assigned to the highest paying jobs. It is important to appreciate the link between the hostile environment evidence and other types of discrimination. It can encourage stereotyping of women

---

[40] Meritor Savings Bank v. Vinson, 477 U.S. 57, 66 (1986).
[41] Hall v. Gus Constr. Co., 842 F.2d 1010 (8th Cir. 1988).

as the sexy, dumb, or weak sex. It is not difficult to understand that a foreman who calls a woman "babe" or pulls her on his lap will not think to nominate that woman for a promotion in the ranks.

There is often a link between stereotyping and a sexualized work environment and the lack of advancement for women. Dr. Eugene Borgida, an expert in industrial psychology with the University of Minnesota-Duluth, states that the preconditions for stereotyping of women are:

1. the rarity of women in the work place
2. a sexualized work environment
3. the lack of clear cut criteria for evaluation of employee performance.[42]

In class-wide discrimination cases, there is first a finding of discrimination based on proof by a preponderance of the evidence that defendant engaged in a pattern or practice of discrimination and that "discrimination was the company's standard operating procedure—the regular rather than the unusual practice."[43] The standards and procedures for proof in class-wide discrimination cases are applicable where treatment of women is as "second class citizens" in the "man's world" not limited to isolated incidents or certain individuals.

Proof of a pattern or practice of discrimination consists of evidence whereby "the plaintiff will produce statistical evidence showing disparities between similarly-situated protected and unprotected employees with respect to hiring, job assignments, promotions and salary, supplemented with other evidence, such as testimony about specific incidents of discrimination."[44] The defendant then has an opportunity to show that the plaintiffs' proof was either "inaccurate or insignificant."[45] Either statistics alone or anecdotal evidence alone can also establish a pattern or practice of discrimination.[46] "A plaintiff in a Title VII suit need not prove discrimination with scientific certainty; rather, his or her burden is to prove discrimination by a preponderance of the evidence."[47]

In proving a pattern and practice of discrimination, plaintiffs generally will not rely on their statistical analysis alone, but also present evidence of discriminatory attitudes, individual instances of discrimination, and the perpetuation of procedures and policies that make discrimination a

---

[42] Dr. Borgida so testified in the first class action sexual harassment case against Eveleth Mines in Minnesota.

[43] Teamsters v. United States, 431 U.S. 324, 336 (1977).

[44] Craik v. Minnesota State University Board, 731 F.2d 465, 470 (8th Cir. 1984).

[45] Teamsters v. United States, 431 U.S. 324, 361 (1977).

[46] Catlett v. Missouri Highway and Transportation Co., 828 F.2d 1260, 1265 (8th Cir. 1987).

[47] Bazemore v. Friday, 478 U.S. 398, 400–401 (1986).

"standard operating procedure." Anecdotes which describe repeated discriminatory actions are a key component of pattern or practice evidence.
Examples of comments that can reveal biases about women include:

- Telling a woman that she does not need to work because her husband makes a good salary
- Accusing women of taking jobs away from men
- That women belong at home or barefoot and pregnant
- Why hire a woman since she will only leave after she gets pregnant
- Women can't handle the stress of the job
- Our clients or customers won't feel comfortable dealing with a woman, and so forth

Another piece of evidence used against employers to show a culture of bias is a failure to adhere to an affirmative action plan (AAP). This has been deemed to demonstrate discriminatory intent.[48] Employers should also be careful to adhere to basic equal employment opportunity principles and practices, including the following:

Systematic and consistent hiring practices.   Whether filling jobs from within the firm or outside, the same interviewing and/or testing process should be applied to all candidates. It is wisest to have job descriptions and specifications when interviewing and hiring qualifications in terms of experience or education for those jobs. This helps to ensure that hiring criteria will be consistently applied to all candidates. Moreover, creating additional experience and education requirements that favor men for a job that does not require them is in itself discriminatory.[49] Because women as a class tend to have less manufacturing experience and less craft training, adding these additional hurdles for an unskilled job can be found to discriminate against women.

Employers using word-of-mouth recruiting to fill open positions should determine whether such recruiting practices are having an adverse impact on women or men (disproportionately excluding one group in comparison to their representation in the available qualified labor pool). If the firm allows hiring of relatives (nepotism), it should establish whether the practice perpetuates exclusion of underrepresented groups (women and minorities for most jobs).

---

[48] Gonzales v. Police Department, City of San Jose, 901 F.2d 758, 761 (9th Cir. 1990); Craik v. Minnesota State University Board, 731 F.2d 465, 472 (8th Cir. 1984); Taylor v. Teletype Corp., 648 F.2d 1129, 1135 n. 14 (8th Cir. 1981).

[49] Griggs v. Duke Power Co., 401 U.S. 431, 433–35 (1971).

An open and objective promotion process, with promotions going to the best-qualified candidates.   The promotions should not solely be a function of the "old boy network." The use of a posting or bidding system that gives access to all who believe that they are qualified for a position, is a more sex-neutral process. Women should not have to meet additional hurdles. Even when a collective bargaining agreement mandates that seniority govern most non-supervisory promotions, women can still be found to consistently occupy lower job classifications and therefore make less money than men with comparable seniority. Women can be directly and indirectly discouraged from posting for higher-paying positions; directly by male supervisors and coworkers who tell them they only are suited for certain jobs, and indirectly by a hostile environment that causes women to gravitate toward the back-office roles where they feel more safe.

Further, in the context of sexual harassment, if an employer cannot demonstrate that positions are filled and promotions made based upon qualifications, then the organization is more vulnerable to claims of sexual favoritism or "quid pro quo" harassment, that is, that positions are filled based on non-job-related reasons. It is well-established in discrimination law that the sole defense for an employer to a discrimination charge is that an employment decision was made based only on job-related criteria—thereby rebutting the implication that immutable characteristics such as race or sex were considered in the decision.

Training opportunities must also be made available equally to all groups of employees.   Particularly when training is the only way to be promoted within the organization, employers must be careful that no employees are unfairly denied the opportunity to train for higher-paying positions.

Consistent disciplinary practices are also a necessary part of preventing actual, or even perceived, unfair treatment.   One group or class of employees should not be disciplined more harshly than others. In some organizations, those in senior positions who are found to have engaged in sexual harassment are spared the full force of the disciplinary process. This is the kind of practice that leads to the big punitive damage awards that have drawn so much attention.

There should be some guidelines for when discipline is warranted, or, at a minimum, managers should be trained to exercise their discretion in a consistent manner. Discipline for performance deficiencies should be documented. This is particularly critical as employees who make a complaint of sexual harassment may claim retaliation if they are disciplined by a supervisor whom they claim has harassed them. The organization should be able to document objectively all performance deficiencies, as well as discussions and coaching relating to addressing those deficiencies.

Compensation should be justifiable based upon objective factors. An organization that has no rational basis for compensation (both base pay and at-risk, such as bonuses) is more vulnerable to charges of unlawful favoritism, or of "quid pro quo" (sleep with me and you'll get a raise) harassment.

A Complaint Procedure Is a Critical Part of the Prevention Strategy

Every employer should have a procedure for addressing sexual harassment complaints. In 1986, the United States Supreme Court, in *Meritor Savings Bank v. Vinson,*[50] gave employers this advice: if you want to have a reasonable chance at avoiding liability for sexual harassment, you should at a minimum,

1. Have a policy in place that informs employees what sexual harassment is and that it is against the law.
2. Provide employees with a mechanism for complaining about harassment that encourages them to raise their concern.
3. Take prompt and appropriate remedial action.
4. Communicate the policy directly to all employees.

The court suggested that while having a procedure, in and of itself, is not sufficient to shield an employer from liability for sexual harassment, if the procedures encourage employees to raise their concerns about sexual harassment, an employee's failure to use them will be given strong consideration. Indeed, many cases have been won by employers due to the strength of their sexual harassment procedures. (A detailed discussion of sexual harassment complaint procedures is contained in **Chapter 3**.)

§ 1.6 Posting and Other State Law Requirements

In addition to the federal laws alluded to in this chapter that can give rise to liability for employers, several state and local governments have their own sexual harassment laws and enforcement agencies (See **Chapter 7** for a review of the agency process).

State Posting Requirements

One example of state regulation of discrimination in the workplace are state posting requirements. Just as states require that employers post Department of Labor information pertaining to wages and hours of work

---

[50] 477 U.S. 57 (1986).

and nondiscrimination, many states require that specific notices regarding sexual harassment be posted. Samples of the postings required by state law are reproduced at Appendixes C through G. States that require some sort of sexual harassment posting include Alaska, California, Connecticut, Delaware, Maine, Massachussetts, New Hampshire, Vermont, Virginia, and Wisconsin. Many of the states have standard posters that can be ordered in bulk from the state Department of Labor and posted.

The states require that certain specific information regarding sexual harassment be posted in conspicuous places. It generally includes a definition of sexual harassment (usually drawn from the EEOC Guidelines), a nonretaliation statement, a complaint procedure, and contact persons within the organization, as well as information regarding outside agencies, responsible for enforcement of the employer's policy and civil rights laws. Several states, including California, Connecticut, and Vermont, require additional steps such as distribution of a policy or training of employees (or just supervisors).

The samples reproduced in Appendixes C through G were customized to incorporate an employer's own complaint procedure. This is required by some states. It may also be preferable, even if not required by state law, as the state posters can only refer employees to the state enforcement agencies to handle their complaints, whereas a customized poster can refer employers to the employer's own internal grievance mechanism—generally firms find it preferable to encourage the internal resolution of matters rather than having to defend against outside agency charges.

State Common Law Claims

There are a number of possibilities some of which may overlap with the Title VII claim and/or be further evidence of the Title VII claim.
These claims include:

- Assault and battery: this involves an unwelcome touching or a threat to engage in an unwelcome touching.
- Defamation: a claim for injury to reputation, either based on a writing (libel) or oral statements (slander).
- Emotional distress: the victim of harassment can claim damages for insomnia, uncontrollable crying or depression, nausea, diarrhea, loss of appetite/weight loss, weight gain, and so forth.
- Loss of consortium: this claim for loss of the enjoyment of the companionship or the services of a spouse, son, daughter or other relative, recognizes that more than just the victim of the harassment can suffer a loss caused by sexual harassment.

- Negligent retention: this theory is based on the employer's duty to keep the workplace safe and free from individuals whom the employer has reason to believe could inflict harm on others, such as through harassment. This could arise from an employer's failure to terminate an individual against whom a claim of sexual harassment has been substantiated.

§ 1.7 Questions and Answers Regarding Legal Issues

The following are a series of commonly asked questions regarding sexual harassment law, with proposed responses. As the law of sexual harassment is still evolving, it is essential that employers seek legal counsel on specific matters rather than relying on any kind of generalization, which can be inapplicable in a specific instance.

Q: What impact, if any, does a sexual harassment policy and sexual harassment awareness training and other "good things" have on a court's consideration of an employer being sued for sexual harassment?

A: The courts have indicated since 1986 when the U.S. Supreme Court decided the case of *Meritor Savings Bank v. Vinson,* that employers should have a policy in place and that if they have such a policy they may be unable to successfully defend against a harassment suit. However, it will do an employer more harm than good to have a policy and procedure in place but fail to follow it systematically.

Once a policy and a complaint procedure are in place, it is less convincing for an employee to argue that they were unaware of them or had no way of alerting management of the harassment and no recourse.

Failure to have a policy in place can result in a court-ordered policy such as that which Eveleth Mines has been compelled by the Minnesota Federal court to implement. (See the Eveleth Mines court-ordered policy reproduced in Appendix A).

Q: What remedies do victims of harassment have if their complaint is substantiated?

A: Victims of harassment can be paid back pay and be reinstated to their job if they were fired or were "constructively discharged", that is, left because they could not endure the hostile work environment. They can elect to transfer to another position (though they should not be compelled to do so). They can recover monetary damages for the pain and suffering they endured during and after the harassment, but they may have to settle for workers' compensation for stress or other physical injury suffered at work as a result of the harassment.

Q: What factors do judges/juries seem to be most influenced by when deciding a sexual harassment case?

A: Judges seem to be most influenced by the employer's diligence in responding promptly and appropriately, that is, "punishment fitting the crime" to complaints; its respect for confidentiality, concern for the complainant, including encouraging complainants to come forward by making the complaint procedure as user-friendly and uninhibiting as is practical; and the speed and rate with which corrective action is administered. Juries will also focus on the nature of the harassment and the behavior of the victim and of the offender. Nature of the harassment includes the number of incidents, the frequency of incidents and the severity of incidents. Behavior of the victim involves an evaluation of whether the incidents were unwelcome.

Q: Is defamation of character a valid concern for employers investigating a charge that may not be substantiated against an individual? Does the conditional privilege usually insulate employers against liability for injury to reputation?

A: Defamation of character is a valid concern. However, most employers exaggerate this concern, as the risk is diminished if a proper investigation is conducted to substantiate the action taken against a harasser. The employer can minimize the risk further by ensuring that all communication is handled in the strictest confidence and information regarding the investigation and any findings made are shared on a "need-to-know" basis only. All steps should be documented so that the record of the investigation is available to justify action taken later if needed. Thorough documentation should be kept in a secured place to prevent unnecessary or unauthorized access.

   As employers have a qualified privilege under the law to investigate claims of harassment, as long as the scope of the investigation is reasonable and there is no intent to ruin anyone's reputation or career in the process, employers run little risk of losing a defamation lawsuit.

Q: What role can/should an attorney play in the investigation or resolution of an in-house sexual harassment complaint? Is there anything that an attorney should not be involved in? What role should attorneys play in drafting a sexual harassment policy for an employer (sometimes the concern is raised that attorneys draft documents that are overly-legalistic)?

A: Attorneys should generally only be involved in an advisory capacity with sexual harassment complaints unless they have evolved into an agency charge or a lawsuit. It is generally advisable for the attorney, even in-house, to avoid actually interviewing witnesses and gathering documentation. First, they might risk losing their work product or attorney-client privilege, and be subject to the discovery process as witnesses, if they interview witnesses and find facts. Second, more information may be obtained by nonlawyers because the witnesses will feel freer to respond, less inhibited.

   With regard to the drafting of the sexual harassment policy, attorneys should review any policy drafted by an employer before it is issued. Outside and in-house counsel can also draft the policy for the employer, but a non-lawyer should always review it and "test drive" it to ensure that it is sufficiently clear and user-friendly. After all, it does no employer good to have a policy and procedure that are not used because employees cannot understand them or are afraid to use them.

Q: How far back in time can the court go in considering incidents claimed to have been sexual harassment?

A: Where a series of unlawful employment practices manifest themselves over time, rather than as a discrete act, *incidents which occurred before the statute of limitations become actionable under a continuing violation theory.*[51] *A plaintiff can prove a continuing violation either by producing evidence of a series of discriminatory acts or by demonstrating that the defendant has a policy of discriminating.*[52] *"Where discrimination is not limited to isolated instances, but pervades a series or pattern of events" which continue into the charge filing period, the events are actionable regardless of when the first event occurred.*[53]

Thus, for example, in *E.E.O.C. v. Rymer Foods,*[54] the E.E.O.C. alleged a pattern of discrimination which extended back six years before the charge was filed and the court found that discriminatory actions against class members in that time period were actionable.

Moreover, where the claim is one of a sexually hostile environment and continuing harassment, courts have often recognize a continuing violation.[55] Hostile environments are particularly susceptible to continuing violation tolling because the acts of discrimination involve the same subject matter; the acts are reoccurring, rather than an isolated decision; and the type of discrimination lacks the degree of permanence that would trigger an awareness of a discreet violation of a right.[56] The focus should be on whether a reasonable person would feel the environment was hostile throughout the period in which a hostile environment is alleged.

In one case, the court found the defendant liable for maintenance of a

---

[51] Satz v. ITT Financial Corp., 619 F.2d 738, 743–44 (8th Cir. 1980).

[52] Bruno v. Western Electric Co., 829 F.2d 957, 961 (10th Cir. 1987).

[53] Laffey v. Northwest Airlines, Inc., 567 F.2d 429, 473 (D.C. Cir. 1976), *cert. denied,* 434 U.S. 1086 (1978).

[54] *See* Non-Traditional Employment for Women v. Tishman Realty and Construction Co., 52 E.P.D. ¶39,715, 61,491 (S.D.N.Y. 1989)(charge alleging discrimination in hiring filed in 1987, claims dating back to 1981).

[55] *See,* e.g., Waltman v. International Paper Co., 875 F.2d 468, 474–76 (5th Cir. 1989); Hansel v. Public Service Co. of Colo., 778 F.Supp. 1126, 1134 (1991).

[56] *Waltman,* 875 F.2d 475.

hostile environment during the entire time the plaintiff worked in the environment. The court held that:

> the sexual harassment suffered by Hansel from 1980 to 1988 was dogged pattern. She was marked from the first day after her probation and the abusive work environment continued beyond the time she filed this lawsuit eight years later. It does not matter that the form of harassment changed over time, nor does it matter that the identity of those responsible changed over time. The continuing violation of Title VII is the hostile environment itself.[57]

Q: How can employers best balance the need to maintain confidentiality of complaints and their legal obligation to take swift and effective action?

A: Once a claim is made, or once an employer has reason to believe that violations are taking place, the employer has a legal obligation to investigate the complaint. However, there is no legal obligation to disclose the identity of the complainant to the alleged harasser. The employer can maintain the identity of the complainant confidential for as long as that does not hinder the effectiveness of the investigation. Most of the witnesses interviewed should be able to remain anonymous as well.

From the alleged harasser's perspective, there is no legal right to due process in the strict sense of the word in the context of sexual harassment investigations in most work settings. In union settings, employees appealing disciplinary action for sexual harassment may be entitled to certain procedural safeguards through the union grievance process that employees in non-union settings are not entitled to by law.

The law provides that employers must take swift remedial action in the event of a substantiated claim of sexual harassment.

Q: Can proven harassers be retained by employers who put them through "rehabilitation" and discipline them? If so, should they be retained? What are the pros and cons for the employer?

A: There are generally two types of harassers: those who know what they are doing is wrong/illegal and cannot usually be rehabilitated and those who do not realize that what they are doing is offensive or illegal and can be made aware through education and will probably cease the offensive conduct. It is neither illegal nor necessarily unwise or unethical to retain someone who harassed an employee as long as that individual has been made to cease the conduct, has been disciplined appropriately, and has been educated. However, the decision to retain a proven harasser is risky as, if they harass again, the employer was unquestionably on notice of the risk and would not only be liable under sexual harassment law but also under tort theories such as negligent retention of the offending employee, and can be subject to punitive damages in an unlimited amount.

---

[57] Hansel v. Public Service Co. of Colo., 778 F. Supp. 1126, 1134 (1991).

The theory of negligent retention is premised on the idea that employers have the duty to ensure that individuals brought into the workplace (not just employees, but also customers, contractors, consultants) do not pose a danger to others in the workplace. Where an employer knew or should have known that someone did pose a risk to the health and safety of others, the employer can be held liable for all reasonably foreseeable consequences of that person's dangerous conduct.

Based upon this theory, if an employer failed to take reasonable steps to investigate the claims against those it retains, the employer can be held liable for that person's violations of law, including sexual harassment. If an employer knew or should have known that a current employee, contractor, or customer poses a potential threat to those in the workplace, but fails to terminate that individual or his/her engagement, the employer can be held liable under the theories of sexual harassment or negligent retention.

While it may seem inconceivable, there are employers who hire individuals who have been dismissed from another organization for substantiated harassment. An employer can be liable under a theory of negligent hiring if it fails to conduct a reasonable investigation into the character and background of those it hires.

Q: What action can employers take with respect to alleged harassers against whom a violation of policy cannot be proven, but where there is ample evidence pointing in the direction of inappropriate conduct?

A: In most cases where an investigation is conducted as it should be, an act of harassment that can be substantiated will be substantiated. It may be necessary in some cases to hire attorneys and/or private investigators, use electronic devices such as recording phone calls with the consent of the harassed employee, employ technical experts such as computer experts where obscene messages are relayed to an employee by computer, and conduct extensive reviews of the alleged harasser's work history, but usually the investigation will yield the correct result.

If the harassment still cannot be substatiated after all of these efforts, then there will have to be a "wait and see" approach to the individual. In addition, that individual, along with his or her entire department, may be required to receive some educational intervention about the sexual harassment policy and about the counseling available through the employer's health insurance plan or Employee Assistance Program.

Q: Who should conduct the investigation of a sexual harassment complaint? In what order should the investigation proceed?

A: The investigation should always follow the established procedure. This lends it greater credibility and prevents claims of favoritism or of unfair treatment to surface. Initially, human resources usually conducts the preliminary background information gathering. Some companies prefer to have a human resources representative (usually fairly high-level) from another part of the organization, whether it's from another business or location, perform the investigation. This can prevent some of the uncomfortable political situations that can arise, and particularly where the accused harasser is a high-level manager, it can avoid any undue influence or even the appearance of any undue influence.

Further, the human resources representative for the unit in which the complaint arose will not have to risk damaging relationships with employees in that unit. One disadvantage is that outside human resources professionals will not be as familiar with the business or the employees of the unit they are investigating, but this can be addressed along the way as the investigation progresses and the professional requires clarification. Conversely, it can be an advantage that the investigator has little or no pre-conceived ideas about the parties to the incident and little or no stake in the outcome.

Other employers use a corporate employee relations officer to conduct all sexual harassment investigations. This affords similar advantages and disadvantages as using an outside human resources professional, and adds an additional advantage of escalating the perceived seriousness of the problem when "corporate" becomes involved.

With each of the above options, keep in mind that there are "formal" and "informal" mechanisms in most organizations for handling complaints. (See **Chapter 3** on Investigations.) To bring "corporate" into the picture when the unit is still trying to resolve a matter informally can have a negative, "chilling", impact on the informal efforts.

As the investigation progresses, it may be advisable to involve legal counsel. Some employers will involve in-house counsel from the outset of an investigation in anticipation of future litigation in an *attempt* to couch all documents and notes generated within the attorney's work product exception to the discovery process. However, the true level of involvement of legal counsel at this stage is often minimal, and many courts will order the disclosure of all notes, memos, witness interviews, and documents generated by human resources and line managers from the investigation conducted, whether or not counsel was informed of the investigation at the time.

While it is not a primary consideration, organizations may wish to consider whether it is worth the substantial additional cost to use in-house or outside counsel at the investigation stage. It may be more appropriate to involve counsel once formal action has been initiated, but organizations will differ in how they make use of legal counsel—some use them only when litigation is involved, even handling all agency matters through human resources professionals, whereas others make frequent use of counsel at all stages of employee relations matters, believing that they can better help to manage potential legal problems before they escalate.

CHAPTER 2

DRAFTING A PREVENTIVE SEXUAL HARASSMENT POLICY

§ 2.1   The Role of a Policy in the Prevention Strategy

A sexual harassment policy is the backbone of an employer's prevention strategy. It empowers management and nonmanagerial employees to effectively prevent and handle sexual harassment.

Acknowledging that once an act of sexual harassment takes place, everyone loses, and that the resolution of sexual harassment complaints is fraught with difficulty, the sexual harassment policy becomes the pivotal focus of the prevention strategy. If the policy is ineffective, the strategy will fail.

The decisions to adopt or amend a policy, of what to include in a policy, and how to administer a policy, are complicated by the fact that the law of sexual harassment is still unsettled in many respects. While legal counsel and consultants can offer some guidance on what components are minimally recommended, they leave the decision about what to include in a policy to the client.

The sample policies reproduced at the end of the chapter are for illustrative purposes only. Each organization has unique needs and culture, as well as different resources to administer a policy successfully. Therefore, the reader is cautioned that policies must be carefully and thoughtfully adapted to respond to the specific needs and constraints of an organization, and not copied wholesale. As with all official personnel documents to which legal liability can attach, legal counsel should always review any policy before it is issued.

§ 2.2   What Is a Policy?

The dictionary definition of policy is "a guiding principle or course of action adopted toward an objective or objectives" or "prudence or practical wisdom." Objective is itself defined as "something that one's efforts are intended to obtain."

Looking at the most basic definition of policy demonstrates that it is not as simple a concept as it appears. The policy must capture both the guiding principle and the course of action (procedure) that will help to prevent sexual harassment. (See **Chapter 3** for more in-depth coverage of procedural issues) While employers' intent behind having a policy can vary, this chapter assumes that the overriding consideration is to prevent sexual harassment from arising in the first place.

Based upon the basic definition, a policy should include:

1. A guiding principle (the company statement prohibiting sexual harassment)
2. A course of action (the procedure for bringing complaints)
3. The objective of the policymaker (articulate the prevention strategy)

Some experts prefer to distinguish between policy and procedure, and only refer to the policy statement, that is, the guiding principle as "the policy." However, for practical purposes, communicating a policy that does not include any specific reference to an enforcement mechanism, that is, the complaint process, is not all that useful to the organization or to its employees. Therefore, most employers give employees information on how to bring a complaint, as well as certain procedural safeguards such as confidentiality, in the document they call "the policy."

§ 2.3   Why Employers Establish Sexual
Harassment Policies

Organizations have different employee relations philosophies: they range from providing employees with a work atmosphere of mutual respect to simply protecting the organization from liability. Both goals are reasonable, however, the philosophical or strategic approach of the organization's policymakers will drive not only the decision of whether to establish a sexual harassment policy, but, more critically, what provisions that policy will contain, and how it will be communicated and used in the organization.

Therefore, before policy decisions are made, an organization must determine the motivation for adopting or amending a policy. As with other key employee relations decisions, senior management's involvement and buy-in at the earliest stages of the process are critical in order to ensure a satisfactory level of compliance.

According to a survey of 156 organizations released by the Bureau of National Affairs' Personnel Policies Forum in 1987, employers established a sexual harassment policy for one or more of the following reasons:

1. In response to the Guidelines issued by the EEOC in 1980 (77%)— 93% of respondents established a policy between 1980 and 1986
2. Out of liability concerns (62%)
3. Because of state/local regulations (25%)
4. Due to employee complaints (10%)
5. Out of concern for employees (2%)

Equal Employment Opportunity Guidelines (EEOC Guidelines)

The Equal Employment Opportunity Commission (EEOC) is the regulatory agency charged with the enforcement of civil rights laws, including discrimination in employment, of which sexual harassment is a subset. The agency issued guidelines to employers regarding how the civil rights laws would be interpreted and enforced, and measures employers can take to prevent sexual harassment and minimize liability.

The Guidelines state: "Prevention is the best tool for the elimination of sexual harassment. An employer should take all steps necessary to prevent sexual harassment from occurring, such as affirmatively raising the subject, expressing strong disapproval, developing appropriate sanctions, informing employees of their right to raise and how to raise the issue of harassment under Title VII, and developing methods to sensitize all concerned."[1]

Employers that wish to take a safe approach to managing sexual harassment should follow the EEOC's guidelines:

1. Affirmatively raise the subject of sexual harassment through issuance of a policy and training programs.

---

[1] *EEOC Guidelines on Discrimination Because of Sex,* 29 C.F.R. § 1604.11 (1990).

2. Express strong disapproval in words through the policy statement and in actions through the resolution process.
3. Develop appropriate sanctions through the disciplinary process: make sure that the punishment fits the crime and enforce the policy in a consistent manner.
4. Inform employees of their rights and their responsibilities, including those of reporting harassment and cooperating in investigations. As part of the reporting system, communicate and enforce a non-retaliation policy.
5. Develop training programs designed to help employees at all levels of the organization understand what sexual harassment is and their role in preventing it.

While the EEOC Guidelines are advisory and do not require employers to adopt a sexual harassment policy, most employers recognize their utility in preventing sexual harassment and in reducing the organization's potential exposure to liability. The Guidelines have been widely accepted by the courts, administrative agencies and arbitrators. (The 1990 EEOC Policy Guidelines are reproduced in § 2.7.)

Liability Concerns

The Civil Rights Act of 1991 gives individuals the right to a jury trial, to compensatory and punitive damages for complaints of discrimination, including sexual harassment. Punitive damages are capped at between $50,000 to $300,000 depending on the number of individuals employed by the organization, however, the Equal Remedies Act legislation has been introduced to uncap damage awards under the Civil Rights Act. Litigation for sexual harassment usually is accompanied by claims for pain and suffering damages, infliction of emotional distress, and assault and battery, for which there are no limits on compensatory or punitive damages.

The potential financial outlays aside, sexual harassment is costly in terms of lost organizational and individual effectiveness. According to a survey conducted by the U.S. Merit Systems Protection Board in 1988, sexual harassment cost the federal government an estimated $267 million in the form of turnover, sick leave, and decreased productivity.

Further, data suggests that the number of sexual harassment charges to agencies is on the rise. The EEOC reports that during the first three quarters of 1993, the agency received 4,963 sexual harassment charges, representing a 24.6 percent increase over the number of such Charges filed in the same period in 1992. For the same time period in 1993, the EEOC obtained $95.9 million in benefits on behalf of individuals claiming workplace discrimination of all kinds, including sexual harassment. This signifies that there is room for improvement in employers' ability to keep claims of harassment within the organization by handling employee complaints more effectively.

There are some states that require that employers have a sexual harassment policy and post it (See **Chapter 1** for details on state law requirements). In addition, state or federal contractors are often required to have a sexual harassment policy in effect in order to qualify for doing business on behalf of the government.

A Policy Can Help to Minimize the Destructive Impact of Sexual Harassment

Employers have good reason to be concerned about the negative impact of sexual harassment on their employees. The following effects of sexual harassment have been identified in studies:

1. "Like women who have been raped, sexually harassed women feel humiliated, degraded, ashamed, embarrassed, and cheap, as well as angry." (MacKinnon 1979)
2. The American Psychiatric Association regards sexual harassment as a "severe stressor."
3. Expert witnesses have testified at trials that victims of sexual harassment suffer from posttraumatic stress disorder (See, for example, *Broderick v. Ruder*[2])
4. Effects identified in several research studies include: anxiety, headaches, sleep and eating disorders, weight loss and gain, crying spells, fear, depression, self-blaming, loss of self-esteem, inability to perform effectively at work or enjoy work, and reduced organizational commitment/increased likelihood of leaving the employer (*See* for example the testimony of K.C. Wagner, a consultant in the area of sexual harassment, in the case of *Robinson v. Jacksonville Shipyards*[3]).

Whether the organization's goal is to avoid liability or to approximate an ideal work setting, adopting a preventive sexual harassment policy will advance that goal. However, the organization's reason for establishing or updating the sexual harassment policy should be agreed upon at the outset.

---

[2] Broderick v. Ruder, 685. F.Supp. 1269 (D.D.C. 1988). In this case, Ms. Broderick recovered substantial damages from her employer, the Securities & Exchange Commission (SEC), for treatment relating to what was diagnosed as posttraumatic stress disorder due to the sexual harassment she endured while working at the SEC.

[3] Robinson v. Jacksonville Shipyards, Inc., 760 F.Supp. 1486 (M.D. Fla. 1991).

It is the single most important driving force for design and implementation decisions, as it reflects the organization's level of commitment to eliminating sexual harassment in the workplace.

Nevertheless, there are certain policy provisions that are advisable for every organization, regardless of strategic approach. These are covered in the following section.

§ 2.4   Necessary or Recommended Policy Provisions—Review of Sample Policies

Policy Statement Against Sexual Harassment (Guiding Principle)

As the EEOC Guidelines suggest, and as numerous courts have reiterated, it is critical for employers to state in no uncertain terms that sexual harassment is against the law and will not be tolerated. Given that the law and most employers prohibit harassment based on any protected characteristic, for example, race, age, religion, national origin, some employers may decide to have one general nonharassment policy.

A powerful demonstration of the organization's commitment to preventing sexual harassment is a clear message from the top, usually from a president, CEO, or director, that the organization's leadership takes the problem of sexual harassment of employees seriously and that it is strictly prohibited. Examples of such statements include:

1. "Sexual harassment is a violation of this organization's standard of conduct and will not be tolerated."

2. "An organization cannot flourish in the absence of an understood and accepted code of conduct that ensures a basic civility and respect for the dignity of every individual. We must make it unmistakably clear to every member of this organization that sexual harassment will not be tolerated."

3. "This organization is committed to a collegial work environment in which all individuals are treated with respect and dignity. Each individual has the right to work in a work environment free of discriminatory practices, including sexual harassment. Sexual harassment, whether verbal, physical or environmental, is unacceptable."

4. "Behaviors which inappropriately assert sexuality as relevant to employee performance are damaging to this environment. This organization deplores this behavior as an abuse of authority and thus it is an official policy that sexual harassment of employees will not be tolerated."

5. "It is this organization's policy to assure a work environment free of sexual harassment."

6. "This organization is proud of its tradition of a collegial work environment in which all individuals are treated with respect and dignity. Each individual has the right to work in a professional atmosphere which promotes equal opportunities and prohibits discriminatory practices, including sexual harassment. At this organization, sexual harassment, whether verbal, physical or environmental, will not be tolerated."

This point was further emphasized by the court in the *Robinson v. Jacksonville Shipyards* case. The court endorsed the testimony of the plaintiff's expert that "sexual harassment can be eliminated through a program . . . that includes a strong policy statement signed by a top-ranking company executive." The policy ordered by the court in that case is reproduced in full in the Appendix. The court went on to enumerate what elements should be included in a sexual harassment policy statement:

> (1) describe with specificity the behaviors that constitute sexual harassment and that are prohibited by the organization; (2) advise employees that sexual harassment may result from the behavior of co-workers as well as the behavior of supervisors; (3) promise and provide confidentiality and protection from retaliation for complainants and witnesses; and (4) provide a number of avenues through which a complaint may be initiated. The policy statement must receive wide, effective distribution.

Human resources managers should bear in mind that the above statement was made in the context of protracted litigation and extremely damaging allegations. In practice, the above language presents some difficulties, as described below.

Definitions of Sexual Harassment

In the 1991 case of *Ellison v. Brady,*[4] the Ninth Circuit held that "a female plaintiff states a prima facie case of hostile environment sexual harassment when she alleges conduct which a reasonable woman would consider sufficiently severe or pervasive to alter the conditions of employment and create an abusive work environment." The court actually endorsed "a reasonable person of the same sex as the victim" standard for determining what may be considered sexual harassment.

The *Ellison* decision recognizes the reality that reasonable men and women can differ as to what behavior they find offensive or intimidating.

---

[4] Ellison v. Brady, 924 F.2d 872 (9th Cir. 1991).

In light of this, employers should include limiting language when enumerating specific behaviors in their policy statement, such as "the following examples of behavior enumerated in the policy statement do not include all those that can be considered sexual harassment, and a finding of harassment depends on all of the circumstances surrounding the incident(s) alleged."

Defining the behavior that constitutes sexual harassment is not as easy as it sounds. It is now well-documented that experts, courts, arbitrators, managers, reasonable women and men cannot always agree on what sexual harassment is. Most employers use the EEOC Guidelines' definitions of sexual harassment to describe prohibited behaviors:

> Harassment on the basis of sex is a violation of Title VII of the Civil Rights Act of 1964. Unwelcome sexual advances, requests for sexual favors, and other verbal or physical conduct of a sexual nature constitute sexual harassment when:
>
> 1. submission to such conduct is made either explicitly or implicitly a term or condition of an individual's employment,
>
> 2. submission to or rejection of such conduct by an individual is used as the basis for employment decisions affecting such individual, or
>
> 3. such conduct has the purpose or effect of unreasonably interfering with an individual's work performance or creating an intimidating, hostile, or offensive working environment.[5]

Numbers 1 and 2 are often referred to as quid pro quo sexual harassment, while Number 3 is referred to as hostile work environment sexual harassment.

Inclusion of the legal definitions is a critical component of the employer's ability to minimize liability. However, because the legal definitions can read too much like "legalese," some employers supplement them with specific examples of conduct such as

- "pressure for sexual favors" or "requests for dates"
- "letters and calls of a personal or intimate nature"
- "touching of another's body"
- "suggestive looks" or "leering"
- "sexual remarks, slurs, jokes, and innuendo"
- "sexually offensive pictures, posters or calendars"
- "wolf whistles or cat calls"
- "demeaning sexual inquiries"

---

[5] *EEOC Guidelines On Discrimination Because of Sex,* 29 C.F.R. § 1604.11 (1988).

The goal is to have a policy that is easy to read and understand. Even a well-trained employment lawyer can read the definition set forth in the EEOC Guidelines and wonder what it means. Employers that want to encourage employees to come forward with their complaints (and thereby minimize charges and lawsuits), and to be able to hold employees accountable for understanding and abiding by the organization's policy may want to include examples of sexual harassment to supplement the legalistic definitions.

The Navy recently undertook to define a range of behaviors to guide employees based on a concept similar to the continuum discussed in **Chapter 1** and elaborated on in **Chapter 6.** They used a green light, yellow light, red light continuum to offer examples of behaviors that were either acceptable (green light), borderline, that is, may be acceptable depending on the circumstances (yellow light), and unacceptable (red light) (See **Chapter 6** for a discussion of training programs).

The difficulty with this approach outside of the training context is that since the law requires employers to assess standards for behavior based on a "reasonable person's" standard, it is potentially misleading, hence misinformation, to give employees the sense that there is certain behavior that is always okay and certain behavior that is never acceptable. For example, "touching which cannot be perceived in a sexual way" is a very subjective notion, that is, what seems asexual to one person may seem like a sexual advance to another, and is best not summarized in a policy, but rather presented in a training program where illustrations and explanations can be used to more fully develop the concepts.

Those drafting the policy may remind employees that the conduct described must be *unwelcome* to constitute sexual harassment. This serves to put supervisors and any would-be harassers on notice that once they perceive that their conduct is unwelcome, it must cease or violate policy and the law. It puts targets of harassment on notice that the sooner they demonstrate that conduct is unwelcome, the sooner the behavior falls into the category of prohibited sexual harassment.

Unwelcome signifies that some level of coercion underlies the interaction between the targeted employee and the aggressor. The U.S. Supreme Court distinguished the term "unwelcome" from the term "voluntary" in the landmark case of *Meritor Savings Bank v. Vinson,*[6] explaining that a subordinate might voluntarily submit to unwelcome sexual advances in order to avoid losing his or her job, but may still consider the advances "unwelcome" in the sense of unwanted or coercive.

As the term "unwelcome" is difficult even for human resources professionals and legal experts to interpret, employers may elect to avoid its use and instead refer to "unwanted" or "coercive" behavior. As long as the

---

[6] Meritor Savings Bank v. Vinson, 477 U.S. 57 (1986).

term "unwelcome" is used in citing the EEOC Guideline definitions, employers should not have to continually repeat this term when referring to examples of sexual harassment, for example, "touching of another's body, including kissing, rubbing up against, or hugging another" versus "unwelcome touching of another's body." It is hard to imagine too many situations where a supervisor would find it necessary to engage in such conduct with a subordinate for job-related reasons—and it is safest not to, whether it is perceived as welcome or not.

Some employers go as far as to prohibit consensual amorous relations among co-workers and/or between superiors and subordinates through a nonfraternization policy. Office romance policies are distinct from sexual harassment policies, but they have interplay. For organizations that have a no-fraternization policy, it may be worthwhile to mention it or at least cross-reference it in the sexual harassment policy. (See Office Romance Policy, § 2.5)

Some employers advise employees that they must demonstrate "unwelcomeness" by immediately objecting to the harassment and confronting the alleged harasser, informing him or her that the conduct is unwelcome and should cease. While employers may want to encourage employees to voice or otherwise demonstrate their objection to offensive conduct, employees have no legal obligation to do so, and as was explained in **Chapter 1,** failure to object is not evidence that the conduct is "welcome." This accounts for the situations where someone in a subordinate position of power feels uncomfortable confronting the alleged harasser directly for fear of reprisal.

Another option is to supplement the legal definitions with stories based on court cases. By using factual accounts from actual court cases rather than from the organization's actual experience, or from hypotheticals which could be attributed to the organization by clever plaintiff's counsel, it is safest to use court cases to illustrate sexual harassment scenarios. An example:

Meet Sandra Bundy

Sandra Bundy was an employee at a public agency where a lot of sexual banter was tolerated. Several of Sandra's supervisors made sexual propositions to her throughout her employment, but she always turned down their advances. She decided to report the sexual advances to the manager above her supervisors, but his response was to invite her to start an intimate relationship with him.

Over the years, Sandra's supervisors denied or delayed her promotions, but they never terminated her. However, when Sandra brought her case to court, the judge found that Sandra was the victim of unlawful sexual harassment, even though she had not lost her job or any job benefits.[7]

If an employer elects to use any examples, stories or scenarios, to illustrate sexual harassment, it is important to include a disclaimer that makes it clear to employees that the illustrations are generic in nature and are not based on any real instances or individuals in the workplace.

Language Regarding Confidentiality

The policy must meet the goal of effectively addressing sexual harassment complaints while providing confidentiality to maximum extent possible. Many policies promise that confidentiality will be maintained to the extent practicable during the course of investigating and resolving complaints. This language acknowledges that confidentiality is of prime importance, but still accommodates the reality of the process which almost always requires some disclosure of the identity of the complainant, the alleged harassers, the witnesses and the acts alleged.

Policies that promise absolute confidentiality to complainants are for the most part misleading. While the names of the complainant and witnesses need not be disclosed up front to the alleged harasser, at some later point disclosure may become unavoidable in order to complete the investigation. An absolute guarantee of confidentiality should be avoided, as it cannot realistically be met.

Language Regarding Nonretaliation

The policy should also inform employees of the organization's and the law's prohibition of retaliation against those who make complaints of sexual harassment or who cooperate in the investigation of such complaints.

Complaint Procedure

The inclusion of a procedure for addressing sexual harassment complaints is essential. It breathes life into the policy statement and lends it credibility. Further, in 1986 the United States Supreme Court in *Meritor Savings Bank v. Vinson*,[8] gave employers this advice: if you want to have a reasonable

---

[7] This story is based on the case Bundy v. Jackson, 641 F.2d 93 (D.C. Cir. 1981).

[8] Meritor Savings Bank v. Vinson, 477 U.S. 57 (1986).

chance at avoiding liability for sexual harassment, you should at a minimum,

1.   Have a policy in place that informs employees what sexual harassment is and that it is against the law.
2.   *Provide employees with a mechanism for complaining about harassment that encourages them raise their concern.*
3.   Take prompt and appropriate remedial action.
4.   Communicate the policy directly to all employees.

The court suggested that while having a procedure, in and of itself, is not sufficient to shield an employer from liability for sexual harassment, if the procedures encourage employees to raise their concerns about sexual harassment, an employee's failure to use them will be given strong consideration. Indeed, many cases have been won by employers due to the strength of their sexual harassment procedures.

However, in addition to the liability reason for having a clearly-articulated procedure, there is the residual benefit that if more employees complain about harassment, harassers will be identified and weeded out of the organization or educated, as the case may warrant, and the preventive end is accomplished. If an employer has a user-friendly complaint procedure more employees are likely to use, keeping complaints within the organization, rather than by default, leaving employees little choice but to seek a forum in the courts or with an enforcement agency.

Summary of Procedure

The procedures should cover to whom complaints can be made, how complaints are handled (including the investigation process, guiding principles such as confidentiality, due process, and nonretaliation), and resolutions (including a statement on discipline).

1.   To whom complaints can be made. The Supreme Court in *Vinson* established the principle that employees should have several channels open to their complaints, not just their supervisor. Employees should be given several alternative contacts for complaints as well.
2.   How complaints are handled.
     The procedure should explain how complaints are processed, for example, steps typically include:
     a.   Interviewing the Complainant and Alleged Harasser
     b.   Conducting an Investigation

   c. Resolving the Complaint, including how long it can take to get a resolution and what the possible outcomes are. Policies generally provide that if an allegation of sexual harassment is substantiated, the harasser is subject to discipline up to and including termination of employment.

   d. Training. The policy should include mention of any training that will be offered to employees and managers in using and administering the policy.

The Objective

Defining the objective up front makes it easier to design and implement a policy that is internally consistent, easy to administer for the organization and easy to use for employees. It facilitates design decisions for all involved to agree on the overall approach to the subject of sexual harassment at the outset.

The objective of preventing of sexual harassment is one that most senior management will buy into. However, the prevention strategy has its costs: without being prepared to effectively train managers in understanding what sexual harassment is and how to handle it, as well as educating employees about their rights and responsibilities, an organization cannot hope to make a preventive approach work. A preventive mind-set assumes recognition that sexual harassment is a costly problem worth addressing and preventing.

§ 2.5   Office Romance Policy Versus Sexual Harassment Policy

The "EEOC Guidelines on Discrimination Because of Sex," Section 1604.11 on Sexual Harassment, provide that:

> Where employment opportunities or benefits are granted because of an individual's submission to the employer's sexual advances or requests for sexual favors, the employer may be held liable for unlawful sex discrimination against other persons who were qualified for but denied that employment opportunity or benefit.

However, in one case, *Mundy v. Palmetto Ford*,[9] decided by the Fourth Circuit Court of Appeals in July 1993, a terminated male employee failed to state a cause of action for sexual harassment where his boss and his female co-worker were intimately involved. The court refused to define

---

[9] 988 F.2d 1010 (4th Cir. 1993).

"sex . . . so broadly as to include an ongoing, voluntary, romantic engagement."

The outcome of this analysis suggests that absent *a pattern* of granting preferential treatment to those who engage in sexual relations with those in a position to grant or withhold job benefits, an employer may not be liable for office romantic relationships.

While sexual bribery and blackmail can be actionable after only one occurrence, generally hostile work environment and sexual favoritism require the demonstration of an ongoing pattern of harassment to be unlawful. There are instances where a single act of sexual harassment, while carrying no reward or punishment for the victim, may be serious enough to create liability, such as where an individual exposes him or herself, grabs someone's body part or gestures with his or her own body part, or seriously threatens an individual in writing or orally.

Consider the headline of the August 8, 1993 issue of the *New York Times* "Federal Investigator is Accused of Sex Harassment." In that case, an investigator with the National Institutes of Health (N.I.H.), who is married, at first denied having had sexual relations with an office manager who reports to him. He later admitted it, but insisted that their relations had been consensual. The office manager's account is that she had sex with her supervisor three times over the year, the first time was consensual and the other two were "under pressure," as the article stated. Apparently this complaint was but one of 80 informal complaints filed in 1992 against the N.I.H. (It has 14,000 employees, according to the article).

The following report appeared in an issue of *The Wall Street Journal*: Some 70 percent of companies "permit and accept" dating among co-workers; the rest "permit but discourage it" and discuss potential problems with couples, according to a survey of 1,493 personnel managers by the Society for Human Resource Management. Potential problems include sexual harassment claims, cited by half of those surveyed, and office gossip, cited by two-thirds.

The greatest concerns for employers in deciding whether to allow office romances are:

- The potential for those romances to turn sour—leaving the firm vulnerable to sexual harassment or other discrimination claims
- The potential for any romantic involvement between subordinate and supervisor to give rise to a claim for favoritism by other employees who are excluded from opportunities because they are not involved with the boss

An office romance policy can help prohibit dating between supervisor and subordinates. While the social relationship between supervisors and subordinates may be amicable during an office romance, if the relationship sours, the employer may have a breeding ground for potential sexual harassment claims. Scenarios that can lead to sexual harassment or sex discrimination claims where office romances are permitted include:

A subordinate and supervisor are dating, and the supervisor accords special treatment to the subordinate. Other employees complain that the subordinate is getting preferential treatment because of his or her relationship with the supervisor. The complaint could be stated as sex discrimination if the claimants can show that the preferential treatment is based on the sex of the subordinate employee.

If the supervisor/subordinate relationship ends due to discord, there is another potential problem. The supervisor may treat the subordinate unduly harshly or take retaliatory measures against the subordinate employee.

Finally, there is the possibility that the supervisor and subordinate would flaunt their relationship openly. If they engage in touching or other demonstrative behavior in the workplace, it could make other employees uncomfortable enough that they would quit their jobs. They may be able to claim that they were forced out of the firm, constructively discharged, and sue for lost wages or successfully file for unemployment benefits.

Analysis of Policy Provisions

The sample policy of Generica Corporation follows the generally-accepted format of a policy statement, enumerating prohibited acts, responsibilities of managerial and nonmanagerial employees, and reporting procedure. The confidentiality statement is well-worded: "To the extent possible, the names of individuals associated with complaints will be maintained in the strictest confidence except to the extent that disclosure is required to conduct an adequate investigation and take any required remedial steps." The only item missing from the policy is a nonretaliation provision.

The XYZ Professional Service Firm policy's language that "at XYZ, sexual harassment whether verbal, physical or environmental, and whether in the workplace itself *or in outside work-sponsored settings* is unacceptable" makes the point that it is not only behavior on-site at the workplace that is covered by the policy—a good point to make. In addition, the XYZ policy reporting options appropriately "recognizes that it is not necessary for an individual to talk directly to an offender if it is uncomfortable," something that many policies fail to articulate so simply. The provision mentioning specific types of responsive action that can be carried out (referral to counseling, withholding a promotion, termination, and so forth) is also effective, but may be risky, as it can build expectations that some firms will not be willing to meet.

The Bonneville Power Administration policy is effective in offering employees "options" on how to respond to harassment or retaliation. Employees will feel more in control of a policy that gives them the option to react the way they are most comfortable doing it: this will make them more likely to come forward. The "confidential harassment hotline" is a good idea, as those handling the hotline calls are presumed to be specifically trained to handle sexual harassment complaints—not always a straightforward process, even for those used to complex employee relations issues. However, the "confidential harassment hotline" option can present some difficulties. First, the confidentiality promised in the first stage of the complaint may not be maintainable throughout an investigation and resolution stages, should they become necessary.

Second, employers receiving calls on a hotline will be deemed to have notice of alleged sexual harassment, giving rise to a legal obligation to take corrective action. Employees should not be given the option of making a complaint in confidence subject to their own decision regarding disclosure (this concept is discussed further in **Chapter 3,** relating to complaint procedures).

Each employer makes the decision as to when and how much information regarding a complaint must be disclosed, and to whom disclosure is needed, in order to fulfill its legal and ethical obligations to stop incidents of harassment of which it has knowledge (or should have knowledge).

The BPA policy is also one of the few that specifically refers to the enforcement of the policy with regard to third parties such as vendors and contractors, noting that the firm may cease doing business with them if they sexually harass employees.

The Megafinancial Service Company policy is useful in its use of a section on "Avoiding harassing behaviors," an unusual statement on work relations between men and women. "In a two-gender work group, neutral relations means that people do not have to be either friends or enemies at work. People can deal courteously without hostility and without the titillation of sexual interest." The conclusions and recommendations offered to managers include a list akin to a "declaration of rights and responsibilities," an effective technique that can be used to capture the "spirit," in addition to the letter of the policy. One statement exemplifying such an attitude is: "Every employee has an obligation to support management's policies and good human relations practices in preventing, removing, reporting, and correcting inappropriate social behaviors at the work site."

The American Bar Association Commission on Women in the Profession has issued a model sexual harassment policy that addresses some of the unique challenges of handling harassment in law firms. It has a comprehensive section on who is covered under the policy which includes court personnel and clients. It also encourages employees to document harassment and keep notes to be able to corroborate their complaints. While this may seem not to be in the organization's best interest, it probably is advantageous for all concerned employees to have to prepare their allegations, particularly if a lawsuit is brought by either party. However, this is a more legalistic approach than might be used in other employment settings where the level of sophistication is more inconsistent. The policy also contains a section on complaint investigation and resolution which is reprinted in **Chapter 3.**

The JSI policy notes that the examples of sexual harassment given is not "exhaustive," a recommended cautionary statement. It also refers to potential individual liability, another unique feature. Individuals in a supervisory capacity can in some jurisdictions be held personally liable for assault, battery, engaging in sexual harassment or aiding and abetting in sexual harassment that they knew about but failed to stop.

The JSI policy also contains a definition of "sexually suggestive" material as material that "depicts a person of either sex who is not fully clothed or in clothes that are not suited to or ordinarily accepted for the accomplishment of routine work." This standard will, of course, vary from one employment setting to another, but there is not much question but that depictions that would qualify as erotica or pornography would not in most cases pass for ordinary work attire.

JSI's definition of retaliation is more comprehensive than most, thereby giving greater notice to those who would be inclined to retaliate of what behavior will be considered reprisal. For instance, the definition includes "refusing to cooperate or discuss work-related matters" with an employee who has made a complaint—otherwise known as giving the employee the cold shoulder, something that employees who have brought complaints are very sensitive to.

JSI's policy is distributed to all new employees at orientation and they must sign to acknowledge its receipt. This is a highly recommended practice. First, it creates a record that shows that each employee has received notice of the policy. Second, it sets the tone from the start of the employment relationship that sexual harassment is something that the organization takes seriously. Supervisory employees must not only acknowledge the policy, they are required to present information regarding the organization's policy to others at periodic employee meetings. This is also an advisable practice: it not only keeps all employees current on the topic, it ensures and demonstrates that supervisors are well-versed in the policy.

The university policy is offered because academia presents some unique challenges for policy drafters. The audience of the policy ranges from nonprofessional staff, to students of all ages, to relatively sophisticated faculty and administrators. Universities also tend to be melting pots of cultural and ethnic diversity.

The sample policy is among the most comprehensive available. It includes a highly-structured complaint process, with a strong emphasis on conciliation. It provides for specific outcomes depending on the finding made. One item in the policy that is controversial is that advice that "persons seeking information will be advised that if they wish to ensure that the discussion remains confidential and that no action is taken without their consent, it is essential that individual names and departments not be disclosed." While this practice may be welcomed by complainants who are afraid to take action and may allow them to voice a concern that they might otherwise harbor in silence, employers may be at risk of having knowledge of the parties involved "implied" or of failing to take appropriate remedial action by giving complainants the option of not naming names. Further, the organization allows potentially grievous violators to continue to break the policy and the law by failing to compel the use of names and other specifics when a complaint is brought forward.

§ 2.6   The Process of Policy Design

The process of designing a sexual harassment policy is unique to each organization. The decision on whom to include in the policy design will vary from organization to organization. Some cultures are more participative than others.

There are advantages to involving line management and human resources, perhaps even employee groups, in the policy design phase of the process:

- Buy-in and acceptance
- Increased saleability of the policy
- Build team spirit for what is a team process
- Reality check
- Gain further understanding and insights
- Customer focus
- A policy that is responsive to, not reactive to, management and employee needs
- Cover all the bases
- Generate ideas from those who will have to use the policy
- Educate through the process of developing the policy

Many human resources professionals find it advantageous to get as broad-based involvement by line managers and key administrators as possible in order to ensure that there is a shared sense of "ownership" in the program.

Disadvantages of the participatory approach include:

- Creates expectations
- Harder to control information
- Harder to make decisions—must seek compromise and consensus
- Time constraints: it will take longer to develop the policy

If you are going to involve employees, line managers, and human resources, consider ways to draw them into the process. To get started on the right track, consider a brainstorming session. Gather a group of experienced human resources professionals and managers together to discuss their views of what the sexual harassment policy should say and do.

Begin by asking participants to select adjectives to describe what they want the policy to be:

—supportive

—clear

—fair

—consistent

—simple

—short

—neutral

—easy to use/user-friendly

—comprehensive

—plain English

What they want to the policy to do:

—educate

—inform

—warn/put on notice

—meet all legal requirements/protect the company

—give complainants options

—deter would-be harassers

What they want the policy to say:

—we care about our employees

—employees should treat each other with respect

—sexual harassment is unacceptable

—sexual harassment will be punished

—sexual harassment is taken seriously

—preventing sexual harassment is every employee's responsibility

—reporting sexual harassment is rewarded not punished

—strict adherence to non-retaliation

—sexual harassment is against the law and against company policy

—we encourage reporting of sexual harassment

Once the initial views of all participants have been considered, consensus should be built on which goals are the most important. Suggestions on specific provisions can be generated through the same process. As the policy progresses, feedback should be solicited from participants who were involved in these initial planning meetings.

Organizations will also differ on whom they involve in drafting the policy. Some will use a consultant, an attorney, in-house counsel or an employee relations/EEO department. Most organizations will vary in how they use lawyers in the process. Some will use them in a consultative role, that is, to review the policy just for legal accuracy once it is drafted by human resources. Others will have lawyers draft the policy for approval by human resources. The only caveat here is that the policy should be user-friendly: easy to read, understand, and to use. Too much legalese can interfere with these goals.

Summary

There is no blueprint for designing sexual harassment policies. This section, perhaps more than any other in this chapter, demonstrates that the development of a sexual harassment policy is more art than science. Beyond certain minimal recommended provisions, employers have wide discretion in a policy's content, organization and style.

Indeed, according to the 1988 *Working Woman* survey in which 165 Fortune 500 companies participated,

- 65% of the companies' policies include a statement prohibiting sexual harassment by supervisory and non-supervisory employees
- 65% include a description of the company's grievance procedure
- 56% include an explanation of disciplinary measures that can be taken against harassers

- 56% promise confidentiality whenever possible
- 47% give assurances against retaliation for victims and witnesses

As the above survey demonstrates, employers do not all agree on what items should be addressed in a sexual harassment policy. While it is advisable that sexual harassment policies address the areas set forth by the EEOC in its Policy Guidelines, the extent and manner of coverage can vary.

A good preventive policy will address each of the points raised in the above EEOC Guidelines. It will. therefore, at a minimum:

1. **Affirmatively raise the subject of sexual harassment.** This is accomplished by adopting a separate sexual harassment policy, in writing, and disseminating it directly to all employees. Effective communication can be accomplished by:

   - Including the policy in the employee handbook
   - Distributing a copy of the policy at new employee orientations
   - Holding mandatory workshops and other educational sessions on sexual harassment that describe and explain the policy
   - Using newsletters, bulletins, and other inter-office publications to periodically feature an item on sexual harassment that includes a review of the policy
   - Offering management and employee training on sexual harassment that covers the policy

2. **Express strong disapproval of sexual harassment.** The policy statement is an effective, and certainly low-cost, way to express the organization's disapproval of sexual harassment.

3. **Inform employees of their rights and responsibilities.** This section generally includes the definition of sexual harassment. Employers should adopt a definition that is at least as stringent as that generally accepted by the courts and the EEOC. However, the definition can be expanded.

4. **Educate and "sensitize" all members of the organization on the problem of sexual harassment.** This is accomplished through the training programs offered by the organization.

§ 2.7   Sample Policies

SAMPLE POLICY 1: GENERICA CORPORATION POLICY ON SEXUAL HARASSMENT

1.0   PURPOSE
To set forth the Company's policy on sexual harassment and to define forms of disciplinary action for violation of the policy.

2.0   APPLICATION
This policy is applicable to all Company organizations and applicants for employment.

3.0   GENERAL PROVISIONS
3.1   Overall Sexual Harassment Policy Statement
It is the policy of the Company that there be no discrimination against any employee or applicant for employment on the basis of sex. In keeping with that policy, the Company will not tolerate acts of sexual harassment by any of its employees. The Company considers sexual harassment to be a major offense, which can result in the immediate suspension or discharge of the offender.

3.2   Prohibited Acts
Sexual harassment is a violation of the Company's rules of conduct. Unwelcome sexual advances, requests for sexual favors, and other verbal or physical conduct of a sexual nature constitute sexual harassment when:

a.   Submission to the conduct is made either an explicit or implicit condition of employment.

b.   Submission to or rejection of the conduct is used as a basis for an employment decision affecting the harassed employee.

c.   The conduct unreasonably interferes with an employee's job performance or creates an intimidating, hostile or offensive work environment.

   The commission of such acts, and of any acts of retaliation against an individual who exercises his or her rights under this policy, is strictly prohibited.

4.0   IMPLEMENTATION
All employees are responsible for the implementation of the provisions under this policy.

5.0   RESPONSIBILITIES
5.1   The Senior Vice President, Administration, is responsible for the overall administration of the Sexual Harassment Policy.
5.2   Each Vice President is responsible for ensuring that the EEO policy is known and implemented within his or her organization, for appointing

EEO representatives to assist in that effort, for referring to such representative or to the Director, EEO Affairs, any complaints or other instances of possible violations of this policy, and for administering appropriate discipline for such violations.

5.3 The Director, EEO Affairs, has the responsibility for investigating alleged acts of sexual harassment in a prompt and confidential manner. In determining whether the alleged conduct constitutes sexual harassment, the totality of the circumstances, the nature of the alleged harassment, and the context in which the alleged incidents occurred will be investigated. Supervisors are responsible for ensuring that their areas of responsibility are free of sexual harassment.

6.0 PROCEDURE FOR REPORTING

6.1 Any employee or applicant for employment who believes he or she is a victim of sexual harassment should report such belief to his or her immediate supervisors, EEO Representative, the Director of Equal Employment Opportunity Affairs, or any member of supervision (as appropriate) and may do so without fear of retaliation. All such complaints, or other instances of possible violations of this policy, shall be investigated by the EEO Representative under the direction of the Director of Equal Employment Opportunity Affairs or referred to the Director of Equal Employment Opportunity Affairs for investigation.

6.2 To the extent possible, the names of individuals associated with complaints will be maintained in the strictest of confidence except to the extent that disclosure is required to conduct an adequate investigation and take any required remedial steps.

6.3 Any report generated as a result of the investigation of a complaint filed under this policy shall ordinarily be maintained as confidential except as to any management representatives who need knowledge of the contents of the report in order to evaluate and/or carry out its recommendations.

7.0 ADVICE & COUNSEL

The Senior Vice President, Administration, and the Director of Equal Employment Opportunity Affairs will provide advice and counsel on this Policy Statement.

SAMPLE POLICY 2: XYZ PROFESSIONAL SERVICE FIRM

FIRM STATEMENT OF PHILOSOPHY

XYZ is committed to a collegial work environment in which all individuals are treated with respect and dignity. Each individual has the right to work in a professional atmosphere that promotes equal opportunities and prohibits discriminatory practices, including sexual harassment. At XYZ, sexual harassment, whether verbal, physical or environmental, and whether in the workplace itself or in outside work-sponsored settings, is unacceptable and will not be tolerated.

DEFINITION OF SEXUAL HARASSMENT

Sexual Harassment constitutes discrimination and is illegal under federal, state and local laws. For purposes of this policy, sexual harassment is defined as it is in the Equal Opportunity Commission Guidelines promulgated in 1980 as unwelcome sexual advances, requests for sexual favors, and other verbal or physical conduct of a sexual nature when (1) submission to such conduct is made either explicitly or implicitly a term or condition of an individual's employment, (2) submission to or rejection of such conduct by an individual is used as the basis for employment decisions affecting such individual, or (3) such conduct has the purpose or effect of unreasonably interfering with an individual's work performance or creating an intimidating, hostile, or offensive working environment.

EXAMPLES OF POTENTIAL SEXUAL HARASSMENT

Sexual Harassment may include a range of subtle and not so subtle behaviors. Depending on the circumstances, these behaviors may include, but are not limited to: unwanted sexual advances; subtle or overt pressure for sexual favors; sexual jokes, flirtations, innuendos, advances, or propositions; verbal abuse of a sexual nature; graphic commentary about an individual's body, sexual prowess, or sexual deficiencies; leering, whistling, touching, pinching, assault, coerced sexual acts, or suggestive, insulting, or obscene comments, or gestures; display in the workplace of sexually suggestive objects or pictures.

Sexual harassment can include harassment between individuals of the same sex.

INDIVIDUALS COVERED UNDER THE POLICY

This policy applies to all employees of XYZ, whether related to conduct engaged in by fellow employees, supervisors, or someone not directly connected to XYZ (e.g., an outside vendor, consultant, client, etc.).

REPORTING AN INCIDENT OF SEXUAL HARASSMENT

XYZ encourages reporting of all perceived incidents of sexual harassment, regardless of who the offender may be. Individuals who believe they have been the victims of sexual harassment or believe they have witnessed sexual harassment should discuss their concerns with a supervisor or with any member of the Sexual Harassment Committee listed on the attachment. See the Complaint Procedures described below.

COMPLAINT PROCEDURE

1. Notification of Appropriate Staff

As noted above, individuals who believe they have been the victim of sexual harassment or believe they have witnessed sexual harassment should discuss their concerns with a supervisor or with any member of the Sexual Harassment Committee listed on the attachment. If you receive information regarding sexual harassment in your capacity as a supervisor, you are obligated to report it to a member of the Sexual Harassment Committee. XYZ encourages individuals who believe they are being harassed to promptly advise the offender that his or her behavior is unwelcome. XYZ also recognizes that it is not necessary for an individual to talk directly to an offender if it is uncomfortable.

2. Timeliness in Reporting an Incident

Prompt reporting of incidents is important so that action may be taken. However, due to the sensitivity of these problems and because of the emotional toll such misconduct may have on the individual, no fixed period has been set for reporting sexual harassment incidents.

3. Investigatory Process

Any reported allegations of sexual harassment will be investigated promptly. The investigation may include interviews with the parties involved, and where necessary, with individuals who may have observed the alleged conduct or may have relevant knowledge. Any reported allegations should be handled in a sensitive and discreet manner.

4. Confidentiality

Confidentiality will be maintained throughout the entire investigatory process to the extent practicable and appropriate under the circumstances to protect the privacy of persons involved.

5. Protection Against Retaliation

Retaliation, against an individual who makes a report of alleged sexual harassment or assists in providing information relevant to a claim of sexual harassment, is a serious violation of this policy. Acts of retaliation should be reported immediately and will be handled appropriately.

6. Responsive Action

Misconduct constituting sexual harassment will be dealt with appropriately. Responsive action may include, for example, training, referral to counseling, and disciplinary action such as warnings, reprimands, withholding of a promotion, reassignment, temporary suspension without pay, compensation adjustments or termination.

7. Reconsideration

If any employee directly involved in a sexual harassment investigation wishes the matter to be reconsidered, that party may submit a written request in a timely manner to the Chairperson of the Sexual Harassment Committee.

CONCLUSION

XYZ has developed this policy to ensure that all its employees and partners can work in an environment free from sexual harassment. XYZ will make every reasonable effort to ensure that its entire population is familiar with the policy and is aware that any complaint received will be investigated and resolved appropriately.

Any employee who has any questions or concerns about this policy should talk with a member of the Sexual Harassment Committee.

SAMPLE POLICY 3: COURT-ORDERED SEXUAL HARASSMENT POLICY: ROBINSON V. JACKSONVILLE SHIPYARDS

Title VII of the Civil Rights Act of 1964 prohibits employment discrimination on the basis of race, color, sex, age, or national origin. Sexual harassment is included among the prohibitions.

Sexual harassment, according to the EEOC, consists of unwelcome sexual advances, requests for sexual favors or other verbal or physical acts of a sexual or sex-based nature where (1) submission to such conduct is made either explicitly or implicitly a term or a condition of an individual's employment; (2) an employment decision is based on an individual's acceptance or rejection of such conduct; or (3) such conduct interferes with an individual's work performance or creates an intimidating, hostile, or offensive working environment.

It is also unlawful to retaliate or take reprisal in any way against anyone who has articulated any concern about sexual harassment or discrimination against the individual raising the concern or against another individual.

Examples of conduct that would be considered sexual harassment or rated retaliation are set forth in the Statement of Prohibited Conduct which follows. These examples are provided to illustrate the kind of conduct proscribed by this policy; the list is not exhaustive.

Jacksonville Shipyards, Inc., and its agents are under a duty to investigate or eradicate any form of sexual harassment or sex discrimination or complaints about conduct in violation of this policy and a schedule for violation of this policy.

Sexual harassment is unlawful, and such prohibited conduct exposes not only JSI, but individuals involved in such conduct, to significant liability under the law. Employees at all times should treat other employees respectfully and with dignity in a manner so as not to offend the sensibilities of a coworker. Accordingly, JSI's management is committed to vigorously enforcing its sexual harassment policy at all levels within the company.

STATEMENT OF PROHIBITED CONDUCT

The management of Jacksonville Shipyards, Inc., considers the following conduct to represent some of the types of acts that violate JSI's sexual harassment policy:

A. Physical assaults of a sexual nature, such as:

1. Rape, sexual battery, molestation, or attempts to commit these assaults; and

2. Intentional physical conduct which is sexual in nature, such as touching, pinching, patting, grabbing, brushing against another employee's body, or poking another employee's body.

B. Unwanted sexual advances, propositions, or other sexual comments, such as:

1. Sexually-oriented gestures, noises, remarks, jokes, or comments about a person's sexuality or sexual experience directed at or made in the presence of any employee who indicates or has indicated in any way that such conduct in his or her presence is unwelcome;

2. Preferential treatment or promises of preferential treatment to an employee for submitting to sexual conduct, including soliciting or attempting to solicit any employee to engage in sexual activity for compensation or reward; and

3. Subjecting, or threats of subjecting, an employee to unwelcome sexual attention or conduct or intentionally making performance of the employee's job more difficult because of that employee's sex.

C. Sexual or discriminatory displays or publications anywhere in JSI's workplace by JSI employees, such as:

1. Displaying pictures, posters, calendars, graffiti, objects, promotional materials, reading materials, or other materials that are sexually suggestive, sexually demeaning, or pornographic, or bringing into the JSI work environment or possessing any such material to read, display or view at work.

A picture will be presumed to be sexually suggestive if it depicts a person of either sex who is not fully clothed or in clothes that are not suited to or ordinarily accepted for the accomplishment of routine work in an around the shipyard and who is posed for the obvious purpose of displaying or drawing attention to private portions of his or her body.

2. Reading or otherwise publicizing in the work environment materials that are in any way sexually revealing, sexually suggestive, sexually demeaning, or pornographic; and

3. Displaying signs or other materials purporting to segregate an employee by sex in any area of the workplace (other than rest rooms and similar semi-private lockers/changing rooms).

D. Retaliation for sexual harassment complaints, such as:

1. Disciplining, changing work assignments of, providing inaccurate work information to, or refusing to cooperate or discuss work-related matters with any employee because that employee has complained about or resisted harassment, discrimination, or retaliation; and

2. Intentionally pressuring, falsely denying, lying about or otherwise covering up or attempting to cover up conduct such as that described in any item above.

E. Other acts:

1. The above is not to be construed as an all-inclusive list of prohibited acts under this policy.

2. Sexual harassment is unlawful and hurts other employees. Any of the prohibited conduct described here is sexual harassment of anyone at whom it is directed or who is otherwise subjected to it. Each incident of harassment, moreover, contributes to a general atmosphere in which all persons who share the victim's sex suffer the consequences. Sexually-oriented acts or sex-based conduct have no legitimate business purposes; accordingly, the employee who engages in such conduct should be and will be made to bear the full responsibility for such unlawful conduct.

SCHEDULE OF PENALTIES FOR MISCONDUCT

The following schedule of penalties applies to all violations of the JSI Sexual Harassment Policy, as explained in more detail in the Statement of Prohibited Conduct. Where progressive discipline is provided for, each instance of conduct violating the policy moves the offending employee through the steps of disciplinary action. In other words, it is not necessary for an employee to repeat the same precise conduct in order to move up the scale of discipline.

A written record of each action taken pursuant to the policy will be placed in the offending employee's personnel file. The record will reflect the conduct, or alleged conduct, and the warning given, or other discipline imposed.

A. Assault

Any employee's first proven offense of assault or threat of assault, including assault of a sexual nature, will result in dismissal.

B. Other acts of harassment by coworkers

An employee's commission of acts of sexual harassment other than assault will result in nondisciplinary oral counseling on alleged first offense, written warning, suspension, or discharge on the first proven offense, depending upon the nature or severity of the misconduct, and suspension or discharge upon the second proven offense, depending on the nature or severity of the misconduct.

C. Retaliation

Alleged retaliation against a sexual harassment complainant will result in non-disciplinary oral counseling. Any form of proven retaliation will result in suspension or discharge on the first proven offense, depending on the nature and severity of the retaliatory acts, and discharge on the second proven offense.

D. Supervisors

A supervisor's commission of acts of sexual harassment (other than assault) with respect to any other employee under that person's supervision will result in nondisciplinary oral counseling on alleged first offense, final warning or dismissal for the first offense, depending on the nature and severity of the misconduct, and discharge for any subsequent offense.

PROCEDURES FOR MAKING, INVESTIGATING AND RESOLVING SEXUAL HARASSMENT AND RETALIATION COMPLAINTS

A. Complaints

JSI will provide its employees with convenient, confidential and reliable mechanisms for reporting incidents of sexual harassment and retaliation. Accordingly, JSI designates at least two employees in supervisory or managerial positions at each of the Commercial and Mayport Yards to serve as investigative officers for sexual harassment issues. The names, responsibilities, work locations, and phone numbers of each officer will be routinely and continuously posted so that an employee seeking such name can enjoy anonymity and remain inconspicuous to all of the employees in the yard in which he or she works.

The investigative officers may appoint "designees" to assist them in handling sexual harassment complaints. Persons appointed as designees shall not conduct an investigation until they have received training equivalent to that received by the investigative officers. The purpose of having several persons to whom complaints may be made is to avoid a situation in which an employee is faced with complaining to the person, or a close associate of the person, who would be the subject of the complaint.

Complaints of acts of sexual harassment or retaliation that are in violation of the sexual harassment policy will be accepted in writing or orally, and anonymous complaints will be taken seriously and investigated. Anyone who has observed sexual harassment or retaliation should report it to a designated investigative officer. A complaint need not be limited to someone who was the target of harassment or retaliation.

Only those who have an immediate need to know, including the investigative officers and/or his/her designee, the alleged target of harassment or retaliation, the alleged harassers or retaliators and any witnesses will or may find out the identity of the complainant. All parties contacted in the course of an investigation will be advised that all parties involved in a charge are entitled to respect and that any retaliation or reprisal against an individual who is an alleged target of harassment or retaliation, who has made a complaint, or who has provided evidence in connection with a complaint is a separate actionable offense as provided in the schedule of penalties. The complaint process will be administered consistent with federal labor law when bargaining unit members are affected.

B. Investigations

Each investigative officer will receive thorough training about sexual harassment and the procedures herein and will have the responsibility for investigating complaints or having an appropriately trained and designated JSI investigator do so.

All complaints will be investigated expeditiously by a trained JSI investigative officer or his/her designee. The investigative officer will produce a written report, which, together with the investigation file, will be shown to the complainant on request within a reasonable time. The investigative officer is empowered to recommend remedial measures based on the results of the investigation, and JSI management will promptly consider and act on such recommendation. When a complaint is made the investigative officer will have the duty of immediately bringing all sexual harassment and retaliation complaints to the confidential attention of the office of the President of JSI, and JSI's EEO Officer. The investigative and EEO officers will each maintain a file on the original charge and follow-up investigation. Such files will be available to investigators, to federal, state, and local agencies charged with equal employment or affirmative action enforcement, to other complainants who have filed a formal charge of discrimination against JSI, or any agent thereof whether that formal charge is filed at a federal, state, or local law level. The names of complainants, however, will be kept under separate file.

C. Cooperation

An effective sexual harassment policy requires the support and example of company personnel in positions of authority. JSI agents or employees who engage in sexual harassment or retaliation or who fail to cooperate with company-sponsored investigations of sexual harassment or retaliation may be severely sanctioned by suspension or dismissal. By the same token, officials who refuse to implement remedial measures, obstruct the remedial efforts of other JSI employees, and/or retaliate against sexual harassment complainants or witnesses may be immediately sanctioned by suspension or dismissal.

D. Monitoring

Because JSI is under legal obligations imposed by court order, the NOW Legal Defense and Education Fund, its designated representative, and, if one is appointed on motion and a showing of need, a representative of the U.S. District Court for the Middle District of Florida are authorized to monitor the JSI workplace, even in the absence of specific complaints, to ensure that the company's policy against sexual harassment is being enforced. Such persons are not ordinarily to be used in lieu of the JSI investigative officers on investigation of individual matters, but instead are to be available to assess the adequacy of investigations. Any individual dissatisfied with JSI's investigation of a complaint may contact such persons in writing or by telephone and request an independent investigation. Such persons' addresses and telephone numbers will be posted and circulated with those of the investigative officers. Such persons will be given reasonable access by JSI to inspect for compliance.

PROCEDURES AND RULES FOR EDUCATION AND TRAINING

Education and training for employees at each level of the work force are critical to the success of JSI's policy against sexual harassment. The following documents address such issues: the letter to be sent to all employees from JSI's chief executive officer/president, the Sexual Harassment policy, Statement of Prohibited Conduct, the Schedule of Penalties for Misconduct, and Procedures for Making, Investigating, and Resolving Sexual Harassment and Retaliation Complaints. These documents will be conspicuously posted throughout the workplace at each division of JSI, on each company bulletin board, in all central gathering areas, and in every locker room. The statements must be clearly legible and displayed continuously. The sexual harassment policy under a cover letter from JSI's president will be sent to all employees. The letter will indicate that copies are available at no cost and how they can be obtained.

JSI's sexual harassment policy statement will also be included in the Safety Instructions and General Company Rules, which are issued in booklet form to each JSI employee. Educational posters using concise messages conveying JSI's opposition to workplace sexual harassment will reinforce the company's policy statement; these posters should be simple, eye-catching and graffiti-resistant.

Education and training include the following components:

1. For all JSI employees: As part of general orientation, each recently hired employee will be given a copy of the letter from JSI's chief executive officer/president and requested to read and sign a receipt for the company's policy statement on sexual harassment so that they are no notice of the standards of

behavior expected. In addition, supervisory employees who have attended a management training seminar on sexual harassment will explain orally at least once every six months at safety meetings attended by all employees the kinds of acts that constitute sexual harassment, the company's serious commitment to eliminating sexual harassment in the workplace, the penalties for engaging in harassment, and the procedures for reporting incidents of sexual harassment.

2. For all female employees: All women employed at JSI will participate, on company time, in annual seminars that teach strategies for resisting and preventing sexual harassment. At least a half-day in length, these seminars will be conducted by one or more experienced sexual harassment educators, including one instructor with work experience in the trades.

3. For all employees with supervisory authority over other employees, including leadermen, quartermen, superintendents, and all employees working in a managerial capacity: All supervisory personnel will participate in an annual, half-day-long training session on sex discrimination. At least one-third of each session (of no less than one and one-half hours) will be devoted to education about workplace sexual harassment, including training (with demonstrative evidence) as to exactly what types of remarks, behavior, and pictures will not be tolerated in the JSI workplace. The president of JSI will attend the training sessions in one central location with all company supervisory employees. The president will introduce the seminar with remarks stressing the potential liability of JSI and individual supervisors for sexual harassment and the need to eliminate harassment. Each participant will be informed that they are responsible for knowing the contents of JSI's sexual harassment policy and for giving similar presentations of safety meetings to employees.

4. For all investigative officers: The investigative officers and their designees, if any, will attend full-day training seminars conducted by experienced sexual harassment educators and/or investigators to educate them about the problems of sexual harassment in the workplace and techniques for investigating and stopping it.

The training sessions for components two to four will be conducted by an experienced sexual harassment educator chosen jointly by JSI and the NOW Legal Defense and Education Fund after receiving bids. In the event of a disagreement between the parties, the parties will refer the matter to an arbitrator chosen by the parties.

SAMPLE POLICY 4: BONNEVILLE POWER ADMINISTRATION POLICY: HARASSMENT-FREE WORKPLACE

POLICY

The Bonneville Power Administration's (BPA) policy is to have a harassment-free work environment where people treat one another with respect. BPA's and our contractors' managers and supervisors have the primary responsibility for creating and sustaining this harassment-free environment (by example, by joint supervision, by coaching, by training, by contract enforcement, and by other means). But all employees, contractor personnel, and visitors must take personal responsibility for maintaining conduct that is professional and supportive of this environment.

ACTION REQUIRED   Managers and supervisors must take immediate action to stop harassment, to protect the people targeted by harassers, and to take all reasonable steps to ensure that no further harassment or retaliation occurs.

LOCATIONS COVERED   The BPA work environment includes areas in and around BPA buildings, facilities, fitness centers, vehicles, food service areas, and break locations, and any other areas or conveyances where BPA employees work or where work-related activities occur, including travel.

DEFINITION   BPA defines harassment as any unwelcome, inappropriate conduct, including retaliation, that causes a BPA or contractor employee or visitor to feel threatened, intimidated, or distressed in the BPA work environment. Examples of harassment include, but are not limited to, the following:

EXAMPLES   Physical conduct: Unwelcome touching; standing too close; inappropriate or threatening staring or glaring; obscene, threatening, or offensive gestures.

Verbal or written conduct: Inappropriate references to body parts; derogatory or demeaning comments, jokes, or personal questions; sexual innuendos; offensive remarks about race, gender, religion, age, ethnicity, sexual orientation, political beliefs, marital status, or disability; obscene letters or telephone calls; catcalls; whistles; sexually suggestive sounds; loud, aggressive, inappropriate comments or other vocal abuse.

Visual or symbolic conduct: Display of pictures of nude, scantily clad, or offensively clad people; display of intimidating or offensive religious, political, or other symbols; display of offensive, threatening, demeaning, or derogatory drawings, cartoons, or other graphics; offensive T-shirts, coffee mugs, bumper stickers, or other articles.

OPTIONS   Individuals who believe they are being harassed or retaliated against should exercise any one or more of the following options as soon as possible:

Tell the harasser how you feel and ask the person to stop the offensive conduct; and/or

Tell a manager or supervisor about the conduct and how you feel about it; and/or

Contact the confidential Harassment Hotline for alternatives on how to deal with the situation.

INTERNAL   In addition, if you are a BPA employee, you may seek help from your administrative officer, an Equal Employment Opportunity (EEO) counselor, the EEO office, the Employee Assistance Program, Employee/ Labor Relations office, your union steward, or the security office.

PENALTIES   BPA staff who engage in harassment will face consequences ranging from verbal warnings and letters of reprimand up to and including termination from BPA employment, depending upon the seriousness of the misconduct. BPA managers and supervisors who do not take action when they know or suspect that harassment is occurring will face the same range of consequences. Contractor staff who engage in harassment may be subject to comparable penalties from their employers, and a contractor who fails to enforce this policy may have its contract with BPA terminated. Visitors who harass may be removed from any BPA workplace and prevented from returning.

SAMPLE POLICY 5: SEXUAL HARASSMENT POLICY PROVISIONS FOR LAW FIRMS

The following sample policy should serve as a guideline to individuals in developing a sexual harassment policy for their workplace. In drafting an effective policy, individuals should take into consideration the unique characteristics and culture of their workplace. We hope the sample policy will serve as a useful starting point for lawyers who are interested in drafting and implementing a sexual harassment policy.

(Excerpted from American Bar Association Commission on Women in the Profession's report, *Sexual Harassment at Work: A Preventive Manual.* © 1990. Reprinted with permission. A copy of the book may be purchased through the American Bar Association's Commission on Women in the Profession, 750 North Lake Shore Dr., Chicago, IL 60611.)

Firm Statement of Philosophy

(Firm Name) is proud of its tradition of a collegial work environment in which all individuals are treated with respect and dignity. Each individual has the right to work in a professional atmosphere which promotes equal opportunities and prohibits discriminatory practices, including sexual harassment. At (Firm Name) sexual harassment, whether verbal, physical or environmental, is unacceptable and will not be tolerated.

Definition of Sexual Harassment

For purposes of this policy, sexual harassment is defined as unwelcome or unwanted conduct of a sexual nature (verbal or physical) when: 1) submission to or rejection of this conduct by an individual is used as a factor in decisions affecting hiring, evaluation, promotion or other aspects of employment; 2) this conduct substantially interferes with an individual's employment or creates an intimidating, hostile or offensive work environment.

Examples of sexual harassment include, but are not limited to: unwanted sexual advances; demands for sexual favors in exchange for favorable treatment or continued employment; repeated sexual jokes, flirtations, advances or propositions; verbal abuse of a sexual nature; graphic, verbal commentary about an individual's body, sexual prowess or sexual deficiencies; leering, whistling, touching, pinching, assaulq coercecd sexual acts or suggestive insulting, obscene comments or gestures; display in the workplace of sexually suggestive objects or pictures.

This behavior is unacceptable in the workplace itself and in other work-related settings such as business trips, court appearances and business-related social events.

Individuals Covered Under the Policy

This policy covers all employees (associates, paralegals, support staff) and partners. (Firm Name) will not tolerate, condone or allow sexual harassment, whether engaged in by fellow employees, supervisors, associates, partners or by outside clients, opposing counsel, court personnel or other non-employees who conduct business with this firm. The firm encourages reporting of all incidents of sexual harassment, regardless of who the offender may be.

Reporting a Complaint

While (Firm Name) encourages individuals who believe they are being harassed to firmly and promptly notify the offender that his or her behavior is unwelcome, the firm also recognizes that power and status disparities between an alleged harasser and a target may make such a confrontation impossible. In the event that such informal, direct communication between individuals is either ineffective or impossible, the following steps should be followed in reporting a sexual harassment complaint.

1. Notification of Appropriate Staff

Individuals who believe they have been subjected to sexual harassment should report the incident to any member of the committee listed below. (The firm should designate a group of individuals within the firm who may receive complaints. These should be individuals of both genders, drawn from a variety of age groups and different levels of seniority.)

An individual also may choose to report the complaint to his/her supervisor. If the supervisor successfully resolves the complaint in an informal manner, this policy requires the supervisor to file a confidential report to (firm management or designated individual) about the complaint and resolution so that the firm will be aware of any pattern of harassment by a particular individual. A supervisor who has not had special training in dealing with sexual harassment complaints is strongly encouraged to consult a trained member of the firm's sexual harassment committee before taking action.

2.   Description of Misconduct

An accurate record of objectionable behavior or misconduct is needed to resolve a formal complaint of sexual harassment.

Verbal reports of sexual harassment must be reduced to writing by either the complainant or the individual(s) designated to receive complaints, and be signed by the complainant. Individuals who believe they have been or currently are being harassed should maintain a record of objectionable conduct in order to effectively prepare and corroborate their allegations.

While (Firm Name) encourages individuals to keep written notes in order to accurately record offensive conduct or behavior, the firm hereby notifies all employees that, in the event that a lawsuit develops from the reported incident, the complainant's written notes may not be considered privileged information, and therefore, confidential unless such notes were originally made in anticipation of litigation.

3.   Timeframe for Reporting a Complaint

(Firm Name) encourages a prompt reporting of complaints so that rapid response and appropriate action may be taken. However, due to the sensitivity of these problems and because of the emotional toll such misconduct may have on the individual, no limited timeframe will be instituted for reporting sexual harassment complaints. Late reporting of complaints will not in and of itself preclude this firm from taking remedial action.

4.   Protection Against Retaliation

The firm will not in any way retaliate against an individual who makes a report of sexual harassment nor permit any partner or employee to do so. Retaliation is a serious violation of this sexual harassment policy and should be reported immediately. Any person found to have retaliated against another individual for reporting sexual harassment will be subject to the same disciplinary action provided for sexual harassment offenders (see "Resolving the Complaint" below).

INVESTIGATING THE COMPLAINT

1.   Confidentiality

Any allegation of sexual harassment brought to the attention of (the firm's appointed committee) will be promptly investigated in a confidential manner so as to protect the privacy of persons involved. Confidentiality will be maintained throughout the investigatory process to the extent practical and appropriate under the circumstances.

2. Identification of Investigators

Complaints will be investigated and resolved by the person on the firm's sexual harassment committee to whom, it was reported. In addition, any of the following individuals may be included in reviewing the investigation and outcome: (list may include a number of appropriate partners or other individuals such as the Director of Human Resources).

3. Investigation Process

In pursuing the investigation, the investigator will try to take the wishes of the complainant under consideration, but should thoroughly investigate the matter as he/she sees fit, keeping the complainant informed as to the status of the investigation. Steps to be taken in the investigation include:

- Confirm name and position of the complainant.

- Identify the alleged harasser.

- Thoroughly ascertain all facts that explain what happened. Questions should be asked in a non-judgmental manner.

- Determine frequency/type of alleged harassment and, if possible, the dates and locations where alleged harassment occurred.

- Find out if there were witnesses who observed the alleged harassment.

- Ask the individual how he/she responded to the alleged harassment.

- Determine whether the harassed individual consulted anyone else about the alleged harassment and take note of who else knows and their response to the disclosure.

- Develop a thorough understanding of the professional relationship, degree of control and amount of interaction between the alleged harasser and complainant. (Does the person control compensation, terms of employment or promotions? Do these individuals work in close proximity to one another and/or on the same projects?)

- Determine whether the alleged harasser has carried out any threats or promises directed at the complainant.

- Does the complainant know of or suspect that there are other individuals who have been harassed by alleged harasser?

- Has the complainant informed other partners or supervisors of the situation? What response, if any, did complainant receive from these individuals?

- Ask complainant what action he/she would like the firm to take as a consequence of the harassment.

- When first interviewing the alleged harasser, remind him/her of the firm's policy against retaliation for making a complaint of sexual harassment.

RESOLVING THE COMPLAINT

Upon completing the investigation of a sexual harassment complaint, the firm will communicate its findings and intended actions to the complainant and alleged harasser.

If the investigator, together with any appropriate review committee, finds that harassment occurred, the harasser will be subject to appropriate disciplinary procedures, as listed below. The complainant will be informed of the disciplinary action taken.

If the investigator, together with a review committee, determines that no sexual harassment has occurred, this finding will be communicated to the complainant in an appropriately sensitive manner.

In the event that no resolution satisfactory to both parties can be reached based on the initial investigation, the matter shall be referred to (name an appropriate individual or group, such as the Managing Partner or Executive Committee or Director of Human Resources). See "Appeals Process" below.

1. Sanctions

Individuals found to have engaged in misconduct constituting sexual harassment will be severely disciplined, up to and including discharge. Appropriate sanctions will be determined by (select the appropriate individual or group of individuals). In addressing incidents of sexual harassment, the firm's response at a minimum will include reprimanding the offender and preparing a written record. Additional action may include: referral to counseling, withholding of a promotion, reassignment, temporary suspension without pay, financial penalties or termination.

Although the firm's ability to discipline a non-employee harasser (e.g. client, opposing counsel, supplier) is limited by the degree of control, if any, that the firm has over the alleged harasser, any employee or partner who has been sub-jected to sexual harassment should file a complaint and be assured that action will be taken.

2. False Accusations

If an investigation results in a finding that the complainant falsely accused another of sexual harassment knowingly or in a malicious manner, the complain-ant will be subject to appropriate sanctions, including the possibility of termi-nation.

3. Appeals Process

If either party directly involved in a sexual harassment investigation is dissat-isfied with the outcome or resolution, that individual has the right to appeal the decision. The dissatisfied party should submit his/her written comments in a timely manner to (select the appropriate reviewers; individual or group of indi-viduals, e.g. Administrative Partners of the firm).

MAINTAINING A WRITTEN RECORD OF THE COMPLAINT

The firm shall maintain a complete written record of each complaint and how it was investigated and resolved. Written records shall be maintained in a con-fidential manner in the office of (name the appropriate individual or appropriate division within the office. The keeper of the records may vary depending on who filed the complaint—associate, partner, paralegal, administrative assistant, etc.).

Written records will be maintained for years from the date of the resolution unless new circumstances dictate that the file should be kept for a longer period of time.

Conclusion

(Firm Name) has developed this policy to ensure that all its employees and partners can work in an environment free from sexual harassment. The firm will make every effort to ensure that all its personnel are familiar with the policy and know that any complaint received will be thoroughly investigated and appro-priately resolved.

SAMPLE POLICY 6: SEXUAL HARASSMENT GUIDELINES FOR MANAGERS AND SUPERVISORS MEGAFINANCIAL SERVICE COMPANY

Sexual harassment is a violation of Title VII. Unwelcome sexual advances, re-quests for sexual favors and other verbal and physical conduct of a sexual nature constitute sexual harassment when, but not limited to:

1. Submission to such conduct is a term or condition of employment;

2. Submission to or rejection of such conduct is used as a basis for employment decisions; and

3. Such conduct unreasonably interferes with an individual's work performance or creates an intimidating or hostile/offensive work environment.

Sexual harassment can occur in a variety of circumstances including but not limited to the following:

- The victim, as well as the harasser, may be a woman or a man. The victim does not have to be of the opposite sex.

- The harasser can be the victim's supervisor, an agent of the employer, a supervisor in another area, a co-worker or a non-employee.

- The victim does not have to be the person harassed but could be anyone affected by the offensive behavior/conduct.

- Unlawful sexual harassment may occur without economic injury to or discharge of the victim.

- The victim has a responsibility to establish that the harasser's behavior/conduct is unwelcome.

EXAMPLES OF SEXUAL HARASSMENT

Touching, caressing, patting on the shoulders or on the buttocks and obscene language may be sexual harassment.

Nonverbal gestures such as winking, leering and ogling are harassment when there is a sexual content to them and when they are repeated and unwanted by the person to whom they are directed.

Names and labels of an endearing nature are harassment when the person to whom they are addressed is annoyed by them.

Using "honey," "sweetie," "dearie," "gal," and "girl" is inappropriate.

PROBLEMS OF REPORTING SEXUAL HARASSMENT

After sexual harassment has been identified by an individual, the next problem is how to report it. How does one report the effects of casual flirting and inappropriate or obscene remarks?

Employees and managers can act as individuals or in small groups to begin to change any unacceptable behavior at work.

As managers begin to recognize sexual harassment behaviors and to accept an employee's report that his/her work is being affected by non-work-related behaviors toward him/her, increases in productivity will be observed.

In business, industry and government, it is probable that sexual harassment is the single largest cause of productivity.

REPRISALS

Reprisals occur after one employee says "no" to a sexual encounter with a fellow employee or supervisor. Reprisals may be more of the same kind of harassment or the harassment may take a different form. When a supervisor feels the pressure to change, he or she may start to find things wrong with the performance of the individual who said "no." Individuals who give the victim support and encouragement may also find themselves the target of criticism.

All employees, supervisors and managers involved need to know what to expect when an employee complains about sex discrimination or harassment. For management to leave the situation alone usually results in the escalation of bad feelings and misperceptions of performance and motives from everyone toward everyone else. Open discussions using clear guidelines are (probably) the best tactic for organizations to take.

AVOIDING HARASSING BEHAVIORS

The baseline from which all other work relationships must be derived is neutral. In a two-gender work group, neutral relations permit all individuals to complete their work assignments. Neutral means that people do not have to be either friends or enemies at work. People can deal courteously without hostility and without the titillation of sexual interest.

SEXUAL HARASSMENT
CONCLUSIONS AND RECOMMENDATIONS

Managers/supervisors should inform employees of Megafinancial Service Company's Sexual Harassment Policy and assist employees who are sexually harassed. It is in the best interests of sexually harassed employees to directly inform the harasser that the conduct is unwelcome and that it must stop. The employee should be advised of Megafinancial Service Company's complaint mechanism or grievance system.

In determining whether alleged conduct constitutes sexual harassment, the totality of the circumstances must be considered. The nature of the sexual advances and the content in which the alleged harassment occurred must be examined.

An employer may be held liable for acts of sexual harassment in the workplace. Managers/supervisors/employers are encouraged to take all steps necessary to prevent sexual harassment from occurring such as:

Affirmatively raising the subject

Expressing strong disapproval

Developing appropriate sanctions

Informing employees of their rights to raise and how to raise the issue of harassment

Developing methods to sensitize all employees

Other related practices: Where employment opportunities or benefits are granted because of an individual's submission to the employer's sexual advances or requests for sexual favors, the employer may be held liable for unlawful sex discrimination against other persons who were qualified but denied that employment opportunity or benefit.

1. Each person has a right to work at the job for which she or he was hired.

2. No employee, supervisor or manager has the right to tease, humiliate, ridicule, be sarcastic or to ignore employees at any level.

3. Every supervisor and manager has an obligation to maintain a working environment free of repeated, unwanted, inappropriate and illegal non-work-related behaviors.

4. Every employee has an obligation to support management's policies and good human relations practices in preventing, removing, reporting and correcting inappropriate social behaviors at the work site.

5. Each work group within the organization must contribute to the total understanding of what constitutes appropriate and unacceptable social and gender-related behaviors on the job.

6. Each organization must establish explicit guidelines so employees and managers will not misunderstand what sexual harassment is and what the procedures and penalties are.

SAMPLE POLICY 7: UNIVERSITY POLICY AND PROCEDURE MANUAL

I. PURPOSE

This section states University policy on sexual harassment and describes the options and resources available to faculty, staff, and students for resolution of sexual harassment problems. It includes procedures for University officials to follow in receiving, reporting, and referring complaints and identifies existing policies for University discipline that apply in matters of sexual harassment. This policy reflects University's continuing determination to deal firmly and fairly with all occurrences through the framework of local reporting procedures and the application of existing policies. Contents of this section are:

II. DEFINITIONS

A. Sexual harassment
The University definition of sexual harassment is based on Equal Employment Opportunity Commission (EEOC) regulations and is as follows:

"Unwelcome sexual advances, requests for sexual favors, and other verbal or physical conduct of a sexual nature constitute sexual harassment when:

1. "Submission to or rejection of such conduct is made either explicitly or implicitly a term or condition of instruction, employment, or participation in other University activity; or

2. "Submission to or rejection of such conduct by an individual is used as a basis for evaluation in making academic or personnel decisions affecting an individual; or

3. "Such conduct has the purpose or effect of unreasonably interfering with an individual's performance or creating an intimidating, hostile, or offensive University environment."

In determining whether conduct constitutes sexual harassment, consideration will be given to the record as a whole and to the totality of circumstances, including the nature of the sexual advances and the context in which the incidents occurred. Certain behavior can be classified as sexual harassment even if a relationship is voluntary in the sense that one was not coerced into participating. A central element in the definition of sexual harassment is that the behavior is unwelcome.

Some acts or practices that have the effect of discouraging individuals of either gender from pursuing academic or professional interests may not constitute sexual harassment because they are not sexual in nature. Such acts may nevertheless constitute illegal sex discrimination if the behavior is directed toward members of one gender and not the other.

B. Sexual harassment complaint

For purposes of this policy, a complaint will be distinguished from a formal grievance. A complaint shall be defined as any meeting or discussion with a University official (e.g., sexual harassment advisor, supervisor, department head, dean, vice chancellor), the purpose of which is to inform the University that sexual harassment may be occurring and to provide them with information sufficient to pursue the complaint. Once this meeting or discussion has occurred, the University is considered by law to be "on notice" and is required by law to investigate such a complaint.

III. GENERAL POLICY STATEMENT

Sexual harassment of faculty, staff, or students is prohibited by University policy and will not be tolerated in any form. Retaliation toward an individual on the basis of her/his bringing a complaint of sexual harassment is also prohibited. The University community will take whatever steps are necessary to protect its faculty, staff, and students from sexual harassment.

A. Assignment of responsibility

1. It is the responsibility of department heads, managers, and supervisors to take whatever action is necessary to prevent sexual harassment if possible and correct it where it occurs. This responsibility involves being aware and sensitive and includes taking disciplinary action when appropriate. It should be made clear through verbal and/or written communication to all parties that inappropriate behavior shall stop immediately and that appropriate administrative action will be taken if necessary. When information or acts come to the attention of these officials, they should immediately determine the facts and ensure that the people involved are informed about this policy. Any nonpersonnel claim or complaint filed through University (e.g., worker's compensation, unemployment insurance) that contains a statement related to sexual harassment should be brought to the attention of the campus or University Personnel Services Manager for review through this policy.

2. In addition, department heads, managers, and supervisors are responsible for providing information to their employees regarding the procedures and resources described in this document. The Sexual

Harassment Education Coordinators, sexual harassment advisors, and administrative support to the sexual harassment advisors (see Exhibit A) are regularly informed concerning current campus procedures and policies. Because of the serious and sensitive nature of sexual harassment and the frequently changing case law in this area, it is strongly recommended that persons with inquiries or complaints be referred to one of these resource people or that, when attempting to resolve sexual harassment complaints within their unit, department heads, supervisors, and managers call on these resources for information.

B. Education

Promoting awareness of the definition and consequences of sexual harassment is an important part of this policy. University will develop programs to sensitize members of the University community to the seriousness of this offense, implement appropriate sanctions, and inform faculty, staff, and students about their right to bring complaints of harassment and the procedures for doing so. The Sexual Harassment Education Offices will provide the University community with a comprehensive educational program.

IV.   FEDERAL REGULATIONS

Sexual harassment is also prohibited by law and by governmental agency regulations. These regulations are rigorous and subject the University to substantial liability if it fails to take positive action to prevent and resolve such behavior.

A. EEOC Title VII regulations state that an employer is "responsible for its acts and those of its agents and supervisory employees with respect to sexual harassment regardless of whether the specific acts complained of where authorized or even forbidden by the employer and regardless of whether the employer knew or should have known of their occurrence." They also state that "an employer is responsible for acts of sexual harassment in the workplace where the employer (or its agents or supervisory employees) knows or should have known of the conduct, unless it can show that it took immediate and appropriate administrative action." The EEOC will examine the circumstances of the particular employment relationships and the job functions performed by the individual in determining whether an individual acts in either a supervisory or agency capacity. Supervisors and other University officials are responsible for knowing these regulations and being informed of the procedures to be used when acts of sex discrimination or sexual harassment are alleged.

B. These standards are also applied as they relate to Title IX regulations of the Education Amendment of 1972, which prohibit discrimination in any Federally funded program.

V. RESOURCES FOR INFORMATION AND COMPLAINT RESOLUTION

Individuals have several alternatives for obtaining assistance in resolving sexual harassment problems. These are described below in order of increasing formality ranging from information only to formal grievance procedures. Any individual with a concern regarding sexual harassment may choose to initiate her/his search for remedy at any of these levels and may pursue more than one option simultaneously. Options include: (a) the Sexual Harassment Information Line (general advice and information); (b) sexual harassment advisors (information, advice, and preliminary review and conciliation services); (c) formal University grievance procedures; (d) complaints filed through outside agencies.

Individuals may also seek information or resolution through the campus or University Employee Relations or Labor Relations Specialists, union representatives, the University Affirmative Action Coordinator, Student Judicial Affairs, and the offices of department chairs, deans, directors, and vice chancellors.

A. Sexual Harassment Information Line (A-CALL/#)

All members of the University community with concerns about sexual harassment are encouraged to seek information and advice by calling the Sexual Harassment Information Line. Any individual who answers the Sexual Harassment Information Line is specifically designated and trained to provide information on sexual harassment, talk with individuals about sexual harassment problems, discuss options for remedy, and make referrals when appropriate. In many instances, he/she can advise those seeking information on effective ways to resolve harassment problems informally on their own.

B. Sexual harassment advisors

In addition to providing general information and advice as described above, sexual harassment advisors provide an option for resolving sexual harassment complaints outside the formal grievance procedure. This process, called preliminary review and conciliation, is described in VIII, below. The goal of this process is to achieve resolution quickly and fairly, and with as much good will and as little damage to individual and institutional well-being as possible.

Advisors do not serve as advocates to any party. Their role is to listen to complaints, review and gather facts, keep records, give information and advice, and attempt to achieve resolution of complaints when appropriate. They follow the provisions stated in this policy as well as those outlined in the guidelines provided during their training program. Although specific advisors are designated for each school, college, and major administrative area (see Exhibit A), an individual may contact and work with any one of the advisors listed. Advisors are nominated by a dean or vice chancellor and appointed by the Associate Vice Chancellor—Employee Relations & Staff Affairs. They are trained through programs implemented by the Sexual Harassment Education Office.

C. Formal University grievance
An individual may choose to bypass completely the preliminary review and conciliation process and file a formal grievance, or may request at any time that the sexual harassment advisor refer her/him to the University grievance process. The persons or positions listed as contacts for filing a formal grievance (Exhibit A) will explain the grievance procedure and may attempt to achieve a satisfactory remedy for the complainant before or during implementation of the grievance procedure. Additional information is provided in X, below.

D. State and Federal agencies
The following resources for redress of alleged sexual harassment and the stated deadlines for filing complaints are subject to change. Complainants are responsible for determining their rights and the agencies' current procedures.

1. State Fair Employment & Housing Commission—365 days from last incident.

2. U.S. Equal Employment Opportunity Commission—300 days (10 months) from last incident.

3. U.S. Office of Federal Contract Compliance—Compliance must be met on a day-to-day basis in accordance with Executive Order 11246.

4. U.S. Department of Education—180 days from last incident or outcome of grievance.

5. Courts (statutes of limitations):

   a. Civil cases

   b. Criminal

VI. CONFIDENTIALITY

A. Information and advice
Persons seeking general information or advice from the Sexual Harassment Information Line or sexual harassment advisors will be told that if they wish to ensure that the discussion remains completely confidential and that no action is taken unless they wish to pursue the matter, it is essential that the inquiry or request for information remain nonspecific and they not disclose any identifying information about themselves or any other party (e.g., names, department or unit). This is necessary because the University is legally obligated to investigate, even without their consent, once it is informed that harassment may be occurring.

B. Making a complaint
Once an individual discloses identifying information, he/she will be considered to have filed a complaint with the University. The confidentiality of the information received, the privacy of the individuals involved, and the wishes of the complainant regarding action by the University cannot be guaranteed, but will be protected to as great a degree as it is legally possible. While the expressed wishes of the complainant regarding confidentiality will be considered, they must be weighed against the responsibility of the University to act upon the charge and the right of the charged party to obtain information about the allegations.

C. Preliminary review and conciliation
When a complainant requests the preliminary review and conciliation services of a sexual harassment advisor, names and units must be identified. During this process, the charged party has a right to the name of the complainant and the charge, but the names of noncomplaining parties, e.g., witnesses, will not be disclosed, and the privacy interests of these noncomplaining parties will be protected.

D. Formal University grievance
If a formal grievance is filed, access to documents is governed by law and by regulations established pursuant to the specific procedure being implemented.

Anyone wishing more information on the issue of confidentiality before filing a complaint is encouraged to call the Sexual Harassment Information Line (A-CALL/#) or to contact one of the sexual harassment advisors (Exhibit).

VIII.   TIME LIMITS

Each University policy or union contract regarding complaint procedures states a time limit for filing complaints or formal grievances. If a complainant experiences further incidents of sexual harassment or retaliation on the basis of bringing a complaint, the deadline becomes 365 days from the most recent offense. A complainant of harassment should not delay in seeking clarification and assistance from a knowledgeable source (see Exhibit) to ascertain the options and applicable time limits (see Exhibit). Time limits for filing formal complaints or grievances of sexual harassment may be waived and exceptions granted for good cause shown.

A. Information and advice
Anonymous discussion on the Sexual Harassment Information Line or a nonspecific request for general information or advice from any University official on a sexual harassment issue does not extend the 365-day time limit for filing a University complaint and requesting preliminary review and conciliation services, nor does it extend the deadline for filing a formal University grievance of sexual harassment.

B.   Making a complaint

The time limit for filing a complaint of sexual harassment with the University is 365 days from the actual date of the incident. Once a complaint has been filed, a request to pursue the preliminary review and conciliation process will automatically extend the 30-day time limit for filing a formal written grievance with the University.

C.   Preliminary review and conciliation

1.   A complainant wishing to work with a sexual harassment advisor toward conciliation, yet preserve the right to file a formal University grievance at a later date, must contact an advisor within 365 days from the time of the incident and sign an Intake Form (Exhibit). The initial period for review and conciliation is up to 30 days. This preliminary review and conciliation period may be extended for 30-day intervals by mutual written agreement of the sexual harassment advisor and the complainant if both parties desire to continue working on the issue and if the advisor believes conciliation is still possible. The time limit for filing a grievance will automatically be extended for the period of time spent in the conciliation process.

2.   The review and conciliation period ends when the sexual harassment advisor sends written confirmation to the complainant that informal efforts to resolve the complaint have been concluded. This will occur when the issue has been resolved satisfactorily, or when the 30-day period for conciliation has ended and an extension has not been requested as described above, or when either the complainant or the advisor feels conciliation efforts are no longer desirable or productive, whichever occurs first. When the review and conciliation period ends, the complainant has 30 days within which to file a formal grievance with the University.

3.   The complainant may, at the time of her/his complaint, bypass the conciliation process and file a formal University grievance. If the conciliation process was begun, he/she may discontinue it at any time and file a formal grievance pursuant to applicable faculty, staff, or student personnel policies or collective bargaining agreements.

D.   Formal University grievance

A formal grievance must be filed with the University within 365 days of the alleged sexual harassment, within 30 days after filing a complaint (if conciliation is not attempted), or within 30 days after a request for preliminary review and conciliation is withdrawn or unsuccessfully concluded.

For an overview of the applicable time limits, see Exhibit.

VIII. CONSULTATION WITH A SEXUAL HARASSMENT ADVISOR

A. Information and advice

1. At the beginning of an initial discussion with a sexual harassment advisor, persons seeking information will be advised that if they wish to ensure that the discussion remains confidential and that no action is taken without their consent, it is essential that individual names and departments not be disclosed. The University is compelled by law to investigate when it has been notified of the possibility of sexual harassment.

2. During the initial interview, the advisor will request information about the event and record it on an Intake Form (Exhibit). The advisor will also provide the complainant with the University's definition of sexual harassment as contained in University policy, explain the options for remedy including suggestions on how he/she can resolve the matter personally, identify the formal University grievance processes and the external resources available, and inform the complainant of pertinent time limits. Advisors use an Information Checklist (Exhibit) during the interview to ensure that the above topics are covered. The Checklist is also used to document what course of action was agreed upon.

3. The advisor keeps the Intake Form and the Information Checklist for up to 30 days while the individual seeking information decides whether or not to request officially the advisor's preliminary review and conciliation services. If, by that time, no further action has been requested or if resolution has been achieved without further action, the forms are sent to the Sexual Harassment Education Office where statistical information is recorded and the forms are placed in the sexual harassment reports file.

4. If, in the initial process of discussion, the person seeking advice conveys specific information regarding the alleged incident (e.g., names, department), the University is then "on notice" that sexual harassment may have occurred, and may be required by law to investigate the incident, even without the consent of the person who has provided the information. Further, the accused has the right to be informed of the charge and the name of the individual making the charge.

5. If a complaint is made, the complainant has 30 days in which to file a formal University grievance or initiate the preliminary review and conciliation process.

B. Preliminary review and conciliation

1. Resolution of problems involving sexual harassment can be especially difficult and is often successfully achieved outside the formal grievance

procedure. If an individual wishes to pursue resolution with the active involvement of the sexual harassment advisor, the next step will include a preliminary review, an activity characterized by communication with others, including the accused, who will have the right to be informed about the charge and the name of the complainant. If the individual decides to proceed with the preliminary review and conciliation process, he/she shall indicate assent by reading and signing the completed Intake Form (Exhibit) and the Preliminary Review Information Sheet (Exhibit). This also automatically extends the filing deadline for a formal grievance for the period of the conciliation process (see also VII, above).

2.   During the preliminary review and conciliation process, the role of the advisor is to question, listen, and record information. At this point, the sexual harassment advisor begins a file on the complaint. Files will include information such as: the names of people contacted and otherwise identified in association with the alleged event(s); questions asked of and responses given by parties interviewed, including signed statements on the accuracy of the interview information obtained by the sexual harassment advisor (see Exhibit); and any other information relevant to the process.

3.   The preliminary review and conciliation process may involve contact with witnesses identified by either the complainant or the accused and other persons considered helpful by the advisor. All such persons shall be reminded of their responsibility to maintain confidentiality in relation to work issues and/or as stated within their individual job descriptions.

4.   When interviewing the alleged harasser, the advisor shall state the nature of the complaint and advise the individual about University policy pertaining to sexual harassment.

C.   **Conclusion of the preliminary review and conciliation process**

1.   At the conclusion of the preliminary review and conciliation process, the sexual harassment advisor will prepare a written summary of the process. The summary shall include the preliminary determinations reached as a result of the interviews and other information gathered, and a general description of the resolution or current status of the complaint.

2.   Upon conclusion of the conciliation efforts, and regardless of outcome, the entire set of records will be forwarded to the sexual harassment reports file maintained by the Sexual Harassment Education Office for the purposes described in IX, below. Both the complainant and the accused will receive notice that such a file exists and that they may request a summary. The Information Practices Act limits the disclosure of certain information. The release of any information contained in the

file will be determined by law and University policy, and the identity of third parties listed in the complaint will be protected to as great a degree as is legally possible. If it becomes necessary to disclose the names of any persons involved, the individual(s) will receive prior notice of such disclosure.

3. With the conclusion of this process, the 30-day time limit begins for the filing of a formal University grievance.

D. Conciliation outcomes

1. If, in the preliminary review, it is determined that sexual harassment may have occurred, the complainant's working or learning environment will be made free of sexual harassment. Further remedies may also occur, as deemed appropriate by law, University policy, or bargaining agreement.

2. If, in the preliminary review, it is determined that sexual harassment may have occurred, the alleged harasser will be accorded appropriate formal due process pursuant to applicable academic, staff, or student personnel policies or collective bargaining agreements.

3. If, in the preliminary review, it is determined that sexual harassment may not have occurred, that determination will be documented in the sexual harassment advisor's summary and forwarded along with the other forms and records to the sexual harassment reports file.

IX. RECORDS

A. Purposes

1. A special file containing documents concerning sexual harassment reports will be maintained by the campus or University Sexual Harassment Education Coordinator. These files will be maintained separately from any other personnel files. The documents are reviewed by the Sexual Harassment Education Coordinator as they are received, and are used:

   a. To compile anonymous statistical information;

   b. To identify areas in which sexual harassment advisors would benefit from additional assistance or training;

   c. To provide support and advice to individual sexual harassment advisors as needed; and

   d. As resource information to sexual harassment advisors actively engaged in a resolution effort.

2. The Associate Vice Chancellor—Employee Relations & Staff Affairs has authority to make decisions regarding the release of information to University administrators who, upon request, and in his/her judgment, have official need for information that is specific to their administrative area of responsibility.

3. File information related to complainants or alleged harassers will be retained for an appropriate period of time. Statistical data compiled for reporting purposes will be retained for at least three years.

B. Contents

The sexual harassment reports file will contain:

1. The Intake Forms and Information Checklists prepared for all reports concerning sexual harassment made to the Sexual Harassment Information Line, Sexual Harassment Education Coordinators, or sexual harassment advisors;

2. All documents from the preliminary review and conciliation efforts of the sexual harassment advisors, including the Preliminary Review Information Sheet, Preliminary Review Interview Sheet, and other forms and documents used to collect information from the alleged harasser, witnesses, or others who provided information concerning the alleged event(s); and

3. A copy of the summary written at the end of the resolution effort. When the inquiring individual chooses not to identify herself/himself or others or not to request the assistance of the University in resolving the issue, the only documents involved will be the unsigned Intake Form and the Information Checklist.

X. FORMAL UNIVERSITY GRIEVANCE PROCEDURES

For grievances of sexual harassment the following policies and procedures set forth how Academic Senate members, non-Senate academic appointees, staff, and students may file a grievance. These policies and procedures also include due process rights and protections for persons accused of sexual harassment. A grievance or an investigation may result in disciplinary or corrective action pursuant to the appropriate academic, Executive, Management and Professional (MAP), Administrative & Professional Staff (A&PS), staff, and student policies or union collective bargaining agreements. Additional information is available from designated staff in the Personnel Services Offices on campus and at University, Academic Affairs, and Student Judicial Affairs, and in personnel manuals located in each department and in the Shields Library Humanities/ Social Sciences reference area.

Note: The various grievance policies cited below outline the proper procedures for filing a University grievance, e.g., information to be included in the grievance, where to file. However, the time limits for filing a complaint or formal grievance related exclusively to sexual harassment, are those specified in VIII, above, and outlined in Exhibit X of this policy.

A. University grievance policies for faculty, staff, and students who are not covered by a collective bargaining agreement:

1. Academic Senate members—Academic Senate Bylaw 335, Bylaws 75 and 87. Where the allegations of sexual harassment are against a faculty member, the complainant may file a complaint with the Chancellor pursuant to the Administration of Faculty Discipline (Academic Personnel Manual Sections 015 and University-015).
    or
    Policy & Procedure Manual Section 380-12.

    Contact: Academic Affairs, 752-3383.

2. Non-Senate academic appointees and residents of the School of Medicine—Academic Personnel Manual Sections 140 and University-140.
    or
    Policy & Procedure Manual Section 380-12.

    Contact: Academic Affairs, Tel. #.

3. Staff employees—Staff Personnel Policy and Procedure 280, Employee Grievances, or 290, Administrative Review; A&PS Program Personnel Policy and Procedure 190, Grievances; MAP Program Personnel Policy 70, Administrative Review; Executive Program Personnel Policy 2, Non-discrimination, or 22, Resolution of Concerns.
    or
    Policy & Procedure Manual Section 380-12.

    Contact: Employee & Labor Relations, Tel. #.

4. Students—Policy & Procedure Manual Section 280-05, Procedures for Student Complaints Charging Prohibited Discrimination. This procedure is available to students who wish to bring complaints about harassment. It provides corrective remedies and serves as the basis for disciplinary sanctions.
    or
    Policy & Procedure Manual Section 380-12.

    Contact: Student Judicial Affairs, Tel. #.

B. Grievance policies and time limits for all faculty, staff, and students who are covered by a collective bargaining agreement:

Refer to the specific collective bargaining contract that governs the terms and conditions of employment to determine appropriate grievance provisions and time limits. However, if a contract permits the substitution of procedures described in this document for the negotiated grievance procedure, the services provided by a sexual harassment advisor may be substituted.

Contact: Appropriate union steward.

XI. FURTHER INFORMATION

Education and training programs for faculty, staff, students, residents, department heads, supervisors, managers, and vendors can be arranged by contacting the Sexual Harassment Education Office or the appropriate sexual harassment advisor. Information regarding the policy and a list of sexual harassment advisors are available in departments or through the Sexual Harassment Education Office. Questions may be directed to the Sexual Harassment Education office (752-2255).

EEOC POLICY GUIDANCE ON SEXUAL HARASSMENT

1. SUBJECT: Policy Guidance on Current Issues Of Sexual Harassment.

2. EFFECTIVE DATE: Upon receipt.

3. EXPIRATION DATE: As an exception to EEOC Order 295.001, Appendix B, Attachment 4, § a(5), this notice will remain in effect until rescinded or superseded.

4. SUBJECT MATTER:

This document provides guidance on defining sexual harassment and establishing employer liability in light of recent cases.

Section 703(a)(1) of Title VII, 42 U.S.C. § 2000e-2(a) provides:

It shall be an unlawful employment practice for an employer—

. . . to fail or refuse to hire or to discharge any individual, or otherwise to discriminate against any individual with respect to his compensation, terms, conditions, or privileges of employment, because of such individual's race, color, religion, sex, or national origin[.]

In 1980 the Commission issued guidelines declaring sexual harassment a violation of Section 703 of Title VII, establishing criteria for determining when unwelcome conduct of a sexual nature constitutes sexual harassment, defining the circumstances under which an employer may be held liable, and suggesting affirmative steps an employer should take to prevent sexual harassment. See Section 1604.11 of the Guidelines on Discrimination Because of Sex, 29 C.F.R. § 1604.11 ("Guidelines"). The Commission has applied the Guidelines in its enforcement litigation, and many lower courts have relied on the Guidelines.

The issue of whether sexual harassment violates Title VII reached the Supreme Court in 1986 in Meritor Savings Bank v. Vinson, 106 S. Ct. 2399, 40 EPD ¶ 36,159 (1986). The Court affirmed the basic promises of the Guidelines as well as the Commission's definition. The purpose of this document is to provide guidance on the following issues in light of the developing law after Vinson:

—determining whether sexual conduct is "unwelcome";

—evaluating evidence of harassment;

—determining whether a work environment is sexually "hostile";

—holding employers liable for sexual harassment by supervisors; and

—evaluating preventive and remedial action taken in response to claims of sexual harassment.

BACKGROUND

A.   Definition

Title VII does not proscribe all conduct of a sexual nature in the workplace. Thus it is crucial to clearly define sexual harassment: only unwelcome sexual conduct that is a term or condition of employment constitutes a violation. 29 C. F. R. § 1604.11(a). The EEOC's Guidelines define two types of sexual harassment: "quid pro quo" and "hostile environment." The Guidelines provide that "unwelcome" sexual conduct constitutes sexual harassment when "submission to such conduct is made either explicitly or implicitly a term or condition of an individual's employment," 29 C.F.R. § 1604.11(a)(1). "Quid pro quo harassment" occurs when "submission to or rejection of such conduct by an individual is used as the basis for employment decisions affecting such individual," 29 C.F.R.§ 1604.11(a)(2).[1] The EEOC's Guidelines also recognize that unwelcome sexual conduct that "unreasonably interferes with

---

[1] See, e.g., Miller v. Bank of America, 600 F.2d 211, 20 EPD ¶ 30,086 (9th Cir. 1979) (plaintiff discharged when she refused to cooperate with her supervisor's sexual advances); Barnes v. Costle, 561 F.2d 983, 14 EPD ¶ 7755 (D.C. Cir. 1977) (plaintiff's job abolished after she refused to submit to her supervisor's sexual advances); Williams v. Saxbe, 413 F. Supp. 665, 11 EPD 10,840 (D.D. C. 1976), rev'd and remanded on other grounds sub nom. Williams V. Bell, 587 F.2d 1240, 17 EPD ¶ 8605 (D.C. Cir. 1978) on remand sub nom. Williams v. Civiletti, 487 F. Supp. 1387, 23 EPD ¶ 30,916 (D.D. C. 1980), (plaintiff reprimanded and eventually terminated for refusing to submit to her supervisor's sexual demands).

an individual's job performance" or creates an "intimidating, hostile, or offensive working environment" can constitute sex discrimination, even if it leads to no tangible or economic job consequences. 29 C. F. R. §[2] The Supreme Court's decision in <u>Vinson</u> established that both types of sexual harassment are actionable under section 703 of Title VII of the Civil Rights Act of 1964, 42 U.S.C. § 2000e-2(a), as forms of sex discrimination.

Although "quid pro quo" and "hostile environment" harassment are theoretically distinct claims, the line between the two is not always clear and the two forms of harassment often occur together. For example, an employee's tangible job conditions are affected when a sexually hostile work environment results in her constructive discharge.[3] Similarly, a supervisor who makes sexual advances toward a subordinate employee may communicate an implicit threat to adversely affect her job status if she does not comply. "Hostile environment" harassment may acquire characteristics of "quid pro quo" harassment if the offending supervisor abuses his authority over employment decisions to force the victim to endure or participate in the sexual conduct. Sexual harassment may culminate in a retaliatory discharge if a victim tells the harasser or her employer she will no longer submit to the harassment, and is then fired in retaliation for this protest. Under these circumstances it would be appropriate to conclude that both harassment and retaliation in violation of section 704(a) of Title VII have occurred.

Distinguishing between the two types of harassment is necessary when determining the employer's liability (<u>see infra</u> Section D). But while categorizing sexual harassment as "quid pro quo," "hostile environment," or both is useful analytically these distinctions should not limit the Commission's investigations,[4] which generally should consider all available evidence and testimony under all possibly applicable theories.[5]

---

[2] *See, e.g., Katz v. Dole,* 709 F.2d 251, 32 EPD ¶33,639 (4th Cir. 1983) (plaintiff's workplace pervaded with sexual slur, insult, and innuendo and plaintiff subjected to verbal sexual harassment consisting of extremely vulgar and offensive sexually related epithets); *Henson v. City of Dundee,* 682 F.2d 897, 29 EPD ¶ 32,993 (11th Cir. 1982) (plaintiff's supervisor subjected her to numerous harangues of demeaning sexual inquiries and vulgarities and repeated requests that she have sexual relations with him); *Bundy v. Jackson,* 641 F.2d 934, 24 EPD ¶ 31,439 (D.C. Cir. 1981) (plaintiff subjected to sexual propositions by supervisors, and sexual intimidation was "standard operating procedure" in workplace).

[3] To avoid cumbersome use of both masculine and feminine pronouns, this document will refer to harassers as males and victims as females. The Commission recognizes, however, that men may also be victims and women may also be harassers.

[4] For a description of the respective roles of the Commission and other federal agencies in investigating complaints of discrimination in the federal sector, *see* 29 C.F.R. § 1613.216.

[5] In a subsection entitled "Other related practices," the Guidelines also provide that where an employment opportunity or benefit is granted because of an individual's "submission to the em-

B. Supreme Court's Decision in Vinson

Meritor Savings Bank v. Vinson posed three questions for the Supreme Court:

(1) Does unwelcome sexual behavior that creates a hostile working environment constitute employment discrimination on the basis of sex;

(2) Can a Title VII violation be shown when the district court found that any sexual relationship that existed between the plaintiff and her supervisor was a "voluntary one"; and

(3) Is an employer strictly liable for an offensive working environment created by a supervisor's sexual advances when the employer does not know of, and could not reasonably have known of, the supervisor's misconduct.

1) Facts—The plaintiff had alleged that her supervisor constantly subjected her to sexual harassment both during and after business hours, on and off the employer's premises; she alleged that he forced her to have sexual intercourse with him on numerous occasions, fondled her in front of other employees, followed her into the women's restroom and exposed himself to her, and even raped her on several occasions. She alleged that she submitted for fear of jeopardizing her employment. She testified, however, that this conduct had ceased almost a year before she first complained in any way, by filing a Title VII suit; her EEOC charge was filed later (see infra at n.34). The supervisor and the employer denied all of her allegations and claimed they were fabricated in response to a work dispute.

2) Lower Courts' Decisions—After trial, the district court found the plaintiff was not the victim of sexual harassment and was not required not required to grant sexual favors as a condition of employment or promotion. (Vinson v. Taylor, 22 EPD ¶ 30,078 (D.D.C. 1980). Without resolving the conflicting testimony, the district court found that if a sexual relationship had existed between plaintiff and her supervisor, it was "a voluntary one . . . having nothing to do with her continued employment." The district court nonetheless went on to hold that the employer was not liable for its supervisor's actions because it had no notice of the alleged sexual harassment; although

---

ployer's sexual advances or requests for sexual favors," the employer may be liable for unlawful sex discrimination against others who were qualified for but were denied the opportunity or benefit. 29 C. F. R. § 1604.11(g). the law is unsettled as to when Title VII violation can be established in these circumstances. See DeCintio v. Westchester County Medical Center, 807 F. 2d 304, 42 EPD ¶ 36,785 (2d Cir. 1986), cert. denied, 108 S. Ct. 89,44 EPD ¶ 37,425 (1987); King v. Palmer, 778 F.2d 878, 39 EPD 35,808 (D.C. Cir. 1985), decision on remand, 641 F. Supp. 186, 40 EPD ¶ 36,245 (D.D.C. 1986); Broderick v. Ruder, 46 EPD ¶ 37,963 (D.D.C. 1988); Miller v. Aluminum Co. of America, 679 F. Supp. 495, 500-01 (W.D. Pa.), aff'd mem., No. 88-3099 (3d Cir. 1988). However, the Commission recently analyzed the issues in its "Policy Guidance on Employer Liability Under Title VII for Sexual Favoritism" dated January 1990.

the employer had a policy against discrimination and an internal grievance procedure, the plaintiff had never lodged a complaint.

The court of appeals reversed and remanded, holding the lower court should have considered whether the evidence established a violation under the "hostile environment" theory. Vinson v. Taylor , 753 F.2d 141, 36 EPD ¶ 34,949, denial of rehearing en banc, 760 F.2d 1330. 37 EPD ¶ 35,232 (D.C. Cir. 1985). The court ruled that a victim's "voluntary" submission to sexual advances has "no materiality whatsoever" to the proper inquiry: whether "toleration of sexual harassment [was] a condition of her employment." The court further held that an employer is absolutely liable for sexual harassment committed by a supervisory employee, regardless of whether the employer actually knew or reasonably could have known of the misconduct, or would have disapproved of and stopped the misconduct if aware of it.

3) Supreme Court's Decision—The Supreme Court agreed that the case should he remanded for consideration under the "hostile environment" theory and held that the proper inquiry focuses on the "unwelcomeness" of the conduct rather than the "voluntariness" of the victim's participation. But the Court hold that the court of appeals erred in concluding that employers are always automatically liable for sexual harassment by their supervisory employees.

a) "Hostile Environment" Violates Title VII—The Court rejected the employer's contention that Title VII prohibits only discrimination that causes "economic" or "tangible" injury: "Title VII affords employees the right to work in an environment free from discriminatory intimidation, ridicule, and insult whether based on sex, race, religion, or national origin. 106 S. Ct. at 2405. Relying on the EEOC Guidelines' definition of harassment,[6] the Court held that a plaintiff may establish a violation of Title VII "by proving that discrimination based on sex has created a hostile or abusive work environment." Id. The Court quoted the Eleventh Circuit's decision in Henson v. City of Dundee, 682 F.2d 897, 902, 29 EPD ¶ 32,993 (llth Cir. 1982):

> Sexual harassment which creates a hostile or offensive environment for members of one sex is every bit the arbitrary barrier to sexual equality at the workplace that racial harassment is to racial equality. Surely, a requirement that a man or woman run a gauntlet of sexual abuse in return for the privilege of being allowed to work and make a living can be as demeaning and disconcerting as the harshest of racial epithets.

---

[6] The Court stated that the Guidelines, 'while not controlling upon the courts by reason of their authority, do constitute a body of experience and informed judgement to which courts and litigants may properly resort for guidance.'" Vinson 106 S. Ct. at 2405 (quoting General Electric Co. v. Gilbert, 429 U.S. 125, 141–142, 12 EPD ¶ 11,240 (1976), quoting in turn Skidmore v. Swift & Co., 323 U.S. 134 (1944).

106 S. Ct. at 2406. The Court further held that for harassment to violate Title VII, it must be "sufficiently severe or pervasive to alter the conditions of [the victim's] employment and create an abusive working environment.'" Id. (quoting Henson, 682 F.2d at 904).

b) Conduct Must Be "Unwelcome"—Citing the EEOC's Guidelines, the Court said the gravamen of a sexual harassment claim is that the alleged sexual advances were "unwelcome." 106 S. Ct. at 2406. Therefore, "the fact that sex-related conduct was 'voluntary,' in the sense that the complainant was not forced to participate against her will, is not a defense to a sexual harassment suit brought under Title VII. . . . The correct inquiry is whether (the victim) by her conduct indicated that the alleged sexual advances were unwelcome, not whether her actual participation in sexual intercourse was voluntary." Id. Evidence of a complainant's sexually provocative speech or dream may be relevant in determining whether she found particular advances unwelcome, but should be admitted with caution in light of the potential for unfair prejudice, the Court held.

c) Employer Liability Established Under Agency Principles—On the question of employer liability in "hostile environment" cases, the Court agreed with EEOC's position that agency principles should be used for guidance. While declining to issue a "definitive rule on employer liability" the Court did reject both the court of appeals' rule of automatic liability for the actions of supervisors and the employer's position that notice is always acquired. 106 S. Ct. at 2408–09.

The following sections of this document provide guidance on the issues addressed in Vinson and subsequent cases.

A. Determining Whether Sexual Conduct Is Unwelcome

Sexual harassment is "unwelcome . . . verbal or physical conduct of a sexual nature. . . ." 29 C. F. R. § 1604.11(a). Because sexual attraction may often play a role in the day-to-day social exchange between employees, "the distinction between invited, uninvited-but-welcome, offensive-but-tolerated, and flatly rejected" sexual advances may well be difficult to discern. Barnes v. Costle, 561 F.2d 983, 999, 14 EPD § 7755 (D.C. Cir. 1977) (MacKinnon J., concurring). But this distinction is essential because sexual conduct becomes unlawful only when it is unwelcome. The Eleventh Circuit provided a general definition of unwelcome conduct" in Henson v. City of Dundee, 682 F.2d at 903: the challenged conduct must be unwelcome "in the sense that the employee did not solicit or incite it, and in the sense that the employee regarded the conduct as undesirable or offensive."

When confronted with conflicting evidence as to welcomeness, the Commission looks at the record as a whole and at the totality of circumstances. . . ." 29 C.F.R. § 1604.11(b), evaluating each situation on a case-by-case basis. When there is some indication of welcomeness or when the credibility of the parties is at issue, the charging party's claim will be considerably strengthened if she made a contemporaneous complaint or protest.[7] Particularly when the alleged harasser may have some reason (e.g., a prior consensual relationship) to believe that the advances will be welcomed, it is important for the victim to communicate that the conduct is unwelcome. Generally, victims are well-advised to assert their right to a workplace free from sexual harassment. This may stop the harassment before it becomes more serious. A contemporaneous complaint or protest may also provide persuasive evidence that the sexual harassment in fact occurred as alleged (see infra Section B). Thus, in investigating sexual harassment charges, it is important to develop detailed evidence of the circumstances and nature of any such complaints or protests, whether to the alleged harasser, higher management, co-workers or others.[8]

While a complaint or protest is helpful to charging party's case, it is not a necessary element of the claim. Indeed, the Commission recognizes that victims may fear repercussions from complaining about the harassment and that such fear may explain a delay in opposing the conduct. If the victim failed to complain or delayed in complaining, the investigation must ascertain why. The relevance of whether the victim has complained varies depending upon "the nature of the sexual advances and the context in which the alleged incidents occurred." 29 C.F.R. § 1604.11(b).[9]

Example—Charging Party (CP) alleges that her supervisor subjected her to unwelcome sexual advances that created a hostile work environment. The investigation into her charge discloses that her supervisor began making intermittent sexual advances to her in June, 1987, but she did not complain to management about the harassment. After the harassment continued and worsened, she filed a charge with EEOC in June, 1988. There is no

---

[7] For a complaint to be "contemporaneous," it should be made while the harassment is ongoing or shortly after it has ceased. For example, a victim of "hostile environment harassment" who resigns her job because working conditions have become intolerable would be considered to have made a contemporaneous complaint if she notified the employer of the harassment at the time of her departure or shortly thereafter. The employer has a duty to investigate and if it finds the allegations true, to take remedial action including offering reinstatement (see infra Section E).

[8] Even when unwelcomeness is not at issue, the investigation should develop this evidence in order to aid in making credibility determinations (see infra).

[9] A victim of harassment need not always confront her harasser directly so long as her conduct demonstrates the harasser's behavior is unwelcome. See, e.g., Lipsett v. University of Puerto Rico, 864 F.2d 881, 898, 48 EPD ¶ 38,393 (1st Cir. 1988)("In some instances a woman may have the responsibility for telling the man directly that his comments or conduct is unwelcome. In other instances, however, a woman's consistent failure to respond to suggestive comments or gestures may be sufficient to communicate that the man's conduct is unwelcome"); Commission Decision No. 84-1, CCH EEOC Decisions ¶ 6839 (although charging parties did not confront their supervisor directly about his sexual remarks and gestures for fear of losing their jobs, evidence showing that they demonstrated through comments and actions that his conduct was unwelcome was sufficient to support a finding of harassment).

evidence CP welcomed the advances. CP states that the feared that complaining about the harassment would cause her to lose her job. She also states that she initially believed she could resolve the situation herself, but as the harassment became more frequent and severe, she said she realized that intervention <u>by</u> EEOC was necessary. The investigator determines CP is credible and concludes that the delay in complaining does not undercut CP's claim.

When welcomeness is at issue, the investigation should determine whether the victim's conduct is consistent, or inconsistent, with her assertion that the sexual conduct is unwelcome.[10]

In <u>Vinson</u>, the Supreme Court made clear that voluntary submission to sexual conduct will not necessarily defeat a claim of sexual harassment. The correct inquiry "is whether [the employee] <u>by her conduct</u> indicated that the alleged sexual advances were unwelcome, not whether her actual participation in sexual intercourse was voluntary." 106 S. Ct. at 2406 (emphasis added). <u>See also</u> Commission Decision No. 84-1 ("acquiescence in sexual conduct at the workplace may not mean that the conduct is welcome to the individual").

In some cases the courts and the Commission have considered whether the complainant welcomed the sexual conduct by acting in a sexually aggressive manner, using sexually-oriented language, or soliciting the sexual conduct. Thus, in <u>Gan v. Kepro Circuit Systems</u>, 27 EPD ¶ 32,379 (E.D. Mo. 1982), the plaintiff regularly used vulgar language, initiated sexually-oriented conversations with her co-workers, asked male employees about their marital sex lives and whether they engaged in extramarital affairs, and discussed her own sexual encounters. In rejecting the plaintiff's claim of "hostile environment" harassment, the court found that any propositions or sexual remarks by co-workers were "prompted by her own sexual aggressiveness and her

---

[10] Investigators and triers of fact rely on objective evidence, rather than subjective, uncommunicated feelings. For example, in *Ukerish v. Magnesium Electron,* 33 EPD ¶ 34,087 (D.N.J. 1983), the court rejected the plaintiff's claim that she was sexually harassed by her co-worker's language and gestures; although she indicated in her personal diary that she did not welcome the banter, she made no objection and indeed appeared to join in "as one of the boys." *Id.* at 32,118. In *Sardigal v. St. Louis National Stockyards Co.,* 41 EPD ¶ 36,613 (S.D. Ill. 1986), the plaintiff's allegation was found not credible because she visited her alleged harasser at the hospital and at his brother's home, and allowed him to come into her home alone at night after the alleged harassment occurred. Similarly, in the *Vinson* case, the district court noted the plaintiff had twice refused transfers to other offices located away from the alleged harasser. (In a particular charge, the significance of a charging party's refusing an offer to transfer will depend upon her reasons for doing so.)

own sexually-explicit conversations" Id. at 23,648.[11] And in Vinson, the Supreme Court held that testimony about the plaintiff 'a provocative dress and publicly expressed sexual fantasies is not per se inadmissible but the trial court should carefully weigh its relevance against the potential for unfair prejudice. 106 S. Ct. at 2407.

Conversely, occasional use of sexually explicit language does not necessarily negate a claim that sexual conduct was unwelcome. Although a charging party's use of sexual terms or off-color jokes may suggest that sexual comments by others in that situation were not unwelcome, more extreme and abusive or persistent comments or a physical assault will not be excused, nor would "quid pro quo" harassment be allowed.

Any past conduct of the charging party that is offered to show "welcomeness" must relate to the alleged harasser. In Swentek v. USAir, Inc., 830 F.2d 552, 557, 44 EPD ¶ 37,457 (4th Cir. 1987), the Fourth Circuit held the district court wrongly concluded that the plaintiff's own past conduct and use of foul language showed that "she was the kind of person who could not be offended by such comments and therefore welcomed them generally," even though she had told the harasser to leave her alone. Emphasizing that the proper inquiry is "whether plaintiff welcomed the particular conduct in question from the alleged harasser," the court of appeals held that "Plaintiff's use of foul language or sexual innuendo in a consensual setting does not waive 'her legal protections against unwelcome harassment.'" 830 F.2d at 557 (quoting Katz v. Dole, 709 F.2d 251, 254 n.3, 32 EPD ¶ 33,639 (4th Cir. 1983). Thus, evidence concerning a charging party's general character and past behavior toward others has limited, if any, probative value and does not substitute for a careful examination of her behavior toward the alleged harasser.

A more difficult situation occurs when an employee first willingly participates in conduct of a sexual nature but then ceases to participate and claims that any continued sexual conduct has created a hostile work environment. Here the employee has the burden of showing that any further sexual conduct is unwelcome, work-related harassment. The employee must clearly notify the

---

[11] *See also Ferguson v. E. I. DuPont deNemours and Co.,* 560 F. Supp. 1172, 33 EPD ¶ 34,131 (D. Del. 1983) ("sexually aggressive conduct and explicit conversation on the part of the plaintiff may bar a cause of action for (hostile environment) sexual harassment")' *Reichman v. Bureau of Affirmative Action,* 536 F. Supp. 1149, 1172, 30 FEP Cases 1644 (M.D. Pa. 1982) (where plaintiff behaved in a very flirtatious and provocative manner" around the alleged harasser, asked him to have dinner at her house on several occasions despite his repeated refusals, and continued to conduct herself in a similar manner after the alleged harassment, she could not claim the alleged harassment was unwelcome).

alleged harasser that his conduct is no longer welcome.[12] If the conduct still continues, her failure to bring the matter to the attention of higher management or the EEOC is evidence, though not dispositive, that any continued conduct is, in fact, welcome or unrelated to work.[13] In any case, however, her refusal to submit to the sexual conduct cannot be the basis for denying her an employment benefit or opportunity; that would constitute a "quid pro quo" violation.

B. Evaluating Evidence of Harassment

The Commission recognizes that sexual conduct may be private and unacknowledged, with no eyewitnesses. Even sexual conduct that occurs openly In the workplace may appear to be consensual. Thus the resolution of a sexual harassment claim often depends on the credibility of the parties. The investigator should question the charging party and the alleged harasser in detail. The Commission's investigation also should search thoroughly for corroborative evidence of any nature.[14] Supervisory and managerial employees, as well as co-workers, should be asked about their knowledge of the alleged harassment.

In appropriate cases, the Commission may make a finding of harassment based solely on the credibility of the victim's allegation. As with any other charge of discrimination, a victim's account must be sufficiently detailed and internally consistent so as to be plausible, and lack of corroborative evidence where such evidence logically should exist would undermine the allegation.[15]

---

[12] In Commission Decision No. 84-1, CCH Employment Practices Guide ¶ 6839, the Commission found that active participation in sexual conduct at the workplace, e.g., by "using dirty remarks and telling dirty jokes," may indicate that the sexual advances complained of were not unwelcome. Thus, the Commission found that no harassment occurred with respect to an employee who had joined in the telling of bawdy jokes and the use of vulgar language during her first two months on the job, and failed to provide subsequent notice that the conduct was no longer welcome. By actively participating in the conduct, the charging party had created the impression among her co-workers that she welcomed the sort of sexually-oriented banter that she later asserted was objectionable. Simply ceasing to participate was insufficient to show the continuing activity was no longer welcome to her. *See also Loftin-Boggs v. City of Meridian,* 633 F. Supp. 1323, 41 FEP Cases 532 (S. D. Miss. 1986) (plaintiff initially participated in and initiated some of the crude language that was prevalent on the job; if she later found such conduct offensive, she should have conveyed this by her own conduct and her reaction to her co-workers' conduct).

[13] However, if the harassing supervisor engages in conduct that is sufficiently pervasive and work-related, it may place the employer on notice that the conduct constitutes harassment.

[14] As the court said in *Henson v. City of Dundee,* 682 F.2d at 912 n.25, "In a case of alleged sexual harassment which involves close questions of credibility and subjective interpretation, the existence of corroborative evidence or the lack thereof is likely to be crucial."

[15] In *Sardigal v. St. Louis National Stockyards Co.,* 41 EPD ¶ 36,613 at 44,694 (S.D. Ill. 1986), the plaintiff, a waitress, alleged she was harassed over a period of nine months in a restaurant at noontime, when there was a "constant flow of waitresses or customers" around the area where the offenses allegedly took place. Her allegations were not credited by the district court because no individuals came forward with testimony to support her.

It is important to explore all avenues for obtaining corroborative evidence because courts may reject harassment claims due to lack of corroborative evidence. *See Hall v. F. O. Thacker Co.,* 24

By the same token, a general denial by the alleged harasser will carry little weight when it is contradicted by other evidence.[16]

Of course, the Commission recognizes that a charging party may not be able to identify witnesses to the alleged conduct itself. But testimony may be obtained from persons who observed the charging party's demeanor immediately after an alleged incident of harassment. Persons with whom she discussed the incident—such as co-workers, a doctor or a counselor—should be interviewed. Other employees should be asked if they noticed changes in charging party's behavior at work or in the alleged harasser's treatment of charging party. As stated earlier, a contemporaneous complaint by the victim would be persuasive evidence both that the conduct occurred and that it was unwelcome (see supra Section A). So too is evidence that other employees were sexually harassed by the same person.

The investigator should determine whether the employer was aware of any other instances of harassment and if so what was the response. Where appropriate the Commission will expand the case to include class claims.[17]

> Example—Charging Party (CP) alleges that her supervisor made unwelcome sexual advances toward her on frequent occasions while they were alone in his office. The supervisor denies this allegation. No one witnessed the alleged advances. CP's inability to produce eyewitnesses to the harassment does not defeat her claim. The resolution will depend on the credibility of her allegations versus that of her supervisor,s. Corroborating, credible evidence will establish her claim. For example, three co-workers state that CP looked distraught on several occasions after leaving the supervisor's office, and that she informed them on those occasions that he had sexually propositioned and touched her. In addition, the evidence shows that CP had complained to the general manager of the office about the incidents soon after they occurred. The corroborating witness testimony and her complaint to higher management would be sufficient to establish her claim. Her allegations would be further buttressed if other employees testified that the supervisor propositioned them as well.

FEP Cases 1499, 1503 (N.D. Ga. 1980) (district judge did not credit plaintiff's testimony about sexual advances because it was "virtually uncorroborated"); *Neidhart v. D.M. Holmes Co.,* 21 FEP Cases 452, 457 (E.D. La. 1979), *aff'd mem.,* 624 F.2d 1097 (5tb Cir. 1980) (plaintiff's account of sexual harassment rejected because "there is not a scintilla of credible evidence to "corroborate [plaintiff's version]").

[16] *See* Commission Decision No. 81-17, CCH EEOC Decisions (1983) ¶ 6757 (violation of Title VII found where charging party alleged that her supervisor made repeated sexual advances toward her; although the supervisor denied the allegations, statements of other employees supported them).

[17] Class complaints in the federal sector are governed by the requirements of 29 C.F.R. § 1613 Subpart F.

If the investigation exhausts all possibilities for obtaining corroborative evidence, but finds none, the Commission may make a cause finding based solely on a reasoned decision to credit the charging party's testimony.[18]

In a "quid pro quo" case, a finding that the employer's asserted reasons for its adverse action against the charging party are pretextual will usually establish a violation.[19] The investigation should determine the validity of the employer's reasons for the charging party's termination. If they are pretextual and if the sexual harassment occurred, then it should be inferred that the charging party was terminated for rejecting the employer's sexual advances, as she claims. Moreover, if the termination occurred because the victim complained, it would be appropriate to find, in addition, a violation of section 704(a).

C. Determining Whether a Work Environment is "Hostile"

The Supreme Court said in Vinson that for sexual harassment to violate Title VII, it must be "sufficiently severe or pervasive 'to alter the conditions of [the victim's] employment and create an abusive working environment.'" 106 S. Ct. at 2406 (quoting Henson V. City of Dundee, 582 F.26 at 904. Since "hostile environment" harassment takes a variety of forms, many factors may affect this determination, including: (1) whether the conduct was verbal or physical, or both; (2) how frequently it was repeated; (3) whether the conduct was hostile and patently offensive; (4) whether the alleged harasser was a co-worker or a supervisor; (5) whether others joined in perpetrating the harassment; and (6) whether the harassment was directed at more than one individual.

In determining whether unwelcome sexual conduct rises to the level of a "hostile environment" in violation of Title VII, the central inquiry is whether the conduct "unreasonably interferes with an individual's work performance" or creates "an intimidating, hostile, or offensive working environment." 29 C.F.R. § 1604.11(a)(3). Thus, sexual flirtation or innuendo, even vulgar language that is trivial or merely annoying, would probably not establish a hostile environment.

1) Standard for Evaluating Harassment—In determining whether harassment is sufficiently severe or pervasive to create a hostile environment, the harasser's conduct should be evaluated from the objective standpoint of a "reasonable person." Title VII does not serve "as a vehicle for vindicating the petty slights suffered by the hypersensitive." Zabkowicz v. Went Bend Co., 589 F. Supp. 780, 784, 35 EPD ¶ 34,766 (E.D. Wis. 1984). See also Ross v.

---

[18] In Commission Decision No. 82-13, CCH EEOc Decisions (1983) ¶ 6832, the Commission stated that a "bare assertion" of sexual harassment "cannot stand without some factual support." to the extent this decision suggests a charging party can never prevail based solely on the credibility of her own testimony, that decision is overruled.

[19] See, e.g., Bundy v. Jackson, 641 F.2d 934, 953, 24 EPD ¶ 31,439 (D.C. Circ. 1981).

Comsat, 34 FEP cas. 260, 265 (D. Md. 1984), rev'd on other grounds, 759 F.2d 355 (4th Cir. 1985). Thus, if the challenged conduct would not substantially affect the work environment of a reasonable person, no violation should be found.

> Example—Charging Party alleges that her coworker made repeated unwelcome sexual advances toward her. An investigation discloses that the alleged "advances," consisted of invitations to join a group of employees who regularly socialized at dinner after work. The co-worker's invitations, viewed in that context and from the perspective of a reasonable person, would not have created a hostile environment and therefore did not constitute sexual harassment.

A "reasonable person" standard also should be applied to the more basic determination of whether challenged conduct is of a sexual nature. Thus, in the above example, a reasonable person would not consider the co-worker's invitations sexual in nature, and on that basis as well no violation would be found.

This objective standard should not be applied in a vacuum, however. Consideration should be given to the context in which the alleged harassment took place. As the Sixth Circuit has stated, the trier of fact must "adopt the perspective of a reasonable person's reaction to a similar environment under similar or like circumstances." Highlander v. K. F. C. National Management Co., 805 F.2d 644, 650, 41 EPD ¶ 36,675 (6th Cir. 1986).[20]

The reasonable person standard should consider the victim's perspective and not stereotyped notions of acceptable behavior. For example, the Commission believes that a workplace in which sexual slurs, displays of "girlie" pictures, and other offensive conduct abound can constitute a hostile work environment even if many people deem it to be harmless or insignificant. Cf. Rabidue v. Osceola Refining Co., 805 F.2d 611, 626, 41 EPD ¶ 36,643 (6th Cir. 1986) (Keith, C. J., dissenting), cert. denied, 107 S. Ct. 1983, 42 EPD ¶ 36, 984. Lipsett v. University of Puerto Rico, 864 F.2d 881, 898, EPD ¶ 38,393 (1st Cir. 1988).

2) Isolated Instances of Harassment—Unless the conduct is quite severe, a single incident or isolated incidents of offensive sexual conduct or remarks generally do not create an abusive environment. As the Court noted in Vinson, "mere utterance of an ethnic or racial epithet which engenders offensive feelings in an employee would not affect the conditions of employment to

---

[20] In *Highlander* and also in *Rabidue v. Osceola Refining Co.,* 805 F.2d 611, 41 EPD ¶ 36,643 (6th Cir. 1986, *cert. denied,* 107 S. Ct. 1983, 42 EPD ¶ 36, 984 (1987), the Sixth Circuit required an additional showing that the plaintiff suffered some degree of psychological injury. *Highlander,* 805 F.2d at 650; *Rabidue,* 805 F.2d at 620. However, it is the Commission's position that it is sufficient for the charging party to show that the harassment was unwelcome and that it would have substantially affected the work environment of a reasonable person.

a sufficiently significant degree to violate Title VII. 106 S. Ct. at 2406 quoting Rogers v. EEOC, 454 F.2d. 234, 4 EPD ¶ 7597 (5th Cir. 1971), cert. denied, 406 U.S. 957, 4 EPD ¶ 7838 (1972)). A "hostile environment" claim generally requires a showing of a pattern of offensive conduct.[21] In contrast, in "quid pro quo" cases a single sexual advance may constitute harassment if it is linked to the granting or denial of employment benefits.[22]

But a single, unusually severe incident of harassment may be sufficient to constitute a Title VII violation; the more severe the harassment, the less need to show a repetitive series of incidents. This is particularly true when the harassment is physical.[23] Thus, in Barrett v. Omaha National Bank, 584 F. Supp. 22, 35 FEP Cases 585 (D. Neb. 1983), aff'd, 726 F.2d 424, 33 EPD ¶ 34,132 (8th Cir. 1984), one incident constituted actionable sexual harassment. The harasser talked to the plaintiff about sexual activities and touched her in an offensive manner while they were inside a vehicle from which she could not escape.[24]

The commission will presume that the unwelcome, intentional touching of a charging party's intimate body areas is sufficiently offensive to alter the conditions of her working environment and constitute a violation of Title VII.

---

[21] See, e.g., Scott v. Sears, Roebuck and Co., 798 F.2d 210, 214, 41 EPD ¶ 36,439 (7th Cir. 1986) (offensive comments and conduct of co-workers were "too isolated and lacking the repetitive and debilitating effect necessary to maintain a hostile environment claim"); Moylan v. Maries County, 792 F.2d 746, 749, 40 EPD ¶ 36,228 (8th Cir. 1986) (single incident or isolated incidents of harassment will not be sufficient to establish a violation; the harassment must be sustained and nontrivial); Downes v. Federal Aviation Administration, 775 F.2d 288, 293, 38 EPD ¶ 35,590 (D.C. Cir. 1985) (Title VII does not create a claim of sexual harassment "for each and every cruel joke or sexually explicit remark made on the job.... [A] pattern of offensive conduct must be proved...."); Sapp v. City of Warner-Robins, 655 F. Supp. 1043, 43 FEP Cases 486 (M.D. Ga. 1987) (co-worker's single effort to get the plaintiff to go out with him did not create an abusive working environment); Freedman v. American Standard, 41 FEP Cases 471 (D.N.J. 1986) (plaintiff did not suffer a hostile environment from the receipt of an obscene message from her coworkers and a sexual solicitation from one co-worker); Hollis v. Fleetguard, Inc., 44 FEP Cases 1527 (M.D. Tenn. 1987) (plaintiff's co-worker's requests, on four occasions over a four-month period, that she have a sexual affair with him, followed by his coolness toward her and avoidance of her did not constitute a hostile environment; there was no evidence he coerced, pressured or abused the plaintiff after she rejected his advances).

[22] See Neville v. Taft Broadcasting Co., 42 FEP Cases 1314 (W.D.N.Y. 1987) (one sexual advance, rebuffed by plaintiff, may establish a prima facie case of "quid pro quo" harassment but is not severe enough to create a hostile environment).

[23] The principles for establishing employer liability, set forth in Section D below, are to be applied to cases involving physical contact in the same manner that they are applied in other cases.

[24] See also Gilardi v. Schroeder, 672 F. Supp. 1043, 45 FEP Cases 283 (N.D. Ill. 1986) (plaintiff who was drugged by employer's owner and raped while unconscious, and then was terminated at insistence of owner's wife, was awarded $113,000 in damages for harassment and intentional infliction of emotional distress); Commission Decision No. 83-1, CCH EEOC Decisions (1963) ¶ 6834 (violation found where the harasser forcibly grabbed and kissed charging party while they were alone in a storeroom); Commission Decision No. 84-3, CCH Employment Practices Guide ¶ 6841 (violation found where the harasser slid his hand under the charging party's skirt and squeezed her buttocks).

More so than in the case of verbal advances or remarks, a single unwelcome physical advance can seriously poison the victim's working environment. If an employee's supervisor sexually touches that employee, the Commission normally would find a violation. In such situations, it is the employer's burden to demonstrate that the unwelcome conduct was not sufficiently severe to create a hostile work environment.

When the victim is the target of both verbal and non-intimate physical conduct, the hostility of the environment is exacerbated and a violation is more likely to be found. Similarly, incidents of sexual harassment, directed at other employees in addition to the charging party are relevant to a showing of hostile work environment. Hall v. Gus Construction Co, 842 F.2d 1010, 46 EPD ¶ 37,905 (8th Cir. 1988); Hicks v. Gates Rubber Co., 833 F.2d 1406, 44 EPD ¶ 37,542 (10th Cir. 1987); Jones v. Flagship International, 793 F.2d 714, 721 n.7, 40 EPD ¶ 36,392 (5th Cir. 1986); cert. denied, 107 S. Ct. 952, 41 EPD ¶ 36,708 (1987).

3. Non-Physical Harassment—When the alleged harassment consists of verbal conduct, the investigation should ascertain the nature, frequency, context, and intended target of the remarks. Questions to be explored might include:

• Did the alleged harasser single out the charging party?

• Did the charging party participate?

• What was the relationship between the charging party and the alleged harasser(s)?

• Were the remarks hostile and derogatory?

No one factor alone determines whether particular conduct violates Title VII. As the Guidelines emphasize, the Commission will evaluate the totality of the circumstances. In general, a woman does not forfeit her right to be free from sexual harassment by choosing to work in an atmosphere that has traditionally included vulgar, anti-female language. However, in Rabidue v. Osceola Refining Co., 805 F.2d 611, 41 EPD ¶ 36,643 (6th Cir. 1986), cert. denied, 107 S. Ct. 1983, 42 EPD ¶ 36,984 (1987), the Sixth Circuit rejected the plaintiff's claim of harassment in such a situation.[25]

---

[25] The alleged harasser, a supervisor of another department who did not supervise plaintiff but worked with her regularly, "was an extremely vulgar and crude individual who customarily made obscene comments about women generally, and, on occasion, directed such obscenities to the plaintiff." 805 F.2d at 615. The plaintiff and other female employees were exposed daily to displays of nude or partially clad women in posters in male employees' offices. 805 F.2d at 623-24 (Keith, J., dissenting in part and concurring in part). Although the employees told management they were disturbed and offended, the employer did not reprimand the supervisor.

One of the factors the court found relevant was "the lexicon of obscenity" that pervaded the environment of the workplace both before and after the plaintiff's introduction into its environs, coupled with the reasonable expectations of the plaintiff upon voluntarily entering that environment." 805 F.2d at 620. Quoting the district court, the majority noted that in some work environments, " 'humor and language are rough hewn and vulgar. Sexual jokes, sexual conversation, and girlie magazines may abound. Title VII was not meant to—or can—change this.' " Id. at 620–21. The court also considered the sexual remarks and poster at issue to have a "de minimis effect on the plaintiff's work environment when considered in the context of a society that condones and publicly features and commercially exploits open displays of written and pictorial erotica at the newsstands, on prime-time television, at the cinema, and in other public places." Id. at 622.

The Commission believes these factors rarely will be relevant and agrees with the dissent in that a woman does not assume the risk of harassment by voluntarily entering an abusive, antifemale environment. "Title VII's precise purpose is to prevent such behavior and attitudes from poisoning the work environment of classes protected under the Act." 805 F.2d at 626 (Keith, J., dissenting in part and concurring in part). Thus, in a decision disagreeing with Rabidue, a district court found that a hostile environment was established by the presence of pornographic magazines in the workplace and vulgar employee comments concerning them; offensive sexual comments made to and about plaintiff and other female employees by her supervisor; sexually oriented pictures in a company-sponsored movie and slide presentation; sexually oriented pictures and calendars in the workplace; and offensive touching of plaintiff by a co-worker. Barbette v. Chemlawn Services Corp., 669 F. Supp. 569, 45 EPD ¶ 37,568 (W.D.N.Y. 1937). The court held that the proliferation of pornography and demeaning comments, if sufficiently continuous and pervasive, "may be found to create an atmosphere in which women are viewed as men's sexual playthings rather than as their equal coworkers." Barbette, 669 F. Supp. at 573. The Commission agrees that, depending on the totality of circumstances, such an atmosphere may violate Title VII. See also Waltman v. International Paper Co., 875 F.2d 468, 50 EPD ¶ 39,106 (5th Cir. 1989), in which the 5th Circuit endorsed the Commission's position in its amicus brief that evidence of ongoing sexual graffiti in the workplace, not all of which was directed at the plaintiff, was relevant to her claim of harassment. Bennett v. Corroon & Black Corp., 845 F.2d 104, 46 EPD ¶ 37,955 (5th Cir. 1988) (the posting of obscene cartoons in an office men's room bearing the plaintiff's name and depicting her engaged in crude and deviant sexual activities could create a hostile work environment).

4) Sex-Based Harassment—Although the Guidelines specifically address conduct that is sexual in nature, the Commission notes that sex-based harassment—that is, harassment not involving sexual activity or language—may also give rise to Title VII liability (just as in the case of harassment based on race, national origin or religion) if it is "sufficiently patterned or pervasive" and directed at employees because of their sex. Hicks v. Gates Rubber Co., 833 F.2d at 1416; McKinney v. Dole, 765 F.2d 1129, 1138, 37 EPD ¶ 35,339 (D.C. Cir. 1985).

Acts of physical aggression, intimidation, hostility or unequal treatment based on sex may be combined with incidents of sexual harassment to establish the existence of discriminatory terms and conditions of.employment. Hall v. Gus Construction Co., 842 F.2d at 1014; Hicks v. Gates Rubber Co., 833 F.2d at 1416.

5) Constructive Discharge—Claims of "hostile environment" sexual harassment often are coupled with claims of constructive discharge. If constructive discharge due to a hostile environment is proven, the claim will also become one of "quid pro quo" harassment.[26] It is the position of the Commission and a majority of courts that an employer is liable for constructive discharge when it imposes intolerable working conditions in violation of Title VII when those conditions foreseeably would compel a reasonable employee to quit, whether or not the employer specifically intended to force the victim's resignation. See Derr v. Gulf Oil Corp., 796 F.2d 340, 343-44, 41 EPD ¶ 36,468 (10th Cir. 1986); Goss v. Exxon Office Systems Co., 747 F.2d 885, 888, 35 EPD ¶ 34,768 (3d Cir. 1984); Nolan v. Cleland, 686 F.2d 806, 812-15, 30 EPD ¶ 33,029 (9th Cir. 1982); Held v. Gulf Oil Co., 684 F.2d 427, 432, 29 EPD ¶ 32,968 (6th Cir. 1982); Clark v. Marsh, 665 F.2d 1168, 1175 n.8, 26 EPD ¶ 32,082 (D.C. Cir. 1981); Bourque v. Powell Electrical Manufacturing Co., 617 F.2d 61, 65, 23 EPD ¶ 30,891 (5th Cir. 1980); Commission Decision 84-1, CCH EEOC Decision ¶ 6839. However, the Fourth Circuit requires proof that the employer imposed the intolerable conditions with the intent of forcing the victim to leave. See EEOC v. Federal Reserve Bank of Richmond, 598 F.2d 633, 672, 30 EPD ¶ 33,269 (4th Cir. 1983). But this case is not a sexual harassment case and the Commission believes it is distinguishable because specific intent is not as likely to be present in "hostile environment" cases.

An important factor to consider is whether the employer had an effective internal grievance procedures. (See Section E, Preventive and Remedial Action). The Commission argued in its Vinson brief that if an employee knows that effective avenues of complaint and redress are available, then the availability of such avenues itself becomes a part of the work environment and overcomes, to the degree it is effective, the hostility of the work environment. As Justice Marshall noted in his opinion in Vinson, "where a complainant without good reason bypassed an internal complaint procedure she knew to be effective, a court may be reluctant to find constructive termination. . . ."

---

[26] However, while an employee's failure to utilize effective grievance procedures will not shield an employer from liability for "quid pro quo" harassment, such failure may defeat a claim of constructive discharge. *See* discussion of impact of grievance procedures later in this section and section D(2)(c)(2), below.

106 S. Ct. at 2411 (Marshall, J., concurring in part and dissenting in part). Similarly, the court of appeals in Dornhecker v. Malibu Grand Prix Corp., 828 F.2d 307, 44 EPD ¶ 37,557 (5th Cir. 1987), held the plaintiff was not constructively discharged after an incident of harassment by a co-worker because she quit immediately, even though the employer told her she would not have to work with him again, and she did not give the employer a fair opportunity to demonstrate it could curb the harasser's conduct.

D. Employer Liability for Harassment by Supervisors

In Vinson, the Supreme Court agreed with the Commission's position that "Congress wanted courts to look to agency principles for guidance" in determining an employer's liability for sexual conduct by a supervisor:

> While such common-law principles may not be transferable in all their particulars to Title VII, Congress' decision to define "employer" to include any "agent" of an employer, 42 U.S.C. § 2000e(b), surely evinces an intent to place some limits on the acts of employees for which employers under Title VII are to be held responsible.

106 S. Ct. at 2408. Thus, while declining to issue a "definitive rule on employer liability," the Court did make it clear that employers are not "automatically liable" for the acts of their supervisors. For the same reason, the Court said, "absence of notice to an employer does not necessarily insulate that employer from liability." Id.

As the Commission argued in Vinson, reliance on agency principles is consistent with the Commission's Guidelines, "which provide in section 1604.11(c) that

> . . . an employer . . . is responsible for its acts and those of its agents and supervisory employees with respect to sexual harassment regardless of whether the specific acts complained of were authorized or even forbidden by the employer and regardless of whether the employer knew or should have known of their occurrence. The Commission will examine the circumstances of the particular employment relationship and the job functions performed by the individual in determining whether an individual acts in either a supervisory or agency capacity.

Citing the last sentence of this provision, the Court in Vinson indicated that the Guidelines further supported the application of agency principles. 106 S. Ct. at 2408.

1. Application of Agency Principles—"Quid Pro Quo" Cases

An employer will always be held responsible for acts of "quid pro quo" harassment. A supervisor in such circumstances has made or threatened to make a decision affecting the victim's employment status, and he therefore has exercised authority delegated to him by his employer. Although the question of employer liability for "quid pro quo" harassment was not at issue in Vinson, the Court's decision noted with apparent approval the position taken by the Commission in its brief that:

> where a supervisor exercises the authority actually delegated to him by his employer, by making or threatening to make decisions affecting the employment status of his subordinates, such actions are properly imputed to the employer whose delegation of authority empowered the supervisor to undertake them.

106 S. Ct. at 2407-8 (citing Brief for the United States and Equal Employment Opportunity Commission as Amicas Curias at 22).[27] See also Sparks v. Pilot Freight Carriers, Inc., 830 F.2d 1554, 44 EPD ¶ 37,493 (11th Cir. 1987) (adopting EEOC position quoted in Vinson opinion); Lipsett, 864 F.2d at 901 (adopting, for Title IX of the Education Amendments, the Vinson standard that an employer is absolutely liable for acts of quid pro quo harassment "whether [it] knew, should have known, or approved of the supervisor's actions"). Thus, applying agency principles, the court in Schroeder v. Schock, 42 FEP Cases 1112 (D. Kans. 1986), held an employer liable for "quid pro quo" harassment by a supervisor who had authority to recommend plaintiff's discharge. The employer maintained the supervisor's acts were beyond the scope of his employment since the sexual advances were made at a restaurant after work hours. The court held that because the supervisor was acting within the scope of his authority when making or recommending employment decisions, his conduct may fairly be imputed to the employer. The supervisor was using his authority to hire, fire, and promote to extort sexual consideration from an employee, even though the sexual advance itself occurred away from work.

2. Application of Agency Principles—"Hostile Environment" Cases

a) Vinson—In its Vinson brief the Commission argued that the employer should be liable for the creation of a hostile environment by a supervisor when the employer knew or had reason to know of the sexual misconduct. Ways by which actual or constructive knowledge could be demonstrated include: by a supervisor when the employer knew or had reason to know

---

[27] This well-settled principle is the basis for employer liability for supervisors' discriminatory employment decisions that violate Title VII. 106 S. Ct. at 2408; see, e.g., Anderson v. Methodist Evangelical Hospital, Inc., 464 F.2d 723, 725, 4 EPD ¶ 7901 (6th Cir. 1972) racially motivated discharge "by a person in authority at a lower level of management" is attributable to employer despite upper management's "exemplary" record in race relations); Tidwell v. American Oil Co., ??? F. Supp. 424, 436, 4 EPD ¶ 7544 (D. Utah 1971) (upper level management's lack of knowledge irrelevant where supervisor illegally discharged employee for refusing to disqualify black applicant discriminatorily); Flowers v. Crouch-Walker Corp., 552 F. 3d ???, ??? 14 EPD ¶ 7510 (7th Cir. 1977) ("The defendant is liable as principal for any violation of Title VII . . . by [a supervisor] in his authorized capacity as supervisor.")

of the sexual misconduct. Ways by which actual or constructive knowledge could be demonstrated include: by a complaint to management or an EEOC charge; by the pervasiveness of the harassment; or by evidence the employer had "deliberately turned its back on the problem" of sexual harassment by failing to establish a policy against it and a grievance mechanism to redress it. The brief argued that an employer should be liable "if there is no reasonably available avenue by which victims of sexual harassment can make their complaints known to appropriate officials who are in a position to do something about those complaints." Brief for the United States and Equal Employment Opportunity Commission as Amicus Curiae at 25. Under that circumstance, an employer would be deemed to know of any harassment that occurred in its workplace.

While the Vinson decision quoted the Commission's brief at length, it neither endorsed nor rejected its position.[28] 106 S. Ct. at 2407-08. The Court did state, however, that "the mere existence of a grievance procedure and a policy against discrimination, coupled with [the victim's] failure to invoke the procedure" are "plainly relevant" but "not necessarily dispositive." Id. at 2408-09. The Court further stated that the employer's argument that the victim's failure to complain insulated it from liability "might be substantially stronger if its procedures were better calculated to encourage victims of harassment to come forward." Id. at 2409.

The Commission, therefore, interprets Vinson to require a careful examination in "hostile environment" cases of whether the harassing supervisor was acting in an "agency capacity" (29 C.F.R. § 1604.11(c)). Whether the employer had an appropriate and effective complaint procedure and whether the victim used it are important factors to consider, as discussed below.

b) Direct Liability—The initial inquiry should be whether the employer knew or should have known of the alleged sexual harassment. If actual or constructive knowledge exists, and if the employer failed to take immediate and appropriate corrective action, the employer would be directly liable.[29]

---

[28] The Court observed that the Commission's position was "in some tension" with the first sentence of section 1604.11(c) of the Guidelines but was consistent with the final sentence of that section. (See supra at 21.)

[29] Barrett v. Omaha National Bank 584 F. Supp. 22, 30-31 (D. Neb. 1983), aff'd, 726 F.2d 424, 33 EPD ¶ 34,132 (8th Cir. 1984); Ferguson v. DuPont Corp., 560 F. Supp. 1172, 1199 (D. Del. 1983); Commission Decision No. 83-1, CCH EEOC Decisions (1983) ¶ 6834. "[A]n employer who has reason to know that one of his employees is being harassed in the workplace by others on grounds of race, sex, religion, or national origin, and does nothing about it, is blameworthy." Hunter v. Allis-Chalmers Corp., 797 F.2d 1417, 1422, 41 EPD ¶ 36,417 (7th Cir. 1986). This is the theory under which employers are liable for harassment by co-workers, which was at issue in Hunter v. Allis-Chalmers. Section 1604.11(d) provides:

With respect to conduct between fellow employees, an employer is responsible for acts of sexual harassment in the workplace where the employer (or its agents or supervisory

Most commonly an employer acquires actual knowledge through first-hand observation, by the victim's internal complaint to other supervisors or managers, or by a charge of discrimination.

An employer is liable when it "knew , or upon reasonably diligent inquiry should have known," of the harassment. Yates v. Avco Corp., 819 F.2d 630, 636, 43 EPD ¶ 37,086 (6th Cir. 1987) (emphasis added) (supervisor harassed two women "on a daily basis in the course of his supervision of them" and the employer's grievance procedure did not function effectively). Thus, evidence of the pervasiveness of the harassment may give rise to an inference of knowledge or establish constructive knowledge. Henson v. City of Dundee, 682 F.2d 897, 905, 29 EPD ¶ 32,993 (11th Cir. 1982); Taylor v. Jones, 653 F.2d 1193, 1197-99, 26 EPD ¶ 31,293 (8th Cir. 1981). Employers usually will be deemed to know of sexual harassment that is openly practiced in the workplace or well-known among employees. This often may be the case when there is more than one harasser or victim. Lipsett, 864 F.2d at 906 (employer liable where it should have known of concerted harassment of plaintiff and other female medical residents by more senior male residents).

The victim can of course put the employer on notice by filing a charge of discrimination. As the Commission stated in its Vinson brief, the filing of a charge triggers a duty to investigate and remedy any ongoing illegal activity. It is important to emphasize that an employee can always file an EEOC charge without first utilizing an internal complaint or grievance procedure[30] and may wish to pursue both avenues simultaneously because an internal grievance does not prevent the Title VII charge-filing time period from expiring.[31] Nor does the filing of an EEOC charge allow an employer to cease action on an internal grievance[32] or ignore evidence of ongoing harassment.[33] Indeed, employers should take prompt remedial action upon learning of evidence of sexual harassment (or any other form of unlawful discrimination), whether from an EEOC charge or an internal complaint. If the employer takes immediate and appropriate action to

---

employees) knows or should have known of the conduct, unless it can show that it took immediate and appropriate corrective action.

Section E(2) of this paper discussed what constitutes "immediate and appropriate corrective action," and is applicable to cases of harassment by co-workers as well as supervisors.

[30] Sexual harassment claims are no different from other types of discrimination claims in this regard. See Alexander v. Gardener-Denver Co., 415 U.S. 36, 52, 7 EPD ¶ 9148 (1974).

[31] See I.U.O.E. v. Robbins & Myers, Inc., 429 U.S. 229, 236, 12 EPD ¶ 11,256 (1976).

[32] The Commission has filed suit in such circumstances, alleging that termination of grievance processing because a charge has been filed constitutes unlawful retaliation in violation of § 704(a). See EEOC v. Board of Governors of State Colleges & Universities, 706 F. Supp. 1378, 50 EPD ¶ 39,035 (D. Ill. 1989) (denying EEOC's motion for summary judgement on ground that ADEA's retaliation provision is not violated if termination of grievance proceedings was done in good faith).

[33] See Brooms v. Regal Tube Co., 44 FEP Cases 1119 (N.D. Ill. 1987), aff'd in relevant part, 881 F.2d 412 (7th Cir. 1989).

correct the harassment and prevents its recurrence, and the Commission determines that no further action is warranted, normally the Commission would administratively close the case.

c) Imputed Liability—The investigation should determine whether the alleged harassing supervisor was acting in an "agency capacity" (29 C.F.R. § 1604.11(c)).[34] This requires a determination whether the supervisor was acting within the scope of his employment (see Restatement (Second) of Agency, § 219(1) (1958)), or whether his actions can be imputed to the employer under some exception to the "scope of employment" rule (Id. at § 219(2)). The following principles should be considered, and applied where appropriate in "hostile environment" sexual harassment cases.

1. **Scope of Employment**—A supervisor's actions are generally viewed as being within the scope of his employment if they represent the exercise of authority actually vested in him. It will rarely be the case that an employer will have authorized a supervisor to engage in sexual harassment. See Fields v. Horizon House, Inc., No. 86-4343 (E.D. Pa. 1987) (available on Lexis, Genfed library, Dist. file). Cf. Hunter v. Allis-Chalmers Corp., 797 F.2d 1417, 1421-22, 41 EPD § 36,417 (7th Cir. 1986) (co-worker racial harassment case). However, if the employer becomes aware of work-related sexual misconduct and does nothing to stop it, the employer, by acquiescing, has brought the supervisor's actions within the scope of his employment.

2. **Apparent Authority**—An employer is also liable for a supervisor's actions if these actions represent the exercise of authority that third parties reasonably believe him to possess by virtue of his employer's conduct. This is called "apparent authority." See Restatement (Second) of Agency, §§ 7, 8; 219(2)(d) (1958). The Commission believes that in the absence of a strong, widely disseminated, and consistently enforced employer policy against sexual harassment, and an effective complaint procedure, employees could reasonably believe that a harassing supervisor's actions will be ignored, tolerated, or even condoned by upper management. This apparent authority of supervisors arises from their power over their employees, including the power to make or substantially influence hiring, firing, promotion and compensation decisions. A supervisor's capacity to create a hostile environment is

---

[34] The fact that an EEO charge puts the employer on notice of sexual harassment means that the question of imputed employer liability under agency principles often will become of secondary importance. It figured critically in the *Vinson* case because the plaintiff never filed an EEOC charge before filing her Title VII lawsuit. Without having given any prior notice of the sexual harassment to anyone, she waited to file her lawsuit until almost a year after she admitted it had ceased. The sexual harassment was alleged to have taken place mostly in private, and she produced no witnesses either to the alleged harassment or to its adverse effects on her. Her case did not include a constructive discharge claim, and the district court found no "quid pro quo" harassment.

enhanced by the degree of authority conferred on him by the employer, and he may rely upon apparent authority to force an employee to endure a harassing environment for fear of retaliation. If the employer has not provided an effective avenue to complain, then the supervisor has unchecked, final control over the victim and it is reasonable to impute his abuse of this power to the employer.[35] The Commission generally will find an employer liable for "hostile environment" sexual harassment by a supervisor when the employer failed to establish an explicit policy against sexual harassment despite plaintiff's failure to pursue internal remedies where the employer's anti-discrimination policy did not specifically proscribe sexual harassment and its internal procedures required initial resort to the supervisor accused of engaging in or condoning harassment).

But an employer can divest its supervisors of this apparent authority by implementing a strong policy against sexual harassment and maintaining an effective complaint procedure. When employees know that recourse is available, they cannot reasonably believe that a harassing work environment is authorized or condoned by the employer.[36] If an employee failed to use an effective, available complaint procedure, the employer may be able to prove the absence of apparent authority and thus the lack of an agency relationship, unless liability attaches under some other theory.[37] Thus, even when an employee failed to use an effective grievance procedure, the employer will be liable if it obtained notice through other means (such as the filing of a charge or by the pervasiveness of the harassment) and did not take immediate and appropriate corrective action.

Example—Charging Party (CP) alleges that her supervisor made repeated sexual advances toward her that created a hostile work environment. The investigation into her charge discloses that CO had maintained an intermittent romantic relationship with the supervisor over a period of three years preceding the filing of the charge in September of 1986. CP's employer was aware of this relationship and its consensual nature. CP asserts, however, that on frequent occasions

---

[35] *See also Fields v. Horizon House, supra* (an employer might be charged with constructive notice of a supervisor's harassment if the supervisor is vested with unbridled authority to retaliate against an employee).

[36] It is important to reemphasize, however, that no matter what the employer's policy, the employer is always liable for any supervisory actions that affect the victim's employment status, such as hiring, firing, promotion or pay. *See supra* at 21-22. Moreover, this discussion of apparent authority recognizes the unique nature of "hostile environment" sexual harassment claims and therefore is limited to such cases.

[37] *Cf. Fields v. Horizon House* ("Apparent authority is created by and flows from the acts of the principal, not from the personal beliefs of the third party.") Moreover, as noted above, an employee would find it difficult to establish a constructive discharge in this situation because she could not show she had no alternative but to resign. Failure to complain also might undermine a later assertion that the conduct occurred or was unwelcome.

since January of 1986 she had clearly stated to the supervisor that their relationship was over and his advances were no longer welcome. The supervisor nevertheless persisted in making sexual advances toward CP, berating her for refusing to resume their sexual relationship. His conduct did not put the employer on notice that any unwelcome harassment was occurring. The employer has a well-communicated policy against sexual harassment and a complaint procedure designed to facilitate the resolution of sexual harassment complaints and ensure against retaliation. This procedure has worked well in the past. CO did not use it, however, or otherwise complain to higher management. Even if CP's allegations are true, the Commission would probably not find her employer liable for the alleged harassment since she failed to use the complaint procedure or inform higher management that the advances had become unwelcome. If CP resigned because of the alleged harassment, she would not be able to establish a constructive discharge since she failed to complain.

In the preceding example, if the employer, upon obtaining notice of the charge, failed to take immediate and appropriate corrective action to stop any ongoing harassment, then the employer will be unable to prove that the supervisor lacked apparent authority for his conduct, and if the allegations of harassment are true, then the employer will be found liable. Or if the supervisor terminated the charging party because she refused to submit to his advances, the employer would be liable for "quid pro quo" harassment.

3. Other Theories—A closely related theory is agency by estoppel. See Restatement (Second) of Agency at § 8B. An employer is liable when he intentionally or carelessly causes an employee to mistakenly believe the supervisor is acting for the employer, or knows of the misapprehension and fails to correct it.

For example, an employer who fails to respond appropriately to past known incidents of harassment would cause its employees to reasonably believe that any further incidents are authorized and will be tolerated.

Liability also may be imputed if the employer was "negligent or reckless" in supervising the alleged harasser. See Restatement (Second) of Agency § 219(2)(6); Hicks v. Gates Rubber Co., 833 F.2d 1406, 1418, 44 EPD ¶ 37,542 (10th Cir. 1987). "Under this standard, liability would be imposed if the employer had actual or constructive knowledge of the sexual harassment but failed to take remedial action." Fields v. Horizon House, Inc., No. 86-4343 (E.D. Pa. 1987). This is essentially the same as holding the employer directly liable for its failure to act.

An employer cannot avoid liability by delegating to another person a duty imposed by statute. Restatement (Second) of Agency at § 492 (1958), Introductory Note, p. 435 ("liability follows if t he person to whom the performance is delegated acts improperly with respect to it"). An employer who assigns the performance of a non-delegable duty to an employee remains liable for injuries resulting from the failure of the employee to carry out that duty. Restatement, §§ 214 and 219. Title VII imposes on employers a duty to provide their employees with a workplace free of sexual harassment. An employer who entrusts that duty to an employee is liable for injuries caused by the employee's breach of the duty. See, e.g., Brooms v. Regal Tube Co., 44 FEP Cases 1119 (N.D. Ill. 1987) (employer liable for sexual harassment committed by the management official to whom it had delegated the responsibility to devise and enforce its policy against sexual harassment), aff'd on other ground, 881 F.2d 412, 420-21 (7th Cir. 1989).

Finally, an employer also may be liable if the supervisor "was aided in accomplishing the tort by the existence of the agency relation," Restatement (Second) of Agency § 219(2)(d). See Sparks v. Pilot Freight Carriers, Inc., 830 F.2d 1554, 44 EPD ¶ 37,493 (11th Cir. 1987); Hicks v. Gates Rubber Co., 833 F.2d at 1418. For example, in Sparks v. Pilot Freight Carriers, the court found that the supervisor had used his supervisory authority to facilitate his harassment of the plaintiff by "repeatedly reminding [he] that he could fire her should she fail to comply with his advances." 830 F.2d at 1560. This case illustrates how the two types of sexual harassment can merge. When a supervisor creates a hostile environment through the aid of work-related threats or intimidation, the employer is liable under both the "quid pro quo" and "hostile environment" theories.

E. Preventive and Remedial Action

1) Preventive Action—The EEOC's Guidelines encourage employers to:

> take all steps necessary to prevent sexual harassment from occurring, such as affirmatively raising the subject, expressing strong disapproval, developing appropriate sanctions, informing employees of their right to raise and how to raise the issue of harassment under Title VII, and developing methods to sensitize all concerned.

29 C.F.R. § 1604.11(f). An effective preventive program should include an explicit policy against sexual harassment that is clearly and regularly communicated to employees and effectively implemented. The employer should affirmatively raise the subject with all supervisory and non-supervisory employees, express strong disapproval, and explain the sanctions for harassment. The employer should also have a procedure for resolving sexual harassment complaints. The procedure should be designed to "encourage victims of harassment to come forward" and should not require a victim to complain first to the offending supervisor. See Vinson, 106 S. Ct. at 2408. It

should ensure confidentiality as much as possible and provide effective remedies, including protection of victims and witnesses against retaliation.

2) Remedial Action—Since Title VII "affords employees the right to work in an environment free from discriminatory intimidation, ridicule, and insult" (Vinson, 106 S. Ct. at 2405), an employer is liable for failing to remedy known hostile or offensive work environments. See, e.g., Garziano v. E. I. DuPont deNemours & Co., 818 F.2d 380, 388, 43 EPD ¶ 37,171 (5th Cir. 1987) (Vinson holds employers have an "affirmative duty to eradicate 'hostile or offensive' work environments"); Bundy v. Jackson, 641 F.2d 934, 947, 24 EPD ¶ 31,439 (D.C. Cir. 1981) (employer violated Title VII by failing to investigate and correct sexual harassment despite notice); Tompkins v. Public Service Electric & Gas Co., 568 F.2d 1044, 1049, 15 EPD 7954 (3d Cir. 1977) (same); Henson v. City of Dundee, 682 F.2d 897, 905, 15 EPD ¶ 32,993 (11th Cir. 1982) (same); Munford v. James T. Barnes & Co., 441 F. Supp. 459, 466, 16 EPD ¶ 8233 (E. D. Mich. 1977) (employer has an affirmative duty to investigate complaints of sexual harassment and to deal appropriately with the offending personnel; "failure to investigate gives tacit support to the discrimination because the absence of sanctions encourages abusive behavior").[38]

When an employer receives a complaint or otherwise learns of alleged sexual harassment in the workplace, the employer should investigate promptly and thoroughly. The employer should take immediate and appropriate corrective action by doing whatever is necessary to end the harassment, make the victim whole by restoring lost employment benefits or opportunities, and prevent the misconduct from recurring. Disciplinary action against the offending supervisor or employee, ranging from reprimand to discharge, may be necessary. Generally, the corrective action should reflect the severity of the conduct. See Waltman v. International Paper Co. 875 F.2d at 479 (appropriateness of remedial action will depend on the severity and persistence of the harassment and the effectiveness of any initial remedial steps). Dornhecker v. Malibu Grand Prix Corp., 828 F.2d 307, 309-310, 44 EPD ¶ 37,557 (5th Cir. 1987) (the employer's remedy may be "assessed proportionately to the seriousness of the offense"). The employer should make follow-up inquiries to ensure the harassment has not resumed and the victim has not suffered retaliation.

Recent court decisions illustrate appropriate and inappropriate responses by employers. In Barrett v. Omaha National Bank, 726 F.2d 424, 33 EPD

---

[38] The employer's affirmative duty was first enunciated in cases of harassment based on race or national origin. See, e.g., United States v. City of Buffalo, 457 F. Supp. 612, 632-35, 18 EPD ¶ 8899 (W.D.N.Y. 1978), modified in part, 633 F.2d 643, 24 EPD ¶ 31,333 (2d Cir. 1980) (employer violated Title VII by failing to issue strong policy directive against racial slurs and harassment of black police officers, to conduct full investigations, and to take appropriate disciplinary action); EEOC v. Murphy Motor Freight Lines, Inc. 488 F. Supp. 381, 385-86, 22 EPD ¶ 30,888 (D. Minn. 1980) (defendant violated Title VII because supervisors knew or should have known of co-workers' harassment of black employees, but took inadequate steps to eliminate it).

¶ 34,132 (8th Cir. 1984), the victim informed her employer that her co-worker had talked to her about sexual activities and touched her in an offensive manner. Within four days of receiving this information, the employer investigated the charges, reprimanded the guilty employee, placed him on probation, and warned him that further misconduct would result in discharge. A second co-worker who had witnessed the harassment was also reprimanded for not intervening on the victim's behalf or reporting the conduct. The court ruled that the employer's response constituted immediate and appropriate corrective action, and on this basis found the employer not liable.

In contrast, in Yates v. Avco Corp., 819 F.2d 630, 43 EPD ¶ 37, 086 (6th Cir. 1987), the court fond the employer's policy against sexual harassment failed to function effectively. The victim's first-level superior had responsibility for reporting and correcting harassment at the company, yet he was the harassers. The employer told the victims not to go to the EEOC. While giving the accused harassers pending investigation, the employer made the plaintiff take sick leave, which was never credited back to them and was recorded in their personnel files as excessive absenteeism without indicating they were absent because of sexual harassment. Similarly, in Zabcowicz v. West Bend Co., 589 F. Supp. 780, 35 EPD ¶ 34,766 (E.D. Wis. 1984), co-workers harassed the plaintiff over a period of nearly four years in a manner the court described as "malevolent" and "outrageous." Despite the plaintiff numerous complaints, her supervisor took no remedial action other than to hold occasional meetings at which he reminded employees of the company's policy against offensive conduct. The supervisor never conducted an investigation or disciplined any employee until the plaintiff filed an EEOC charge, at which time one of the offending co-workers was discharged and three others were suspended. The court held the employer liable because it failed to take immediate and appropriate corrective action.[39]

When an employer asserts it has taken remedial action, the Commission will investigate to determine whether the action was appropriate and, more important, effective. The EEOC investigator should, of course, conduct an independent investigation of the harassment claim, and the Commission will reach its own conclusion as to whether the law has been violated. If the Commission finds that the harassment has been eliminated, all victims made whole, and preventive measures instituted, the Commission normally will administratively close the charge because of the employer's prompt remedial action.[40]

---

[39] See also *Delgado & Lehman,* 665 F. Supp. 460, EPD ¶ 37,517 (E.D. Va. 1987) (employer failed to conduct follow-up inquiry to determine if hostile environment had dissipated); *Salazar v. Church's Fried Chicken,* 44 FEP Cases 472 (S.D. Tex. 1987) (employer's policy inadequate because plaintiff, as a part-time teenage employee, could have concluded a complaint would be futile because the alleged harassers was the roommate of her store manager); *Brooms vs. Regal Tube Co.,* 44 FEP Cases 1119 (N.D. Ill. 1987) (employer liable when a verbal reprimand proved ineffective and the employer took no further action when informed of the harassers persistence).

[40] For appropriate procedures, see §§ 4.4 (e) and 15 of Volume I of the Compliance Manual.

CHAPTER 3

SEXUAL HARASSMENT COMPLAINT PROCEDURE

§ 3.1 The Role of Complaint Handling in the Prevention Strategy

The complaint procedure, when it works, can play a critical role in preventing sexual harassment and, at a minimum, in minimizing the consequences of sexual harassment to the organization by enabling the organization to be alerted to actual and potential violations. If the organization is trying to prevent sexual harassment from arising in the first place, the complaint procedure will tell victims how to take action, warns would-be harassers that they cannot readily conceal their wrongdoing as the complaint procedure can bring it to light, and sends a message to the organization that sexual harassment is deviant behavior that can be legitimately and fully prosecuted within the system.

If the organization's goal is to prevent liability if sexual harassment does occur, a complaint procedure is also an important line of defense. The dictum in the landmark U.S. Supreme Court case *Meritor Savings Bank v. Vinson*[1] hinted that where the employer prohibits sexual harassment and publishes an effective complaint procedure that is designed to encourage victims to come forward, if the victim does not take advantage of that procedure, the employer may be shielded from liability. While this is not yet accepted law, it is the direction that many courts seem to be taking, and shows that weight will be given to the employer's procedure when considering the issue of liability.

An analysis by the Equal Employment Advisory Council, a management advocacy and research group based in Washington, D.C., points out that two cases following the U.S. Supreme Court's 1993 decision in *Harris v. Forklift Systems* demonstrate the importance of complaint procedures that enable employers to take prompt corrective action. In the 1993 case of *Saxton v. AT&T,* the 7th Circuit decided that the plaintiff would be required to "produce evidence of a significant shortcoming in AT&T's response in order to hold the company liable under Title VII." The plaintiff alleged she was constructively discharged due to her supervisor's treatment of her after she rebuffed his sexual advances. The court found that the employee had not filed a complaint with the company ombudsperson until about a year after the alleged harassment and that AT&T had made a timely and thorough investigation of the complaint. The plaintiff's claim failed "because she had not demonstrated that AT&T failed to take prompt and appropriate remedial action upon discovering the harassment."[2]

In another case decided in 1993, *Nash v. Electrospace System,* the Fifth Circuit ruled that the company's prompt remedial action provided a defense to Title VII liability. The plaintiff asserted that she was harassed by her supervisor who asked her personal questions about her sex life and, she alleged, made anonymous telephone calls to her home. She did not raise her concern until after she received a performance review containing some criticism.[3] Her complaint was handled promptly by the Director of

---

[1] Meritor Savings Bank, FSB v. Vinson, 477 U.S. 77 (1986).

[2] Saxton v. AT&T, 63 F.E.P. Cas. (BNA) 625 (7th Cir. 1993).

[3] Employers often assert that employees who first complain about sexual harassment after they have received a negative performance review lack credibility. While it may be the case that some employees will claim sexual harassment as a way of retaining their job in the face of possible termination due to poor performance, I believe that such employees are in the minority. Most employees who bring sexual harassment complaints do believe that they have been harassed. The possible reasons that complaints sometimes coincide with critical performance evaluations are two: first, employees who are subject to sexual harassment may, in fact, suffer a decline in the quality or quantity of their work because of harassment, and this is something to explore, particularly when there is a prior record of satisfactory performance. Second, supervisors engaging in sexual

Human Resources, including several witness interviews. The complainant was given a transfer to an equivalent position in another department with no loss in pay or benefits. The court found the employer's actions demonstrated "a model of prompt, sensitive employer handling of these very traumatic cases."[4]

The EEOC Policy Guidance on Current Issues of Sexual Harassment (reproduced in **Chapter 2**) also provides that "[i]f the Commission finds that the harassment has been eliminated, all victims made whole, and preventive measures instituted, the Commission normally will administratively close the charge because of the employer's prompt remedial action."

Therefore, developing and disseminating effective complaint procedures to accompany the organization's sexual harassment policy buys employers some peace of mind.

Finally, the development and dissemination of formal complaint procedures tend to over time encourage managers to take initiatives to prevent sexual harassment from arising in their area in order to avoid embarrassment, having their management ability questioned, and paying all or part of potential charges or lawsuit settlements if a problem arises during their watch.

A word of caution: the dissemination of a credible complaint procedure is apt to trigger an initial surge and sustained increase in usage for a wide variety of complaints and inquiries. The complaint procedure can fail, even when done with the best intentions, if the administrative support for the procedure is not adequate. Many organizations will have to staff up existing departments or create a new function to handle complaints. The investigation and resolution of sexual harassment complaints are highly time-consuming and intensive, as will be explored further below. **Chapter 5** offers a more comprehensive discussion of ongoing administrative needs in support of a preventive strategy.

The investigation of sexual harassment claims is a major component of the complaint procedure, and is critical to the successful implementation of any viable sexual harassment policy. Without a thorough and consistent investigation process, the policy will not be used. Word will get around that the company performs a cursory and one-sided inquiry, and that no effort is made to protect the parties or witnesses to the investigation from retaliation. This chapter also presents techniques and strategies for

---

harassment are likely to find other ways of abusing the system, including retaliating against a subordinate who is not cooperating with requests for sexual favors or participating in sexual banter. Retaliation can take the form of a recommendation for termination, a poor performance appraisal and passing an employee over for a salary increase or a promotion.

[4] Nash v. Electrospace System, 63 F.E.P. Cas. (BNA) 765 (5th Cir. 1993).

performing effective investigations into allegations of sexual harassment to ensure that the complaint procedure remains credible.

§ 3.2   Formal versus Informal Complaint Procedures

There are a variety of processes that can be referred to as complaint procedures. They range from a process as informal as "Tell the harasser to stop" to a rigid four step process culminating in a final appeal to a committee whose decision is final. Informal and formal complaint procedures each have a distinct role to play in an organization's effective handling of sexual harassment. The principles and concepts described in the chapter generally apply to both formal and informal complaint handling.

Informal Complaint Procedures

Informal complaint mechanisms have several characteristics in common:

- They generally are used at an early stage of the complaint process.
- They involve minimal paperwork, data gathering and witness interviews.
- They tend to be contained, involving either only the victim and the alleged perpetrator, or perhaps one other intermediary.
- They are carried out at the lowest possible level of the organizational hierarchy.
- They are typically adaptable to comport with the style and state-of-mind of the victim, and end when the complainant is satisfied with the outcome, which can happen at any stage of the discussions.
- They tend to focus more on resolving the matter than on making a finding of guilt or innocence. Typically, the complainant has a say in the discipline or remedy involved in the resolution.

Informal complaint procedures include:

- Letting the alleged harasser know directly that his/her conduct is unwanted, such as by stating a clear objection at the time of an incident or by writing a letter to him or her describing the unwanted behavior and demanding that it cease. (A sample "Dear Harasser" letter is provided in § 3.10.)

- Speaking with a colleague or an official in the organization about the harassment and obtaining advice on how to approach a harasser and request that offensive behavior cease
- Having a meeting with the harasser, at which an observer of the complainant's choice is present, to discuss the behavior found to be offensive and agreeing on acceptable limits to behavior in the future
- In the case of an office romance gone sour, the couple should be encouraged to inform their management and/or human resources of the situation and request some kind of guidance or alternate arrangement, particularly when theirs was a reporting relationship. As is discussed further in **Chapter 5,** it should not be the subordinate who is routinely transferred, as this may serve to aggravate an already volatile situation

Individuals electing to make use of informal procedures should be followed-up with by their management, colleague or whomever is involved as a third-party, to ensure that the matter has been resolved to the complainant's satisfaction and consistent with company policy and applicable laws. If informal means cannot bring about a satisfactory outcome, formal recourse should be pursued. The organization is in a far worse position if it knows of the harassment but then fails to address it adequately. The outcome of informal complaint procedures should be documented similarly to the outcome of a formal process (see below).

Advantages/Disadvantages of Informal Process

Informal complaint mechanisms enable complaints to be resolved with less disruption to the organization and the parties than formal procedures. This is an advantage if the goal is to correct behavior toward one individual that he or she found to be offensive. However, the goal of preventing future incidents of harassment may be placed at a disadvantage by the use of an informal process for the following reasons:

- There tends to be little or no discipline associated with an informal process, thus the disincentive to repeat offenders can be minimal.
- There tends to be minimal fact finding, with the emphasis more on restoring harmony, thus problem behavior may continue unchecked since no "finding of misconduct" is made.
- For those who may have observed the harassing behavior, though not directly targeted by it, there may be a misperception that the organization took no action to correct the situation or to provide a remedy to the victim.

- If informal complaints and their resolution go undocumented by the organization, the organization may underestimate the scope of the problem of sexual harassment and fail to address it adequately.
- The organization has less control over informal processes and thus is less able to monitor and/or stop retaliation if it occurs following and informal complaint.

Informal complaint mechanisms are most appropriate when the following occurs:

- There is not a substantial discrepancy in the power positions of the complainant and the alleged harasser.
- The complaint is not against a multiple offender, either involving several acts of harassment against one individual or harassment of several individuals.
- The complaint does not involve a repeat offender who has already been disciplined for harassment against the same individual or others.
- The complaint does not include an allegation of physical touching or assault.
- The complaint does not involve third parties such as customers or suppliers with which the organization does business.
- The alleged harasser was not a "knowing" harasser, that is, the harasser did not act intentionally and expressed regret as well as a commitment to change.
- The victim will not come forward under a formal or more intimidating procedure.

Many organizations prefer to use informal mechanisms when upper-level or high-profile employees are involved on either side of the complaint. This is beneficial in preserving the reputation of the parties, and in some cases, the morale of the organization. However, this benefit should be weighed against the preventive value of formally resolving such complaints. Such high-profile cases are often cited as evidence that the organization takes sexual harassment seriously. Such examples can serve to dissuade would-be harassers from violations, and persuade victims to come forward. In some cases, victims will be discouraged from bringing complaints for fear of ruining another person's career and attracting wider attention to themselves. Research presented in *American Psychologist* (May 1991) suggests that most victims of sexual harassment state that they simply want an end to the offending behavior rather than punishment of the offender and that women may prefer to use informal procedures to resolve conflicts. Indeed, many HR managers can relate to this finding as it is very common for complainants to go as far as stating that they do not want anything done at all, just to discuss the matter and leave it at that.

Informal complaint mechanisms offer a middle ground between doing nothing and taking a more full-blown, drawn-out formal approach.

Formal Complaint Procedures

Formal complaint procedures are commonly what people refer to when discussing sexual harassment complaints. They have a beginning—the complaint is made verbally or in writing—, a middle—the complaint is investigated and findings are made as a result—, and an end—some recommended action to resolve the complaint. The typical characteristics of formal complaint procedures are

- Rely on written documentation, such as a written report from the complainant, a written finding of facts and recommendation, and documentary evidence
- Are invoked longer after the action occurred than with informal mechanisms
- Involve witness interviews and data gathering to support findings and recommended action
- Tend to spread the information regarding the complaint beyond the parties and an intermediary to include a fact-finding committee or a management review board of some kind. Appeals are often carried out at the highest levels of the organization
- Their goal is to arrive at a resolution that remedies wrongdoing—there is a determination of guilt or innocence of the alleged offender, and disciplinary and remedial action reflect the determination made
- The procedures used are rigid and applied consistently. They end when the organization is satisfied that the policy has been enforced. Typically, the organization, often without input from the complainant, makes the decision on disciplinary and/or remedial action. A sample Complaint Withdrawal form is provided at § 3.15 which exemplifies the measures which must be taken to stop formal procedures once they are invoked. With an informal process, the complainant's written withdrawal of the complaint would not be necessary, though it is not unwise to fashion a form that acknowledges the complainant's consent to and understanding of the terms of the resolution, even for informal complaint handling.

An example of a formal complaint procedure:

A complaint procedure that requires (a) a written intake sheet to be completed by the complainant or summarized by an intake officer and submitted to a centralized department; (b) a written response from the alleged harasser; (c) an investigation that involves interviewing witnesses and gathering documents to substantiate the claim; (d) a formal fact-finding process, either by a designated respresentative or a committee; (e) a written report of findings and recommended action to resolve the complaint; (f) an appeals process, after which the decision is final and binding.

The reporting methods for formal procedures can also include a hotline that triggers a formal responsive process; a written complaint to a high-level manager in the business unit in which the complainant works; a report to an impartial administrator such as an ombudsperson who will invoke the formal complaint mechanism on behalf of the complainant. (See § 3.7.)

Advantages/Disadvantages of Formal Process

Formal complaint procedures have the following advantages:
- Lending consistency to the complaint process thereby ensuring greater quality control especially when parts of the process are delegated to line managers.
- Documenting the process from the intake through to final resolution, thereby protecting the organization against attacks from both parties to the complaint of either unfair treatment or inadequate procedures.
- Offering greater protection to both the complainant and the alleged harasser by ensuring that basic procedural safeguards such as confidentiality and nonretaliation are observed.
- Ensuring that the organization's policy and standards for behavior are followed by providing, for example, that certain violations will trigger specific disciplinary measures, without leaving room for a negotiated outcome as occurs with informal procedures.

The chief disadvantage of formal complaint mechanisms is that they do not always achieve the end of encouraging victims of harassment to come forward. This may be particularly the case with a lower-level employee for whom the procedures seem intimidating. One way to overcome this is to have a company representative whose function in the complaint process is to assist the complainant and/or to allow complainants to select an advocate of their choice from within the organization. Many universities recognize this need, and provide for such assistance. The University of California Davis whose policy is reproduced in **Chapter 2** maintains a running list of volunteers to assist in the complaint process. The list includes male and female faculty members, administrators, and students. Individuals can bring their complaints to any advisor on the published list to initiate the formal process.

It is most appropriate to use a formal process in the following circumstances:

- An informal process would be inappropriate.
- The alleged harasser is belligerent and uncooperative.
- The complainant is a union employee, as the formal grievance procedure may be used by the union representing either or both of the parties to the complaint during or after the employer's investigation and findings.

Employers should offer both formal and informal complaint handling to employees. In this way, employees may, in most instances, select the process with which they are most comfortable to handle their complaint. Having both types of mechanisms helps to ensure that more employees will come forward with complaints of alleged sexual harassment and gives employees little excuse for not making use of the system and little need to go to an outside agency or an attorney for resolution.

Centralized or Decentralized Complaint Procedure?

Should the sexual harassment complaint function be centralized or decentralized? This is a difficult question, as it can be examined from several perspectives: legal liability, cost, control or power, and customer focus.

A major objective of decentralization is to move more decisionmaking to a level closer to where day-to-day problems arise. The issue is whether the decentralized decisionmaking due to the organization along lines of business of many firms is appropriate for some or all of the phases involved in sexual harassment complaint handling.

Typically, the role of the centralized personnel function has evolved to one of consultant or adviser to the personnel specialists in the operating units or to local line managers with administrative responsibility.

In a 1991–92 study of 1,289 U.S. companies by the Bureau of National Affairs (BNA), BNA found that "employee relations activities that are most likely to be handled exclusively by Human Resources include EEO compliance/Affirmative Action (88 percent), exit interviews (86 percent), and attitude surveys (78 percent) . . . HR is rarely excluded from the other labor relations functions". (BNA Bulletin to Management, p.5)

Some parts of the employee relations function seem to be more advantageously handled through a decentralized structure than others. For example, according to the BNA study, 88 percent of the companies surveyed that have an EEO Compliance/ Affirmative Action function stated that it was handled by the HR department only, with 11 percent of the activities being handled by the HR department and another department (not identified) and only one percent delegating the responsibility for this activity outside of the HR department. Other activities, such as suggestion systems, were handled more frequently outside of the domain of the HR department, with 47 percent being handled by the HR department only, 36 percent being handled by the HR department and another department, and fully 17 percent being handled entirely by a non-HR entity. HR rarely can match the expertise of line managers in judging business-related suggestions.

Sexual harassment complaints have corporate-wide impact. For instance, if the organization is sued by an employee in one area and is found not to be in compliance, there is a chance that other areas of the organization will be subject to scrutiny in the discovery process, and the entire organization's finances and reputation will be at risk.

A Customer-Focused Analysis

If sexual harassment complaints were decentralized such that each business unit could conduct its own investigations and handle its own complaints, would that be an acceptable system? It depends on whose perspective you take.

1. **The Business Unit**

   From the business units' perspective, they will conceivably enjoy the greater autonomy of carrying out policies and procedures in a way that more closely fits their culture and responds to their needs. They would welcome the reduced bureaucracy in not having to run everything through "Corporate." On the other hand, they will have to expend their own limited resources on non-revenue-generating personnel matters.

2. **The Corporate Entity**

   From the perspective of the shareholders or the board organization greater uniformity in the handling of sexual harassment complaints, which represent a potential exposure to the shareholders may be more desirable. After all, when the company is sued, it is not just the business unit's name appearing on the lawsuit (even though the business unit may end up footing the bill for the litigation). Centralization in high-risk and strategic areas of employee relations such as sexual harassment enables the organization to shape policy, change policy, and enforce policy more efficiently. While it may be necessary to train line managers to recognize and prevent sexual harassment, they do not necessarily need to be trained to conduct investigations and resolve complaints, as long as they are given clear direction on whom to contact upon discovery of a problem.

3. **Employees Want a Fair and Safe Complaint Process**
    From the employees' vantage point, while the business unit managers are arguably closest to their employees and best know their needs, they also are closer to the alleged harasser. Complainants may prefer, that is, feel safer, turning to a "corporate" entity that is not connected to their business unit to bring a complaint.

4. **Human Resources Generalists' Perspective**
    The business unit human resources generalists generally want as much support as possible from the corporate entity so that they do not have to spend time and resources re-inventing the wheel and can spend more of their time being proactive. However, they do not necessarily want corporate intervention in actual decisionmaking. They may want corporate to play an advisory-only role in sexual harassment complaint handling.

A Case Study.   No one would dispute that sexual harassment is a high-risk employee relations issue. It is a highly-regulated area which can have severe impact on all involved. In this case, Janet is an employee who has been subject to unwelcome advances by a company technician. She is usually left alone with him while he conducts repairs. She decides to complain about his conduct to her supervisor.

Janet's supervisor Lisa is poorly trained on how to handle sexual harassment issues. She immediately notifies her boss Mary who also knows little about company policy on handling sexual harassment claims. Mary contacts the manager in charge of technical assistance and tells him that a certain technician has been harassing an employee, and that he should be terminated immediately. The technician is terminated on the spot.

Let's look at how this process worked and determine if customers have been well-served.

Janet confides that she is extremely angry that everyone knows it was she who made the complaint and that she was never consulted in the process. Her feelings and concerns were not acknowledged, and she was not included in the resolution. Further, she questions the result of the process, as she still believes that she is at risk because the technician lives in her neighborhood, and now that she has caused his termination, she fears retaliation. She has lost faith in her managers and in the system that she thought was designed to protect her.

From Lisa and Mary's perspective, they have expended time and energy on a matter that disrupted the entire department and caused them much personal grief. They were unsure whether they took the right action, but felt that as they had taken immediate action, they did what was legally required. Neither of them has been through the company's sexual harassment training, deeming it low priority compared to just getting their regular work completed. Besides, they never thought they would have to deal with a real situation. They are concerned that Janet has become distant from them, and does not seem appreciative of their swift action on her behalf. They are pleased that the resolution only took a few days, rather than a few weeks or longer as it used to take when "Corporate" became involved. They also felt very powerful when they fired the perpetrator on their own.

From the alleged harasser's perspective, and that of the predominantly male group he works with, there is no fairness in a system that gives him no opportunity to defend himself or even tell his side of the story. He has never received any sexual harassment training and cannot recall ever having seen the company's policy. He feels that his name has been unjustly "smeared," and that he will probably never be able to get another job because the company will bad-mouth him. He is unaware of what the company's policy is on references, and no one has informed him of it (the company does not give references).

The company does in fact have a sexual harassment policy. However, since the employee relations function was decentralized two years ago, all of the training activity and the dissemination of information relating to the sexual harassment policy have all but been discontinued. Even changes made to the policy were publicized via a memo sent inter-office mail to managers. Some read it prior to inserting it into the personnel policy manual most of them never open and some of them did not. Individual businesses have complete ownership for the employee relations activities in their area.

The organization has not been well-served in this case. No one is satisfied with the outcome. Company policy was not followed, the alleged harasser is threatening to sue for defamation of character and the employee who complained has exhibited low morale and declining performance. She has told other employees that you cannot trust the company to protect you.

In effect, the decentralized design of the complaint handling has created a loss of control, meaning that while Corporate staff still sets goals and establishes standards, there is no monitoring of line of business staff activity to ensure compliance, provide feedback, or create acceptable limits on deviation from established standards. There is also a lack of coordination, such that one line of business may follow corporate policy very closely and others may disregard it altogether, with the result of employees belonging to the same organization receiving vastly different treatment.

This inconsistent treatment of individuals across the organization poses its own risks, just as it would if a securities firm enforced insider trading prohibitions in one area but allowed it to go unchecked in another.

What would the company's options be in terms of re-designing the sexual harassment complaint handling function?

Re-centralize sexual harassment complaint handling. This is a direct control mechanism that would ensure that company policy is strictly followed in each case. Corporate representatives investigate and resolve all complaints because they pose uniquely sensitive issues for all involved and pose a high risk to the organization of legal exposure and damage to its reputation. As the information generated from incidents of sexual harassment crosses horizontal and/or vertical reporting lines and is not centrally-located, those staffing the centralized function need a high level of influence and professionalism to make up for the diminished speed of the process. They may delegate some of the procedure to local representatives, but probably still need to provide constant guidance along the way.

Critical variables are those involving significant risk. Is sexual harassment strategically important enough to keep under central control because the risk associated with loss of control is too great? This depends on the company's philosophy toward sexual harassment and its level of risk-aversion.

The direct expense involved with decentralization would be the cost of space, staff and other overhead costs for a group generating no revenue. While the group may effectuate cost savings if lawsuits are averted and may reduce opportunity cost for managers by relieving them of some of the burdens associated with employee relations activities, these savings are speculative. Indirect costs include the time and energy that line managers and business generalists will have to spend "doing things right" at the direction of the Corporate staff.

Design a decision management mechanism that allows some decisions to be made centrally and others at the unit level, though consistent with Corporate goals and standards. Formal mechanisms can be used such as establishing rules or guidelines that dictate exactly how sensitive matters like sexual harassment are to be handled, and then training individuals on the use of the guidelines. Informal mechanisms, such as policy manuals, rewards and recognition, and performance review systems, also can help to retain some control and coordination in the process. It is possible to encourage compliance by including management of personnel matters as a criterion that managers will be evaluated, and hence rewarded, on. This is the most commonly used complaint handling structure.

Line of business managers, being understandably more focused on meeting their business needs than on employees' needs, are probably more content with the decentralized system, being spared the "heavy hand," and the additional maintenance cost, of "Corporate." However, it is uncertain whether they are better-served by a decentralized complaint handling function.

§ 3.3 Basic Components of a Complaint Procedure

The procedures should cover to whom complaints can be made, how complaints are handled (including the investigation process, guiding principles such as confidentiality and nonretaliation), and resolutions (including a statement on discipline).

To whom complaints can be made.   The Supreme Court in *Meritor Savings Bank v. Vinson* clearly established the principle that employees should have several channels open to their complaints, not just their immediate supervisor. This principle recognized the theory that sexual harassment, particularly of the quid pro quo variety, is a power play more than it is an expression of sexual desire, and that it often is perpetrated by supervisors and managers against their subordinates.

Employees should be given several alternative reporting channels including:

1. A supervisor, manager, or human resources representative to whom they would feel comfortable reporting the incidents
2. An ombudsperson within the organization who is not aligned with any department or business area. This could also be an Industrial Relations, Employee Relations, Affirmative Action, EEO Officer, or their equivalents. Note that the court in the *Robinson v. Jacksonville Shipyards*[5] case found the complaint procedure to be inadequate because it did not offer an alternative to complaining to the company's industrial relations department representative

Secondary reporting options could include:

1. An Employee Assistance Program (EAP) may be able to counsel employees who are distressed from sexual harassment and encourage them to seek redress through appropriate channels
2. A co-worker. While co-workers do not have the authority to take action on behalf of a complainant, they are able to encourage the complainant to seek help through the appropriate channels. Some employers may feel that it is better for those who believe that they are being harassed to talk with a co-worker than to suffer in silence
3. Complaint procedure. This section can also cover how complaints can be made, such as if they may be made orally or must be made in writing on a specific form, and so forth. This section can also

---

[5] 760 F. Supp. 1486 (M.D. Fla. 1991).

include time limits, for example, the complaint must be made within 90 days of the incident.

How complaints are handled.   The procedure should explain how complaints are processed.

1. Interviewing the Complainant and the Alleged Harasser. Most procedures begin with an interview with the complainant and the alleged harasser followed up by an investigation. Sometimes witnesses will be interviewed before the alleged harasser if there is a concern that the alleged harasser might intimidate witnesses into silence or persuade them not to cooperate. However, this need not be disclosed in a summary of procedures as it is more an investigation strategy. (See § 3.14.)

2. Confidentiality. At the outset, it is important to address the issue of confidentiality with parties to the complaint. While it would be nice to be able to guarantee the confidentiality of the complaint process, it is virtually impossible to take prompt and appropriate remedial action, which employers are required by law to do, without identifying the complainant and the alleged harasser and revealing the details of the allegations. However, complainants should be reassured that the allegations and their identity will only be disclosed on a strict "need-to-know" basis. This should be thoroughly explained to the parties and witnesses.

3. Nonretaliation. The procedure should also inform employees of the organization's and the law's prohibition of retaliation against those who make complaints of sexual harassment or cooperate in the investigation of such complaints.

4. Due process. It is important to reassure all parties that they will have the opportunity to tell their side of the story. This should include a procedure that requires that those accused of sexual harassment have the opportunity to respond fully to the allegations against them. This, of course, requires that the identity of the accuser be revealed at some point in the process, but not always at the outset. Again, as a matter of strategy, not necessarily for inclusion in a proceedural summary, the investigator may reserve disclosure of the complainant's name until after the alleged harasser has had the opportunity to speculate on the victim's identity. (See § 3.14.) There is no law requiring this provision. It is a matter of the organization's chosen approach or "culture."
   The main concerns that organizations have are:
   - Those accused of sexual harassment may sue the employer and the accuser for defamation of character for injury to their reputation;

- Simply being accused of sexual harassment may tarnish a person's reputation or even ruin a career if not handled with discretion. Organizations may consider this a compelling enough reason to consider building a due process safeguard into the process.

5. Investigation. The procedure should detail how information is gathered, how it is used, and how it is stored. This can outline who is interviewed, the kinds of information gathered, the typical duration of the investigation, and the role that the parties to the investigation are expected to play.

6. Resolution. The resolution section of the procedure should give employees a clear sense of how long it can take to get a resolution and what the possible outcomes are. Policies generally provide that if an allegation of sexual harassment is substantiated, the harasser is subject to discipline up to and including termination of employment. (See § **3.13.**)

The court in the *Ellison v. Brady*[6] case suggested that "the reasonableness of an employer's remedy will depend on its ability to stop harassment by the person who engaged in harassment. In evaluating the adequacy of the remedy, the court may also take into account the remedy's ability to persuade potential harassers to refrain from unlawful conduct." Essentially, when deciding on the discipline of harassers, bear in mind not only that the punishment should fit the crime, but also the deterrent impact, if any, that the organization wishes to have on other potential harassers.

A controversial issue is whether the policy should provide for discipline of those found to have made false charges of sexual harassment. If your organization is considering such a provision, explore how it relates to the goal of preventing sexual harassment, that is, will it have a chilling effect, and discourage employees with meritorious cases from coming forward for fear that if it's their word against the harasser's, they will be accussed of bringing a false claim? Or they may be intimidated from reporting behavior that they think is sexual harassment but they are not positive, so they will not risk being wrong. Is it more important to protect those who are falsely accused or to encourage those who are harassed to speak out without fear of repercussions? Both needs are compelling. These are questions that must be resolved by each organization based on its employee relations philosophy and culture.

7. Appeal. An appeal process is not legally required, and many organizations do not include it as a step in the complaint procedure. They

---

[6] 924 F.2d 872 (9th Cir. 1991).

believe that if a thorough investigation was conducted, the decisions made based on that investigation's findings should be final, and not subject to challenge except through external processes, such as an arbitration or lawsuit. Other employers see in the appeal an additional check to ensure that the parties have every opportunity to "make their case."

Employers who elect to use an appeal procedure must decide the following:

- Whether the parties can be represented by the person of their choice either from within or outside the organization and whether this representation can be by an attorney
- Whether the appeal will require written arguments, whether certain specified time limits for filing the appeal must be met, and whether new evidence may be introduced
- Who will hear and rule on the appeal
- Other procedural matters such as is the appeal handled in writing, by public or private hearings, can there be witness examinations, will there be a transcript, and so forth

§ 3.4   Investigating Complaints of Sexual Harassment

The Investigation Process

Before an investigation begins, the organization must determine the following:

The purpose and scope of the investigation, namely, to verify the allegations made by the complainant or to investigate whether sexual harassment in the form of a hostile work environment permeates a certain department or division

Who will conduct the investigation, that is, whether the investigation will be done by a designated individual, a team with corporate and business unit representation, an attorney, one man and one woman, and so forth

Any applicable time limits, such as, all investigation must be completed within 15 days of the date the complaint was made

Any applicable safeguards, such as, all complaints must be brought immediately to the attention of legal counsel and/or the HR department

These determinations will vary from employer to employer, depending on available resources, corporate politics, the perceived need to address the problem of sexual harassment, the size and type of the organization, and so forth. However, there are certain basic components of an investigation that each corporation should incorporate into their process.

The investigation is generally a five step process as follows:

Receive and review the complaint.   This involves reviewing the oral or written complaint. This step occurs in both formal and informal processes. The complaint should be reviewed carefully and an analysis made of what additional information will be needed to substantiate it. Some organizations may decide to involve legal counsel immediately upon reciept of a complaint in the hope of being able to invoke the attorney-client privilege or the work product privilege for all evidence gathered and reports made relating to the complaint. In most cases, however, the facts gathered in the course of the investigation, whether proceeding at the request of or with the involvement of legal counsel, will be discoverable by an agency or in a lawsuit. There should also be consideration of whether immediate intervention is necessary given the nature of the allegations made. Such would be the case when physical touching, assault or offensive visual depictions are involved. A meeting may then be arranged with the complainant to supplement whatever information is deemed to be missing at this preliminary stage.

An oral complaint should be conducted in a private office away from the day-to-day distractions of the workplace. The same principles of witness interviewing discussed below should be followed when meeting with the complainant. Additionally, as the meeting is likely to evoke high emotion, be prepared with tissues, aspirin, and the telephone number of a nearby counselor.

Some employers advocate having a third party observer in the room when the initial complaint is being made. This decision should be made taking all of the circumstances into account, including

- Is the complainant likely to become violent or unduly hostile (always keep the office door unlocked in the event that you do interview the complainant or the alleged harasser alone)
- Is there an individual who is not part of the formal complaint process but whom either the complainant or the organization would like to have present during the meeting for their support or expertise
- Is the complainant likely to be intimidated in a "two against one" situation
- Is there a reasonable basis to doubt the credibility of the complainant, such that having a witness present during the meeting will protect the organization's

The same issues arise with respect to recording the meeting. When meeting with the parties and all witnesses to a complaint, detailed notes should be made either during the meetings or immediately thereafter. Explain to interviewees that the notes will help you to recall what they said so that you do not have to requestion them later. However, making a record via electronic means may be illegal in some states without the prior knowledge of the complainant. Second, taping can have a chilling effect on a number of complainants who may feel inhibited sharing highly embarrassing details on audio or video tape. If procedures are supposed to be designed to encourage employees to come forward, this type of intrusive technique can dissuade some potential complainants. However, it offers an indisputable record of the first, often most spontaneous discussion with complainant.

Develop an investigation plan.   Part of this will involve developing an initial strategy of how to tackle the complaint most effectively and quickly, as prompt remedial/corrective actions are required. This will depend on the nature of the facts alleged. Establish goals and timetables for achieving each phase of the investigation, determine, with the complainant's input, which witnesses to interview and what data to gather, and give the complainant some sense for how the investigation will proceed.

Gather facts.   This stage involves meeting with additional witnesses and the alleged harasser. Whatever procedural guidelines were followed in meeting with the complainant should be considered when interviewing the alleged harasser, for example, if the meeting with the complainant was taped so should the meeting with the alleged harasser. It is best to proceed first with interviews of key witnesses, from those identified by either or both of the parties, and add more only as needed. This will minimize the impact of the complaint on the organization. Gather general personnel documents, such as personnel files, disciplinary documents, and performance evaluations, as well as any documentary evidence of the harassment, such as notes, comics, posters, etc.

Analyze the information gathered.   Once the investigator is satisfied that a critical mass of information relating to the complaint has been gathered, he or she should analyze the data in light of the questions sought to be answered at the outset. For example, if the question was "Did George give Anne a bad performance review in retaliation for her turning down his requests for dates and rebuffing his physical advances?" then the analysis may proceed as follows:

Step One: What evidence have I gathered regarding the specific allegation of physical advances? Requests for dates? Look to interviews with witnesses who work with the two parties who may have observed such advances and/or requests by George and Anne's reactions. Perhaps the witnesses could recall dates or occasions when the events occurred.

Step Two: What evidence have I gathered regarding Anne's past and current job performance? This could include a review of any references regarding Anne if she is a new employee or any prior evaluation of her performance by the same supervisor George or by previous supervisors. This could also encompass evidence about Anne's performance tendered by Anne herself or by co-workers, peers, or customers. At a minimum, the specifics in George's contested evaluation should be proved or disproved by the evidence gathered.

Step Three: What evidence have I gathered regarding George's supervisory skills generally and specifically as they relate to performance evaluations of subordinates? Consider interviews with other employees who are currently or have been under George's supervision. Review all performance evaluations gathered, looking for consistency of the standards applied in the evaluations, any differences in the evaluation of men and women subordinates, and the adherence to any applicable corporate guidelines on competing performance evaluations.

Step Four: What evidence have I gathered that speaks to the credibility of the parties or any of the witnesses? This step should be covered regardless of the issue being investigated, as in any legal proceedings, credibility would be a determining factor. This involved identifying statements made that are inconsistent and/or unsupported by the evidence gathered, reconciling contradictory versions of the same events from different witnesses, considering motives, fears, and the characters of the parties and witnesses, and so forth.

Make and convey findings and a proposed resolution. Findings may be published in some form depending on the formality of the process. Making findings involves an assessment of all of the evidence, after the analysis is completed, based upon whether it is more likely than not that the events alleged took place. This finding is similar to the preponderance of the evidence standard used by courts in most civil cases. Findings based upon Anne's allegations might include:

1. Anne has demonstrated a history of performance problems, as evidenced by the fact that she has received negative feedback periodically and has shown some improvement over time.

2. Anne's performance has declined sharply over the past six weeks. This can be attributed mainly to a divorce which she and others have described as "ugly" and "emotionally draining" for Anne. She has had difficulty focusing on her work.

3. George has physically touched Anne as observed by several witnesses who saw him patting her on the back, putting his arm around her,

and massaging her shoulders. Two witnesses observed Anne politely remove George's hands from her body. George then ceased the touching. These incidents took place during the past two months according to witnesses. There were no direct observations of requests for dates.

4. George's record as a supervisor is mixed. While his technical skills are superior and his ability to manage the operations has proven satisfactory, he has been inconsistent in managing his people. He has not completed performance evaluations of a number of his subordinates, and in the past, he sometimes rated an employee's performance with insufficient or no supporting information. This has been found to be the case with Anne's evaluation.

5. While Anne and witnesses acknowledge that Anne's lack of concentration at work has negatively affected her performance, her performance evaluation points to few specific instances. These instances which are noted have also been observed by co-workers in other departments or other employees who received satisfactory performance evaluations.

6. Witnesses observed that George is known to be single and is believed to be fond of Anne. He had mentioned to at least two witnesses that he thought Anne's husband was "scum." Witnesses described Anne as somewhat timid, but generally pleasant. She did not speak to anyone at work about George.

7. George has only supervised two other women during his employment with this organization, and neither of them had complaints regarding his treatment. Neither had received performance evaluations from him but had been rated as fully satisfactory employees.

Proposed resolution:

Based upon the above findings, the following resolution will be adopted.

Anne and George will both receive performance warnings. Anne will be given the benefit of specific feedback regarding her performance problems and how to improve them. There will be no specific time limit given for improvement. George will be given feedback by his manager regarding his management style and any corrections thereto and shall be given training on sexual harassment prevention and on evaluating employee performance. Both parties will be told that they are expected to improve in their respective areas and that further measures could be taken if there is no demonstrated improvement within a reasonable timeframe.

Anne will be offered information regarding the firm's counseling services and encourage, though not compelled, to seek assistance in managing in these turbulent times for her.

George will be told that any further evidence of inappropriate behavior, such as unwelcome touching and repeated requests for dates, will result in either loss of managerial responsibility (demotion) or termination of employment, depending on the violation. Anne will be informed of this warning as George will be concerning her warning, and both will be instructed that they are bound to maintain these matters confidential and that the firm and the law strictly prohibit any form of reprisal as a result of these proceedings.

Witness Interviewing Techniques

Knowing how to interview a witness is a critical skill for an investigator. It enables the investigator to elicit valuable information and it helps to build a mutual trust between the interviewer and interviewee. Consider some of the following techniques (see also **Chapter 6** for a review of a video on interviewing):

- Give interviewees your undivided attention. Most people feel unimportant if you answer or accept telephone calls or visits in your office while they are meeting with you. If at all possible, postpone all telephone calls and office meetings while you are interviewing witnesses. It helps if you meet them in a conference room or other area outside of your office where you are less likely to be interrupted.

- Maintain eye contact with witnesses as much as possible. Explain to them that there will be moments when you will have to take notes, but that they should not interpret this as a lack of attention to what they are saying. Even if you are bored and distracted, avoid demonstrating this: do not look out the window, do not look down at the floor, do not play with your pen or otherwise fidget.

- Be alert. If you are out on a date with a person who means something to you, you generally would not spend the time yawning. Do not do this in the presence of witnesses, as it can easily be interpreted as a lack of interest or respect for the process.

- Listen to witnesses. In order to encourage openness, you must listen carefully to what witnesses have to say—and to how they say it. Is there regret, fear, insecurity, hostility, or some other emotion in their voice? If so, you should make note of that emotion. If you only focus on getting to your next question, rather than on the answers, you will miss valuable follow-up opportunities.

- Observe witnesses. You also must observe witnesses' body language. Does their posture convey anger, sarcasm, depression? Do they seem to be holding something back? If you are not focusing on the physical expression, you may be missing important signs that go to credibility and that should be explored further.

- When interviewing complaintants, convey that you understand their concerns. Victims become very upset when it appears that the listener has either not heard or has not understood something they have said. A good technique to use is to recap what the victim has said in your own words at regular intervals to verify that you have understood his or her statements correctly.

- Ask open-ended questions. Leading questions are those which convey the asker's expected answer, for example, "You only put your arm around her because you felt badly for her, I suppose?" It is far more effective to use open-ended questions during most of an interview, saving leading or specific questions for the end when the ground has not been already covered without prompting the witness. Examples of open-ended questions are: "How would you characterize your working relationship with X?" "Have there been any incidents over the past six weeks that you think might have upset X?" As the individual describes incidents you need only follow up with such statements as "Then what happened?" or "How did she react?" or "What did you say when she did that?" and so forth.

  Leading questions should be used to confirm or deny specific facts alleged such as: "Did you call her at home on Friday night September 15?" and "Did you then drive to her home even though she told you she preferred you left her alone?"

- Convey that you understand the alleged complainant's and harasser's feelings. At the heart of empathy is the ability to relate to another person's emotions. By occasionally interrupting the discussion after an emotional moment to state that you appreciate the pain or discomfort that they must be feeling, you will make the victims of sexual harassment feel more comfortable about expressing emotions and you also will enhance their trust in the relationship with you. The alleged harasser will feel frustrated and defensive, and conveying that you understand these feelings can help bring the level of anger down a notch or two.

One possible drawback is that on occasion alleged victims or perpetrators will make it difficult for you to draw the line between your role as a professional, whether a line manager, human resources representative, or an attorney, and that of a counselor. Interviewers must exercise caution in advising employees on emotional issues. Depending on your position, some emotional counseling is a necessary part of the job.

However, when you find that you are delving into areas that border on delivering advice on psychological issues, it is always best to explain your discomfort to the interviewee and to make a referral to a more qualified professional. Maintain a current list of the names and telephone numbers of several mental health professionals, including the firm's EAP, if any, to whom you feel confident sending employees, as they will often need emotional support during the investigation of a sexual harassment complaint.

In addition, when meeting with the parties, try to estimate the following:

Time frame.   How long will it be before the first report back to the parties? How long will each phase of the investigation take? When can the parties expect the matter to be concluded?

Complexity.   What obstacles will present themselves? Did you prepare the parties for the possibility of their arising?

Likely Result.   What might the final outcome be? What will each completed phase add to the final outcome?

Effort.   How much effort will be required from the parties at the outset and during the course of the investigation, that is, assembling documents, attending matters, gathering information responding to follow-up questions?

Tips on Handling Common Interview Problems

A common obstacle that occurs when meeting with an alleged harasser is a threat to sue the employer for defamation of character (injury to reputation) if the investigation proceeds. As discussed in **Chapter 1,** employers have a legal obligation to investigate claims of sexual harassment. It is helpful to explain to the alleged harasser that the harassment is just an allegation until substantiated and that the firm takes all such matters seriously and that the investigation is for everyone's protection, including the alleged harasser's, as false allegations will be uncovered as well. Of chief concern to the alleged harasser is the firm's commitment to preserving the confidentiality of matters and the parties concerned. It should be explained that only those who need to know specifics in order for the allegations to be confirmed or refuted will be granted limited disclosure of that information pertinent to their testimony. However, in the end it should be conveyed that:

- The firm will proceed with the investigation as it is required to do, with due respect for all procedural safeguards
- Each employee, including alleged perpetrators, has an obligation to cooperate fully with investigations of any alleged wrongdoing
- Any form of retaliation, whether direct or indirect, is strictly prohibited and all witnesses shall be so advised. Violation of this prohibition will lead to disciplinary actions up to and including termination

Another common challenge to interviewers is to avoid pre-judging the witnesses or the outcome of the complaint. Maintaining and appearing to maintain impartiality throughout the process is critical to its success. However, at times the investigation will feel like a ping-pong match, with the investigator changing his or her assessment of the case with each new witness or document uncovered. Avoid drawing any conclusions until that critical mass of evidence is in, otherwise you may inadvertently drive the investigation in a certain direction. Make sure that you have emotional support during an investigation, as interviewers often bear the brunt of people's anger, pain, fear, and other emotions in the process.

§ 3.5 Procedural Safeguards: Confidentiality, Due Process, and Documentation

The Confidentiality Dilemma

One of the major concerns expressed by employees who bring complaints is whether the matter will remain confidential. Confidentiality is an extremely complex matter: the courts require employers to take quick and decisive action on any complaint of sexual harassment, including a prompt and thorough investigation, but they also require employers to establish a complaint mechanism that encourages employees to come forward with complaints. Therein lies the dilemma of handling sexual harassment: how to encourage employees to come forward with complaints when we cannot promise them confidentiality beyond that which is practicable in light of the need for a thorough investigation.

In the context of sexual harassment complaints, confidentiality means that the information will be limited only to persons in the organization who have a *need to know about the information.* Those involved in a sexual harassment investigation can ask themselves at each turn whether they are appropriately limiting disclosures to those who need to know the information in order to conduct an effective investigation and find all of the necessary facts.

It is difficult to explain this to employees. When employees who have been harassed contact the employer representative who handles harassment complaints, whether they be their supervisor, manager, EEO officer, or HR representative, they are generally emotionally distraught and launch right into their complaint without considering that there may be limited disclosure of their indentity or of the facts that they relate. The employer representative should reassure employees of confidentiality so that they feel safe enough to bring their complaints forward, but should also advise employees at the outset of the limits of confidentiality once an investigation is undertaken.

Many complainants will react by saying that they do not want anything done about their complaint. However, the employer representative must explain to the complainant that they have a legal and ethical obligation to undertake an investigation of the facts and to take disciplinary action against the alleged harasser if a violation of the sexual harassment policy is substantiated.

Therefore, the employer representative has to explain the "need to know" concept to complainants. Below are suggestions of ways to discuss confidentiality with complainants. It is always best to advise complainants before they disclose their complaint that all complaints are kept as confidential as possible, depending on their nature, but that there is an obligation to investigate all allegations of sexual harassment.

Suggested sample language:

- I appreciate how difficult it is to bring a complaint and how vulnerable you must feel. But I want to assure you that confidentiality will be maintained to the maximum degree possible throughout the investigation and resolution of your complaint. Only those individuals who are needed to resolve your complaint effectively will be involved in the process.
- I will do everything I can to handle this in a sensitive and discrete manner and to limit the people who know about the situation. However, I hope that you understand that as a firm, we have a legal and ethical obligation to stop any further harassment from going on in this organization. You have an important part to play in helping us rid the organization of people who harass or, at the very least, identify individuals or departments in need of training and education regarding sexual harassment. I look forward to working with you and will keep you apprised of developments along the way, including of whom has knowledge of your complaint.
- I can try to avoid using your name, at least initially, especially in preliminary discussions with the alleged harasser, but allowing me to use your name in the investigation and for exploring solutions will probably allow more to be accomplished, and will be critical for my being able to offer you a full remedy and protect the organization from further incidents.
- In certain cases, such as those involving criminal incidents or multiple complaints about the same person, your identity may need to be revealed. When this does happen, you will be advised about it. Remember, the firm has a nonretaliation policy which we take very seriously. If you feel that any reprisals are being carried out, no matter how slight, please notify me immediately so that I can intervene.
- We will make every effort to maintain confidentiality and allow you to help us determine who should be told and when, because we want the

system to work, and for employees like yourself to bring their complaints to us.

- In order to assure complete confidentiality of this matter, let me remind you that you play an important part, and must avoid discussing the matter with other people.

While the complainant has concerns about confidentiality of the complaint due to concerns about embarrassment, reputation, career mobility, and retaliation, the alleged harasser shares all of those same concerns and should also be briefed on the mutual commitment to confidentiality. The alleged harasser also has concerns about telling his or her side of the story.

Due Process

One concern unique to the alleged harasser is whether he or she will have an opportunity to tell his or her side of the story. Alleged harassers are rightfully concerned about due process—and employers should share this concern. If harassment is substantiated, both the harasser and the employer may be held liable should a lawsuit be brought, though in many jurisdictions the employer will be liable for the acts of the harasser and the harasser will be not held individually liable (see **Chapter 1**). Therefore, the employer has a strong interest in giving alleged harassers a full and fair hearing.

Particularly when the investigation process is decentralized, investigators must be made to understand the importance of due process. Even in light of horrendous allegations, they must be sure not to bypass the critical step of hearing the alleged perpetrator's version of the incident before arriving at a resolution.

Suggestions about Maintaining Documentation

There are several reasons to maintain documentation of sexual harassment complaints.[7] It is important to maintain documentation of complaints and to keep the documents in a central place and secure. This assures consistency of handling complaints and is necessary for making the system

---

[7] The suggestions in this section are reproduced with permission from Susan W. Brecher. © 1992 Cornell University Inc./Susan W. Brecher. All rights reserved.

work and for making sure the employer is meeting all of its legal obligations.[8]

Because of the sensitive nature of the matter there is always the concern, however, that documentation discourages employees from using the system because they fear that confidentiality will not be maintained. This is especially true when a complaint is handled informally.

To balance these concerns documentation should be kept in a separate confidential locked file and accessibility should be extremely limited. The documentation could consist of a single confidential memorandum with the following information:

- date of the complaint
- nature of the complaint
- name of the person complained about (unless the complainant would not reveal the person)
- the name of the complainant (unless the organization chooses not to require disclosing the complainant's name)
- the department or unit involved
- the action taken

If notes were kept by the complaint handler, the original of the notes should also be attached and copies should not be kept. The locked confidential file should be accessible to a very limited number of people (ideally only two) and should only be used in relationship to the complaint process.

The memorandum should be sent to a person who can review the way the situation was handled to be sure there are no additional legal concerns. In addition, the person can maintain the locked confidential file, keeping the memoranda in alphabetical order based upon the name of the person complained about. This will allow the person to be sure there have not been multiple complaints about a person and review for patterns of discrimination.

Ideally, the person who maintains the file should be an attorney. This may allow an attorney-client privilege to protect the documents in the file from discovery during litigation. Even if a privilege does not attach, it

---

[8] For example, the standard which the EEOC has established for sexual harassment complaints is whether the employer **knew or should have known** about a problem. In a system where the employer does not have a central place to maintain documents and employees are allowed to complain to different people, each complaint handler may not be aware that there have been multiple complaints about one person. If ultimately one person were to go to the EEOC to complain, the EEOC may assert that the employer should have known about each or the prior complaints and imposed more stringent disciplinary action because there were so many complaints.

may help employers to limit who can see the documents for purposes of litigation. Regardless, the locked confidentiality file certainly shows the employer's commitment to maintaining confidentiality and limiting who has access to information which could be detrimental to all employees.

Finally, before adopting this system, be sure to check federal, state and local laws regarding employee personnel files, and rights of access and of privacy of personnel documents.

In addition to the above recommendations, be aware of the following potential problems:

1. If either a complainant or an alleged harasser against whom a complaint was brought but not substantiated, separates from the organization, it is still essential to maintain the matter of the complaint in confidence and any related documents in a separate, confidential file. As long as the matter was resolved, it should never come back to haunt either of the parties.

2. The organization must also be cautious when giving references regarding individuals who were parties to a complaint. Either party may be in a position to sue the firm if they lose career opportunities due to inappropriately disclosed information.

A good overview of maintaining an investigator's file is contained in § 3.11.

§ 3.6   Sample Sexual Harassment Complaint Handler's Models

Model 1

SEXUAL HARASSMENT COMPLAINT HANDLER'S MODEL[9]

1. COMPLAINT INTAKE (Meeting with the Complainant)
    1.0 If possible, prepare for the meeting.
        1.01 Prior to the meeting with the Complainant, gather background information about the situation.
        1.02 Try to have another person present during the interview, if appropriate. That person can take notes and ultimately be available to verify the discussion that took place during the meeting.
    1.1 Identify the purpose of the meeting.
        1.11 Make the Complainant comfortable.

---

[9] Reprinted with permission of Susan Brecher. © Copyright 1992, CORNELL UNIVERSITY, INC./SUSAN W. BRECHER All rights reserved.

      1.12   Explain the process.

      1.13   Explain your role.

      1.14   Discuss that confidentiality will be maintained as much as possible.

      1.15   Where appropriate, ask if you can take notes to be sure you understand the facts.

  1.2   Probe for information.

      1.21   Ask the Complainant to start chronologically and explain what happened.

      1.22   Ask open-ended questions, (i.e., how can I help you, what would you like to talk about, can you tell me more).

      1.23   While explaining, have the individual provide as many details as possible, (i.e., who, where, who else saw it; dates, times and places; specific examples or exact words used, etc.).

      1.24   Ask how the Complainant reacted or responded to the situation. (Do not say: Why did you keep this to yourself so long?)

      1.25   Ask if the Complainant has any witnesses that can support their information or provide any relevant additional information.

      1.26   Ask if the Complainant has any relevant documentation or physical information (evidence) they can provide you.

      1.27   If you have taken notes, ask the Complainant to review them and confirm the accuracy of your understanding.

  1.3   Explain the steps to be taken in the complaint process.

      1.31   Assure the Complainant of no retaliation.

      1.32   Ask the Complainant what outcome they would like.

      1.33   Ask the Complainant what they would like you to do for them.

      1.34   Review what can be expected from the process and what next steps you will be taking. Try to assure the person of impartiality.

      1.35   Set a time to get back to the complainant.

      1.36   Inform the complainant that they should feel free to come see you if they need to discuss the issue or to provide more information. (Open door policy)

      1.37   Discuss again that confidentiality will be maintained as much as possible. Set boundaries of confidentiality.

      1.38   Remind the complainant that to assure confidentiality, they must avoid discussing the matter with other people.

      1.39   Refrain from committing to a specific action.

2. INVESTIGATING THE COMPLAINT

  2.0   Determine whether this is an EEO matter.

      2.01   What, if any, written policies or procedures are affected by this situation?

      2.02   Are there any organizational practices affected by this situation?

      2.03   Are there any issues that affect EEO and other departments?

      2.04   Screen and reroute inappropriate complaints.

  2.1   Develop an understanding of problem

      2.11   Develop an understanding of the organizational (departmental) structure that applies to the situation.

2.12 Consider the political situation, including the risks to the individual and the organization.

2.13 Restate the problem in terms of the policy or practice involved.

2.2 Determine whether any issues require immediate attention, i.e., separating people, notifying other management before a scheduled action is taken.

2.3 Determine whether this is an informal or formal complaint.

2.31 Think about the depth of investigation necessary to respond to this complaint.

2.32 Review whether the steps required by the complaint procedure have been followed thus far, and what additional steps will need to be followed.

2.4 Involve or notify appropriate management. (Keep this in mind during all steps of the investigatory process.)

2.41 Consider whether you need to discuss this with your boss.

2.42 Consider whether you need to seek advice from an attorney.

2.43 Consider whether other departments can provide some expertise, i.e., labor relations, health and safety, security, etc.

2.44 Consider whether you need to inform any managers from the complainant's department.

2.45 Consider whether any people outside your organization are involved and need to be notified.

2.5 Consider the methods available for "investigating" the complaint. (Any one or all or these methods may be necessary.)

2.51 Determine whether you need to meet with any managers who may have information.

2.52 Determine whether you need to meet with the accused person.

2.53 Determine whether you need to collect any relevant documents, i.e., policies, employee files, etc.

2.54 Determine whether you need to view any relevant sites, take pictures or gather any physical information (evidence).

2.55 Determine whether you need to conduct additional meetings with the complainant.

2.56 Determine whether you need to meet with any witnesses.

2.57 Determine whether you need to meet with any persons from outside the organization.

2.6 Structure and conduct the investigation.

2.61 Determine investigatory methods which may be appropriate and in what order to carry them out.

2.62 Establish a tentative time frame for conducting the investigation.

2.63 Maintain contact with the complainant during the investigatory process.

2.64 Develop appropriate documentation of the investigatory process.

3. DEVELOPING COMPLAINT RESOLUTIONS

3.0 Involve or notify appropriate management. (Keep this in mind during all stages of this process.)

3.01 Consider whether you need to discuss this with your boss.

3.02 Consider whether you need to seek advice from an attorney.

3.03 Consider whether other departments can provide some expertise, i.e., labor relations, health and safety, security, etc.

3.04 Consider whether you need to inform any managers from the complainant's department.

3.1 Generate alternative solutions or interventions. (Any one, all of these, or more creative interventions may be appropriate.)

3.11 Consider whether the complainant can be empowered to speak directly with the accused on their own.

3.12 Consider whether a meeting with both parties is appropriate.

3.13 Consider whether the accused requires training, counseling or disciplinary action.

3.14 Consider whether any personnel actions are necessary for the person complaining, i.e., transfers, providing job opportunities, etc.

3.2 Select appropriate solution(s) or intervention(s).

3.21 Consider the political situation, including the risks to the individual and the organization.

3.22 If possible, prior to selecting a solution or intervention, discuss the facts and conclusions with another person who can provide neutrality and another perspective.

3.23 Establish management support for the solution.

3.24 Determine which solutions or interventions may be appropriate and in what order to carry them out.

3.25 Determine the managers necessary to help implement the interventions.

3.26 Consider whether to meet with the complainant to discuss whether the interventions or solutions will help resolve the matter and be effective and practical.

3.27 Present the resolutions or interventions to the involved persons.

3.3 Monitor and follow up on the complaint.

3.31 Meet with the person who complained and summarize the events.

3.32 Set a time in the future to check back with the person who complained and possibly the other party.

3.33 Be sure that everything agreed upon by the parties is actually happening.

3.34 Be sure that appropriate action was taken with the accused

3.35 Determine whether follow up is necessary with the workgroup or witnesses involved in the investigation to assure that accurate information has been provided, where appropriate, and group morale has been addressed.

3.4 Prepare and review documentation.

3.41 Send appropriate memoranda to the parties.

3.42 Review notes and documents and determine which ones are necessary to keep.

3.43 Forward documentation to a secure confidential file.

4. EVALUATING THE COMPLAINT HANDLING PROCESS
   4.0 Review your skills as a complaint handler.
   4.1 Speak with other complaint handlers about their experiences, making sure you protect confidentiality.
   4.2 Check back with the Complainant and other parties to find out how well the system has worked, i.e., was it quick enough; was the matter handled thoroughly; did all parties think it was fair; etc.
   4.3 Where a multiple entry system is being used, review the process for coordination and consistency.
   4.4 Analyze complaints for trends or patterns. If found, look for global preventive interventions or solutions.
   4.5 Conduct surveys to make sure employees are aware of the system, know how to use it, and feel that it is working.
   4.6 Is the policy and procedure disseminated regularly?
   4.7 Are the managers and supervisors receiving training?

§ 3.7 Sample Reporting Procedure Notice

Reporting an Incident of Sexual Harassment

Organizations should encourage the reporting of all perceived incidents of sexual harassment, regardless of who the offender may be. Individuals who believe they have been the victim of sexual harassment or believe they have witnessed sexual harassment should discuss their concerns with a supervisor or with any other designated representative in the organization. See the Complaint Procedures described below.

Complaint Procedure

1. Notification of Appropriate Staff
   As noted above, individuals who believe they have been the victim of sexual harassment or believe they have witnessed sexual harassment should discuss their concerns with a supervisor or with any other designated individual. If you receive information regarding sexual harassment in your capacity as a supervisor, you are obligated to report it. The organization encourages individuals who believe they are being harassed to promptly advise the offender that his or her behavior is unwelcome. The firm also recognizes that it is not necessary for an individual to talk directly to an offender if it is uncomfortable.

2. Timeliness in Reporting an Incident
   Prompt reporting of incidents is important so that action may be taken. However, due to the sensitivity of these problems and because

of the emotional toll such misconduct may have on the individual, no fixed period has been set for reporting sexual harassment incidents.

3. Investigatory Process

    Any reported allegations of sexual harassment will be investigated promptly. The investigation may include interviews with the parties involved, and where necessary, with individuals who may have observed the alleged conduct or may have relevant knowledge. Any reported allegations should be handled in a sensitive and discreet manner.

4. Confidentiality

    Confidentiality will be maintained throughout the entire investigatory process to the extent practicable and appropriate under the circumstances to protect the privacy of persons involved.

5. Protection Against Retaliation

    Retaliation, against an individual who makes a report of alleged sexual harassment or assists in providing information relevant to a claim of sexual harassment, is a serious violation of this policy. Acts of retaliation should be reported immediately and will be handled appropriately.

6. Responsive Action

    Misconduct constituting sexual harassment will be dealt with appropriately. Responsive action may include, for example, training, referral to counseling, and disciplinary action such as warnings, reprimands, withholding of a promotion, reassignment, temporary suspension without pay, compensation adjustments or termination.

7. Reconsideration

    If any employee directly involved in a sexual harassment investigation wishes the matter to be reconsidered, that party may submit a written request in a timely manner to the Director of Human Resources.

§ 3.8 Sample Sexual Harassment Complaint Summary

SEXUAL HARASSMENT INFORMATION SUMMARY

(Reprinted with permission)

(1) Date Report Received _____

(2) Please provide the following information about the <u>person filing the report</u> with you.

Status: administrator (a) _____ faculty (b) _____ P&S staff (c) _____

merit staff (d) _____ graduate assistant (e) _____

undergraduate student (f) _____ graduate student (g) _____

Gender: male _____ female _____

Department or administrative unit (if appropriate): _____

(3) Please provide the following information about the <u>person about whom the report is filed</u>.

Status: administrator (a) _____ faculty (b) _____ P&S staff (c) _____

merit staff (d) _____ graduate assistant (e) _____

undergraduate student (f) _____ graduate student (g) _____

Gender: male _____ female _____

Department or administrative unit (if appropriate): _____

(4) Date(s) of reported incident(s) _____

Where did the reported incident(s) occur? _____

(5) Briefly describe the incident(s) as reported: _____

_____

_____

(6) Using the classifications and examples provided on the back, categorize the incident(s) being reported (check all that apply).

"sexist comments" (a) _____ "sexual comments" (b) _____

"undue attention" (c) _____ "invitations" (d) _____

"physical advances" (e) _____ "sexual propositions" (f) _____

"sexual bribery" (g) _____ other (i) _____

(7)   What action was requested by the person filing the report with you?

_____

_____

(8)   What action did you take in response to the information reported to you?

_____

_____

(9)   Has the person reported the incident(s) described above to another university official prior to telling you about it? What action did you take in response to the information reported to you?   Yes   No

(10) Should further involvement by the Affirmative Action Office be initiated?   Yes   No

(11) Feel free to provide additional comments on the back of this form.

Person receiving the report   _____   _____
                                          Name   Department

_____   _____
       Signature   Date

Questions about completing this summary should be directed to the Assistant Affirmative Action Officer. Upon completion, return this form (labeled confidential) to her.

CATEGORIES AND EXAMPLES OF SEXUAL HARASSMENT BEHAVIOR

Category	Examples
sexist comments	comments or jokes (verbal or visual) that are stereotypical or derogatory to members of one sex
sexual comments	unwanted jokes (verbal or visual), questions, teasing, or remarks that are sexual in nature; inquiries of sexual behaviors or values
undue attention	sexually suggestive looks or gestures; leaning over; leering at one's body; cornering

invitations	unwanted, repeated pressure for personal dates; pressure for personal (non-professional) letters or phone calls
physical advances	kissing, hugging, pinching, fondling, patting, grabbing, touching
sexual propositions	clear invitation for sexual encounter but involving no threats or promises
sexual bribery	explicit sexual propositions which include or strongly imply job-related or education rewards or punishments
sexual assault	actual or attempted rape

§ 3.9 Sample Procedural Guidelines for Law Firms

COMPLAINT AND INVESTIGATION PROCEDURES FOR LAW FIRMS
(Excerpted from Commission on Women in the Profession. Reprinted with the permission of the American Bar Association, Commission on Women in the Profession. All rights reserved.)

Investigating the Complaint

1. Confidentiality

Any allegation of sexual harassment brought to the attention of (the firm's appointed committee) will be promptly investigated in a confidential manner so as to protect the privacy of the persons involved. Confidentiality will be maintained throughout the investigatory process to the extent practical and appropriate under the circumstances.

2. Identification of Investigators

Complaints will be investigated and resolved by the person on the firm's sexual harassment committee to whom it was reported. In addition, any of the following individuals may be included in reviewing the investigation and outcome: (list may include a number of appropriate partners or other individuals such as the Director of Human Resources).

3. Investigation Process

In pursuing the investigation, the investigator will try to take the wishes of the complainant under consideration, but should thoroughly investigate the matter as he/she sees fit, keeping the complainant informed as to the status of the investigation. Steps to be taken in the investigation include:

_____ Confirm name and position of the complainant.

_____ Identify the alleged harasser.

_____ Thoroughly ascertain all facts that explain what happened. Questions should be asked in a nonjudgmental manner.

_____ Determine frequency/type of alleged harassment and, if possible, the dates and locations where alleged harassment occurred.

_____ Find out if there were witnesses who observed the alleged harassment.

_____ Ask the individual how he/she responded to the alleged harassment.

_____ Determine whether the harassed individual consulted anyone else about the alleged harassment and take note of who else.

_____ Develop a thorough understanding of the professional relationship, degree of control and amount of interaction between the alleged harasser and complainant. (Does the person control compensation, terms of employment or promotions? Do these individuals work in close proximity to one another and/or on the same projects?)

_____ Determine whether the alleged harasser has carried out any threats or promises directed at the complainant.

_____ Does the complainant know of or suspect that there are other individuals who have been harassed by the alleged harasser?

_____ Has the complainant informed other partners or supervisors of the situation? What response, if any, did complainant receive from these individuals?

_____ Ask the complainant what action he/she would like the firm to take as a consequence of the harassment.

_____ When first interviewing the alleged harasser, remind him/her of the firm's policy against retaliation for making a complaint of sexual harassment.

Resolving the Complaint

Upon completing the investigation of a sexual harassment complaint, the firm will communicate its findings and intended actions to the complainant and alleged harasser.

If the investigator, together with any appropriate review committee, finds that harassment occurred, the harasser will be subject to appropriate disciplinary procedures, as listed below. The complainant will be informed of the disciplinary action taken.

If the investigator, together with a review committee, determines that no sexual harassment has occurred, this finding will be communicated to the complainant in an appropriate sensitive manner.

In the event that no resolution satisfactory to both parties can be reached based on the initial investigation, the matter shall be referred to (name an appropriate individual or group, such as the Managing Partner or Executive Committee or Director of Human Resources). See "Appeals Process" below.

1. Sanctions

Individuals found to have engaged in misconduct constituting sexual harassment will be severely disciplined, up to and including discharge. Appropriate sanctions will be determined by (select the appropriate individual or group of individuals). In addressing incidents of sexual harassment, the firm's response at a minimum will include reprimanding the offender and preparing a written record. Additional action may include: referral to counseling, withholding of a promotion, reassignment, temporary suspension without pay, financial penalties, or termination.

Although the firm's ability to discipline a nonemployee harasser (e.g. client, opposing counsel, supplier) is limited by the degree of control, if any, that the firm has over the alleged harasser, any employee or partner who has been subjected to sexual harassment should file a complaint and be assured that action will be taken.

2. False Accusations

If an investigation results in a finding that the complainant falsely accused another of sexual harassment knowingly or in a malicious manner, the complainant will be subject to appropriate sanctions, including the possibility of termination.

3. Appeals Process

If either party directly involved in a sexual harassment investigation is dissatisfied with the outcome of resolution, that individual has the right to appeal the decision. The dissatisfied party should submit his/her written comments in a timely manner to (select the appropriate reviewers; individual or group of individuals, e.g. Administrative Partner of the firm).

Maintaining a Written Record of the Complaint

The firm shall maintain a complete written record of each complaint and how it was investigated and resolved. Written records shall be maintained in a confidential manner in the office of (name the appropriate individual or appropriate division within the office. The keeper of the records may vary depending on who filed the complaint—associate, partner, paralegal. administrative assistant, etc.).

Written records will be maintained for _____ years from the date of the resolution unless new circumstances dictate that the file should be kept for a longer period of time.

Conclusion

(Firm Name) has developed this policy to ensure that all its employees and partners can work in an environment free from sexual harassment. The firm will make every effort to ensure that all its personnel are familiar with the policy and know that any complaint received will be thoroughly investigated and appropriately resolved.

§ 3.10 —Sample Dear Harasser Letter

A DEAR HARASSER LETTER

Dear:

Over the weekend I thought about our conversation last Friday, and I decided to let you know how I feel about what happened.

Perhaps the joke I told you led you to believe that pinching my rear end would be acceptable. For that reason, I am giving you the benefit of the doubt, and I may not pursue this further. But I want to say clearly, and unequivocally that I consider your pinching my rear end inappropriate and offensive. In addition, I ask that you never repeat that behavior, either in the workplace or in any social situation in which you and I may be together.

In fact, in the future you should probably act under the assumption that pinching *any* woman's rear end at work would be judged a violation of this university's policy prohibiting sexual harassment, passed by the Senate.

I consider this matter closed and hope you and I will continue to have an amicable working relationship in which we respect each other's professional roles.

Sincerely,

§ 3.11 —Sexual Harassment Investigator's Guidebook

SEXUAL HARASSMENT IN EMPLOYMENT INVESTIGATOR'S GUIDEBOOK*

Prepared by

Marilyn I. Pearman, State Women's Program,
California State Personnel Board

and

Mary T. Lebrato, Ph.D., Sexual Harassment in Employment Project,
California Commission on the Status of Women

November 1984

Chapter 2

CONDUCTING AN INVESTIGATION OF A SEXUAL
HARASSMENT COMPLAINT

SECTION A.
THE ROLE OF THE INVESTIGATOR

The primary responsibility of the investigator is to obtain all of the information pertinent to the complaint and to reduce this information to a form which will allow a conclusion to be drawn. A successful investigator develops a story. It should include what witnesses saw and heard, as well as other evidence which allows a conclusion to be drawn; in this case, a conclusion regarding whether or not sexual harassment occurred.

It is important that the investigator act as a neutral factfinder. Personal opinions of the investigator regarding the facts or circumstances of the complaint or the merit of the allegations should not be communicated to anyone during the investigation. The investigator should always be cognizant of confidentiality and other special considerations which are discussed more fully below. The investigator should remain impartial, but not insensitive.

The specific tasks assigned to an investigator may vary from process to process or from employer to employer. The role, however, remains the same: to seek out and evaluate evidence which will allow a determination as to whether or

---

* Reprinted with the permission of the California Commission on the Status of Women, State of California.

not sexual harassment occurred. The nature and extent of your role must be clear.

Make sure that as the investigator, you are aware of what is expected of you in this process *prior* to initiating the investigation. Clarifying the process and your role will assure that everyone has a clear understanding of that role and will eliminate misunderstandings during the process.

SECTION B.
A DEFINITION OF
SEXUAL HARASSMENT

Sexual harassment is *unwanted* sexual attention. Such attention is generally directed toward someone who is not in a position to *freely* refuse the advances, such as an employee dependent upon a supervisor's favorable evaluation for promotion.

Sexual harassment may take many forms including harassment which is verbal ("if you go out with me I'll get you a promotion."), visual (pornographic posters), physical (sexual assault, offensive touching), and gestural (leers and obscene gestures).

Sexual harassment may occur in many contexts (school, street, work). In the work setting, as author Lyn Farley notes in *Sexual Shakedown,* sexual harassment often forces a choice between one's economic livelihood and one's sexual integrity. Such behavior is clearly inappropriate in the work context,

In sorting out whether or not subtle behavior is sexual harassment, it is helpful to consider whether a reasonable person would be embarrassed to see his / her behavior described in the newspaper or to his/ her family and friends.

The remainder of Chapter I is intended to provide the reader with information of particular importance in the investigation of sexual harassment complaints and to discuss the actual conduct of an investigation from determining jurisdiction to the presentation of investigative findings.

SECTION C.
SPECIAL CONSIDERATIONS
REGARDING SEXUAL HARASSMENT

There are a number of issues that must be given special considerations by the investigator in a sexual harassment discrimination case. These include:

• Confidentiality.

• The possibility of criminal charges or defamation actions being brought into the process.

- The role of past complaints in investigations of sexual harassment.

- How sexual harassment affects a person.

- Inappropriate focus on harasser's intent.

- The volatile nature of sexual harassment as an issue in the workplace.

- Myths about sexual harassment.

- The reputation of the accused.

Confidentiality

It is essential that the investigator follow prescribed procedures and maintain confidentiality regarding the course and conclusions of any investigation until it is completed. In sexual harassment, the investigator may find that the actual facts of the complaint and the sensitive nature of the specific allegations may require special efforts to maintain confidentiality. For example, an investigator may find that the case includes allegations of explicit sexual activities, sexual assault and other allegations which may be extremely upsetting and embarrassing to the complainant and to the alleged harasser should they become generally known. Where an investigator might normally freely share and discuss a case with other investigators or EEO staff, in this instance, the entire investigation should be completed with stricter confidentiality considerations. The investigator should also be aware that because this issue is such a sensitive one and because it is possible that the allegations may not be substantiated, any breach of confidentiality may unnecessarily cause harm to the reputation of the accused harasser. The final report, regardless of the findings, should be kept confidential in secure files with very limited access.

Criminal Charges or Defamation Actions

The investigator should also be aware that charges may be brought in a sexual harassment case which might not be expected in other types of discrimination complaints. Criminal charges, such as sexual assault, rape, attempted rape, assault and battery, etc., may be filed with local law enforcement agencies. The investigator should be aware of the pending charges, yet proceed with the discrimination complaint investigation. The outcome of the criminal charges is based on a different set of legal standards The decision in the criminal investigation does not either prove or disprove the presence of discrimination in the workplace.

It is also sometimes the case that the alleged harasser will file a tort action (such as defamation) when he/she hears of the complaint. It is essential that the investigator make note of any such action which may indicate reprisal for filing a complaint. Investigate further to determine if there is reprisal. Strict adherence to confidentiality considerations may avoid complaints of defamation by the alleged harasser.

Role of Past Complaints

It is important to avoid the temptation to review past complaints from the same complainant which do not involve the current incident. For example, an employee may have filed a sexual harassment complaint against a previous employer. This past complaint and its resolution have no bearing whatsoever on the present investigation. Review of these documents only serves to introduce bias into the investigation. For this reason, the investigator should never request, review, or refer to past complaints unless they involve allegations against the same individual(s).

The Effects of Sexual Harassment

Another special consideration in sexual harassment cases is the effect the harassment has on the complainant. In some case, these effects may prevent the complainant from assisting in the investigation. All discrimination has a negative effect on the individual's work and personal life, but sexual harassment can be particularly devastating because it forces a person to choose between their sexual integrity and their economic livelihood. Further, it requires a discussion of personal sexual issues which has no place in the employment setting. Effects of sexual harassment include: depression, inability to sleep, loss or gain of weight, emotional and psychological disorders and other physical and mental manifestations. It is not unusual to find emotional effects so severe that the individual is almost incapable of discussing the harassment incidents.

It is important for the investigator to be aware that the complainant may exhibit any number of stress effects, the consequences of which may lead the investigator to the erroneous conclusion that the individual is failing to cooperate fully in the investigation or that they are not credible.

Inability to fully discuss the incidents, failure to provide documentation in a timely manner and other problems may be only an indication that the complainant is experiencing extreme stress. The investigator should be aware that the individual may be cooperating to the best of her/ his ability. A skilled investigator will take this into consideration and not allow the investigation to be biased by the current emotional or psychological state of the complainant.

It is appropriate for the investigator to make the complainant aware of other resources, such as counselors, support groups, workers' compensation personnel, physicians, attorneys,[10] or other community specialists available to assist the complainant in making it through this difficult process.

---

[10] Most employers would not consider referring employees to outside attorneys. Some employees may ask about their right to sue, and in those cases, they should be advised that this is always a right that they are free to pursue.

Inappropriate Focus

A common mistake made by investigators is the tendency to analyze the "intentions" of the sexual harasser instead of focusing on the impact of the harasser's action on the complainant. Whether or not harassment occurred depends upon the effect of the acts upon the individual's employment or work-environment and not upon whether or not the acts were intended to cause harm. For example, a work environment which is characterized by sexual teasing, sexual jokes and innuendo may be an offensive and hostile work environment to an individual even though the perpetrators intend such actions to be "good fun." Likewise, a supervisor who seeks dates from subordinates may only intend to be friendly, while the effect is that the subordinates feel, due to the supervisor's position, that dating the supervisor is being made a condition of continued employment.

Sex as a Volatile Workplace Issue

Sexual harassment, by virtue of the fact that it is "of a sexual nature", can be a very volatile issue to investigate. Investigators must anticipate the strong feelings of coworkers and witnesses about sexual harassment as an issue and about the intentions of the individuals involved. There may be a tendency on the part of co-workers to immediately take sides, to express disbelief that it occurred and/or to "blame the victim" in much the same way as rape victims are blamed for being raped. The investigator must take into account these reactions when planning and conducting the investigation.

Myths

There are a number of common falsehoods regarding sexual harassment that the investigator should be aware of prior to conducting an investigation. Often an investigator will allow these myths to color the conclusions she/ he reaches. Discussed below are the most common of these myths and the correct information.

Myth 1: If a woman was sexually harassed, she must have asked for it, or at least, failed to discourage it.

It is not the responsibility of the employee to stop sexually harassing behavior. If a harasser is in a position of power, the victim may be coerced or feel forced to submit to sexual advances. Even in cases of co-worker harassment, it may be difficult for an individual to say "no" or it may be that the harasser(s) refused to take "no" for an answer.

Myth 2: People invite sexual harassment by the manner of their dress.

Sexual harassment occurs regardless of the type or style of clothes worn. Further, the investigator should understand that the manner of dress of the complainant is *not* at issue in a sexual harassment complaint. A perpetrator of sexual harassment may not use the complainant's manner of dress as a defense or excuse for sexually harassing behavior. In addition, an employer may be held liable for sexual harassment charges if he/she required the wearing of clothes that resulted in sexual harassment by a third party.

Myth 3: Most charges of sexual harassment are false and are used as a way to get back at supervisors or co-workers.

It is difficult to complain about sexual harassment because very often the complainant is not believed, and may suffer embarrassment and retaliation for filing a charge. Complainants have much to lose and little to gain by filing false charges considering the difficulty of pursuing a complaint.

Myth 4: People invite sexual harassment by their "lifestyles".

Regardless of the lifestyle (such as single, divorced, gay or lesbian, feminist) of an individual, it is not an excuse or justification for subjecting him/ her to unwanted sexual attention. People should not be treated as a sexual conquest or challenge. Further, if the investigator discovers during the course of the investigation, personal information (e.g., sexual orientation) about the complainant, the investigator must make sure that this information does not bias her/ his findings.

The Accused's Reputation

Another pitfall for the investigator is the tendency to disbelieve the complainant because there were no witnesses and because the accused harasser has never harassed anyone else or because he/she has a good reputation. Although evidence of past harassment of others by the accused may help corroborate the complainant's allegations, the opposite does not hold true. The lack of evidence that an individual has harassed others does *not* Constitute evidence that no harassment occurred. Sexual harassment, especially sexual assault, attempted rape and other serious offenses most often occurs in private, with no witnesses present, and may be perpetrated by an individual who is otherwise known to be a "model" employee. The investigator must carefully evaluate the testimony of the complainant and the alleged harasser, as well as any other relevant evidence, before reaching a conclusion.

All of these special considerations combine to make the sexual harassment complaint perhaps the most difficult of discrimination complaints to investigate. Because these cases are so difficult, it is essential that the investigator be trained in investigation and discrimination issues. It is also recommended that the investigator have experience with other types of discrimination investigations before beginning a sexual harassment discrimination investigation.

SECTION D.
STEPS IN CONDUCTING AN
INVESTIGATION

The following is a list of steps which must be completed in the conduct of any investigation of a sexual harassment complaint. In the remainder of the chapter, five major areas in this process are discussed in more detail.

1. Review the complainant's statement of discrimination to determine the basis(es) for the complaint and to gain an understanding of the issues presented.
2. Determine jurisdiction.
3. Open and organize an investigative file.
4. Thoroughly review all statements, evidence and documents currently contained in the file in order to become well acquainted with the facts of the case and to assist in planning the investigation.
5. Limit the scope of inquiry.
6. Plan the investigation by making lists of witnesses to interview and evidence to gather.
7. Determine additional or clarifying information needed from the complainant, alleged harasser, employer, and witnesses.
8. Plan the interviews carefully. Prepare a list of questions to ask.
9. Conduct interviews.
10. Gather supporting documentation and evidence.
11. Visit the worksite, if necessary.
12. Analyze the information.
13. Make a determination of findings.
14. If sexual harassment is found, determine/recommend appropriate remedy.
15. Write and present the investigators report of findings.

SECTION E.
DETERMINING JURISDICTION (This section does not apply to private employers.)

The first issue in the conduct of the investigation is verification that jurisdiction for the investigation of the sexual harassment complaint exists. Although in most cases this will be pre-determined prior to assignment of the case, there have been many instances where jurisdictional issues are not resolved prior to the investigation. This results in an investigation being completed with no ability to offer remedy or provide resolution. Listed below are four examples of jurisdictional issues within State civil service. They may also be applied to situations in private or other public employment.

Example One:

A complaint of sexual harassment is filed by a full-time State civil service employee. In the complaint, she charges that the departmental Deputy Director, an exempt employee (non-civil service), made sexual advances. As the departmental EEO investigator, you are assigned to investigate. Do you have jurisdiction since a noncivil service employee is charged?

Quite clearly, yes. A discrimination complaint is a charge by an individual against the employer. As a representative of the employer, you are assigned to investigate any and all charges made by employees of the department. It is true, in this case that because the individual charged is "exempt" from civil service, there may be no jurisdiction to take adverse action against the exempt employee under the usual civil service rules for adverse actions. However, this would be a consideration in the investigator's recommendation of remedy, should a finding of sexual harassment be made. It has no bearing on your jurisdiction over harassment against the complaining party.

Example Two:

A number of employees of a State department report that a client who visits their office subjects them to verbal sexual comments on a regular basis. They file a complaint and request an investigation. As the departmental EEO investigator, do you have jurisdiction?

Again, yes. Remember that the employer is responsible for preventing discrimination and harassment of all departmental employees regardless of the source of the harassment or discrimination.

Example Three:

A State employee in your department is charged with harassment of a welfare recipient. Do you have jurisdiction?

Yes. The case would most likely proceed on the basis of inappropriate conduct proscribed, for example, by California Government Code Section 19572(m, q, w or x) which authorizes adverse action for discourteous treatment of the public or other employees, violation of board rule, unlawful discrimination, including harassment, and unlawful retaliation, respectively. Further, other department policy or code relating to the delivery of services may proscribe discriminatory acts against the public.

Example Four:

You are asked to investigate a complaint of sexual harassment of an employee in *another* department charging one of your departmental employees. Do you have jurisdiction?

The other department is responsible for the investigation of the discrimination complaint filed by their employee. However, your department may conduct an investigation to determine whether or not punitive or adverse action should be taken against your employee. In most instances, this investigation would be made by those responsible for determining adverse action for improper behavior not by the EEO investigator.

Employers may also be subject to the regulations of the Federal Equal Employment Opportunity Commission (EEOC), the State Department of Fair Employment and Housing (DFEH), State and Federal Title IX and any other local ordinances or regulations relating to contracts that may be applicable. For instance, EEOC has jurisdiction over those employees who work for an employer having 15 or more employees and effective January, 1985 DFEH has jurisdiction for harassment complaints only over any employer. Local regulations vary. Employers using governmental monies or having governmental monies may also be subject to regulations which prohibit discrimination in the delivery of services and/or in employment.

It is essential that the investigator know her/ his jurisdictional boundaries and satisfy those limitations prior to beginning the investigation.

SECTION F.
ORGANIZING THE INVESTIGATIVE FILE

The accuracy of the determination and the effectiveness of the investigator in providing a satisfactory resolution will depend to a great degree on the organization and quality of the investigator's file and report. It is essential that the investigative file be maintained in an organized manner. This will facilitate the completion of the investigation should the assigned investigator be unable to complete it. It will also assure that the investigator completes all necessary steps.

A suggested method of organization is found on the following page. However, regardless of the method used, it is critical that it be documented in the report and that all essential items be included. This method follows closely the method used by the EEOC.

Organizing the file in this manner will assure that no essential elements of the investigation have been forgotten. Good organization will enable anyone reviewing the file to understand the issues and how the determination was made.

SAMPLE FILE FORMAT

Case identification name/ number

Table of Contents

Statement of Complaint/ Charge

Timeframes/ Deadlines for Completion of Case

Jurisdictional Items

Complainant's Statement

Statements of Complainant's Witnesses

Statements of Employer(s) and Employer's

Witnesses

Employer's Records and Documents

Statements of Other Witnesses

Tour of Worksite

Investigator's Analysis

Investigator's Notes

List of Witnesses/Persons Contacted

Other Relevant Information

Irrelevant Information

SECTION G.
LIMITING THE SCOPE OF INQUIRY

One objective of the investigator is to limit the scope of inquiry by restricting the investigation to the specific allegations of sexual harassment at issue.

The scope of inquiry is limited to the relevant immediate environment in which the complainant experienced discrimination or "harm." The investigation will be limited to the gathering of information within the organizational structure where the complainant suffered harm. Limiting the scope of inquiry to only the relevant, disputed issues will create the basis for a clear and concise investigation.

This is accomplished by completing a series of steps which address the issues of the case.

1. Examine the charge or statement of discrimination. Determine and clarify the specific allegations by reviewing the statement of the complainant and

any supporting evidence, witness statements or affidavits submitted by the complainant.

2. Contact the complainant to verify that all allegations are included and to request additional information if the original statement fails to identify specific areas of individual harm or if clarification is needed.

3. Identify issues which are not disputed.

4. Identify issues which have already been investigated.

5. Identify charges which are not relevant to employment discrimination or are not material to this investigation.

6. Isolate remaining issues which will be the subject of the investigation.

Failure to limit the scope of inquiry is a common mistake of investigators. It results in a long, unclear process which makes it difficult to reach a well-reasoned conclusion.

SECTION H.
CONDUCTING A THOROUGH
INVESTIGATION

Although the role of the investigator may vary somewhat from one organization to another, the essential duty of all investigators is to assure that a complete and thorough investigation is conducted. The task of determining when it is complete is often difficult for the inexperienced investigator.

An investigation can only be considered complete when there are no further worthwhile avenues of inquiry. The investigator must make a judgment as to whether or not to continue based on the following indicators:

• The nature of the case. This is based on: (1) the nature of sexual harassment charges; (2) the possible extent of the harassment and the number of individuals involved; (3) whether or not there is an indication of continued harassment; and (4) whether retaliation is occurring or has occurred.

• If additional evidence seems warranted, will the particular evidence affect a determination of the outcome? Does the lack of evidence relate to the charge as a whole or to a specific allegation which is not essential to the determination?

• Will further investigation facilitate reaching a resolution to the complaint?

- How much investigative time is necessary to obtain additional evidence? The investigator must weigh the importance, relevance, and need for the additional evidence sought against the amount of time necessary to obtain it in order to determine whether or not to continue.

For example, investigators often fail to interview the alleged harasser because statements from several witnesses "clearly" substantiate the allegations. While such an investigation may be sufficient to determine that harassment occurred, the investigator has failed to consider an essential source of evidence which may reveal further information.

No investigation should be considered complete merely because there appears to be enough evidence available to support a conclusion one way or the other. Thoroughness and a serious effort to fully investigate all sources of evidence are the only proper tests establishing the time to terminate an inquiry.

SECTION I.
WRITING THE INVESTIGATIVE REPORT

A discrimination complaint investigative report includes a cover memorandum of investigator's findings and the information contained in the case file as indicated in Section F, above. It must be clear, concise, accurate and complete. The report serves as a written record of the facts of the complaint and is used to make a determination.

The report should be written to include all necessary details. Partial information or evidence may lead to an incorrect conclusion. Include all relevant information, but leave out anything irrelevant. Be as brief as possible.

The reader should be able to understand the report and conclusions without having to ask additional questions of the investigation.

The reader must be able to rely on the information found in the report. Accuracy is an absolute must. Inaccurate information in any part of the report will cause the reader to question the reliability of the entire report as well as the conclusion of the investigator.

It is the investigator's responsibility to present clear findings as to whether or not discrimination occurred. It is essential that the investigator reach and state specific conclusions on each allegation based upon the evidence gathered during the investigation. The investigator's skill at presenting the facts and conclusions will ultimately determine whether or not the complaint is satisfactorily resolved.

The investigator's findings must at least include the following:

1. A finding and conclusion for each allegation. (A finding of merit or no merit to the allegation(s) of discrimination.)

2. Appropriate jurisdictional information.

3. Evidence and rationale for each conclusion.

4. Findings regarding other violations or inappropriate actions which were not discrimination-based. such as improper personnel transactions, violations of the Information Practices Act, or generally poor management practices.

5. Proposed remedy(ies), if discrimination has been found.

Normally, the memorandum of investigator's findings serves as a summary of the report and is written as a cover memorandum to the final draft of the investigator's report. It is a summary which includes the who, what, why, when, where and how of the complaint in a clear and concise manner. The evidence supporting the findings should be referenced and the conclusions and recommendations clearly stated. The remainder of the report is merely an organized compilation of the various evidence gathered during the conduct of the investigation.

Section 3.12 presents a sample format for a memorandum of investigator's findings. Although the format may vary, the investigator's findings should include all essential elements.

§ 3.12   —Sample Memorandum of Investigator's Findings

SAMPLE MEMORANDUM OF INVESTIGATOR'S FINDINGS

To: Manager/ Employer Date: June 13, 1984

From: Investigator
Re: Case Name/Number

I. Allegation   Recommendations

   1. Sexual Harassment   Merit
   2. Sexual Harassment (Refusal to Hire)   No Merit
   3. Retaliation   Merit

II. Jurisdiction

The complainant is employed by the Department of Public Works as a full-time civil service employee. The complainant met all requirements for timely filing of the complaint.

Alleged violations: Oct. 12 and 26, 1983
Departmental decision: Apr. 10, 1984
Complaint filed: Nov. 19, 1983
Appeal filed: May 6, 1984

III. Evidence / Rationale for Recommendations

On October 12, 1983, the supervisor of Section IV approached the complainant and requested that she spend the evening with him to discuss her upcoming work performance evaluation. She refused the supervisor. She felt that she was being asked to comply with sexual favors in return for a good rating. The complainant subsequently received a poor performance report.

The supervisor admits asking the complainant out, but denies that her refusal to go out with him was a factor in her poor performance report. The draft copy of the performance report, given to the complainant prior to the alleged harassment of October 12, 1983, indicates that the supervisor rated her superior on two factors and above average on four factors. However, the supervisor's ratings on the final report dated October 26, 1983 completed after the harassment of October 12, 1983 were much lower. The supervisor is unable to explain why he changed the report. Therefore, there is evidence that the lowered performance report ratings were a result of her refusal to comply with the sexually harassing advances.

The complainant further alleged that she was denied a job in another unit based on the poor performance report. However, the supervisor of that unit has no awareness of the sexual harassment complaint and has no affiliation or association with the supervisor of Section IV. There is no evidence that this supervisor had any knowledge of either the refusal of the complainant to date the supervisor of Section IV or the fact that she had filed a formal complaint.

Further he was able to provide a copy of the rating sheets of all competitors which indicated that the ratings of the complainant were consistent with reports previous to October 12, 1983, and appeared to represent a fair estimate of complainant's ability to perform the job. The rating sheets also indicated that the performance reports were not seen by the raters and had no bearing on the decision not to hire the complainant. Therefore, it does not appear that sexual harassment was a factor in the decision not to hire the complainant.

Finally the complainant alleged that she was subjected to verbal abuse, loss of overtime and was given unequal work assignments as reprisal for filing the discrimination complaint. Co-workers, records of work assignments and overtime payroll records all verify that after filing the complaint on November 19, 1983, the complainant received different types of work assignments than she had been receiving prior to that date. She was also verbally harassed by the supervisor and was refused requested overtime work which prior to the complaint she had routinely been given. Therefore, the evidence supports the claim of retaliation for filing a discrimination complaint.

IV. Other Violations

There were no other violations or incidents of discrimination found.

V. Proposed Remedies

The complainant has requested to be moved to another unit within the department, to have her personnel file purged of all references to poor performance related to this incident and to have the supervisor formally reprimanded. Management states that it would be a hardship to move her to another unit, but that they agree to provide the other remedies.

I recommend that the complainant's request for remedy be granted in full. The evidence regarding the retaliation indicates that the complainant should be allowed to move to another unit regardless of the "hardship" involved for management.

§ 3.13   Sample Notice of Withdrawal of Complaint

NOTICE OF WITHDRAWAL OF COMPLAINT OF SEXUAL HARASSMENT

COMPLAINANT' S NAME:
TITLE AND DEPARTMENT:
DATE COMPLAINT FILED:
DEPARTMENT HEAD NOTIFIED:

I HEREBY WITHDRAW THIS COMPLAINT AND AGREE THAT NO FURTHER ACTION IS REQUIRED ON IT.

_____   _____
COMPLAINANT'S SIGNATURE   DATE

CHAPTER 4

SEXUAL HARASSMENT RESOLUTION

§ 4.1   The Preventive Role of Resolutions

The court in the *Ellison v. Brady*[1] case suggested that "the reasonableness of an employer's remedy will depend on its ability to stop harassment by the person who engaged in harassment. In evaluating the adequacy of the remedy, the court may also take into account the remedy's ability to persuade potential harassers to refrain from unlawful conduct." Essentially, when deciding on the discipline of harassers, bear in mind not only that the punishment should fit the crime, but also the deterrent impact, if any, that the organization wishes to have on other potential harassers.

A 1992 *Working Woman* survey of 9,600 readers and 106 personnel executives at Fortune 500 firms revealed that too often the perception of employees is that violators go unpunished: 60% of readers said that sexual harassment complaints are ignored or that harassers received only token reprimands. They reported that nothing was done to the harassers for 55 percent of the women who reported harassment. By contrast, the survey of personnel managers revealed that 82 percent of them believe that most offenders receive punishment that is justified. Since the deterrent effect can only be achieved when the proper perception prevails, employers

---

[1] Ellison v. Brady, 924 F.2d 872 (9th Cir. 1991).

should publicize in communications and training programs that substantiated cases of harassment have led to disciplinary action. They may even want to offer a few illustrations when conducting training sessions (without naming names, of course) based on real cases of the firm's (these real case scenarios should probably not be disseminated in writing lest they fall into the wrong hands).

Resolutions can operate to deter harassment if they are appropriate to the incidents involved by reflecting the nature of the incidents, their gravity, the number of incidents involved, the mind-set of the harasser, and the harm to the victim.

§ 4.2 Alternatives for Dealing with Harassers

Discipline of harassers, depending on the shade of gray involved in their conduct and how dark or light it is, can include the following options, all of which should be documented and supported by evidence following a thorough investigation:

- verbal warning
- written warning
- probation with or without pay
- demotion
- job transfer
- termination
- pay reduction
- bonus reduction or elimination

The word will be spread that an individual has been accused of sexual harassment. Often, the victim or the alleged harasser will speak about it with others in the office—often in a effort to muster support. This means that it is critical for the resolution of the matter to send the right message: to clear a name unequivocally when no harassment is found and discipline as harshly as warranted when harassment is substantiated. At some firms, where lower to middle management or nonmanagerial employees are concerned, it is often easier to make the severity of the discipline fit the severity of the violation, up to and including termination. However, when a high-level manager, a revenue generator, or a long-service employee are involved, some employers may be more reluctant to apply the harsher disciplinary options.

There is a value in recognizing those employees for their contribution in all of the positive means available such as through compensation and rewards. However, it is difficult for a sexual harassment program to have credibility when discipline is not administered consistently-regardless of status in the firm. The role of Human Resources managers is generally to recommend appropriate disciplinary action, and in these instances, they might recommend more severe discipline than management is inclined to dole out in an effort to protect the employer and its employees from further harm—economic and otherwise. Retaining an offender, even where a harsh reprimand is issued, can expose the employer to further liability in the long run if the offensive conduct continues.

Depending on the severity of the harassment, it is also questionable from an ethical standpoint to retain an individual who seems inclined to disregard other employees. Human Resources may need to enlist the aid of in-house or outside counsel for "objective" guidance about disciplining, including terminating, a high-level or long-term player in the organization.

Should action short of termination be warranted, as is most often the case, the following options may be considered:

- terminating an offender then hiring him back on as a "consultant," with no contact with alleged victim
- reassigning the offender to another business area or location
- placing the offender where he will operate as an "individual contributor" rather than in a supervisory or managerial role
- in almost all cases, training on sexual harassment prevention and managerial skills is recommended, with an emphasis on deterrence factor to protect the employer and potential harassment victims. Behavioral changes are mandatory, and are achieved through greater awareness, understanding and skills development.
- have the manager of the area in which harassment occurred or was alleged send a letter to employees regarding nonharassment. A desk drop is a good way to distribute this communication. The letter will put the harasser on notice
- split up the victim and alleged harasser by having one of them move to a different location or department
- ensure that the harasser has no direct or indirect input on the complainant's performance reviews

Assuming some degree of violation occurred, considerations in deciding on disciplinary action include:

- was the harassment knowing or intentional (while this has no impact on liability for the harassment, it may be relevant to the discipline imposed) or "unaware"

- did the behavior show a complete disregard for others
- was there a demonstrated abuse of power or trust
- what harm came to the victim
- the relationship between the parties (peers or supervisor-subordinate)
- frequency of the conduct considered to be harassing
- what work environment existed—(traditionally male? use of obscene language or presence of sexually explicit materials, and so forth)

All considerations should be based on evidence, not mere speculation of the decision maker. Decisions based on speculation are often challenged in court.

Employers wishing to apply a system to the discipline decision can give each of the above factors a different weight, and depending on a total "severity score," i.e., the harassment's shade of gray, administer corresponding discipline. For example, if there is a supervisory or reporting relationship, add a substantial weight to the "abuse of power" factor. If the harasser was told to stop, or the harasser had been through a training program, but the prohibited behavior continued, add a substantial weight to that harasser's "knowledge" factor.

Disciplining False Accusers

It is recommended to not specifically address in the policy how the organization will deal with false allegations of sexual harassment. This should be handled on a case-by-case basis, especially since the cases are so rare. Advertising that false accusations can lead to discipline can have a chilling effect, and works against the objective of encouraging employees to come forward with complaints. Considering that courts and experts on sexual harassment can differ as to the definition of sexual harassment, it is understandable that employees may not be sure whether what they are experiencing is sexual harassment or something else, for example, rudeness, affection, cultural differences, and so forth. Therefore, they should not be discouraged from raising concerns which may turn out not to substantiate sexual harassment but are not "false" claims.

By publicizing that those who bring "false" claims will be punished, employers may be tacitly discouraging a wide range of "gray area" concerns from being raised, going against the letter and spirit of the sexual harassment laws. Further, it is difficult to define just what a "false" claim is. If it is a statement that is made with malice and ill will, and that has no reasonable basis whatsoever in fact, the person falsely accused will have recourse through the legal system for libel (written) or slander (oral). Therefore, there is no reason to thus jeopardize the effectiveness of the resolution process.

§ 4.3   Alternative Remedies for the Victim

Victims of sexual harassment suffer severely. Harassment can precipitate:

- career setbacks
- low morale
- physical symptoms, including insomnia, crying, loss of appetite, extreme weight gain or loss, headaches, back pain, and others often associated with a high level of stress or emotional upheaval
- intimacy problems
- fear for their safety
- withdrawal from the community, friends and family
- severe depression

When seeking a resolution of a sexual harassment complaint, share information with the victim. By being open with the victim, you will be able to learn more information about him or her that can be helpful in decisionmaking later. For instance, the victim might share with you that she has been wanting to transfer out of the area where she is (and where the harasser is) for a while due to career interests. Or the victim might explain that she would feel more comfortable working in a different area. As stated earlier, one has to be very cautious when exploring transfer options, as this can often end up looking, and feeling to the victim, like reprisal for making the complaint.

An example of this was conveyed in a *New York Times*[2] article reporting how a female employee of the National Institutes of Health was "outraged that she was being asked to move" following her complaint of sexual harassment against her supervisor. She was allegedly asked to move even after her supervisor admitted to having been sexually involved with her, though he alleged it was consensual. She reportedly suggested that if anyone should be transferred, it should be him, not her. The resolution attempted by the National Institutes of Health raises some concerns. First, remedies for sexual harassment complaints should be reasonably calculated to end the harassment. By transferring the victim, the organization sends a message that there was something *she* did wrong, and moving her away is a resolution to the problem. This may not dissuade other harassers from engaging in unlawful conduct. Second, a remedy should place the victim in the same position she would have been in if there had been no harassment. This is the essence of a "make whole" remedy, and generally involves a reinstatement, not a transfer. Keep in mind that unless the victim expresses a desire to be transferred, she has the right not to be

---

[2] *New York Times,* Sunday, August 8, 1993 (Section L, page 30).

transferred, and other means will have to be considered during the pendency of the claim. At a minimum, the reporting relationship should be suspended.

While the victim's wishes are not the only consideration in fashioning a remedy to sexual harassment, it is a primary factor.

- Discuss options with the victim as to how he or she would like the matter resolved and the harasser handled (you should have a good sense in advance of the meeting as to setting reasonable expectations for the victim about what the organization can do for him/her)
- Bring up counseling, not just for the victim but also for the alleged harasser. Some organizations may want to try a joint counseling session where the victim and alleged harasser air their feelings in a non-threatening environment. If they reach an understanding, this may lead to a positive outcome
- If the victim raises a desire to leave the firm, be prepared to discuss a severance arrangement and an agreement to Release of Liability. Know what your authority is ahead of time so that you can resolve the matter as quickly as possible, thereby reducing the chances of making the victim feel frustrated or lose trust.

When documenting resolutions, do not include any reference to the complaint or the outcome in either of the parties' personnel file. Instead, safeguard the documentation in a separate, secured file that should be kept by the personnel manager or the department manager. Once a matter has been resolved, it is inappropriate for it to continue to haunt either of the parties. The complainant should never have to suffer any repercussions, such as a reputation as a "troublemaker," for having brought a complaint, and the harasser, once having been "rehabilitated" or having had the matter dismissed, should not be prejudiced by the stigma of having a complaint made against him or her.

§ 4.4 Alternative Dispute Resolution

All employers are aware of the time and expense litigation involves. With sexual harassment cases on the rise, a growing trend toward alternative dispute resolution (ADR) in organizations, including arbitration and mediation, are being explored as a means of resolving complaints outside of the traditional channels.

Some state laws allow employers to deter lawsuits by providing employees with an "alternative method of dispute resolution," often arbitration. While ADR does restrict an employer's managerial discretion by allowing a neutral decisionmaker the right to decide employment-related disputes, legal costs and the potential for inflated jury verdicts are greatly reduced. As the cap on damage awards under the State and Federal Civil Rights laws are raised or removed altogether, employers should consider the value of ADR. In addition, arbitrators often do not award attorneys' fees and are restricted by practice and/or law from awarding punitive damages. Arbitrators who reverse employers' decisions are more apt to reinstate employees and grant back pay, rather than to award exaggerated lost back pay and future damages. Rather than award an employee hundreds of thousands of dollars for sexual harassment, an arbitrator is more likely to order the reinstatement of the harassed employee, the discipline of the harasser, up to and including termination, the development and dissemination of a sexual harassment policy subject to the complainant's and arbitrator's approval, and mandatory training on sexual harassment throughout the organization on an ongoing basis. Further, legal expenses are reduced as pre-hearing discovery is generally limited and the time it takes to get the dispute resolved is far shorter.

Ensuring Fairness of the Arbitration Process

In order for most arbitration procedures to hold up under judicial review, they must satisfy the concept of "elementary fairness." According to the Michigan Supreme Court, for example, arbitration procedures should at a minimum provide the following:

- Adequate notice to the employee
- The right to present and rebut evidence and argument
- A formulation of the legal and factual issues
- A rule specifying when the final decision will be rendered, and
- An impartial decisionmaker

Mediators may be appointed from within the firm, as long as they have a reputation and record of being unbiased and fair. Human Resources managers not aligned with particular management groups, ombudspersons, and well-respected senior managers may be selected. A committee may also serve as a mediating body. Mediators are most often brought in from outside the organization, and the number of firms offering professional mediation services is increasing steadily.

The EEOC is piloting a new mediation program that offers the parties to a charge the opportunity to mediate a resolution before going to litigation. The employee submits the claim to a mediator and the employer may elect to participate. The parties can withdraw from the process at any time. Early figures show that 557 charging parties were offered this option, and 451 (81 percent) opted to try it. Settlements were reached in about 40 percent of the mediations.

There is some indication that the scope of arbitration agreements is expanding. Recently the U.S. Supreme Court held that an agreed-to arbitration clause in an employment agreement that provided for the arbitration of any dispute, claim or controversy, including employment claims, can preclude a discrimination lawsuit.[3] Employees in two separate cases involving the securities industry have been compelled to arbitrate age and race discrimination claims. Central to the Supreme Court's ruling was the fact the employee previously agreed, in writing, to the arbitration procedure. More employers may wish to consider adding mandatory ADR procedures to their employment arrangements.

Challenge to Arbitration Awards

Generally, courts are restricted to reviewing arbitration awards for specific grounds for impeachment as provided under the applicable state statute (most states have such a statute). For example, pursuant to Louisiana law, which appears to reflect the arbitration law of most jurisdictions, there are only four bases for a finding of impeachment of an arbitrator:

- Where the award was procured by corruption, fraud, or undue means
- Where there was evident partiality or corruption on the part of the arbitrators or any of them
- Where the arbitrators were guilty of misconduct in refusing to postpone the hearing, upon sufficient cause shown, or in refusing to hear evidence pertinent and material to the controversy, or of any other misbehavior by which the rights of any party have been prejudiced
- Where the arbitrators exceeded their powers or so imperfectly executed them that a mutual, final, and definite award upon the subject matter was not made.[4]

As it is difficult to overturn arbitration awards, employers do not have to fear years of endless expensive appeals as much as with lawsuits. For a comprehensive discussion of arbitration of sexual harassment cases, two articles have been attached in the appendix to this chapter.

---

[3] See Fletcher v. Kidder, Peabody, 62 F.E.P. 599 (N.Y. Ct. App. 1993).

[4] *See In Re Dissolution of Mouton and Jeansonne,* 573 So.2d 257 (La. App. 1991). *See also* Cashman v. Sullivan and Donegan, P.C., 578 A.2d 167 (Conn. App. 1990).

Designing an ADR

While some organizations are governed by regulations that require their employees to arbitrate disputes, including discrimination and sexual harassment, most employers must find a way to encourage employees to use ADR. An ADR is only effective if it is used. Employers should seek employees' input in the design of an ADR system to ensure that they will use it rather than resort to the courts or government agencies.

Maintain confidentiality by ensuring that only those involved in the case know about it:

Limit disclosures to those who need to know. With sexual harassment, employers don't have to reveal the name of the complaining employee to the manager, only need to say "an employee has brought a complaint against you alleging," etc. . . .

In addition to confidentiality, employees generally expect the following safeguards in an ADR system:

- Impartial-a fair decision not biased toward management
- Impartiality so that employees are not treated differently based on their level, title, position ("clerical") or if their management doesn't like them
- Respect for employees
- Due process: the parties have a full opportunity to present their point of view

Typically, employees think that they cannot get a "fair shake" from management. The ADR must overcome this perception by addressing employees' fear of repercussions, including loss of job, negative impact on promotions/performance reviews/training opportunities, for using the ADR. This perception can also be overcome by giving employees the opportunity to select a representative of their choice for the mediation process, generally from within the organization.

Promoting the Use of ADR

- Promote the system and its merits: managers, HR and employees should know about it
- Get support from the top-down for the system
- Ensure that employees using the system are treated equally regardless of race, sex, age, national origin, etc.

§ 4.5 Tests Used by Arbitrators in Deciding Whether to Uphold Discipline of a Harasser

While arbitration can be made optional or may be mandatory depending on the employment setting (union, nonunion), the following principles governing arbitration of matters relating to sexual harassment will generally apply. The following information offers management and unions insight into how arbitration works to resolve these complex issues, and in striking a balance between the rights of the harassed and the harasser. Employers should be particularly interested in the insight to be gained on how to make disciplinary actions stick. The seven tests described below were articulated by arbitrator Carroll Daugherty in the *Enterprise Wire Co.* case.

The Seven Tests[5]

The most probable type of sexual harassment case to face an arbitrator will be one where the grievant is accused of sexual harassment. There are several intrinsic questions to be addressed by the arbitrator.

1. Did the employer provide the employee with forewarning or foreknowledge of the possible or probably disciplinary consequences of the employee's conduct?

In general, there are two requirements for "good" notice—knowledge of the rules and knowledge of the consequences. This requires effective communication on the part of management, and in many instances, documentation of the grievant's knowledge of the rules and the consequences. For the employer, notice of rules poses no dilemma for the capital crimes of sexual harassment, it is only in the area of sexual harassment lesser felonies and misdemeanors that notice as a test of just cause becomes problematic.

In a perfect work world, all rules and consequences are written and all employees are aware of them. In reality, there are many loose ends with respect to knowledge of the rules and the consequences of breaking them. Labor arbitrators are aware of that fact and know that it would be almost impossible to catalogue and update all rules related to misconduct. As a result, there are exceptions to formal notice requirements.

It is an established practice in labor arbitration to hold employees accountable for the laws and mores necessary for social or industrial order.

---

[5] This material is taken from S. Crow, J.C. McKoen, Jr., *Sexual Harassment: New Challenges for Labor Artibitrators.* Arbitration Journal (now Dispute Resolution Journal) (June 1992) published by the American Arbitration Association. Reprinted with permission.

Even in the absence of well-communicated rules, employees are expected to know that some conduct will not be tolerated by management. In situations of insufficient formal notice of rules and consequences, arbitrators will hold grievants responsible for knowing that serious sexual harassment offenses, for example, sexual assault or *quid pro quo* propositions, can result in discharge. On the subject of notice in a sexual harassment case involving sexual advances by the grievant toward another employee, [Arbitrator] Haemmel said:

> [The] grievant cannot complain of receiving no express warnings; such male versus female aggressions on the job predate the very first collective bargaining agreement and such a prohibition remains part of the unwritten law of the shop. When the grievant closed the door and pulled down the shades of Mrs. L.'s office, he was acting out his knowledge that such actions were improper.

Since many of the issues of sex-related conduct and hostile environments remain unresolved, the formal notice requirements of rules and penalties may be troublesome in arbitration cases involving sexual harassment, lesser felonies and misdemeanors. Clearly, some behavior—for example, some forms of sexual horseplay—will be construed as sexual harassment. Not so clear are those situations in which an employee's conduct, albeit tasteless and offensive, is repugnant to many other employees, irrespective of their gender. An example is an employee who habitually tells other employees, male or female, off-color jokes with sexual punch lines. Since the employee makes no gender distinction in choice of an audience, if a female employee complains, does the joke-telling create a hostile environment?

Compounding the problem for employers is the fact that many companies are still in an employee behavioral transition due to the increasing presence of females in the workplace. We recall, but do not mourn, the demise of the "rites of passage" that occurred in practically all male-related professions. Whether subtle or overt, for years a certain form of harassment awaited newcomers to many professions. When overt, these rites were not wholly asexual, and what's more, the behavior was routinely ignored by many employers.

Fortunately, the rites of passage began to abate as long-established discrimination against women began to crumble. Many employers saw the hiring of women as an opportunity to end much of the hazing and intimidation in the workplace. However, residuals of these mores, euphemistically called "horseplay," still exist and are unconsciously sanctioned by employers. When employers do not react to horseplay or aggressive behavior in the workplace, they may unwittingly create an environment that may seem hostile to women. A male employee may act aggressively or engage in horseplay and his employer will dismiss the behavior as "normal" and "harmless." However, a woman may interpret this same behavior as sexually threatening. These differing perceptions, therefore, routinely challenge employers to meet formal notice requirements with respect to sexual harassment rules and penalties.

Certainly, companies cannot catalogue all behaviors that may constitute sexual harassment. However, they must demonstrate to the arbitrator's satisfaction that they have done their homework in spelling out the rules and penalties for sexual harassment, particularly in the vague area of sexual harassment, lesser felonies and misdemeanors. Without this, and regardless of whether the alleged sexual harassment is a major or minor offense, they must be able to demonstrate that prevailing social and workplace values indicate that certain conduct is unacceptable.

2. Was the employer's rule or managerial order reasonably related to the orderly, efficient, and safe operation of the employer's business, and to the job performance that the employer might rightfully expect of the employee?

The acid test for this criteria of just cause is the business relatedness of the rules concerning sexual harassment. It should be relatively easy for employers to establish that rules related to sexual harassment are job related and based on business necessity. Establishing the reasonableness of sexual harassment rules will be a problem only when sexual harassment misconduct occurs away from the workplace.

For many reasons, sexual harassment, like harassment of any kind, is contrary to the business purpose of organizations. First, employees who harass other employees are spending company time engaged in activity unrelated to their job. Second and more important, the productivity of the harassment victims is seriously impaired. A person who is upset or worried about harassment is preoccupied and does not perform efficiently. Much of their mental energy is devoted to the incidents of harassment, and as a result, their focus is diverted from the tasks at hand. Surely, employees beset with anxiety about harassment are not as productive as they could be. What's more, employees preoccupied with the threat of harassment are prone to accidents, absenteeism, and turnover. Last, and as a practical matter, sexual harassment is contrary to federal law and unless an organization establishes rules against sexual harassment and enforces them, the threat of legal liability is ever present.

For these reasons, establishing the reasonableness of sexual harassment rules should be relatively easy and should not be questioned at arbitration. However, what if the incidents of sexual harassment occur off the job? How reasonable are rules that govern behavior when employees are not at work? A scenario, albeit improbable, can be presented wherein sexual harassment occurs away from work with no sex-related misconduct once the perpetrator and the victim return to the job. If the perpetrator has influence over the work or status of the victim or works closely with the victim, it will not matter if the sexual harassment happens off the job. The psychological impact of sexual harassment on the victim carries over to the workplace and productivity may be impaired. Here, the rule is reasonable. Beyond that simple example, the arbitrator must be convinced that sexual harassment away from work is demonstrably linked to business necessity. Arbitrators will be particularly interested in the nature of the working relationship between the perpetrator and the victim. More specifically, how much influence does the perpetrator have on the victim's status as an employee?

3. Did the employer, before administering the discipline to the employee, make an effort to discover whether the employee did in fact violate or disobey a rule of order of management?

The proper investigation of a sexual harassment situation should not differ from that of any other disciplinary situation. Generally speaking, and according to Koven and Smith [footnote omitted], two things are important for a proper investigation. First, management must demonstrate that it thoroughly and properly examined all the evidence associated with the allegations. This requires management to consider all sides of the dispute, to collect all verbal, documentary, physical and related evidence, and to conduct the investigation promptly before disciplinary action is taken. Second, management must apply due process. The relatedness and application of the concept of due process in arbitration are controversial; nevertheless, most arbitrators will require proof that the grievant received notice of the allegations, was given the right to confront accusers and to present evidence in his own behalf, and was accorded the right to counsel if required.

4. Was the employer's investigation conducted fairly and objectively?

Of all [Arbitrator] Daugherty's tests of just cause, the requirement of a fair investigation seems to be out of place within the context of labor arbitration. Certainly, fairness and objectivity are important; however, research indicates that fairness of the investigation is rarely cited by arbitrators. Moreover, in the approximately 400 pages devoted to the tests of just cause, Koven and Smith used only six pages to discuss the issues related to the fairness of the investigation.

By and large, what is important, however, is that a fair investigation in a sexual harassment situation is no different from the same investigation in any disciplinary circumstance. More specifically, management must show that their investigative approach was fair and objective. In other words, the investigation was conducted in an impartial fashion and was not based on a self-fulfilling, preconceived notion of guilt on the part of the grievant.

However, one problem could develop if the arbitration involves a female grievant as a victim of sexual harassment. Conceivably, the union could claim that management's investigation was not conducted fairly or objectively because it was approached from a male's point of view.

5. Was there substantial evidence to support the accusation of sexual harassment?

Surely, the most important test of just cause will be proof of misconduct. However, establishing or discrediting proof of misconduct in labor arbitration will be particularly problematic for the advocates. There have been few true experimental studies about sexual harassment; there are fewer policy-capturing studies related to judgments about sexual harassment, and there are no policy-capturing studies about sexual harassment in arbitral contexts. Most of the general research relates to frequency of sexual harassment, and labor arbitration research is based primarily on qualitative analyses of published cases.

We believe that [researcher] York's study and Koven and Smith's work [footnotes omitted] are good approaches to the issues of establishing proof of sexual harassment for the arbitrator. York used a sample of equal opportunity officers from educational settings in his study of sexual harassment decision issues. While one cannot comfortably generalize the decision-making processes of EEO officers to labor arbitrators, the results of York's study are useful to help establish a theoretical base for the discussion of proof of misconduct in sexual harassment cases. Koven and Smith's standards for evaluating harassment as mitigation in "but for" cases are also helpful in proving sexual harassment misconduct. Based on York's findings, arbitrators are likely to weight three aspect of sexual harassment most heavily—evidence of coercion, the victim's reaction, and job consequences.

Coercion—There should be evidence that the person charged with sexual harassment implicitly or explicitly behaved in a way that coerced the victim to respond in a way contrary to his or her free will. One can quickly see the difficulties here. What is implicit and explicit behavior? How can it be corroborated? What constitutes coercion? How can these conditions be proven to the arbitrator's satisfaction?

The frequency and degree of coercion will also be important. An arbitrator will view a grievant who persists in sex-related behavior, such as requests for dates and lewd language, differently from a grievant who did the same thing once, or infrequently. On the other hand, arbitrators will probably be unequivocal in their response to coercive "sex or else" demands.

Victim's Reaction—We know at least two things from the Thomas-Hill debacle. The victims of sexual harassment should not wait 10 years to complain; nor should they be so clinical and dispassionate when they do. If sex-related behavior is offensive, the victim should deal with it immediately and directly. At arbitration, the person who complains about sexual harassment may have to prove that not only was the sexual harassment not encouraged, but also, that it was *discouraged*. This is easier said than done. Many people are sexually aggressive and their overtures require nothing less than the verbal equivalent of a knee drop to the groin. Worse still, if the sexually aggressive person is pathological or naive, ignoring their behavior may send them the wrong message. When ignored, they are likely to believe that their actions are either welcome or, at least, *not* unwelcome.

The concept of innocent until proven guilty is deeply imbedded in the collective American value system. That reality, coupled with what we believe may be an intrinsic suspicion about the veracity and complicity of victims of sexual abuse, may make it more important for the advocates to effectively demonstrate that the victim of sexual harassment reacted appropriately.

Job Consequences—It is crucial to show that unfavorable job consequences resulted after the incident of sexual harassment. If the person accused of sexual harassment is a bargaining unit employee, the situation becomes more challenging. It will be necessary to show that the worker's behavior contributed, in some tangible way, to negative employment outcomes. A statement citing stress, or "mental cruelty," or a hostile environment, will not be sufficient in and of itself. Instead, the sexual harassment behavior must be shown to be job-related. For example, the behavior caused the victim to perform poorly, miss work, have accidents, or resign. Of course, if the complainant is a coworker with a history of poor performance and poor work habits, the alleged negative job consequences will appear to be a pretext. The employer may be able to show that the most important negative job consequence is the threat of litigation had the employer not taken action to eliminate the situation.

As mentioned before, the arbitrator may hear a case wherein sexual harassment is a mitigating issue. For example, a grievant disciplined for poor performance acknowledges the poor performance but attributes it to a hostile environment due to sexual harassment. Or a grievant curses a supervisor, then claims it was provoked by sexual harassment. Here, the burden of proof belongs to the union, and Koven and Smith's research suggests that a strong showing is necessary for the union to prevail. Koven and Smith's findings originate from cases where race or sex discrimination was the mitigating factor; in our opinion, however, there is no essential difference in cases where sexual harassment is the mitigating factor. Based on the Koven and Smith research, arbitrators will probably rely on the following standards.

Proof that the harassment occurred: This situation is no different from what we already covered about establishing proof in the previous sections.

A consistent pattern: The union must show that the harassment occurred on a continuing basis and not just in isolated incidents. A lesson from the Thomas-Hill controversy suggests that timing will be important to arbitrators. More specifically, the union will be hard pressed to show mitigation if the pattern of harassment showed signs of abating in the time frame immediately preceding the disciplinary action against the grievant.

A demonstrable effect: The union must show that the sexual harassment would have been intimidating to "a reasonably mature individual" to the extent that performance was negatively affected. A demonstrable effect is particularly interesting in light of the controversy swirling about the reasonable man, reasonable woman, or reasonable person standard. The game of labor arbitration is, by and large, played on a male-dominated field, and women are, by and large, the victims of sexual harassment. Accordingly, at arbitration, there may be a juxtaposition of contrasting values, attitudes and beliefs about the "demonstrable effect" of sex-related behaviors.

The company must have known: Simply stated, the union must show that the grievant notified management of the sexual harassment. Arbitrators will probably be persuaded if the union can show that the grievant's complaint was unequivocal, that it was made to an appropriate member of management, and that the company failed to take action. Equally important will be the company's track record of affirmative action when an incident of sexual harassment was reported. Certainly, if the company has a history of immediate action to remedy sexual harassment situations, the union will have difficulty showing that the company must have known.

6.   Has the employer applied rules, orders and penalties even-handedly and without discrimination to all employees?

This is a straightforward and accepted test for showing just cause. The employer must show that its action did not depart from past practice and that it did not discriminate in any manner. The test of equal treatment may be problematic in sexual harassment labor arbitrations. Sexual harassment, particularly the concept of a hostile environment, is a relatively new facet of industrial jurisprudence, and we suspect that some companies may have a past practice of tolerating some forms of sexual harassment. We also suspect that some companies, to a certain extent, tolerate conduct that creates tension for others. In short, aggressive behavior, whether related to sexual harassment or not, has been tolerated in many work settings for a long time. If we are correct, a grievant disciplined for creating a hostile environment may be able to show that the company's action departs from a past practice of tolerance. In such a situation, management will have to show that those practices have been eliminated and that new policies were introduced and properly communicated.

Another possible problem related to this test is that allegations of sexual harassment are still directed primarily at males. This is understandable to an extent. Historically, men have been more sexually aggressive than women, and it was not uncommon for men to take the sexual initiative with women in any social context, including work. Only recently have romantic overtures become such a legal problem that employers must require men to "chill out" at work. And, it seems to us, that this is exactly what many employers have done—told *men* to "chill out." If our suspicions are correct that many organizations direct their efforts to modify sex-related misconduct to male employees, they may have difficulty at arbitration in proving equal treatment.

7. Was the degree of discipline administered by the employer reasonably related to the seriousness of the employee's proven offense, and to the employee's service record with the employer?

For several reasons, this test of just cause in sexual harassment cases will involve more than simply deciding if the penalty fits the crime. First of all, sexual harassment is manifested in several degrees of offensiveness. It is not like theft where a simple dollar amount can distinguish a felony from a misdemeanor. Some sex-related misconduct is the workplace equivalent of a capital offense and requires the ultimate penalty—discharge. Other forms of sexual harassment run the gamut from simple misdemeanors to lesser felonies to serious felonies, and are more appropriately handled with progressive discipline. Or should that be the case? Is sexual harassment so *malum in se* that summary discharge is appropriate irrespective of the form it takes?

Second, as mentioned above, there is still a great deal of controversy over what constitutes sexual harassment. At this point, sexual harassment, particularly the concept of a hostile environment, defies operational definition, and our understanding of the related issues is still evolving. There is no question when defining conduct like sexual assault or *quid pro quo* sexual harassment that these behaviors warrant discharge. However, if we have yet to define the crimes of sexual harassment, how can we determine if the penalties are appropriate?

Third, in what way has the company's past complacency and inaction contributed to the acts of sexual harassment? For example, if an organization has tolerated a certain degree of aggressive behavior in the past and continues to do so, can it not be held accountable for the acts of employees to the extent that its penalties against the perpetrators of sexual harassment are unreasonable?

Last, other questions deserve consideration in the evolving nature of appropriate penalties in sexual harassment cases. For example, what role do mitigating circumstances like tenure and work record play in deciding if the penalty is appropriate? Does sexual harassment have such a chilling effect on the productivity of some employees that it is best to remove the guilty party altogether? Once the mark of sexual harassment is fixed on employees, are they forever the pariah of the workplace, unworthy of even a transfer?

Arbitrators anxiously await the advocates' rationales for determining the appropriate penalties in sexual harassment cases. We suspect that arbitrators will not break any new ground in this area. They will accept summary discharge for the more serious forms of sexual harassment and expect progressive discipline for less offensive varieties of sexual harassment. Additionally, arbitrators will look for the traditional pitfalls in progressive discipline. For example, past disciplinary records are either nonexistent, "fuzzy" in their meaning, or stale, there was no opportunity to improve, the employer was "building a case" against the grievant, or the discipline was not promptly imposed.

We realize we have only touched the surface of sexual harassment in arbitral frameworks. Time and research will be necessary to see how arbitrators resolve the issues and develop the decisional standards for sexual harassment in arbitral contexts.

§ 4.6   Arbitration Process

Arbitrators use the same standards as enforcement agencies and courts in reviewing complaints of harassment or disciplinary action brought before them. The following material analyzes actual arbitration decisions relating to sexual harassment of the hostile environment and quid pro quo variety.

Standards Used by EEOC[6]

In determining whether the alleged conduct constitutes sexual harassment, the Commission will look at the record as a whole and the totality of the circumstances, such as the nature of the sexual advances and the context in which the alleged incidents occurred. The determination of the legality of a particular action will be made from the facts, on a case-by-case basis.

Inherent in the EEOC's definition is that sexual harassment is based upon the perceptions of the victim. As well, sexual harassment is perceived

---

[6] The material in this section is taken from A. Gomey and J. Monat, *Decisional Standards Used by Arbitrators,* Labor L. J. 712–18 (Oct. 1986). Reprinted with permission from the October 1986 issue of the Labor Law Journal, published and copyrighted 1986 by CCN Incorporated, 4025 W. Peterson Ave., Chicago, Ill. 60646. All rights reserved.

by victims to be an issue of power.[7] Consequently, the problems of burden of proof and the standards for evidence are potentially vague. The Guidelines have been interpreted broadly by the EEOC.

Courts have addressed two different types of sexual harassment under Title VII of the Civil Rights Act of 1964. The first, which we will call "Type A," is the "quid pro quo" type of harassment; for example, "sleep with me or you won't get the promotion." In this case, requiring sexual activity as a quid pro quo for a promotion is an additional burden placed by the manager on women but not on men.[8]

Where we will call "Type B" harassment is where there is no traditional "employment opportunity" affected; rather, a "sexually offensive work environment" is created. A sexually offensive work environment discriminates against women in the "conditions" of employment.[9]

Employer Liability

A second issue that courts have faced is the question of employer liability. The United States Supreme Court case of *Meritor Savings Bank, FSB v. Taylor* offers guidelines for determining employer liability. The Court rejected a "strict liability" standard for harassment by supervisors. However, the Court stated that it would not make a definite ruling on the issue. Instead, the Court expressed interest in common law "agency" principles, leaving open for future cases a more detailed ruling. Despite this uncertainty, the thrust of the Court's discussion is: Where there is supervisor-generated harassment, the employer will be liable only where it had actual knowledge or where the harassment was "so pervasive and so long continuing" that the employer "must have become aware of it." In addition, employer liability for supervisory harassment would seem to be found only where it had actual or constructive knowledge of the harassment and was ineffective in stopping the harassment.

In the case of *co-worker* harassment an analysis similar to that of supervisory harassment is used. Co-worker harassment is almost always Type B (sexually offensive work environment) rather than Type A (quid pro quo harassment). Usually a co-worker cannot require a quid pro quo before the co-worker victim receives a promotion or pay-raise. In these cases, the rules seem more clearly defined: The employer will be liable only if it knew or should have known, *and* did nothing (or was ineffective)

---

[7] E.G.C. Collins, and T.B. Blodgett, *Some See It . . . Some Won't,* Harvard Business Review, March–April, 79–97 (1981); J. James, *Sexual Harassment,* 10 Public Personnel Management Journal, 402–407 (1981).

[8] *See* Phillips v. Smalley Maintenance Services, Inc., 32 E.P.D. ¶33,802 (11 Cir. 1983).

[9] Katz v. Dole, 709 F.2d 251 (4th Cir. 1983).

in correcting the situation.[10] Discussion in both supervisor and co-worker harassment cases has generally focused on several points.

1. If the harassment was done quietly or privately, and if the victim did not report it, and the employer did not otherwise learn of it, then no employer liability.[11]
2. Where the harassment is public or in the open, or if the victim reported it, then courts may decide that the employer knew or should have known about it and should have corrected it.[12]
3. After the company has knowledge of the harassment, corrective action by the company must result in the harassment stopping. A variety of methods are open to the company, including verbal warning, written warning, suspension, transfer, or termination—all of which should be directed at stopping the harassment.[13]
4. The victim need not prove that she resisted: the test is whether the sex-related conduct was "unwelcome." However, it has been recognized as a company defense if the victim "gave as good as she got" and was a willing participant in the give and take.[14]

Harassment by or of third parties, such as customers, follows roughly the same analysis as co-worker harassment; i.e., no employer liability unless the employer had or should have had knowledge, and failed to correct the situation. Strict liability for supervisory actions has been challenged in a case now awaiting decision before the United States Supreme Court.

In *Meritor Savings Bank, FSB v. Vinson,*[15] the plaintiff filed under the Type B "sexually offensive work environment" theory, claiming her supervisor was causing the offensive environment. The lower court ruled in favor of plaintiff under the strict liability standard discussed above. The defendants appealed on the grounds that, without a quid pro quo, the employer should be held liable only if it "knew or had reason to know" of the offensive environment. The Supreme Court may conclude that only Type A (quid pro quo) supervisory harassment will lead to strict liability and that Type B (environment) supervisory harassment will lead to liability only if there is employer knowledge by someone in the company in a position of authority other than the harassing supervisor.

---

[10] Zabkowicz v. West Bend Co., 589 F.Supp. 780 (E.D. Wis. 1984).

[11] Scott v. Sears Roebuck & Co., 605 F.Supp. 1047 (N.D. Ill. 1985).

[12] Katy v. Dole, 709 F.2d 251 (4th Cir. 1983).

[13] Hosemann v. Technical Laterals, Inc., 554 F. Supp. 659 (R.I. 1982).

[14] Meritor Savings Bank v. Vinson, 477 U.S. 57 (1986); Gan v. Kepro Circuit Systems, Inc., 27 E.P.D. ¶32,379 (D.Mo. 1982).

[15] 477 U.S. 57 (1986).

Sexual Harassment in Arbitration

The review of arbitration awards published in *Labor Arbitration Reports* (BNA) and *Labor Arbitration Awards* (CCH) reflects over two dozen decisions involving sexual harassment reported since 1981. The awards found did not appear to break new ground but instead tended to adopt or rely upon standards used by the courts and the compliance agencies. The reasons for this will be discussed later.

In arbitration, the charging party has the burden of proof, but it is not an onerous burden.[16] Commentators have suggested that the grievant show evidence in five areas to meet the prima facie burden of proof. The five points include: (1) a showing of continued or repeated abuse, (2) threat of adverse impact on employment conditions if there is no sexual submission, (3) a showing that the victim tried to stop the harassment, (4) a showing that the victim reported the harassment to management, (5) a showing of a generally abusive or harassing environment.[17]

Typical conduct found by courts to be sexual harassment include discipline and discharge, assignments to undesirable shifts or jobs, onerous tasks, dress codes, touching the victim's body, and verbal abuse, especially comments about a woman's anatomy.[18]

Proof of such conduct in either an arbitration or court forum, however, becomes a serious problem for the grievant.[19] Harassment often takes place when there are few, if any, witnesses or where the harassment is not obvious.[20] Women often do not report harassing conduct to managers because they are either embarrassed or fearful.[21] There may, for example, be a fear of retaliation.

---

[16] P. Linenberger, *What Behavior Constitutes Sexual Harassment?* 34 Labor L. J., 238–47 (April 1983).

[17] P. Linenberger, *What Behavior Constitutes Sexual Harassment?* 34 Labor L.J., 238–47 (April 1983); P. Linenberger and T.J. Keaveny, *Sexual Harassment in Employment*, Human Resources Management, 11–16, (Spring 1981); P. James, *Sexual Harassment Claims of Abusive Work Environment Under Title VII*, Harvard L. R., pp. 1449–67 (1984); Bakery and Confectionary Union, 81–2 ARB ¶8566 (1981).

[18] Robson v. Eva's Supermarket, 30 F.E.P. 1212 (1983); Marentette v. Michigan Host., Inc., 24 F.E.P. 1665 (1980); *Bundy v. Jackson,* 24 E.P.D. ¶31,439, 24 F.E.P. (1981).

[19] T. Hunt, *A Plaintiff's Attorney Perspective on Sexual Harassment Cases,* SPIDR Conference, Los Angeles, CA, Jan. 12, 1984.

[20] Gateway United Methodist Youth Center, 75 L.A. 1177 (1980).

[21] New Industrial Techniques, Inc., 84 L.A. 915 (1985); Vernitron Piezoelectric Div., 84 L.A. 1315 (1985); A. Gomez, *Arbitration Sexual Harassment Cases: Management's Perspective,* American Arbitration Association Workshop on Sexual Harassment, Los Angeles, CA, Feb. 13, 1985; R.H. Faley, *Sexual Harassment: Critical Review of Legal Cases with General Principles and Preventive Measures,* 35 Personnel Psychology, 583–601 (1982).

Some arbitrators require victims to have reported alleged sexual harassment to management.[22] In *Dayton Power and Light,* the arbitrator ruled that the victim had to have told the offender that such conduct was offensive. Running away from the harasser was insufficient proof that the verbal or physical conduct was offensive. That the accuser responded in kind is a defense against a charge of sexual harassment in any forum, including arbitration.[23]

Just Cause Causes

Most sexual harassment grievances arrive as "just cause" causes rather than as violations of discrimination or other clauses (such as seniority or work assignment).[24] That is, the arbitrations do not arise from a sexual harassment grievance filed by a disciplined alleged harasser. In a review of forty-three published arbitration awards on sexual harassment over a twenty-year period, it was found that all arrived at arbitration as grievances involving the discipline or discharge of the harasser.[25] In a discipline setting, the burden of proof for the harassment typically moves from a mere "preponderance of the evidence" to "convincing and substantial."[26] For example, in *Rockwell International Corp.,*[27] a quality control inspector was discharged for a persistent, corroborated course of sexually harassing conduct. The discharge was upheld as reasonable under the circumstances. The same result was reached for similar facts in *United Electric Supply.*[28]

Management has the burden of proof in discharge cases moving against a grievant, usually male, who has been discharged or disciplined for sexually harassing conduct. Establishing the fact of sexual harassment has, in effect, been shifted subtly to the victim from the company and the grievant. Most practitioners agree that this is the typical form of sexual harassment cases in the arbitration forum.[29]

---

[22] Paccar, Inc., 72 L.A. 769 (1979); Dayton Power and Light, 83-1 ARB ¶8068, 80 L.A. 19 (1982).

[23] Meijer, Inc., 83 L.A. 570 (1984); Paccar, Inc., 72 L.A. 769 (1979).

[24] *See, e.g.,* University of Missouri Health Sciences Center, 92-1 ARB ¶8133 (1982).

[25] R. Meiners, *An Arbitrator's Perspective on Sexual Harassment Cases,* SPIDR Conference, Los Angeles, CA, Jan. 12, 1984.

[26] Gateway United Methodist Youth Center, 75 L.A. 1177 (1980); U.S. Army Signal Center, 78 L.A. 120 (1982).

[27] 85-2 ARB ¶8546, 85 L.A. 246 (1985).

[28] 82 L.A. 921 (1984).

[29] A. Gomez, *Arbitration Sexual Harassment Cases: Management's Perspective,* American Arbitration Workshop on Sexual Harassment, Los Angeles, CA, Feb. 13, 1985; J. Kaplon, *A Union Attorney's Perspective on Sexual Harassment Cases in Arbitration,* American Arbitration Association Workshop, Los Angeles, CA, Feb. 13, 1985; T. Hunt, *A Plaintiff's Attorney Perspective on Sexual Harassment Cases,* S. Linnick, *Sexual Harassment: An Expensive Proposition,* SPIDR Conference, Los Angeles, CA, Jan. 12, 1984.

Arbitrators have routinely upheld discharge as the appropriate remedy for sexual harassment, especially: where there was a prior warning to the harasser;[30] where the course of conduct extended over a lengthy period of time;[31] where the sexual harassment combined with an otherwise poor work record;[32] or where the circumstances of the harassment were aggravated.[33] Discharges have also been upheld for a single kiss on the cheek;[34] and for posting seven "obscene" drawings in the work area.[35]

However, other arbitrators have held that discharge was too harsh a discipline for the harasser and required that progressive discipline should have been imposed. An arbitrator ruled that an employer's laxity condoned that harassing behavior, and the discharged employee was reinstated but without backpay in light of the gravity of the offense.[36] Moreover, an employer must not overreact when there is no evidence of intent to intimidate and harass, especially where "victim" testified she took the crude comments as a joke.[37] In *Meijer, Inc.,*[38] a discharge was reduced to a long suspension because the male victim apparently willingly participated in the by-play. In a colorfully written award, the arbitrator details unusual male-male sexual harassment, including the observation that "[T]he cold storage warehouse seems persistently to have incubated hot thoughts. Grown men, married with families, and with no apparent homosexual inclinations frequently cavorted like satyrs when unobserved by females or [supervisors] . . . [Playful] humping was so frequent that employees were careful to find a protective wall before bending to tie a shoelace."

In *County of Ramsey,*[39] a discharge was reduced to a thirty-day suspension without pay on condition that the employee participate in six months of therapeutic counseling. The arbitrator in *Sunshine Mining Co.*[40] upheld a suspension imposed on a male employee for verbal abuse of female co-workers. In *Cavol, Inc.,*[41] a male employee was given a written

---

[30] United Electric Supply, 82 L.A. 921 (1984).

[31] New Industrial Techniques, Inc., 84 L.A. 915 (1985); Rockwell Int'l, Corp., 85-2 ARB ¶8546, 85 L.A. 246 (1985).

[32] Hayes Int'l. Corp., 81 L.A. 99 (1983).

[33] Zia Co., 82 L.A. 640 (1983).

[34] Care Inns, Inc., 83-2 ARB ¶8517, 81 L.A. (1983).

[35] Alumax Extrusions, Inc., 81 L.A. 722 (1983).

[36] David R. Webb Co., Inc., 84-1 ARB ¶8290 (1984).

[37] Louisville Gas & Electric, 83-2 ARB ¶8552, 81 L.A. 730 (1983).

[38] Meijer, Inc., 83 L.A. 570 (1984).

[39] 86-1 ARB ¶8521, 86 L.A. 249 (1986).

[40] 77 L.A. 1259 (1981).

[41] 239 AAA Awards 10 (1978).

reprimand for verbal abuse directed to female employees. A single, ambiguous comment regarding sex made by a male co-worker to a female worker, on the other hand, did not warrant any discipline, and the grievant was reinstated with full backpay.[42]

Harassing Environment

Arbitrators have recognized that harassment of non-employees such as company customers or passersby will support imposition of discipline. In *City of Rochester,*[43] offensive comments made by a repairman to women walking by on the sidewalk resulted in a six-month suspension. *Pepco*[44] involved an employee who made advances to a customer's teenage daughter; that award similarly resulted in a long-term suspension. A therapist who made sexually-oriented remarks to clients was given a thirty-day suspension on condition that he submit to therapeutic counseling in *County of Ramsey.*[45]

Another common fact situation arising in collective bargaining agreement disputes are those involving a Type B claim, that is, a hostile or intimidating work environment. This may arise, for example, where the victim formerly had been having an affair on her own volition with a co-worker or supervisor. The jilted male then spreads rumors leading to the hostile environment. If the male is a supervisor, the woman may be the victim of unfair documentation to create a poor work record, denial of a promotion, or other adverse employment condition.

When cases arise under discrimination clauses in the contract, as in a Type B (environment) claim, the burden of proof clearly falls on the union representing the grievant-victim. The five points noted above become important to an arbitrator making a factual determination about alleged sexual harassment.[46]

Although no published award has set out clear standards of unacceptable behavior in sexual harassment cases, the *Harvard Law Review* suggests one approach:

> The proper standard to evaluate the conduct alleged is an objective one from the perspective of a "reasonable victim." Such a standard would protect women from offensive behavior that "diverges from male and female

---

[42] Washington Scientific Ind., 83 L.A. 824 (1983).

[43] 82 L.A. 217 (1983).

[44] 83 L.A. 449 (1984).

[45] 86-1 ARB ¶ 8521, 86 L.A. 249 (1986).

[46] Gateway, Paccar, Inc., 72 L.A. 769 (1979); Dayton Power and Light, 83-1 ARB ¶8068, 80 L.A. 19 (1982); U.S. Army Signal Center, 78 L.A. 120 (1982); National Archives, 73 L.A. 737 (1979).

perceptions of appropriate conduct." This standard would protect the male defendant from overly sensitive grievants unless she had communicated to him that she was offended while the preponderance of evidence would allow the "reasonable victim" to prevail.[47]

Normally, arbitrators use a "preponderance of the evidence" or "reasonable evidence" standard in these non-discipline cases.[48] Often, under either a Type A or Type B matter, credibility questions are central. One arbitrator's reasoning is worth noting. In the *Gateway United Methodist Youth Center,* the arbitrator (who happened to be a woman) reinstated a custodian at a home for emotionally disturbed children discharged for allegedly harassing and molesting an adolescent resident.

She said, "[I] cannot find convincing proof that the grievant committed the offense. I see no compelling reason to doubt the account of the incident by either the grievant or by the female resident. . . . No witness could state clearly and unambiguously that he or she saw the incident occur. [There were] contradictions, ambiguities, and assumptions. . . . While I am reluctant to assess [the victim's] credibility, I am convinced of enough proof." The arbitrator detailed a very careful weighing of the credibility factors against the high standard of proof required for discharge cases.

The *Gateway* arbitrator followed an approach consistent with the general tests of credibility used by most arbitrators. An arbitrator should look at the witnesses' demeanor,[49] relationship of victim and harasser,[50] consistency with other facts and evidence,[51] internal consistency,[52] corroboration,[53] and motivation to lie.[54] "There is no way to be absolutely sure of the true state of the facts."[55] The trauma caused by the harassment has been considered as a mitigating circumstance where the victim's testimony contained some conflicts and lack of factual recall.[56] Some threats are so serious (e.g., rape) that for a woman to have made the charge of harassment carries extra credibility weight because of the risk of adverse publicity.[57]

---

[47] *Sexual Harassment Claims of Abusive Work Environment Under Title VII,* 97 Harvard L. Rev., 1449–67 (1984).

[48] National Archives, 73 L.A. 737 (1979).

[49] King Soopers, Inc., 86 L.A. 254 (1985); Care Inns, Inc., 832 ARB ¶8517, 81 L.A. (1983).

[50] Vernitron Piezoelectric Div., 84 L.A. 1315 (1985).

[51] New Industrial Techniques, 84 L.A. 915 (1985).

[52] Care Inns, Inc., 85-2 ARB ¶8517, 81 L.A. (1983).

[53] Rockwell Int'l Corp., 85-2 ARB ¶8546, 85 L.A. 246 (1985).

[54] Hayes Int'l Corp., 81 L.A. 99 (1983); A. Gomez, *Arbitration Sexual Harassment Cases: Management Perspectives,* American Arbitration Workshop on Sexual Harassment, Los Angeles, CA, Feb. 13, 1985.

[55] Paccar, Inc., 72 L.A. 769 (1979).

[56] Fisher Foods, 80 L.A. 133 (1983).

[57] St. Regis Paper, 74 L.A. 1281 (1980).

Where the victim does not testify at the hearing, arbitrators are reluctant to discredit the alleged harasser's denials of wrongdoing. They may therefore overturn the discipline imposed.[58]

Remedies

Once arbitrators have found sexually harassing conduct in violation of the labor agreement, the employer's responsibility becomes "strict liability" only in superior/subordinated cases.[59] For co-worker harassment, management has the responsibility to maintain a nonharassing environment.[60] Once management has investigated and found sexual harassment, it must take actions to correct and remedy the situation. Action must be prompt; having a policy is not enough. Unless the conduct is truly "egregious," the application of progressive discipline may be accepted.[61]

In a discussion regarding remedy, an arbitrator refused to order that a male employee apologize to a female employee for his abusive language. The arbitrator noted that a disciplinary suspension had already been imposed, and that he had no authority to augment the discipline imposed.[62]

Why have so few sexual harassment cases gone to arbitration? Among several factors, the most important reason seems to be that the approach through the state and federal courts and EEOC agencies permits the awarding of compensatory and often, punitive damages plus attorneys' fees.[63] Also, well-established law gives the victim access to the courts and compliance agency machinery at the same time as the grievance procedure.[64] The victim-grievant may, therefore, have dual or triple remedial pathways.

Second, arbitration is influenced increasingly by external law. Since the historic *Steelworkers* trilogy, in which one of the grounds for overturning an arbitrator's award was that it was contrary to law, the use of external law in arbitration has become substantial. Sexual harassment is a relatively new issue in the arbitration forum, and it may be prudent for consistency

---

[58] Veterans Administration Med. Center, 82 L.A. 25 (1984); Pepco, Inc., 83 L.A. 449 (1984).

[59] R. Meiners, *An Arbitrator's Perspective on Sexual Harassment Cases,* SPIDR Conference, Los Angeles, CA, Jan. 12, 1984.

[60] U.S. Customs Service, 82-1 ARB ¶8072 (1982); University of Missouri Health Services Center, 92-1 ARB ¶8133 (1982).

[61] Knouse Foods Corp., 81-1 ARB ¶8117 (1980).

[62] Sunshine Mining Co., 77 L.A. 1259 (1981).

[63] J.F. Wymer, *Compensatory and Punitive Damages for Sexual Harassment,* Personnel Journal, 181–4 (March 1983); A. Gomez, *Arbitration Sexual Harassment Cases: Management Perspectives,* American Arbitration Association Workshop, Los Angeles, CA, Feb. 13, 1985.

[64] Zia Co., 82 L.A. 640 (1983).

to use the same standards of conduct as applied in other forums for retaining the looser standard of evidence and proof traditionally used by arbitrators. Most contract clauses about discrimination in labor agreements provide no specific standards. Consistency with external law on substantive criteria may therefore be desirable.

Finally, other theories might be developed to deal with sexual harassment charges under labor agreements. Charges alleging breaches of the duty of fair representation, safety and health clauses, or specific work rule clauses might be raised.[65]

Typical Contract Provisions

Article X: Rights of Management.   The management of the company and the direction of the workforce are vested exclusively in the company, and this shall include and shall not be limited to the right to hire, properly classify, promote, transfer, layoff, or release employees for lack of work, and for just cause to discharge, suspend, or discipline employees, provided that the exercise of such rights shall not conflict with the provision of this Agreement.

Article XV: Nondiscrimination.   The company agrees to continue its present nondiscriminatory policy offering equal opportunities for available jobs to qualified employees without regard to sex, race, creed, color, national origin, age or handicap. Neither the company nor the union, in carrying out their obligations under this agreement, will discriminate in any manner whatsoever against any employee because of sex, race, creed, color, national origin, age or handicap. To the extent that the law or any final order of a cognizant court with which the company and the union are required to comply is in conflict with any of the provisions of this Agreement, such law or final order will supersede the said provisions of this Agreement.

§ 4.7   Restoring the Workplace after a Sexual Harassment Complaint

The departments in which complaints are made can suffer substantial disruption in the aftermath of a complaint. These matters can divide individuals into camps, lower productivity, and raise fears. Part of the

---

[65] S.K. Blumberg, *Sexual Harassment in City Hall,* 45th National Conference, American Society for Public Administration, Apr. 10, 1984; B.N. McClennan, *Sex Discrimination in Employment and Possible Liabilities of Labor Unions,* 33 Labor L. J., 26–35.

follow-up to the resolution process is ensuring that the department is restored to some semblance of harmony.

This can be best achieved by periodically reaffirming the employer's commitment to a harassment-free work environment. This message should come from a unit head or department manager. There should also be a clear statement prohibiting any form of reprisal against those who bring complaints or participate in their investigation, with a warning that disciplinary action could result from such retaliatory behavior. The group should be reminded that they are to avoid gossip and other nonproductive use of their time. Employees who work in a team environment should be reminded that their performance is evaluated in part on their ability to work well with all team members. Finally, employees should be advised of any EAP or other counseling available to assist them if they feel any residual distress.

CHAPTER 5

ADMINISTRATION OF THE PREVENTIVE POLICY

§ 5.1   Preventive Management Practices and Audit

This chapter explores the different ways for determining what your organization's level of knowledge is about sexual harassment and describes some tools you can use to assess how well the message gets out that sexual harassment is unacceptable in the organization.

There are many ongoing activities that an employer can engage in to support the preventive strategy. A number of them are discussed in the following sections. Certain ongoing management practices such as the following are recommended:

- Periodically reissue a memo to all employees reiterating the firm's policy and complaint procedure
- Include a statement prohibiting sexual harassment and reproduce the organization's policy in handbooks, supervisory manuals, ethics policies and manuals, and any communication regarding how employees are expected to treat one another and customers

- Based upon the results obtained through any of the tools described throughout this chapter, including the audit that follows, report back periodically, but not less than once per year, to management and/or administration, on how the organization is addressing the issue of sexual harassment
- Be sure to follow up training sessions with additional information and insights identified during those sessions. The Bonneville Power Administration's sample training follow-up materials in § 5.7 offer an excellent illustration of this highly-effective technique.

As with all documents and data relating to sexual harassment and other sensitive personnel matters, the reports generated should be kept in a secured file, not widely disseminated, and all those receiving such documentation or data should be advised in writing of its confidential nature. Unless such information is produced in response to litigation at counsel's request, it probably would be discoverable by an agency or in a lawsuit and should be written with that consideration in mind.

§ 5.2 Climate Surveys

One option for ascertaining the extent of sexual harassment in the workplace is to include an item relating to sexual harassment in the organization's general climate survey. A climate survey is used to gauge the employment environment and generally covers a wide array of topics from benefits and compensation to supervisor-subordinate relations. Sample climate surveys are reproduced in **Figures 5–1** and **5–2**. It is usually comprised of statements followed by some form of rating scale which enables the employee to rate the statement for degree of agreement or accuracy in his or her case.

Many organizations conduct climate surveys periodically to determine the level of employee satisfaction. You can take this opportunity to include a question or two specifically about sexual harassment that are designed to measure the current level of awareness about what sexual harassment is and how the organization addresses it. It is difficult to separate the issue of sexual harassment from that of climate in organizations. As the experts on quality in organizations tell us, climate has everything to do with quality. In their ground-breaking work *Driving Fear Out of the Workplace,* Kathleen Ryan and Daniel Oestreich, originators of the "Just Say No" to drugs campaign, present research finding that "EEO Practices," including sexual harassment, is one of the primary "undiscussables" in organizations. They define "undiscussables" as "a problem or issue that someone hesitates to talk about with those who are essential to its resolution" and "the fact that it is not discussed represents a potential barrier to doing

HUMAN RESOURCE CLIMATE SURVEY ®

Questionnaire

You are about to take part in a very important task. The answers that you give to the questions in this booklet will serve as a guide to your organization in planning improvement efforts. The survey is an opportunity for you and your co-workers to present your views of the organization, the people you work with and your job. No individual's answers will be identified, so we encourage you to be straightforward in responding to each question.

To protect confidentiality, no names are to be placed on the survey answer sheets. Instead, you will be given a code number which, along with your answers, will be fed into a computer to prepare employee group results. The summarized results will be shared with you.

Figure 5–1. Sample climate survey.

INSTRUCTIONS

1. Your survey administrator will give you a work group code number to place on your answer sheet. The code number is used by the computer to summarize group responses. Please enter only the code number in the box provided at the top, right hand side of your answer sheet. *Do not* write your name on the answer sheet.

2. Mark your answers on the separate answer sheet using a black, soft lead pencil (No. 2). The answer sheet is processed by a machine which reads only pencil marks. Please do not mark any answers in this booklet.

3. The circle you choose for your answer should be filled in completely. If you wish to change an answer, erase the circle completely, then mark your new choice.

4. Each question has five possible responses. Fill in the numbered circle of your choice, for each question. If you do not find a numbered circle that fits your exact needs, choose the one closest to it.

5. If you find a question where you simply have no information on which to base an answer, skip the question and go on to the next one. We encourage you to answer all questions, if possible.

6. Your survey administrator will explain the meaning to the following terms from the questionnaire:

> Organization
> Supervisor
> Work Group
> Department or unit

7. There is no time limit for taking the survey. Please take the time to read each question carefully before you answer.

Thank you for your cooperation.

Figure 5–1 (*continued*).

HUMAN RESOURCE CLIMATE SURVEY®

1. To what extent is this organization generally quick to use improved work methods? ① ② ③ ④ ⑤   1.

2. To what extent does this organization have a real interest in the welfare and satisfaction of those who work here? ① ② ③ ④ ⑤   2.

3. To what extent does this organization try to improve working conditions? ① ② ③ ④ ⑤   3.

4. To what extent does this organization have clear-cut, reasonable, goals and objectives? ① ② ③ ④ ⑤   4.

5. To what extent are work activities sensibly organized in this organization? ① ② ③ ④ ⑤   5.

6. How adequate is the amount of information you get about what is going on in other departments or units? ① ② ③ ④ ⑤   6.

7. To what extent are people above your supervisor receptive to suggestions and ideas coming from subordinates? ① ② ③ ④ ⑤   7.

8. To what extent are you told what you need to know to do your job in the best possible way? ① ② ③ ④ ⑤   8.

9. To what extent are the equipment and resources you have to do your work with adequate, efficient, and well-maintained? ① ② ③ ④ ⑤   9.

10. To what extent do you look forward to coming to work each day? ① ② ③ ④ ⑤   10.

- 1 -   Continued on next page ☞

Figure 5–1 (*continued*).

HUMAN RESOURCE CLIMATE SURVEY®

11. To what extent are there things about working here (people, policies, or conditions) that encourage you to work hard?   ① ② ③ ④ ⑤   11.

12. To what extent do you feel free to suggest changes that would allow you to perform your job more effectively?   ① ② ③ ④ ⑤   2.

13. To what extent do changes occur as a result of your suggestions?   ① ② ③ ④ ⑤   13.

14. People at all levels of an organization usually have information that could be of use to decision makers. To what extent is information widely shared so that those who make decisions have access to such information?   ① ② ③ ④ ⑤   14.

15. When decisions are being made, to what extent are the persons affected asked for their ideas?   ① ② ③ ④ ⑤   15.

16. In this organization, to what extent are decisions made at those levels where the most adequate and accurate information is available?   ① ② ③ ④ ⑤   16.

17. To what extent do different units or departments plan together and coordinate their efforts?   ① ② ③ ④ ⑤   17.

18. How are problems between units or departments usually resolved?   *Note: For Question 18, use the responses listed below the question.*   18.

Nothing is done - the problems usually grow worse .... ①

Little is done about these problems — they continue to exist .... ②

The problems are appealed to a higher level in the organization — .... ③
but often still are not resolved.

The problems are appealed to a higher level in the .... ④
organization — and are usually decided there.

The problems are worked out at the level where they .... ⑤
appear, through mutual effort and understanding.

19. To what extent are you satisfied with the persons in your work group?   ① ② ③ ④ ⑤   19.

20. To what extent are you satisfied with your supervisor?   ① ② ③ ④ ⑤   20.

© 1990 HRCSI   - 2 -   Continued on next page ☞

Figure 5–1 (*continued*).

HUMAN RESOURCE CLIMATE SURVEY®

21. To what extent are you satisfied with your job? ① ② ③ ④ ⑤ 21.

22 To what extent are you satisfied with this organization? ① ② ③ ④ ⑤ 22.

23. Considering your skills and the effort you put into your work, to what extent are you satisfied with your pay? ① ② ③ ④ ⑤ 23.

24. To what extent are you satisfied with the progress you have made in this organization up to now? ① ② ③ ④ ⑤ 24.

25. To what extent are you satisfied with your chances for getting ahead in this organization in the future? ① ② ③ ④ ⑤ 25.

26. To what extent are you satisfied with the fringe benefits programs (hospitalization, life insurance, retirement benefits, etc.)? ① ② ③ ④ ⑤ 26.

27. To what extent are you satisfied with the pay for your job, compared with other jobs in the community which require the same skills? ① ② ③ ④ ⑤ 27.

28. To what extent have you received the training you need to perform well in your job? ① ② ③ ④ ⑤ 28.

29. To what extent are your skills and abilities being used? ① ② ③ ④ ⑤ 29.

30. To what extent do the supervisors you know seek out and use ideas developed by subordinates? ① ② ③ ④ ⑤ 30.

- 3 -   Continued on next page ☞

Figure 5–1 (*continued*).

HUMAN RESOURCE CLIMATE SURVEY®

TO A VERY LITTLE EXTENT
TO A LITTLE EXTENT
TO SOME EXTENT
TO A GREAT EXTENT
TO A VERY GREAT EXTENT

31. To what extent are your job objectives the result of discussion and mutual agreement between you and your supervisor? ① ② ③ ④ ⑤ 31.

32. To what extent do you understand how your job fits in with other work going on in this organization? ① ② ③ ④ ⑤ 32.

33. To what extent does doing your job well lead to recognition and respect? ① ② ③ ④ ⑤ 33.

The following questions are about your supervisor, the person to whom you directly report. When a question has two parts please answer both parts.

---

34. To what extent is your supervisor receptive to suggestions and ideas from your work group? ① ② ③ ④ ⑤ 34.

How friendly and easy to approach is your supervisor?

35. This is how it is **now** ① ② ③ ④ ⑤ 35.
36. This is how I'd **like** it to be ① ② ③ ④ ⑤ 36.

When you talk with your supervisor, to what extent does he/she pay attention to what you are saying?

37. This is how it is **now** ① ② ③ ④ ⑤ 37.
38. This is how I'd **like** it to be ① ② ③ ④ ⑤ 38.

To what extent is your supervisor willing to listen to your problems?

39. This is how it is **now** ① ② ③ ④ ⑤ 39.
40. This is how I'd **like** it to be ① ② ③ ④ ⑤ 40.

- 4 -   Continued on next page ☞

Figure 5–1 (*continued*).

HUMAN RESOURCE CLIMATE SURVEY®

How much does your supervisor encourage people to give their best effort?

> 41. This is how it is **now**   ① ② ③ ④ ⑤   41.
> 42. This is how I'd **like** it to be   ① ② ③ ④ ⑤   42.

To what extent does your supervisor maintain high standards of performance?

> 43. This is how it is **now**   ① ② ③ ④ ⑤   43.
> 44. This is how I'd **like** to to be   ① ② ③ ④ ⑤   44.

To what extent does your supervisor encourage the persons who work for him/her to work as a team?

> 45. This is how it is **now**   ① ② ③ ④ ⑤   45.
> 46. This is how I'd **like** it to be   ① ② ③ ④ ⑤   46.

To what extent does your supervisor encourage people who work for him/her to exchange opinions and ideas on job-related problems?

> 47. This is how it is **now**   ① ② ③ ④ ⑤   47.
> 48. This is how I'd **like** it to be   ① ② ③ ④ ⑤   48.

To what extent does your supervisor use group meetings to solve problems of vital concern to the work group?

> 49. This is how it is **now**   ① ② ③ ④ ⑤   49.
> 50. This is how I'd **like** it to be   ① ② ③ ④ ⑤   50.

- 5 -   Continued on next page ☞

Figure 5–1 (*continued*).

HUMAN RESOURCE CLIMATE SURVEY®

To what extent does your supervisor provide help, training, and guidance so that you can improve your performance?

51. This is how it is **now**   ① ② ③ ④ ⑤   51.
52. This is how I'd **like** it to be   ① ② ③ ④ ⑤   52.

To what extent does your supervisor provide the help you need so that you can schedule work ahead of time?

53. This is how it is **now**   ① ② ③ ④ ⑤   53.
54. This is how I'd **like** it to be   ① ② ③ ④ ⑤   54.

To what extent does your supervisor offer new ideas for solving job-related problems?

55. This is how it is **now**   ① ② ③ ④ ⑤   55.
56. This is how I'd **like** it to be   ① ② ③ ④ ⑤   56.

57. To what extent does your supervisor have realistic performance expectations?   ① ② ③ ④ ⑤   57.

58. To what extent does your supervisor have confidence and trust in you?   ① ② ③ ④ ⑤   58.

59. To what extent do you have confidence and trust in your supervisor?   ① ② ③ ④ ⑤   59.

60. To what extent does your supervisor handle well the *technical* side of his/her job - for example, general expertise, knowledge of job, technical skills needed in the profession or trade?   ① ② ③ ④ ⑤   60.

- 6 -   Continued on next page ☞

Figure 5–1 (*continued*).

HUMAN RESOURCE CLIMATE SURVEY®

> **The following questions are about your work group, that is, you and others who report to the same supervisor.**

How friendly and easy to approach are the persons in your work group?

    61.   This is how it is **now**   ① ② ③ ④ ⑤   61.
    62.   This is how I'd **like** it to be   ① ② ③ ④ ⑤   62.

When you talk with persons in your work group, to what extent do they pay attention to what you are saying?

    63.   This is how it is **now**   ① ② ③ ④ ⑤   63.
    64.   This is how I'd **like** it to be   ① ② ③ ④ ⑤   64.

To what extent are persons in your work group willing to listen to your problems?

    65.   This is how it is **now**   ① ② ③ ④ ⑤   65.
    66.   This is how I'd **like** it to be   ① ② ③ ④ ⑤   66.

How much do persons in your work group encourage each other to give their best efforts?

    67.   This is how it is **now**   ① ② ③ ④ ⑤   67.
    68.   This is how I'd **like** it to be   ① ② ③ ④ ⑤   68.

To what extent do persons in your work group maintain high standards of performance?

    69.   This is how it is **now**   ① ② ③ ④ ⑤   69.
    70.   This is how I'd **like** it to be   ① ② ③ ④ ⑤   70.

       - 7 -   Continued on next page ☞

Figure 5–1 (*continued*).

HUMAN RESOURCE CLIMATE SURVEY®

How much do persons in your work group encourage each other to work as team?

71. This is how it is **now**   ① ② ③ ④ ⑤   71.
72. This is how I'd **like** it to be   ① ② ③ ④ ⑤   72.

To what extent do persons in your work group work toward <u>team</u> goals?

73. This is how it is **now**   ① ② ③ ④ ⑤   73.
74. This is how I'd **like** it to be   ① ② ③ ④ ⑤   74.

To what extent do persons in your work group help you find ways to do a better job?

75. This is how it is **now**   ① ② ③ ④ ⑤   75.
76. This is how I'd **like** it to be   ① ② ③ ④ ⑤   76.

To what extent do persons in your work group provide the information or help you need so that you can plan, organize and schedule work ahead of time?

77. This is how it is **now**   ① ② ③ ④ ⑤   77.
78. This is how I'd **like** it to be   ① ② ③ ④ ⑤   78.

To what extent do persons in your work group offer each other new ideas for solving job-related problems?

79. This is how it is **now**   ① ② ③ ④ ⑤   79.
80. This is how I'd **like** it to be   ① ② ③ ④ ⑤   80.

- 8 -   Continued on next page ☞

Figure 5–1 (*continued*).

HUMAN RESOURCE CLIMATE SURVEY®

For the following questions, think of your work group as a team which includes your supervisor.

81. To what extent do persons in your work group know what their jobs are and know how to do them well?   ① ② ③ ④ ⑤   81.

82. To what extent is information about important events and situations shared within your work group?   ① ② ③ ④ ⑤   82.

83. To what extent does your work group emphasize meeting its objectives successfully?   ① ② ③ ④ ⑤   83.

84. To what extent is your work group able to respond to unusual work demands placed on it?   ① ② ③ ④ ⑤   84.

85. To what extent do you have confidence and trust in the persons in your work group?   ① ② ③ ④ ⑤   85.

86. To what extent does your work group plan together and coordinate its efforts?   ① ② ③ ④ ⑤   86.

87. To what extent does your work group make good decisions and solve problems well?   ① ② ③ ④ ⑤   87.

88. To what extent is there freedom from favoritism in your work group?   ① ② ③ ④ ⑤   88.

89. To what extent does your work group plan and coordinate work activities effectively with other related work groups?   ① ② ③ ④ ⑤   89.

90. To what extent are the performance goals of your work group clearly defined?   ① ② ③ ④ ⑤   90.

Figure 5–1 (*continued*).

You may be given questions to answer in addition to those in this booklet. Please use the extra spaces on your answer sheet to mark your responses. Thank you for your help.

210 East Huron
Ann Arbor, MI 48104
(313) 668-1303

Figure 5–1 (*continued*).

HRCS X

Code Number ☐☐☐☐☐☐

HUMAN RESOURCE CLIMATE SURVEY

From the list below, please check only three factors or conditions which if improved or corrected would contribute most to increasing your own effectiveness or performance. For each of the three factors or conditions checked please provide an example or specific item that needs to be improved.

FACTOR / CONDITION		EXAMPLE
More cooperation from other areas, departments, shifts		
Improved supervision		
Improvements in tools, and/or equipment		
More authority in my job		
More and/or better information		
Improvement in work environment		
Clearer definition of responsibilities		
Additional manpower		
Better planning and/or scheduling		
More and/or improved training		
Improved company/employee relations		
Other:		

THIS IS AN IMPORTANT PART OF THIS SURVEY. DO NOT LEAVE THIS UNANSWERED!

_____% Using a percentage, indicate your estimated increase in effectiveness if the items checked above were improved or corrected.

© Bauer & Associates, Inc.

BAUER
& ASSOCIATES, INC.

Figure 5–1 (*continued*).

ADDITIONAL COMMENTS

I.   This organization's major strengths are:

II. The major problems facing this organization are:

III. To achieve its potential this organization needs to:

Please use the following page for any other comments you wish to make.

Figure 5–1 (*continued*).

Other comments:

Figure 5–1 (*continued*).

Bauer & Associates, Inc. was founded in 1978 by Robert and Sandra Bauer. Initially the focus of the first was in the area of organization and management development consulting. From the start, survey methodology was extensively used in organization diagnosis, identification of problem areas and opportunities for improvement, assessment of leadership styles, survey feedback, problem solving and action planning, and assessment of organization change over time.

During 1978, the *Human Resource Climate Survey I* questionnaire was created, based on the organization research of Dr. Rensis Likert. Since 1978, this questionnaire has been administered to over 200,000 survey participants in business, health care, and government organizations. *HRCS I* is the principal survey questionnaire used in support of the firm's *Work Climate Improvement Process,* which has been implemented in a number of client organizations over the years; GTE, Mead Corporation, Phillips Petroleum, Haworth, PHH Group, among others.

In 1979, the first generation of survey processing software was developed internally to give B & A total capability in all phases of the survey process, from questionnaire design through processing, analysis and feedback of survey results. This capability continues to be enhanced each year, including improvement in computer systems and laser printing, and continuing refinement of our proprietary survey processing software.

Figure 5-1 (*continued*).

Form 5-2
Sample Client Survey

Sexual Harassment Survey
Minnesota Legislature
1992

The sexual harassment policy developed for the entire legislature has been in effect for a year. To assess the effectiveness of the policy and training, we are asking all members and employees to complete this anonymous survey.

PLEASE RETURN IN THE ENCLOSED ENVELOPE
BY FRIDAY, JANUARY 10, 1992 to
Janet Lund, Director
Legislative Coordinating Commission
St.Paul, Minnesota 55155

Thank you for your timely assistance on this important matter.

I.   DEMOGRAPHICS

1. In what area of the legislature do you work?   ____ House
____ Senate
____ LCC (Commissions, Revisor's, Library)

2. What is your position?   ____ Partisan   ____ Non-partisan

3. What is your gender?   ____ Female   ____ Male

4. What is your age?   ____ 25 or under ____ 36-45
____ 26-35   ____ 46-55

5. How long have you worked for the legislature?   ____ 5 years or less
____ 6-10 years
____ over 10 years

6. Please check the category which best describes your position:
____ Page, clerk, word processor, or receptionist
____ Legislative assistant, secretary, aide, or other administrative support
____ Fiscal analyst, attorney, librarian, committee administrator, administrative assistant, public information staff, researcher, writer, media services staff, or technical/computer staff
____ Supervisor, manager, director
____ Legislator (skip question 7)

7. What is your job status?   ____ Permanent ____ Session only / other

(Reprinted with permission of the Minnesota Legislature Coordinating Commission, Minnesota Legislature.)

Figure 5–2. Sample climate survey.

II. TRAINING

1. Have you read the legislature's sexual harassment policy manual? ____ Yes ____ No

2. Did you attend a sexual harassment training session provided by the legislature? ____ Yes ____ No

   If NO, skip to page 3.
   If YES, would you want to attend a refresher training session in 1992? ____ Yes ____ No

3. If a video was used at the training session that you attended, did you find ti beneficial? ____ Yes ____ No
   ____ Don't know
   ____ Not applicable

4. Which of the following did you find helpful in the training session? Check all that apply.

   ____ Role playing   ____ Lecture
   ____ Question & Answer   ____ Facilitator
   ____ Overhead   ____ Small Group Discussion
   ____ Video   ____ Sexual Harassment Policy Manual

5. What would be the most useful to include in any future training? Check all that apply.

   ____ Role playing   ____ Lecture
   ____ Question & Answer   ____ Facilitator
   ____ Overhead   ____ Small Group Discussion
   ____ Video   ____ Sexual Harassment Policy Manual
   ____ Other

6. Did the training increase your understanding in the following areas?

   A. Your ability to recognize sexual harassment and sexually offensive behavior ____ Yes ____ No

   B. Your awareness of options for dealing with sexual harassment and sexually offensive behavior ____ Yes ____ No

   C. Your awareness of options for dealing with sexual harassment policy ____ Yes ____ No

   D. Youe knowledge of how to report sexual harassment and sexually offensive behavior ____ Yes ____ No

2

Figure 5–2 (*continued*).

III. Experience

1. During the past year have you experienced sexual harassment or sexually offensive behavior in the work environment? If yes, please note the following on the table:

- the kind and number of offending incidents you experienced during the past year;
- the offender's relationship to you;
- the code(s) [see below] for the action(s) you took; and
- the effect of the actions.

To distinguish among multiple incidents of the same type with significantly different offenders, actions or effects, please use the lines marked "Other" at the bottom of the table.

	Number of Incidents	OFFENDER IS				Action(s) you took: See codes 1-13 below:	EFFECT OF ACTION		
		Subordinate	Peer (LEGISLATIVE)	Superior	NON LEGISLATIVE		Made things worse	Made no difference	Made things better
A. Unwelcome sexual comments, compliments, innuendoes, or suggestions about one's clothing, body, or sexual activity									
B. Turning work discussions into sexual topics such as sexual practices or preferences, or telling sexual jokes or stories									
C. Requesting or demanding sexual favors or suggesting that there is any connection between sexual behavior and any term or condition of employment, whether that connection be positive or negative									
D. Use of obscene or sexual words or phrases or the use of unwelcome words such as "sweetheart," "stud," "honey," "'babe," or "hunk"									
E. Displaying sexually explicit pictures or objects in the work area									
F. Giving personal gifts of a sexual nature									
G. Making sexually suggestive facial expressions or gestures									
H. Making unwelcome visits to the home or hotel room of a staff person or a legislator									
I. Kissing, touching, patting, pinching, or brushing against a person's body									
J. Sexual contact, intercourse, or assault									
K. Other (describe)_____									

(Please use the reverse side (page 4) for comments) or explanations.

Codes for action(s) taken:

1. I went along with the behavior.
2. I made a joke of the behavior.
3. I ignored the behavior or did nothing.
4. I avoided the person(s).
5. I asked/told the person to stop.
6. I threatened to tell or told others.
7. I transferred, disciplined, or gave a poor performance rating to the person.
8. I reported the behavior to a supervisor or other officials.
9. I requested an internal investigation.
10. I consulted an attorney.
11. I requested an investigation by an outside agency.
12. I filed a discrimination complaint with the Human Rights Department.
13. I did something other than the actions listed above. (Please explain on reverse side)

3

Figure 5–2 (*continued*).

III.   **Experience** (continued)

         2. Do you have any comments or explanations regarding the experiences you noted on the
            preceding table?

IV.   **OPEN QUESTIONS**

         1. What do you think about the reporting procedures in the sexual harassment policy? Please
            explain.

            _____ No opinion

         2. Do you have any comments or recommendations for change in:

            A. the policy?

            B. the reporting policy?

            C. the training?

4

Figure 5–2 (*continued*).

V.   RESPECT IN THE WORKPLACE

The following questions deal with issues that may be specifically covered under the sexual harassment policy. The information provided by your answers may be useful in continuing efforts to encourage respect and sensitivity in the workplace. Thank you.

1. Have you experienced or witnessed offensive behavior or insensitivity in any of the following areas?
Is YES, to whom was the behavior directed? Check all that apply.

OFFENSIVE BEHAVIOR   **IT WAS DIRECTED TO:**
OR INSENSITIVITY

	<u>YOU</u>	**ANOTHER PERSON**	**A CLASS OR GROUP**
A. Race, color or national origin	____	____	____
B. Age	____	____	____
C. Gender	____	____	____
D. Religion or creed	____	____	____
E. Physical or mental disability	____	____	____
F. Sexual or affectional orientation	____	____	____
G. Status with respect to public assistance	____	____	____
H. Marital status	____	____	____
I. Chemical dependency recovery	____	____	____
J. Other_____	____	____	____

2. Please give examples of the offensive behavior or insensitivity, and indicate the frequency of the behavior.

3. Have you tried reporting the offensive behavior or insensitivity? If yes, what were the results?

5

Figure 5–2 (*continued*).

quality work or building an effective work relationship." (See *Introduction* regarding the "systemic" view of sexual harassment.)

Many experts link the prevalence of sexual harassment with the type of culture and "systems" that permeate the workplace. William White, director of Training and Consultation for The Lighthouse Training Institute, explains that "a strong organizational culture can promote sexual harassment if aberrant values have been incorporated into the culture that legitimize disrespect and abuse towards a targeted group of workers. Weak organizational cultures can promote sexual harassment by failing to socialize members with values, attitudes, standards and taboos that would inhibit harassing and exploitive behavior." There is increasing discussion in organizations ravaged by re-organizations, reductions in force, and other jarring experiences, about what kind of culture was allowed to stagnate the organization. Organizations that are now called upon to not only react quickly to the marketplace, but also engage in constant "environmental scanning" and anticipate their customers' needs, are examining forces that shape them from inside and outside. These organizations use climate surveys and other means to scan their internal customer base as well—a useful exercise to help identify and, in some cases, rectify values that are shaping dysfunctional behaviors, like sexual harassment.

To construct a couple of climate survey items, consider first what data you would like to generate out of the process about sexual harassment. A statement in the survey might read: "I am aware of the organization's policy on sexual harassment." This will help the organization to determine what the general level of awareness is with respect to company policy. Another item to include is: "I am comfortable raising the issue of sexual harassment in the organization." This will help the organization assess how effective the policy and complaint procedure are at encouraging employees to come forward, a critical component in avoiding liability. Another area to explore is the extent to which employees believe that they have been subjected to a quid pro quo or hostile work environment type of sexual harassment: "I have never been asked to comply with sexual favors in exchange for some form of job advancement or enhanced compensation" vs. "My workplace (management) is respectful in its dealings with women employees (and customers)."

This approach poses some risks, particularly for organizations not truly prepared to implement change:

- May raise concerns which might otherwise have remained dormant or unidentified.
- If the results are documented and discovered somehow in the course of litigation or by an Agency audit, they could work in the organization's or in the plaintiff's favor, depending on the outcome and, if applicable,

whether the organization has taken any decisive action to ameliorate the situation.

- The level of awareness may be raised to a point where the organization receives more inquiries or complaints than it is prepared to handle effectively.
- Politically, management of the organization may react defensively to the inclusion of such references in the survey.
- An individual may make a complaint on the climate survey form that cannot be traced back, and you will be unable to take any corrective action on his or her behalf.

Generally speaking, the organization should be prepared to deal with the data generated by the climate survey, or it is better to not undertake the survey at all. This is not only advisable in terms of liability concerns, but also in terms of employee morale: there is nothing more demoralizing to employees and frustrating to human resources managers than to have cultivated a deep-seeded, underlying cynicism toward valuable research assessment tools like climate surveys.

The benefits can be summarized as the same points made above, but viewed from a different perspective. For instance, it is beneficial for an organization seeking to improve its climate to undertake a climate survey that raises topics such as sexual harassment. A beneficial by-product, not a "risk," is that you raise the awareness level regarding sexual harassment and send a message that the organization is concerned about the treatment of its employees.

§ 5.3 Focus Groups

Some organizations make extensive use of focus groups, a term borrowed from the marketing profession to describe discussion groups with consumers about products being developed for market. Typically, small groups of employees are assembled and a discussion is lead by a facilitator or moderator about specific topics, with questions designed to elicit candid and spontaneous reactions. An organization can also use focus groups to learn more about sexual harassment among employees. This is a risky technique, and may not even be recommended due to the highly sensitive and confidential nature of sexual harassment. Discussions about sexual harassment can also be highly-unpredictable, with individuals blurting things out and expressing overwhelming anger or pain about personal experiences.

If an organization decides to conduct focus groups including the topic of sexual harassment, Human Resources managers and/or professional trainers should act as facilitators and should lay clear ground rules for the session—and still be prepared for the unexpected. Ground rules might include: "The company is concerned about sexual harassment and wants to learn more about how employees feel about it and what their needs might be for further information and policies regarding sexual harassment. However, we appreciate that sexual harassment is a very sensitive subject, and we therefore request that you refrain from naming individuals or discussing individual complaints which should be raised in private through our employee complaint procedure. We have pamphlets on that as well as our Employee Assistance program (EAP) which we will make available at the end of the session."

§ 5.4 Exit Interviews

This is the "it's never too late to learn" technique. Unfortunately, the first time that many employers learn that an individual has been sexually harassed is during their exit interview as they are leaving the organization—usually as a resignation. Sexual harassment is generally not included as a standard subject matter in an exit interview or on an exit opinion survey form, but is generally raised in connection with an open question such as "is there anything else that you would like to tell me about your experience with us that influenced your decision to leave?" Such open-ended questions are valuable for just this reason, as you do not want to learn about the sexual harassment allegation for the first time in the unemployment compensation process or in a complaint filing.

Your open-ended question can even be more directly focused on climate or management issues that are more likely to generate a hidden concern about sexual harassment, such as "did you have any concerns about the way you or the department was managed?" or "did you find that the organization's value or 'respect for others' was observed in your experience with the firm?" A sample exit interview form is reproduced in **Form 5-1.**

FORM 5-1
SAMPLE EXIT INTERVIEW FORM

Your candor in completing the information requested below is greatly appreciated. This is a confidential form.

Name: _____

Department: _____

Date of Hire: _____

Date of Last Day Worked (or To Be Worked): _____

Reason for Leaving the Firm: _____

_____

Is there anything about your experience at the firm that can be improved? If yes, please suggest how.

_____

_____

Is there anything that you would like to report regarding any experience you had at the firm that you would like to be resolved.

_____

_____

Address and phone number where you can be reached for follow-up:

_____

_____

§ 5.5   Orientation

Orientations offer a potentially powerful opportunity to set the stage for behavior and values in the organization. Unfortunately, many employers do not take advantage of this opportunity. How many of the readers of this book have given serious thought to the content of the new employee orientation? Probably not many, and this is why states like Connecticut have legislated that sexual harassment training will be given to all new supervisors, whether they are new to the organization or not. It is a win-win proposition to offer some information about sexual harassment in an orientation: the individual benefits by being empowered through knowledge and information about his or her rights and responsibilities, and the organization benefits by having placed all new hires on notice that this behavior will not be tolerated, thereby sending a strong message about organizational climate.

Some raise the concern that orientation is supposed to be a positive forum to welcome new employees and make them feel good about the organization and that affirmatively raising the topic of sexual harassment has a negative impact. While there may not be any surveys conducted on this topic, many employees would probably interpret coverage of this topic at orientation as a positive statement about climate—not as a source of anxiety, except of course for those who might have been otherwise inclined to sexually-harassing behavior or fond of using intimidation tactics as a substitute for coaching and counseling employees.

§ 5.6   Suggestion and Complaint Systems

Other sources of data concerning sexual harassment in the workplace include information gathered through existing suggestion systems. If feasible, it might be helpful to include a specific category for suggestions relating to sexual harassment in the suggestion system tracking mechanism. In addition, many employers already have a complaint mechanism in place, particularly union grievance procedures and Ombudsman systems in academic institutions. If you do not already have a system in place to capture and report data concerning sexual harassment complaints, you may want to build that into the process. Always consider the critical requirement of maintaining confidentiality by ensuring that any reporting aggregates data without reference to names or other identifiers that might compromise the confidentiality of the process.

§ 5.7   Sample Training Follow-up Memo from Bonneville Power Administration with Implementation Guidance

FROM ADMINISTRATOR'S OFFICE
Memorandum[1]

Steven G. Hickok
Executive Assistant Administrator—A
Harassment-Free Workplace Policy

TO: All BPA Managers and Supervisors

Attached is the new BPA policy on maintaining a harassment-free workplace.

Please read it carefully so you understand its full implications, including those of the last paragraph.

Many of you were Involved in training/consultation sessions in the January-March period that helped us develop and refine this policy statement, and we are very

---

[1] This memo and the following materials are reprinted with the permission of Bonneville Power Administration.

grateful for your contributions. To avoid confusion, please discard all earlier copies and drafts of this policy. It went through many changes.

In transmitting this final version to you, I want to respond to two issues that surfaced repeatedly in the training/consultation sessions: (1) jobrelatedness, and (2) sexual orientation.

(1) Earlier drafts described harassing conduct as being "unwelcome, inappropriate, non-job-related." That means all three conditions must be present in order for the conduct to be harassing. (In addition, the perceiver of the conduct must feel at least one of the following: "threatened, intimidated or distressed.") However, we know harassment could occur in a situation that most would agree is job-related, so in later drafts we dropped "non-job-related" as a required condition. This created some difficulty for supervisors who rightly use some pretty strenuous language and behavior in correcting an employee's behavior. But if we retained "non-job-related" in the definition, we did not want it to easily excuse what is otherwise harassing behavior. Our solution is to retain "non-job-related" but define it in a way that does not make it an easy out. Therefore, note in the policy that if conduct Is job-related It is not harassment, as long as the conduct is an acceptable part of successful job performance. (It might be okay for a foreman to yell at an apprentice who Is engaged in a procedure that could threaten injury to a crew member; whereas, such yelling might be inappropriate in a different on-the-job setting, such as in a performance appraisal interview).

(2) We were asked over and over why BPA would include sexual orientation as an example of things you cannot harass employees about, especially since it is not a basis for prohibited discrimination under the Civil Rights Act's Title VII. The answer is that this policy is about harassment, not discrimination. Anyone can be the target of harassment; and we will not tolerate it, whatever the reason. (Harassing a person because of race or religion is probably discrimination prohibited by the Civil Rights Act, but that's another matter.) Anyone working at a BPA worksite must maintain non-harassing behavior. All must get along with their fellow workers. One may personally disapprove of aspects of another's character, off-the-job behavior, or affiliations (which may include homosexuality, having an affair with a neighbor's spouse, or Communist Party membership), but that does not permit one to harass. BPA, by this policy, does not condone or condemn any such character trait, off-the-job behavior, or affiliation. Furthermore, if employees wish to network through a "Pluralism Council" (one of the recommendations of the Employee Support Sounding Board), BPA will not interfere with the operation of a "gay and lesbian" network or other networks so long as they do not interfere with job performance and the accomplishment of our mission.

> Many of you asked for guidance in the form of questions-and-answers and sample cases that would walk through analyses of potential harassment situations. We have attached such guidance.

> As I have said to nearly each and every one of you, the greater part of the responsibility for creating and sustaining a harassment-free workplace rests

with you. You have my personal support and that of the Administrator in implementing and enforcing this policy.

Purpose of this Paper

The purpose of this Paper is to provide BPA managers and supervisors with initial guidance on how to deal with potential harassment situations under BPA Is Harassment-Free Workplace Policy. The Paper is divided into General Procedures for Handling Possible Harassment Situations, and Examples of How to Handle Some Possible Harassment Situations.

Note: This Paper should never be used as a substitute for explicit guidance from upper management and/or appropriate BPA support services in specific harassment situations.

§ 5.8   General Procedures for Handling Possible Harassment Situations

In responding to a possible harassment situation, managers and supervisors first should ask themselves the following question:

Do I have enough information to find that the alleged or suspected conduct occurred?

If "No":

Obtain relevant information through personal observations and talking with potential witnesses and/or the accused.

If necessary, seek advice from within your chain of command and/or from appropriate support services.

Document your actions and findings, and go on to the next question.

If "Yes":

Go on to the next question.

Can the conduct I have found constitute harassment under the BPA Policy?

If "No":

Consult with your chain of command and/or appropriate support services for advice.

Document your actions, particularly your response to the complaining party.

If the complaining party is dissatisfied, advise the designated department.

Take immediate, appropriate, action to stop the harassment and protect/support the victim.

Document your actions, and the reasons for your actions.

Check back with the victim and the harasser periodically, and monitor the work place to ensure the person has contacted the harassment Hotline for options.

Check that no further harassment or retaliation occurs.

Determine whether training, counseling, and/or team building may help heal the work place, and obtain the necessary commitments.

If I have found harassment, is some form of discipline appropriate for the harasser?

Consult with the Employee/Labor Relations (ELR) unit and/or General Counsel (GC) unit. If you decide to impose some discipline, document your reasons for selecting a particular action.

§ 5.9 Examples of How to Handle Possible Harassment Situations

Example 1—Sexual Banter, Off-Color Racial Cartoon

Paul advises Karen, his supervisor, that he is deeply offended by his co-workers, ongoing and open sexual banter, and by a blatant anti-Japanese cartoon posted on the employee bulletin board in his section. Paul states that he has not confronted his coworkers because last year they made life miserable for a woman who complained about similar issues.

Enough Information?

Unless Karen has personally observed the sexual banter and cartoon, she must verify Paul's information through personal observation or, if necessary, interviews with relevant witnesses, including the alleged perpetrators.

Note: If the sexual banter is open and ongoing, as Paul asserts, and if the offensive cartoon is posted on the employee bulletin board, a court could find that a reasonable supervisor in Karen's position should have known about this conduct at or about the time it occurred; See "Responses to Legal Questions Concerning the Harassment-free Workplace Policy" Question L4.

Harassment under BPA's Policy?

The conduct Paul described is harassment because it is inappropriate and non-job-related, and Paul finds it unwelcome and distressing. Paul's perceptions are not unreasonable, even if others do not object to the conduct, and even if the conduct is not intended to offend Paul. This is because, in the BPA workplace, sexual banter is inappropriate if anyone finds it unwelcome, and derogatory racial commentary in any form always is inappropriate.

Immediate Action?

Karen has several options, depending on Paul's willingness to talk about his concerns and the sensitivity of Paul's coworkers to his concerns. Karen can:

- Talk with the group as a whole about what constitutes inappropriate conduct under the Policy, and help the group identify conduct that is acceptable and unacceptable, including what materials may and may not be put on bulletin boards and walls.
- Talk with Paul's coworkers, individually or as a group, and let them know that their conduct can be/is perceived as offensive under the Policy, and must stop (this includes removing the anti-Japanese cartoon from the bulletin board).
- Provide training on harassment and diversity issues to help the group understand the sensitivities of others and become more aware of the kinds of things that can be offensive.
- Assert support for the Policy and its goal to allow all employees to work in a positive environment where individuals respect one another.
- Address the importance of the work group learning to work well together, even where differences of opinion arise, and point out the inappropriateness of retaliation as a way to deal with these differences.
- Talk with Paul about what has occurred, and assure him that he will be protected from further harassment and/or retaliation.
- Advise Paul of support services, such as the Employee Assistance Program (EAP), that may be of use to him in dealing with his feelings around these harassment issues.
- Evaluate whether support services, including Mediation, may help work group members deal more effectively with these issues.
- Monitor the workplace and check with Paul *and* his coworkers periodically to ensure that the environment continues to be harassment-free.
- Document actions and reasons.

Discipline appropriate at this time?

If there is no evidence that Paul's coworkers intended to harass or demean him, and if the coworkers now appear to be sensitive to Paul's concerns, there is little reason to believe that the conduct will recur. Thus, discipline probably is not appropriate.

If the conduct was intentional harassment, or if the conduct recurs, Karen should consult with ELR and/or GC to determine whether a letter of warning or other discipline may be appropriate.

If Paul's coworkers retaliate against him (through offensive jokes, demeaning comments, sarcasm, silence, exclusion, or other means) for complaining, Karen must take some disciplinary action. This is particularly important if Karen finds that the same coworkers retaliated last year against the woman who complained of similar issues. If retaliation is allowed to occur, individuals will not come forward to report harassment in the future.

Example 2—Contractor Employee Harassed by BPA Employee

Ellen is an on-site contractor employee. She advises Marv, a BPA supervisor, that she is being sexually harassed by Bill, one of Marv's subordinates. Ellen states that she has told Bill that she is not interested in him, but he keeps hanging around her work station, pestering her for dates, and calling her at home.

Procedural complications?

Ellen's allegations involve sexual harassment by a BPA employee against a contractor employee. Therefore, Marv must not try to resolve this situation alone, because it involves some very complex issues.

Marv's first step should be to notify the appropriate Contracting Officer's Technical Representative (COTR) of the situation. The COTR then will arrange to get Ellen's contractor supervisor involved, and help orchestrate a coordinated, cooperative effort to investigate and resolve this complaint. If Marv does not know the COTR, or is unsure how to proceed, he should get help from his chain of command, administrative officer, And/or Harassment Hotline.

Marv also should encourage Ellen to contact her contractor supervisor directly, and to call the Hotline for more options on how she might want to handle the situation.

Enough information?

Unless Marv personally observed Bill's behavior, Marv must take action to verify Ellen's allegations. Marv can do this through personal observations, or through interviews with Bill and other potential witnesses. If contractor employees are to be interviewed, Marv should work through the COTR and the contractor supervisor. All of Marv's actions in dealing with this matter should be documented.

Harassment under BPA's Policy?

Bill's conduct, as described by Ellen, is harassment. Once Ellen told Bill she was not interested in his attentions, he was obligated to stop the conduct, even if he thought that she was just being coy, or that she would "come around" to him eventually.

Immediate action?

Marv must tell Bill to stop his unwelcome behavior, both inside and outside the work place. Marv should coordinate with the contractor supervisor and, if it should become necessary, with BPA Security or local law enforcement officials, to make sure that Ellen feels safe and protected as possible.

Marv also should monitor the workplace, and check back with the contractor supervisor periodically to ensure that no further harassment or retaliation is occurring. If the work environment is trained and uncomfortable for Ellen and/or Bill, it may be useful for BPA to consider some additional options. This might involve BPA approving Ellen's special use of SPA's EAP, Mediation, and/or other appropriate support services. It also might include BPA and/or the contractor exploring temporary or permanent details or transfer options.

Note: If any work related changes are contemplated, BPA should ensure that the victim (in this case, Ellen) is not pressured into accepting a move away from her current position or become disadvantaged in any other way. Any proposed employment action against Bill should be thoroughly reviewed by ELR and/or GC, and properly documented by Marv.

Discipline appropriate at this time?

If Bill was aware that his sexual advances toward Ellen were unwelcome, yet continued the behavior, some formal discipline, such as a letter of warning, may be necessary. This will ensure that Bill understands that he must take such rejections seriously.

If Bill also engaged in this behavior toward other contractors or BPA employees, it may be necessary to impose more severe discipline. This is because of the intentional, repeated nature of Bill's actions.

On the other hand, if Bill sincerely did not understand Ellen's rejections, regrets his unwelcome behavior, and has not engaged in similar behavior toward others, Marv may conclude that discipline is inappropriate. Marv should make this decision about discipline only after consulting with ELR, GC, and other Appropriate chain of command and support personnel.

Example 3—Abusive/Demeaning Management Style

Keith, an EPA manager, is known for his abrupt and volatile manner. Although he often is supportive of his subordinates, he can be openly cruel. For example, he periodically humiliates subordinates who have not performed up to his standards by shouting at them in a loud, strident, and abusive manner, often in front of other managers, supervisors, and employees.

It is apparent at meetings that some of Keith's subordinates are unwilling to speak up in front of him, and several currently are seeking transfers to other areas.

Enough information?

Because Keith's humiliation of subordinates is open, ongoing, and public, other managers and supervisors reasonably should know about his conduct.

Harassment under BPA's Policy?

Keith's abusive management style is harassment because it is unwelcome, inappropriate, and non-job-related, and it causes employees to feel threatened, intimidated, and/or distressed. The fact that Keith's behavior may be in response to his subordinates' perceived job-related deficiencies does not make the behavior appropriate or acceptable under BPA's Policy. This is because the behavior shows Keith's lack of respect for his subordinates, and negatively affects the ability of these subordinates to perform their duties.

Immediate action?

Any manager or supervisor who observes Keith's conduct has an obligation to take immediate action and document it. Depending on the manager's or supervisor's relationship with, and position relative to, Keith, that action could include:

- Alerting Keith's supervisor to his behavior, and its effect on the workplace.
- Discussing the matter with the Hotline, the EEO Office, or another manager or supervisor, and getting help on available options.
- Discussing with Keith his behavior and BPA's Policy, helping him see why he should stop, and perhaps referring him to support services.

Discipline appropriate at this time?

As a manager, Keith has the primary responsibility to create and sustain a harassment-free work environment within his work group. His actions to the contrary seriously affect BPA's ability to carry out its Policy.

Therefore, BPA management must take effective action to stop Keith's behavior so that employees will perceive that management is supportive of the Policy.

Management should consider the following options:

Counsel Keith and provide him, with appropriate training on how to manage effectively.

Provide Keith with the opportunity for EAP counseling to help him control his outbursts.

Address Keith's behavior as a conduct problem and issue him a letter of warning or other discipline.

Address Keith's behavior as a performance problem, rate him appropriately for his management shortcomings, and establish a performance improvement plan.

Relieve Keith of his supervisory responsibilities.

Involve Keith and his work group in team building sessions that deal with, and help heal, the effects of Keith's negative management style.

In addition, BPA management must hold accountable those managers and supervisors who were aware of, but failed to take action to stop, Keith's harassment of his subordinates. Accountability can come in the form of counseling or discipline, as discussed above.

Example 4—Employee Request for Confidentiality

Mike, a lineman, approaches Steve, his former supervisor, and asks if they can talk privately. Mike says that he needs some advice about how to handle a problem he has been having with some members of his new crew. Mike makes it clear that he wants his concerns to stay private. When Steve agrees to talk with Mike privately, Mike describes a situation that could be harassment under BPA's Policy.

Procedural complications?

As a supervisor, Steve is obligated under the BPA Policy to take action when he knows or suspects that harassment has occurred. Mike's request for privacy cannot change that obligation, nor can Steve's initial agreement to keep Mike's concerns private.

Steve should discuss his obligation with Mike, and try to obtain Mike's consent to let Steve deal with the problem as confidentially as possible. If the problem is not severe and/or life threatening, Steve may want to talk to Mike about how he wants to handle the problem. If Mike wants to try to deal with the problem himself, Steve should give him a brief period of time to do that, while closely monitoring what happens and documenting his actions.

If the problem is indeed harassment, and it is not resolved within a short time, Steve will have to take further action. This must include notifying Mike's supervisor of what had occurred, and may also include getting guidance from the chain of command, administrative officer, Harassment Hotline, and/or other support services.

Enough information?

Because Steve is not the supervisor for Mike's crew, he could reasonably leave any investigation of Mike's concerns to Mike's supervisor. Nevertheless, it may be useful for Steve to observe what Mike has described, if possible, particularly if Mike is trying to handle it himself. This may later be helpful to Mike's supervisor if he becomes engaged in the situation. He could then rely on Steve's observations, and not call as much attention to Mike, in dealing with the situation.

Immediate action?

For Steve, immediate action may consist of getting enough information from Mike to understand the situation and his concerns, helping Mike find the best way to resolve the problems with his new crew, monitoring the outcome, and documenting his actions.

Discipline?

As in other examples, discipline for any alleged harassers will depend on whether harassment occurred, the intent of the harassers, the harassers' willingness to conform their conduct, to what is required by the Policy, and other relevant factors that can be addressed by Mike's supervisor with help from ELR and GC.

Example 5—Supervisor Knowledge; Religious Harassment; Diversity

Michelle's supervisor overhears a group of her employees complaining loudly about "stupid Ruth's stupid objections" to having Christmas decorations in the office, and how she has ruined the holiday season for everyone. Ruth is not present, and Michelle does not know if Ruth has heard these complaints from her coworkers.

Enough information?

Michelle personally has observed comments in the work place that are demeaning and derogatory toward Ruth because of her religious or other beliefs. Because Michelle is a supervisor and the potential for harassment is high, she must take action at this point.

Harassment under BPA's Policy?

The demeaning and derogatory comments about Ruth and her beliefs indicate that a harassment situation may exist. The fact that a whole group of coworkers, rather than just a single coworker, is complaining can make the comments more threatening, intimidating, or distressing to Ruth.

Although the comments reasonably relate to the group's work environment, they are inappropriate and non-job-related because they are destructive to a positive work environment where people respect one another, and they have nothing to do with job performance. The fact that Ruth may not be present at the time the comments are made does not mean that she may not be disadvantaged as a result of this behavior. Michelle may surmise that such comments could not be welcomed by Ruth.

The potential for harassment is extremely high.

Immediate action?

Michelle should consider the following options:

- Talk with the group, confer with group members individually, about the conduct and its potential affect on Ruth and the work environment.
- Get advice from support services, including EEO, ELR, and EAP, about how to handle the diversity aspect of religious observances.
- Talk with Ruth to understand her feelings about the Christmas decorations, determine whether she is aware of the group's conduct, and find out what she is comfortable doing in terms of a group discussion about this issue.
- Facilitate, or get someone from Human Resources or Mediation to facilitate, a discussion with the whole work group about diversity issues, being sure that everyone is heard.

- Attempt to work out a middle ground that will allow each member of the work group to feel that his/her religious beliefs are honored and respected during holiday seasons.
- Document actions.

Discipline appropriate at this time?

If the group is amenable to these discussions, and to greater sensitivity toward differences, there is no need for any disciplinary action. If the group remains hostile toward Ruth, or takes action to harass or alienate her because of her beliefs, some discipline is appropriate. Michelle should consult with ELR before taking such action.

Example 6—Offensive Comments at Customer Work Site

Kathleen, a new program manager, regularly must attend meetings at customer offices. At one meeting, a customer representative tells stories about his recent trip to San Francisco and all the "queers" he saw. During the meeting, two customer representatives make offensive comments about local Indian tribes and their inability to handle "wampum" and fire water. Kathleen, the only woman and the only person of color at the meeting, decides not to respond to these comments. When she returns to BPA, she tells Greg, her supervisor, what happened, and asks how she can handle this. Greg acknowledges that he has heard similar comments during the meetings he has attended with the same customer.

Enough information?

While the specific information that Kathleen presented must be verified, Greg's similar experiences over time reasonably suggest that Greg has enough information at this time to take action. Because Kathleen has asked for Greg's advice in how to handle the situation, Greg should find out if Kathleen wants guidance in how to confront the offenders, or if she wants him to intervene on her behalf.

Harassment under BPA's Policy?

The offensive comments Kathleen described about gays and American Indians constitute harassment under the Policy, even though the comments were made off BPA premises by non-BPA employees. This is because, at the time of the comments, Kathleen was engaged in work-related activity for SPA.

Immediate action?

Because these are customer actions at a customer facility, BPA has no direct control. Greg should check with his chain of command, administrative officer, Harassment Hotline, and/or the COTR (if BPA has a program contract relationship with this customer) regarding how he and/or Kathleen best can handle this situation. If Kathleen wants to try to deal with it herself, Greg should monitor the situation carefully and intervene only if necessary, and/or if Kathleen asks him to intervene. Such intervention could include a telephone call to the customer, with a follow-up letter enclosing a copy of the BPA Policy.

If the customer does not respond appropriately to Kathleen or Greg, Greg should notify his next level manager so that additional steps can be taken. Until the situation is resolved, Greg should give Kathleen the option of having a substitute cover this customer meeting.

Discipline appropriate at this time?

BPA has no authority to take disciplinary action to encourage the customer to conform its representative's conduct to the BPA Policy. However, BPA can make the customer, its officers, and/or its board of directors aware of the problems that the behavior causes for BPA and its employees.

Example 7—Retaliation

Six months ago Evan told Sharon, his supervisor, that he was very distressed with the way she "harassed" and "bad mouthed" certain employees during meetings. Sharon stopped her behavior, but since that time, Evan has noticed that Sharon has become very cool toward him. She seldom gives him the good assignments he used to get, and she frequently does not include him in important discussions and meetings. Recently, Sharon told Evan that she could not recommend him for a training class that he had been scheduled to attend because his work quality had dropped. Evan believes that Sharon is retaliating against him, and has approached Sharon's supervisor, Dan, with this information.

Enough information?

Unless Dan has personally observed the described changes in Sharon's behavior toward Evan, he must verify Evan's allegations. Dan also must determine whether Evan's work assignments have changed and, if so, whether there is a work-related reason for any change. Dan can do this through talking with Sharon and relevant witnesses. He also can review the work assignments and work performance of individuals in Sharon's work group.

Harassment under BPA's Policy?

The conduct Evan described is retaliation if Sharon is acting because of Evan's harassment complaint. Regardless of how Sharon feels about the complaint or its merit, she may not use the complaint to affect adversely his work assignments and work environment.

Immediate action?

If Dan determines that retaliation has occurred, he must take action to stop it, correct its effects, and prevent its recurrence. He can do this by ensuring that Evan is:

- Given appropriate job assignments and training opportunities.
- Provided with relevant experiences he may have lost because of retaliation.
- Rated fairly on his performance appraisal.
- Included in all appropriate discussions and meetings, and protected from any further retaliation, including isolation and exclusion.

In addition, Dan should consider one or more of the following:

- Counseling Sharon about her conduct, and determining whether discipline is appropriate, given the conduct and Sharon's status as a supervisor.
- Providing Sharon with training on harassment issues and supervisory skills.
- Monitoring Sharon's future treatment of Evan.
- Bringing in a Human Resources professional to do team building or "healing" within the work group.
- Relieving Sharon of her supervisory duties.

Discipline?

As in other examples, discipline will depend on many factors.
Dan should consult with ELR and GC before taking action.

CHAPTER 6

SEXUAL HARASSMENT TRAINING

§ 6.1   **The Preventive Role of Training**

§ 6.2   **Sexual Harassment Awareness Training**

§ 6.3   **Sexual Harassment Videos**

§ 6.4   **Management Training**

§ 6.5   **Sample Training Programs**

§ 6.1 The Preventive Role of Training

It has been widely acknowledged that it is difficult to define sexual harassment. This problem is reflected in the judicial system, where the "reasonable person" standard has been replaced by the so-called "reasonable woman" standard and then recast as the "reasonable person in the same situation as the plaintiff" standard. As one litigator has aptly stated it, it comes down to the reasonable judge standard. The point is that there is very little agreement on what constitutes sexual harassment, even among "reasonable" men and women, beyond the overt, blatant variety which is less frequent than more subtle forms. The Supreme Court has acknowledged that sexual harassment has both an objective and a subjective component to it. For employers, the challenge of training employees in what constitutes sexual harassment and what conduct to avoid/prohibit is made all the more difficult by the lack of clear guidance. Training is an opportunity for employers to educate employees on how to recognize and prevent harassment, as well as how to make and resolve complaints.

§ 6.2 Sexual Harassment Awareness Training

Because of the difficulty in defining sexual harassment, many employers approach the training from an "awareness" perspective. This approach is premised on the belief that if employees and managers are sensitized to the issues involved with sexual harassment, they will make efforts to question their behavior and that of others if it could possibly be construed as offensive or could be found illegal. While there is no magic to the order in which material is covered, there should be a rationale to how you choose to unfold the training. Some preliminary recommendations include the following:

- Employees attending sexual harassment training sessions are nervous and uncomfortable. There may be some initial outbursts of nervous laughter or some jokes made by participants to attempt to lighten things up.

This behavior is usually not a reflection of the participants' level of regard for the seriousness of the session, but rather a release of nervous tension. The trainer may want to be prepared with a statement reaffirming the firm's commitment to educating employees and to prevention, without necessarily stifling the initial giggles or comments (as long as they are not potentially offensive to others) as some employees will interpret the trainer's silence as agreement and will feel that the environment is intimidating.

- Consider whether to have a man and a woman lead each session. This can be an effective strategy to lend balance to the session.
- Carefully review the decision to videotape a session. While this can be a useful training tool, it may cause some participants to withdraw.
- Be aware that men often come into sexual harassment training sessions prepared for "male bashing." This can be addressed early by emphasizing that men and women can be harassed and by including some such scenarios in the training program.
- Consider cautiously the decision to train management and nonmanagement employees together. The advantages to training employees of all levels together is that everyone will be reading the same materials and nonmanagement employees have the benefit of witnessing first-hand that management has knowledge of how to properly handle such matters. Disadvantages include:

The risks that managers in the session will *not* be knowledgeable and will show their ignorance to employees who report to them or even make comments that can exacerbate an environment that is already hostile.

Nonmanagement employees may feel intimidated and not free to ask questions, particularly about incidents they feel management may not have handled appropriately, even if using hypotheticals.

- Make sure that top management support is secured and communicated prior to rolling out a training program. This will help the trainer to respond to resistant participants such as those who think that the training is a waste of time pulling them away from revenue-generating endeavors or that the training dredges up things that are better left buried.
- Consider having a phased roll-out of training whereby a few groups are trained at a time and then there is a waiting period during which feedback about the sessions can be received and changes made to the programs as warranted. The feedback should probably not be in writing but obtained informally in meetings and by telephone. Some of the comments received could be damaging to the organization if written and later used in litigation.
- Formulate a strategy and program goals at the outset. The goals will vary depending, in part, on how well-informed employees are on the subjects of harassment and discrimination generally. In some organizations, this is new information and the goals will be to inform employees about the basics, such as, what is harassment, how complaints are made and resolved, employee responsibility, and so forth. In other firms where the awareness concerning harassment is greater, one of the goals might be to offer an additional phase of learning such as assertiveness training, coaching and counseling, witness interviewing skills, use of gender neutral language, and managing diversity. For organization located in states that require training, one of the goals is compliance. (See **Form 6-1** for Connecticut Posting and Training Requirements as an example.)
- Select and train trainers carefully. Before implementing and training, ensure that the trainers themselves are sensitized to the issues that are likely to be raised in sessions, to the organization's strategy, and are well-versed in the organization's sexual harassment policy and procedures, disciplinary process, and all applicable laws.

The University of California-Davis uses sexual harassment advisors to act as mediators in sexual harassment complaints, and are an informal alternative to making a formal complaint in departments. They are located in various units throughout the campus and Medical Center. According to the University of California-Davis guidelines for the function of an advisor, each advisor must possess a high level of commitment to assisting victims of sexual harassment, have sufficient personal and organizational power to be effective and must be viewed as fair and objective. In addition, they must

- learn policy and laws related to sexual harassment and communicate them accurately to others

FORM 6-1
CONNECTICUT POSTING & TRAINING REQUIREMENTS

Regulations for
Sexual Harassment Posting &
Training Requirements

Regulations of Connecticut State Agencies
Sections 46a-54-200 — 46a-54-207
Effective February 24, 1993

Connecticut Commission on
Human Rights & Opportunities
90 Washington Street, Hartford, CT 06106
203/566-3350

Reprinted with permission.

Sexual Harassment Posting & Training Regulations

Effective Feb. 24, 1993

Section 46a-54-200. Definitions

For purposes of sections 46a-54-200 through 46a-54-207, inclusive:

(a) "Sexual Harassment" means any unwelcome sexual advances or requests for sexual favors or any conduct of a sexual nature when 1) submission to such conduct is made either explicitly or implicitly a term or condition of an individual's employment, 2) submission to or rejection of such conduct by an individual is used as the basis for employment decisions affecting such individual, or 3) such conduct has the purpose or effect of substantially interfering with an individual's work performance or creating an intimidating, hostile or offensive working environment.

(b) "Employer" includes the state and all political subdivisions thereof, including the General Assembly, and means any person or employer with three or more persons in his employ.

(c) "Employer Having Fifty or More Employees" means the state and all political subdivisions thereof, including the General Assembly, and means any person or employer who has a total of fifty or more persons, including supervisory and managerial employees and partners, in his employ for a minimum of thirteen weeks during the previous training year.

(d) "Employee" means any person employed by an employer, but shall not include any individual employed by his parents, spouse or child, or in the domestic service of any person.

(e) "Supervisory Employee" means any individual who has the authority, by using her or his independent judgment, in the interest of the employer, to hire, transfer, suspend, lay off, recall, promote, discharge, assign, reward or discipline other employees, or responsibility to direct them, or to adjust their grievances or effectively to recommend such actions.

(f) "Commission" means the Commission on Human Rights and Opportunities created by section 46a-52 of the Connecticut General Statutes.

(g) "Training year" means the period of time from October first in any calendar year through September thirtieth in the following calendar year.

Section 46a-54-201. Posting Requirement For Employers Having Three Or More Employees

(a) Employers with three or more employees must post notices to employees concerning the illegality of sexual harassment and remedies available to victims of sexual harassment.

(b) Such information shall include, but is not limited to:

(1) The statutory definition of sexual harassment and examples of different types of sexual harassment;

(2) Notice that sexual harassment is prohibited by the State of Connecticut's Discriminatory Employment Practices Law, subdivision (8) of subsection (a) of section 46a-60 of the Connecticut General Statutes;

(3) Notice that sexual harassment is prohibited by Title VII of the 1964 Civil Rights Act, as amended, 42 United States Code section 2000e et. seq.; and

(4) The remedies available, including but not limited to:

(A) Cease and desist orders,

(B) Back pay,

(C) Compensatory damages, and

(D) Hiring, promotion or reinstatement;

(5) Language to the effect that persons who commit sexual harassment may be subject to civil or criminal penalties;

(6) The address and telephone number of the Connecticut Commission on Human Rights and Opportunities; and

(7) A statement that Connecticut law requires that a formal written complaint be filed with the Commission within one hundred and eighty days of the date when the alleged sexual harassment occurred; and

(8) Any and all notices so posted will have the heading, "**SEXUAL HARASSMENT IS ILLEGAL,**" in large bold-faced type.

(c) The Commission strongly recommends, but does not require, that the poster include:

Sexual Harassment Posting & Training Regulations

(1) A statement concerning the employer's policies and procedures regarding sexual harassment and a statement concerning the disciplinary action that may be taken if sexual harassment has been committed; and

(2) A contact person at the place of employment to whom one can report complaints of sexual harassment or direct questions or concerns regarding sexual harassment;

(d) A model poster is appended to these regulations, labeled Appendix A.

Section 46a-54-202. Where To Post

Employers must place, and keep posted, notices in prominent and accessible locations upon its premises where notices to employees are customarily posted. Notices must be posted at each employer facility in such a manner that all employees and applicants at that facility will have the opportunity to see the notices on a regular basis.

Section 46a-54-203. When To Post

(a) All employers with three or more employees shall post notices as soon as practicable after the effective date of these regulations, but no later than forty-five (45) days after the effective date of these regulations.

(b) An employer shall promptly replace notices that are removed, destroyed or defaced.

Section 46a-54-204. Posting And Training Requirements For Employers Having Fifty Or More Employees

(a) An employer having fifty (50) or more employees shall comply with the posting requirements set forth in sections 46a-54-200 through 46a-54-207, inclusive.

(b) An employer having fifty (50) or more employees must also provide two hours of training and education to all supervisory employees of employees in the State of Connecticut no later than October 1, 1993 and to all new supervisory employees of employees in the State of Connecticut within six months of their assumption of a supervisory position. Nothing in these regulations shall prohibit an employer from providing more than two hours of training and education.

(c) Such training and education shall be conducted in a classroom - like setting, using clear and understandable language and in a format that allows participants to ask questions and receive answers. Audio, video and other teaching aides may be utilized to increase comprehension or to otherwise enhance the training process.

(1) The content of the training shall include the following:

(A) Describing the federal and state statutory provisions prohibiting sexual harassment in the work place with which the employer is required to comply, including, but not limited to, the Connecticut discriminatory employment practices statute (section 46a-60 of the Connecticut General Statutes) and Title VII of the Civil Rights Act of 1964, as amended (42 U.S.C. section 2000e, and following sections);

(B) Defining sexual harassment as explicitly set forth in subdivision (8) of subsection (a) of section 46a-60 of the Connecticut General Statutes and as distinguished from other forms of illegal harassment prohibited by subsection (a) of section 46a-60 of the Connecticut General Statutes and section 3 of Public Act 91-58;

(C) Discussing the types of conduct that may constitute sexual harassment under the law, including the fact that the harasser or the victim of harassment may be either a man or a woman and that harassment can occur involving persons of the same or opposite sex;

(D) Describing the remedies available in sexual harassment cases, including, but not limited to, cease and desist orders; hiring, promotion or reinstatement; compensatory damages and back pay;

(E) Advising employees that individuals who commit acts of sexual harassment may be subject to both civil and criminal penalties; and

(F) Discussing strategies to prevent sexual harassment in the work place.

(2) While not exclusive, the training may also include, but is not limited to, the following elements:

(A) Informing training participants that all complaints of sexual harassment must be taken seriously, and that once a complaint is made, supervisory employees should report it immediately to officials designated by the employer, and that the contents of the complaint are personal and confidential and are not to be disclosed except to those persons with a need to know;

(B) Conducting experiential exercises such as role playing, coed group discussions and behavior modeling to facilitate understanding of what constitutes sexual harassment and how to prevent it;

(C) Teaching the importance of interpersonal skills such as listening and bringing participants to understand what a person who is sexually harassed may be experiencing;

(D) Advising employees of the importance of preventive strategies to avoid the negative effects sexual harassment has upon both the victim and the overall productivity of the work place due to interpersonal conflicts, poor performance, absenteeism, turnover and grievances;

(E) Explaining the benefits of learning about and eliminating sexual harassment, which include a more positive work environment with greater productivity and potentially lower exposure to liability, in that employers--and supervisors personally--have been held liable when it is shown that they knew or should have known of the harassment;

(F) Explaining the employer's policy against sexual harassment, including a description of the procedures available for reporting instances of sexual harassment and the types of disciplinary actions which can and will be taken against persons who have been found to have engaged in sexual harassment; and

(G) Discussing the perceptual and communication differences among all persons and, in this context, the concepts of "reasonable woman" and "reasonable man" developed in federal sexual harassment cases.

(d) While not required by these regulations, the Commission encourages an employer having fifty (50) or more employees to provide an update of legal interpretations and related developments concerning sexual harassment to supervisory personnel once every three (3) years.

Section 46a-54-205. Effect Of Prior Training

An employer is not required to train supervisory personnel who have received training after October 1, 1991 that:

(1) substantially complies with the required content of the training set forth in subsection (c)(1) of section 46a-54-204; and

(2) was provided in a classroom setting and lasted at least two hours.

Section 46a-54-206. Trainers

An employer required to provide training by these regulations may utilize individuals employed by the employer or other persons who agree to provide the required training, with or without reimbursement.

Section 46a-54-207. Recordkeeping

(a) The Commission encourages each employer required to conduct training pursuant to Public Act 92-85 to maintain records concerning all training provided.

(b) Such records may include, but are not limited to:

(1) documents sufficient to show the content of the training given, such as the curriculum;

(2) the names, addresses and qualifications of the personnel conducting the training;

(3) the names and titles of the personnel trained and the date or dates that each individual was trained;

(c) The Commission encourages employers to maintain any such records for a minimum of one year, or if a discriminatory practice complaint is filed involving personnel trained, until such time as such complaint is finally resolved.

- attend regularly scheduled Sexual Harassment Advisor education programs
- develop annual goals and an educational program for the unit or department and submits them to the Sexual Harassment Education Director or Coordinator in coordination with the unit head
- provides in-service education on sexual harassment to departments, utilizing the assistance of the Sexual Harassment Education Director or UCDMC Coordinator when necessary
- functions as a resource and referral person for questions and/or problems concerning sexual harassment

The skills, knowledge and ability of Advisors should, include:

- sensitivity to women and men, and knowledge of gender issues
- sensitivity to and knowledge of gay, lesbian, and bisexual issues
- ability to initiate and conduct interviews and thorough investigations
- utilize appropriate techniques in mediation and negotiation
- knowledge of sexual harassment issues
- knowledge of when to refer complainant/accused to other resources
- awareness and understanding of the cultural diversity, political, and/or traditional practices of the campus community
- strategic and problem-solving ability
- ability to confront
- ability to manage multiple roles (for example, that of advisor, mediator, and investigator)
- ability to coordinate training programs within designated unit
- deals objectively and compassionately with emotionally distressed individuals
- ability to learn laws and policies about sexual harassmemt
- ability to write clearly and keep accurate records
- ability to maintain confidentiality

Awareness of Consequences

The best way to gain and retain the attention of employees in training them on being more aware of sexual harassment is to explain how they can be personally impacted by their failure to take the matter seriously. This can begin with a review of the organization's policy, values, commitment, as well as all of the pertinent laws and regulations.

A review of the consequences for employees can include:

- Potential disciplinary action, up to and including termination
- Becoming involved in a lawsuit or agency enforcement action, either as a witness or as an individual respondent
- Suffering embarrassment and loss of reputation in the community/at work
- Permanent career damage, loss of future career opportunities
- Loss of income and inability to collect unemployment benefits.

Cite specific instances within the company of employees who have suffered from their failure to become more aware of consequences of their conduct or that of their subordinates. Draw on situations from higher and lower levels of the organization (make sure that they accurately reflect the organization's practice).

Don't Forget the Victims

Review the consequences to men and women victimized by sexual harassment:

- They quit or are unjustly fired from their job (economic and professional consequences)
- They suffer emotional pain, humiliation and loss of self-esteem
- Their pain and suffering impacts their entire family
- Their career can suffer a setback
- They lose faith in the company and in their colleagues

There may be a fine line between examining the range of consequences to sexual harassment victims and the perception that employees who raise a concern will be adversely impacted. This might be a good point at which to raise the importance of dealing with sexual harassment immediately rather than letting it get to the point where it can have a destructive impact on all involved. It is also a good time to emphasize that the organization attempts to minimize the negative impact of sexual harassment on victims who report it by maintaining confidentiality as circumstances permit, by prohibiting retaliation and offering protection from further abuse by suspending the harasser or otherwise separating the harasser and victim.

Awareness of Sexual Harassment Behavior

Once you have raised the level of interest around the consequences of sexual harassment, it seems only fair to next define what behavior can constitute sexual harassment—in practice and in theory. It is important to remind the audience up front that there is no clear-cut guidance and that the determination of whether behavior is harassive or not is highly circumstantial. This can be reinforced by the use of "quizzes" or "role play" where participants are confronted with simulated or real situations and asked to determine if they constitute sexual harassment. **Forms 6-2** and **6-3** illustrates such training tools. The correct answer should almost always be "maybe, depending on the circumstances."

There are usually no right or wrong answers as to what is sexual harassment outside of the blatant situations that are easily identified. While the author wishes to provide as much information as possible to readers, it is best to have in-house or outside counsel work with you on responses to the questionaire that they are comfortable with as they can vary depending on state and local laws. The goal of the training is to raise awareness of what could be considered sexual harassment, not to make employees legal or psychological experts. Where there are situations that more likely than not would be considered sexual harassment, this can be indicated by the trainer. Likewise, where case scenarios are drawn from arbitrations or court cases where the outcome was a finding of sexual harassment, this can be indicated.

In addition, no training on sexual harassment behavior would be complete without some discussion of body language. According to psychology experts like Deborah Tannen and Tuan Nguyen, men and women interpret body language differently. For employees to learn more about this topic, consider not only discussing the theory, but also using role plays to explore the typical way that men and women interpet certain behavior. Likewise, employees should be explained the firm's protocol, if any, on when and how, if ever, touching in the workplace might be appropriate. (The standard is generally whether it is job-related such as when certain jobs require some physical contact.)

Focus groups or surveys can be used to help the organization to identify how effectively it is dealing with sexual harassment and those problem areas that need to be addressed through training. There is a significant risk associated with running focus groups on sexual harassment, the session must be carefully planned and run in such a way as to avoid the disclosure of specific incidents and allegations. This is a delicate process, and given the emotional nature of the topic, even the most experienced facilitator may not be able to keep a participant from blurting out an alleged violator's name or declaring him or herself a victim. If this risk can be managed, focus groups with a good cross-section of employees from across the organization can offer a valuable data-gathering opportunity, a multi-dimensional approach that is ostensibly far richer than a pencil and paper approach.

Training is usually best handled with the aid of a video to demonstrate scenarios of prohibited conduct and appropriate resolutions. What follows

FORM 6-2

CONFIDENTIAL SEXUAL HARASSMENT QUESTIONNAIRE

CONFIDENTIAL SEXUAL HARASSMENT QUESTIONNAIRE

Situation (Part A)	Would it be Sexual Harassment?		Are you currently aware of or have you recently observed this behavior within the organization?		
	Yes	No	Yes	Uncertain	No
1. Mr. (Ms.) X (Supervisor) habitually posts cartoons on a central bulletin board containing sexual related materials.	Yes	No	Yes	Uncertain	No
2. Mr. (Ms.) X (Supervisor) constantly tells sexually related jokes to female (male) subordinates. They seem to share his sense of humor.	Yes	No	Yes	Uncertain	No
3. Mr. (Ms.) X (Supervisor) asks a female (male) subordinate for a date which she (he) willing accepts.	Yes	No	Yes	Uncertain	No
4. Mr. (Ms.) X (Supervisor) enjoys patting or pinching female (male) subordinates as a way of providing encouragement.	Yes	No	Yes	Uncertain	No
5. Mr. (Ms.) X (Supervisor) kisses a female (male) subordinate on the cheek when wishing her (him) a happy birthday.	Yes	No	Yes	Uncertain	No

1

2

		Yes	No	Uncertain	Yes	No
6.	Mr. (Ms.) X (Supervisor) often touches subordinates on the shoulder when talking to them.	Yes	No	Uncertain	Yes	No
7.	Mr. (Ms.) X (Supervisor) brushes up against a female (male) subordinate whenever he (she) passes by her (him) in the hallway.	Yes	No	Uncertain	Yes	No
8.	Mr. (Ms.) X (Supervisor) terminates a female (male) subordinate for not complying with his (her) requests for sexual favors. He (she) has recently given the subordinate a positive performance appraisal.	Yes	No	Uncertain	Yes	No

Situation (Part A)	Would it be Sexual Harassment?		Are you currently aware of or have you recently observed this behavior within the organization?		
	Yes	No	Yes	Uncertain	No
9. Mr. (Ms.) X (Supervisor) has on several occasions, had sexual intercourse with a female (male) subordinate on and off company premises.	Yes	No	Yes	Uncertain	No
10. Mr. (Ms.) X (Supervisor) posts a wall calendar in his (her) office that shows female (male) models clad in skimpy swim suits.	Yes	No	Yes	Uncertain	No
11. Mr. (Ms.) X (Supervisor) denies a raise to a female (male) subordinate soon after he (she) is turned down on a request to meet for dinner.	Yes	No	Yes	Uncertain	No
12. Mr. (Ms.) X (Supervisor) has a habit of staring at a female (male) subordinate whenever she (he) walks past his (her) desk.	Yes	No	Yes	Uncertain	No
13. Mr. (Ms.) X (Supervisor) in the presence of others often asks a female (male) secretary to "Be a good girl (boy) and get the coffee."	Yes	No	Yes	Uncertain	No
14. Mr. (Ms.) X (Supervisor) habitually calls all female employees "sweetie" or "honey."	Yes	No	Yes	Uncertain	No

3

4

	Yes	No	Uncertain	Yes	No
15. Mr. (Ms.) X (Supervisor) takes the female (male) secretary to lunch on "Secretaries' Day."	Yes	No	Uncertain	Yes	No
16. Mr. (Ms.) X (Supervisor) often asks a female (male) employee for her (his) opinion regarding issues such as sex education courses taught in the public schools in their town.	Yes	No	Uncertain	Yes	No
17. Mr. (Ms.) X (Supervisor) recommends that a female (male) subordinate wear revealing attire at work because a particular client likes people to be dressed that way.	Yes	No	Uncertain	Yes	No

Situation (Part A)	Would it be Sexual Harassment?		Are you currently aware of or have you recently observed this behavior within the organization?		
18. Mr. (Ms.) X (Supervisor) fails to promote a female (male) subordinate for not granting sexual favors.	Yes	No	Yes	Uncertain	No
19. Mr. (Ms.) X (Supervisor) sends the book, "Joy of Sex" to a female (male) subordinate as a gag gift.	Yes	No	Yes	Uncertain	No
20. Mr. (Ms.) X (Supervisor) invites a female (male) subordinate to accompany him (her) to a two-day business meeting in another city.	Yes	No	Yes	Uncertain	No
21. Mr. X (Supervisor) seems to lean and peer over the back of a female employee whenever she wears a low cut dress.	Yes	No	Yes	Uncertain	No
22. Mr. (Ms.) X (Supervisor) tells a female (male) job applicant that she (he) won't be hired unless she (he) agrees to have sexual intercourse.	Yes	No	Yes	Uncertain	No
23. Mr. X (Supervisor) frequently rolls up the sleeves on his long sleeve shirt at meetings attended by female subordinates.	Yes	No	Yes	Uncertain	No

6

	Yes	No	Uncertain	Yes	No
24. Mr. (Ms.) X (Supervisor) gives a subordinate a substantial raise even though she (he) has repeatedly rejected the bosses' sexual overtures. The secretary files a grievance charging sexual harassment.	Yes	No	Uncertain	Yes	No
25. Mr. (Ms.) X (Supervisor) gives a female (male) subordinate a nice present on her (his) birthday.	Yes	No	Uncertain	Yes	No
26. Mr. (Ms.) X (Supervisor) asks a female employee to massage his (her) shoulders.	Yes	No	Uncertain	Yes	No

Situation (Part A)	Would it be Sexual Harassment?			Are you currently aware of or have you recently observed this behavior within the organization?	
	Yes	No	Uncertain	Yes	No
27. Mr. X (Supervisor) looks up the skirt of female subordinate who often wears her skirts short. He has not made remarks or improper advances toward her.	Yes	No	Uncertain	Yes	No
28. Mr. (Ms.) X (Supervisor) follows a female (male) subordinate into the women's (men's) bathroom.	Yes	No	Uncertain	Yes	No
29. Mr. X (Supervisor) frequently walks around the work area where women are present with his fly unzipped.	Yes	No	Uncertain	Yes	No
30. Mr. (Ms.) X (Supervisor) invites a female (male) subordinate to meet him (her) at a bar which features female (male) exotic dancers.	Yes	No	Uncertain	Yes	No
31. Mr. X (Supervisor) takes his shirt off while playing volleyball at a company party. Female employees are playing volleyball too.	Yes	No	Uncertain	Yes	No

7

	Yes	No	Uncertain	Yes	No
32. Mr. (Ms.) X (Supervisor) likes to play comedy tapes that feature obscene language and jokes that are clearly derogatory toward the opposite sex. Female (male) subordinates can hear the radio through the thin walls but, to-date, nobody has complained.	Yes	No	Uncertain	Yes	No
33. Mr. X (Supervisor) is writing a memo and asks a female secretary how to spell the word, "brassiere."	Yes	No	Uncertain	Yes	No
34. Mr. (Ms.) X (Supervisor) stands very close to a female (male) subordinate whenever talking to her (him).	Yes	No	Uncertain	Yes	No

Situation (Part A)	Would it be Sexual Harassment?		Are you currently aware of or have you recently observed this behavior within the organization?		
35. Mr. X (Supervisor) hires an authentic belly dancer to perform at the firm's Christmas party attended by all employees.	Yes	No	Yes	Uncertain	No
36. Mr. (Ms.) X (Supervisor) invites a female (male) subordinate and a few of her (his) friends to come over to his (her) apartment for a hot tub party.	Yes	No	Yes	Uncertain	No
37. Mr. (Ms.) X (Supervisor) repeatedly asks a female (male) employee about her (his) love life.	Yes	No	Yes	Uncertain	No
38. Mr. (Ms.) X (Supervisor) sends his (her) secretary a birthday card that features a backside view of a naked person.	Yes	No	Yes	Uncertain	No
39. Mr. (Ms.) X (Supervisor) tells a female (male) employee that she (he) must wear tight clothing for safety reasons.	Yes	No	Yes	Uncertain	No

10

No

Yes

Uncertain

Yes   No

40. Mr. (Ms.) X (Supervisor) walks up to a group of subordinates who are talking about sexual harassment and jokingly says, "I wish someone would harass me."

Situation (Part B)	Would it be Sexual Harassment?			Are you currently aware of or have you recently observed this behavior within the organization?	
1. A male clerk asks a female clerk for a date which she refuses. He decides to keep asking until she says yes.	Yes	No	Uncertain	Yes	No
2. Male (female) workers whistle every time female (male) employees walk by their work area.	Yes	No	Uncertain	Yes	No
3. A married female employee and a married male employee are having an affair.	Yes	No	Uncertain	Yes	No
4. Male employees repeatedly use vulgar language when talking to each other. Two female employees often overhear what is said and find it offensive.	Yes	No	Uncertain	Yes	No
5. A male repair technician who works for another firm asks female employees for dates every time he comes to repair equipment. They always say no but he persists anyway.	Yes	No	Uncertain	Yes	No

FORM 6-3
TEXAS COMMISSION ON HUMAN RIGHTS TRAINING WORKBOOK

TEXAS COMMISSION ON HUMAN RIGHTS
SEXUAL HARASSMENT
COMPLIANCE WITH EQUAL EMPLOYMEMT OPPORTUNITY LAW
TRAINING WORKBOOK FOR SUPERVISORS AND MANAGERS

COMPLIANCE WITH EQUAL EMPLOYMENT OPPORTUNITY LAW ON SEXUAL HARASSMENT

Course Participants: Supervisors and Managers
Length of Course: Four Hours

Excerpts Reprinted with permission of the Texas Commission on Human Rights (P.O. Box 13493, Austin, Texas 78711)

EXERCISE I
SEXUAL HARASSMENT AS SEX-BASED EMPLOYMENT DISCRIMINATION

Please determine whether the following are true, false or maybe.

T F M   1. A man as well as a woman may be the victim of sexual harassment, and a woman as well as a man may be the harasser.

T F M   2. The victim does not have to be of the opposite sex of the harasser.

T F M   3. The victim does not have to be the person to whom unwelcomed sexual conduct is directed. He or she may be someone who is affected by such conduct when it is directed toward another person.

T F M   4. The victim does not have to complain to the harasser or report the harassment to his/her supervisor or employer in order for the employer to be held responsible for the unlawful conduct when committed by a supervisory employee.

T F M   5. If the harasser is a non-supervisory employee, the employer is not responsible for the act committed by the harasser unless he/she knew or should have known and failed to take immediate and appropriate corrective action.

T F M   6. Sexual harassment is a violation of Title VII of the Civil Rights Act of 1964 and the Texas Commission on Human Rights Act.

T F M 7. Sexual harassment includes unwelcomed sexual advances, requests for sexual favors, and other verbal or physical conduct of a sexual nature.

T F M 8. Submission to the requests for sexual favors does not negate the victim's rights to file a sexual harassment complaint.

T F M 9. If an employee is receiving benefits (promotions, increases, etc.) as a result of a voluntary sexual relationship with a supervisor/manager, employees being denied these same benefits are eligible to file a complaint of sexual harassment.

T F M 10. It is the intent of the harasser, rather than the perception of the victim, which determines if sexual harassment took place or not.

T F M 11. Explicit sexual language and provocative dress by an employee may be taken into account when that employee files a complaint of sexual harassment.

T F M 12. If the harasser is requesting sexual favors from both male and female employees, these employees may file a valid complaint/charge of sexual harassment under Title VII and the Texas Commission on Human Rights Act.

MAJOR LAWS PROHIBITING EMPLOYMENT DISCRIMINATION

Title VII of the Civil Rights Act of 1964, as amended in 1972, 1978 and the Civil Rights Act of 1991

The most prominent source of anti-bias employment rules is Title VII of the Civil Rights Act of 1964. It forbids discrimination in all areas of the employeremployee relationship, from advertisement for new employees through termination or retirement, on the basis of race, color, sex (including pregnancy, childbirth or abortion), religion or national origin. The Civil Rights Act of 1991 included additional provisions to Title VII reversing or reinforcing certain U.S. Supreme Court decisions, damages for intentional discrimination and removal of exemptions for previously-exempted employees of elected officials.

Texas Commission on Human Rights Act of 1983, as amended

Prohibits discrimination in employment transactions because of race, color, national origin, religion, sex, age or disability status by public and private employers in the State of Texas.

Texas Penal Code, as amended (71 st Session Texas Legislature)

Texas Penal Code was amended to include sexual harassment. Under this amendment to the Penal Code there must be a showing of intent on the part of the harasser. A violation of this amendment is a Class A Misdemeanor.

PERSONNEL TRANSACTIONS COVERED UNDER EEO LAW

1. It is an unlawful employment practice for an employer to fail or refuse to hire or to discharge an individual or otherwise to discriminate against an individual with respect to compensation or the terms, conditions, or privileges of employment because of race, color, disability, national origin, religion, sex or change.

2. It is an unlawful employment practice for an employer to limit, segregate, or classify any employee or applicant for employment in a way that would deprive or tend to deprive an individual of employment opportunities or other-wise adversely affect the status of an employee because of race, color, disability, religion, sex, national origin or age.

3. It is an unlawful employment practice to retaliate or discriminate against a person who as opposed a discriminatory practice or who has made or filed a charge, filed a complaint, testified, assisted or participated in any manner in an investigation, proceeding or hearing under the TCHR Act.

4. It is an unlawful employment practice for an employer to aid, abet, incite or coerce a person to engage in discriminatory practice.

5. It is an unlawful employment practice to willfully interfere with the performance of a duty or the exercise of a power by the Commission, one of its staff or its representatives.

6. It is an unlawful employment practice to willfully obstruct or prevent a person from complying with the provisions of the TCHR Act or a valid rule or order issued under the TCHR Act.

REFERENCE: PART 1604-EEOC GUIDELINES ON DISCRIMINATION BECAUSE OF SEX

1604.11   Sexual harassment.

(a) Harassment on the basis of sex is a violation of Sec. 703 of Title VII. Unwelcome sexual advances, requests for sexual favors, and other verbal or physical conduct of a sexual nature constitute sexual harassment. When (1) submission to such conduct is made either explicitly or implicitly a term or condition of an individual's employment (2) submission to or rejection of such conduct by an individual is used as the basis for employment decisions affecting such individual or (3) such conduct has the purpose or effect of unreasonably interfering with an individual's work performance or creating an intimidating, hostile, or offensive working environment.

(b) In determining whether alleged conduct constitutes sexual harassment, the Commission will look at the record as as a whole and at the totality, of the circumstances such as the nature of the sexual advances and the context in which the alleged incidents occurred. The determination of the legality of a particular action will be made from the facts on a case by case basis.

(c) Applying general Title VII principles, an employer, employment agency, joint apprenticeship committee or labor organization (hereinafter collectively, referred to as "employer") is responsible for its acts and those of its agents and supervisory employees with respect to sexual harassment regardless of whether the specific acts complained of were authorized or even forbidden by, the employer regardless of whether the employer knew or should have known of their occurrence. The Commission will examine the circumstances of the particular employment relationship and the job junctions performed by the individual in determining whether an individual acts in either a supervisory or agency, capacity.

(d) With respect to conduct between fellow employees, an employer is responsible for acts of sexual harassment in the workplace where the employer (or its agents or supervisory employees) knows or should have known of the conduct, unless it can show that it took immediate and appropriate corrective action.

(e) An employer may also be responsible for the acts of nonemployees with respect to sexual harassment of employees in the workplace, where the employer (or its agents or supervisory employees) knows or should have known of the conduct and fails to take immediate and appropriate corrective action. In reviewing these cases the Commission will consider the extent of the employer's control and another legal responsibility which the employer may have with respect to the conduct of such non-employees.

(f) Prevention is the best tool for the elimination of sexual harassment. An employer should take all steps necessary to prevent sexual harassment from occuring, such as affirmatively raising the subject, expressing strong disapproval, developing appropriate sanctions, informing employees of their right to raise and how to raise the issue of harassment under Title VII, and developing methods to sensitize all concerned.

(g) Other related practices: Where employment opportunities or benefits are granted because of an individual's submission to the employer's sexual advances or requests for sexual favors, the employer may be held liable for unlawful sex discrimination against other persons who were qualified for but denied that employment opportunity, or benefit.

(Title VII, Pub. L. 88-352.78, Stat.253 (42 U.S.C. 2000e et seq.))

LEGAL THEORY OR PROOF FORMULA FOR DETERMINING A VIOLATION OF FAIR EMPLOYMENT LAW

Regardless of the specific allegations on a complaint of employment discrimination, a violation of fair employment law will be determined on the basis of the following legal theory or proof formula:

Disparate Treatment: The Complainant was or was not treated differently than persons not of the Complainant's same class under like or similar circumstances who are like or similarly situated. *(McDonnell Douglas Corp. vs. Green) [5EPD 8067] 411 U.S. 792 (1973)]*

THREE APPROACHES IN ANALYZING EVIDENCE IN A CASE OF EMPLOYMENT DISCRIMINATION

Regardless of the nature of evidence and information supplied by the Respondent or Complainant in a case of employment discrimination, including any documents or testimony, such evidence will be analyzed in the following ways:

1. Direct Evidence of Employment Discrimination

    Example: Evidence confirms that the Charging Party was fired because of her pregnant condition.

    Example: Evidence reveals that White co-workers used racial epithets on the work site.

    Example: Evidence revealed that supervisors or co-workers committed unwanted sexual acts of a vital or physical nature against the Complainant.

2. Comparative Data

    Example: Black widget makers were not terminated as was White Com plainant for theft of company property.

    Example: A male was promoted to a supervisory position who was less qualified for the supervisory position than a female, after she complained to management about sexual harassment.

3. Statistical Analysis

    Example: A disproportionate number of Blacks are rejected for assembler positions compared to Whites rejected, based on availability in the labor force within the recruitment area,on the basis of non-job-related qualifications.

INVESTIGATIVE STAGES IN DETERMINING A VIOLATION OF EEO LAW AND BURDEN OF PROOF (SEXUAL HARASSMENT)

I.   Complainant Establishes a Prima Facie Case of Employment Discrimination

II.   The Respondent Articulates Defense and Substantiates the Factual Basis for the Employment Decision

III.   The Employer's Defense is Examined as a Pretext to Employment Discrimination

CRITERIA TO MEASURE COMPLIANCE WITH EEO LAW

A.   Objectivity: For a personnel decision, policy, practice or requirement to meet the test of objectivity, the criteria must be measurable in quantifiable terms as opposed to a subjective judgment. (author's note: this is not the case for all jobs, as some involve tasks that are not readily measurable in objective terms. In these types of jobs, the remaining three criteria take on greater importance.)

B.   Job Relatedness: For a personnel decision, policy, practice or requirement to be job related, the criteria must have a direct relationship to the work to be performed.

C.   Consistent Application: For a personnel decision, policy, practice or requirement to be consistent, the criteria must be applied in the same manner to all like or similarly situated employees under like or similar circumstances without regard to protected class status.

D.   Uniform Effect: For a personnel decision, policy, practice or requirement to be uniform, the criteria must have a uniform impact without regard to protected class status and should not have a disproportionate effect on a particular protected class.

EXERCISE II

The following exercise allows you the opportunity to apply the four factors we have discussed in terms of personnel decisions, policies, practices or job requirements. You are to select the answer that is most appropriate for each question. (author's note: the message should be that a personnel decision must meet all of the criteria below in order to on its face be in compliance with EEO law and policy)

PERSONNEL TRANSACTION:	IS THE DECISION OBJECTIVE Yes No	ARE THE CRITERIA JOB-RELATED Yes No	CAN IT BE CONSISTENTLY APPLIED Yes No	DOES IT HAVE A UNIFORM EFFECT Yes No
1. Discharge a supervisor for sexual harassment.				
2. Require all employees, other than victim, to report incidents of sexual harassment or be subject to discipline.				
3. Discharge an employee for a bad attitude or insubordination.				
4. Give all the secretaries a subscription to Playboy magazine.				
5. Require all secretaries to have a high school diploma.				

is a discussion of sexual harassment videos by a video reviewer, along with the reviewer's rating of the videos. The author urges trainers to review as many videos as possible as some will be more amenable to their culture and specific training needs than others. The reviews represent the exclusive opinion of the reviewer.

§ 6.3 Sexual Harassment Videos[1]

One of the first things you will notice about the sexual harassment videos on the market is that most are relatively new. Sexual harassment, of course, has been around for thousands of years but nothing brought the issue more to public attention than the now fabled Clarence Thomas hearings.

It has been two years since that public confrontation on television, and since that time a wide spectrum of video producers has released a plethora of tapes. They are a remarkably similar lot. In fact, you really can't go wrong. Even the videos I put in the "acceptable" category would probably do the job for most situations. That sameness made it difficult to decide which tapes to recommend. There are, however, some truly excellent programs.

Most Comprehensive and Best

"What once was considered acceptable behavior, may not now be considered to be so at work," summarizes the theme of Audio Graphics' excellent entry into sexual harassment training tapes. Taking the tactic that companies need to clearly understand the legal issues and change employee behavior, the paired tapes—*Sexual Harassment: Understanding the Law* and *Sexual Harassment: Handling the Complaint*—demonstrate what constitutes harassment and the consequences of those actions.

In the first 30-minute program, a group of middle managers gather to discuss the firing of one of their colleagues. His offense? He did nothing to stop a pattern of unacceptable behavior on the job of those he managed. Through sometimes acrimonious debate with a company attorney and their own manager, they come to understand the implications of Title 7 legislation.

The tape presents behavioral issues and does not grapple with attitudes. For example, the program points out the financial implications of sexual harassment such as low productivity, absenteeism, and employee turnover. That may be the only way to reach certain audiences.

---

[1] Reprinted from *View* Newsletter with permission. The opinions expressed in the reviews represent those of *View* Newsletter's editorial staff and not necessarily those of the author.

The second program consists entirely of acted sequences that illustrate to employees and managers how to handle incidents of sexual harassment. It deals directly with very tough issues: a lesbian coming on to a prospective employee during a job interview, a telephone repairman harassing a receptionist, sexually related joking about an overweight, black woman, a highly placed and attractive woman requiring a younger, married man to perform, and even guys teasing a co-worker about the size of his sexual organ. Tough stuff.

The vignettes illustrate these issues not only as wrong way/right way but also as wrong way/another wrong way/right way. This approach develops the concepts in a more subtle and less clear cut manner. Audio Graphics is careful to include a good mix of blacks and whites, men and women, white collar and blue collar individuals so the tape will be useful for just about any audience. The acting is always top notch and the production values fine.

A Subtle Approach

We all think of sexual harassment as men making inappropriate remarks or advances to women. One of the problems with many of the tapes I viewed was that they presented only the obvious examples. But the issue of sexual harassment can often be complex and difficult.

Advantage's new program, *Sexual Harassment: Serious Business,* shows us that it can be that and much more. The program also illustrates how sexual harassment can damage worker productivity and even product quality.

In one scene, for instance, we see an attractive female employee flirting with her superior. Things get out of hand in the department as he spends more and more of his time with her. The department begins to fall apart and their relationship poisons the whole environment. It's not sexual harassment as we normally think of it but clearly a hostile work environment has been created.

Another terrific scene shows how a false accusation can also wreak havoc upon manager/employee relationships and upon the company for which they work. The sequence is used to reinforce the importance of conducting thorough and unbiased investigations into sexual harassment complaints.

Advantage's tape depicts both office and factory scenes. Too many programs don't. It's well produced and provides solid guidelines.

Vignettes for Discussion

A couple of distributors list programs that contain a number of scenes of possible sexual harassment for discussion. The scenes are open ended and provide grist for the training mill by bringing the real world into the corporate training room.

The best of these comes from BNA. Titled *A Costly Proposition,* the tape presents five open-ended situations. A couple are not particularly subtle but all seem realistic and challenging. The final sequence even presents two views of the same situation to illustrate how difficult it can be to decide who did what to whom.

In this sequence, a man and a woman are on a business trip. His business associate suggests they go up to her room to work on a report they must deliver the next day. Everything goes fine until he gets up to leave. In her version, after she gives him a friendly peck on the cheek, he grabs her and kisses her aggressively. His version, which we also see, shows that the peck on the cheek is merely a prelude to a mutual kiss. Whom do we believe?

American Media distributes a similar program though the sequences are much shorter. Titled *Sexual Harassment: Is It or Isn't It?,* the tape presents fourteen short scenarios. Some tend to be fairly obvious examples but a few showcase some difficult problems. In one, a man looks a woman up and down. At first she doesn't see him. Is there harm in this?

In another scenario, a woman insists that a man she works with pose for a picture with her. At the last second, she kisses him on the cheek. Later she puts the picture on her desk. Is this harassment? Good question. American Media's program delivers some fine supplementary material for in-house sessions.

Practical Advice

Several programs outline practical methods about what to do to prevent or stop sexual harassment. Spelling out its objectives right from the start, BNA's *How to Manage Sexual Harassment Situations* outlines specific questions and practical methods about how to talk to the alleged recipient, how to respond appropriately, how to avoid key mistakes, how to talk with the harasser, and finally, how to intervene when a complaint is not made.

The tape uses a series of illustrative scenarios that not only show how to act but also variations in the recipient's behavior that demand different approaches. How to Manage sets up a good example at the beginning. A man makes an aggressive pass at a female co-worker in the cafeteria. It's obviously another instance in an on-going pattern of behavior.

The first time the woman complains to her supervisor, the manager handles it badly with advice such as "Don't you think you're overreacting." We then see the meeting replayed correctly. In a long sequence, the manager clearly illustrates both how to question the complainer and appropriate responses.

The best part of the video comes later. The program first replays the scene with the complaining worker deciding to resolve the harassment problem herself. The tape demonstrates what the manager should do in this instance as well as another situation in which the recipient does not want the manager to do anything. By illustrating the same circumstance with these variations, the program helps managers understand typical behavior and demonstrates how they should react.

American Media's *Sexual Harassment in the Workplace: Identify, Stop, Prevent* also develops a detailed analysis. Starting with the EEOC guidelines, the program spends a great deal of time defining what constitutes sexual harassment. It all comes down to an inappropriate use of power.

Although the opening sequence in a company conference room tends to be much too talky, the remainder does a good job of analyzing specific incidents. Each short scene illustrates specific issues raised by company employees. For example, if a woman dresses provocatively does that change the situation? Or what if someone gets a job because they acquiesce to sexual advances?

The program offers some solid guidance and develops an effective review. In fact, the program has one of the better sections on prevention of any of the tapes reviewed. One criticism: the conference room scenes portray a talk by a consultant to a small group of company managers. Only one of these managers is a woman.

The Legal Issues

BNA offers another similar though more legally oriented approach in its three part series *Preventing Sexual Harassment*. The first tape, *The Risk,* establishes the concrete consequences of harassment in the workplace: a costly legal judgment against the fictitious Zycore company. The program then steps back and enacts what led up to the court case. It is not what happened as much as the errors that both managers and employees at Zycore make that counts. One of the major mistakes: the lack of a specific policy.

Tape two, *Minimizing the Risk,* uses the wrong way/right way technique to show what the managers in part one should have done to prevent the lawsuit. The program does not deal with the personal consequences of sexual harassment but only how to handle its occurrence and the complaints it engenders.

A Shared Responsibility, the final segment, deals with prevention but doesn't actually show us how to do so. It relies more upon narration and bullet points than the others and is the weakest of the three.

The Human Cost

The last recommended tape, *Coastal's Ending Sexual Harassment,* carries the subtitle Using Communication and Consideration. That indicates the program's orientation. Pitching human sensitivity as the key, the program zeroes in on the two primary standards: hostile environment and quid pro quo.

Though this program also starts out with too much talk, we finally get two extended stories that illustrate each concept. The scenes work because they develop the action from beginning to end. In the second, for example, a female employee has become tired of her co-workers playing a pornographic computer game. Though she asks them to stop, they mock her requests. It is only after she goes to her manager that she gets results.

The program stresses that many men don't realize the consequences of their actions. It is only through a manager's follow-up that people change their behavior. We see that follow-up and its result. The tape asks the question that many programs ask, "Would I behave like this if my mother was in the room."

In similar fashion the program looks at a quid pro quo example, this one going all the way to court.

If all the tapes have one major fault, even some of the recommended ones, it's that they tend to portray exaggerated scenes. Those are the easy ones to understand. It is the more subtle efforts such as those of Audio Graphics' or Advantage's tapes that really teach us something.

See **Table 6-1** for a summary of available videos.

§ 6.4 Management Training

While the focus for nonmanagement employees should mainly be on defining and recognizing sexual harassment and learning to address it either directly with each other, or if that is not an option, then through a more formal complaint mechanism, managers and supervisory employees have a higher responsibility to the organization. They must be trained in recognizing harassment, but also in stopping it, preventing it, counseling about it, investigating it, and resolving it.

Chapter 3 presented a complaint handler's model that demonstrates the breadth of an investigator's role. The material which follows presents information on that role that can be used in training complaint handlers.

Table 6-1

Summary of Available Videos

TITLE	DIST.	LENGTH	COST	AUDIENCE	COMMENTS
Recommended					
A Costly Proposition	BNA	32:00	$875	All levels	Realistic open-ended vignettes set up discussion about sexual harassment. Most scenes are not clear cut nor obvious and one even presents two versions. Effective and helpful.
Ending Sexual Harassment: Using Consideration (1993)	Coastal	25:00	$495	Managers	Though limited in scope, the program presents a very human approach to the problem. Two long vignettes present a detailed analysis of Quid Pro Quo and Hostile Environment.
How to Manage Sexual Harassment Situations (1993)	BNA	30:00	$895	Managers	Reviewed in March, 1993. Program outlines specific questions and practical methods about how to talk to the alleged recipient, how to respond appropriately, how to avoid key mistakes, how to talk with the harasser, and finally, how to intervene when a complaint is not made.
Preventing Sexual Harassment (1992)	BNA	27, 28, & 13	$495	Managers	Reviewed in November, 1992. Three-part program highlights The Risk, Minimizing the Risk, and how all is a Shared Responsibility. Most of the scenarios work well and "wrong way/right approach" is instructive.
Sexual Harassment: Understanding the Law (1992)	Audio Graphics	30:00	$695	Managers and supervisors	Reviewed in January, 1993. Through sometimes acrimonious debate, managers and supervisors come to understand the implications of Title VII. The group reviews "Quid Pro Quo" behavior and the more difficult to understand "Hostile Work Environment." Though format is a problem, it's the most thorough program around.
Sexual Harassment: Handling the Complaint (1992)	Audio Graphics	30:00	$695	All levels	Reviewed in January, 1993. Deals directly with very tough issues: a lesbian coming on to a prospective employee during a job interview, a telephone repairman harassing a receptionist, sexually related joking about an overweight, black woman, and others. Best program around.
Sexual Harassment in the Workplace...Identify. Stop. Prevent. (1990)	American Media	21:00	$575	Managers	Very short vignettes illustrate most aspects of harassment issues. Includes segments on women harassing men, men and men, and women and women. Good guidelines on what to do.
Sexual Harassment: Is It or Isn't It? (1993)	American Media	12:00	$495	All levels	Short scenes presented for discussion. Some are pretty obvious but others do present more subtle situations. Good supplement for training sessions.

Table 6-1 (*continued*)

TITLE	DIST.	LENGTH	COST	AUDIENCE	COMMENTS
Sexual Harassment: Serious Business (1993)	Advantage	24:00	$495	All levels	Excellent program that develops the more subtle side of sexual harassment. Includes scenes that most of the other programs don't touch--even one on a false accusation. Very effective.
Acceptable					
All the Wrong Moves (1987)	Dartnell	23:00	$495	Managers	Defines three problem areas and illustrates them with acted scenes. Lawyer defines problem areas. Sequences present rather obvious examples and program needs more graphic reinforcement. A bit dated.
Employee Awareness: Sexual Harassment (1993)	AIMS	19:00	$375	Manufacturing Employees	Fairly general approach. Hits key areas but not in organized manner. Too many office scenes in "industrial version" which is disappointing. A needed area. Good review at end about what constitutes harassment and what to do.
Handling the Sexual Harassment Complaint (1990)	American Media	12:00	$495	Managers	Straightforward presentation of steps managers should take when employees make harassment complaint. Section on prevention is weak. Characters seem a bit plastic and unreal.
How to Recognize and Confront Subtle Sexual Harassment (1993)	BNA	27:00	$895	All levels	Reviewed in March, 1993. The program doesn't deliver on its promise. Video doesn't illustrate particularly subtle behavior nor, more importantly, does it delineate the business relationships of the individuals involved. To its credit it does add a new standard--Equal Initiation or Participation--to the mix.
Person to Person: Creating Respectful Workplaces (1993)	Video Publishing	28:00	$695	Managers	Reviewed in March, 1993. Program takes a slightly different tack, arguing that respectful behavior can be the guide. It claims people agree on what is respectful. Actually, people in the program don't agree and the video ends up proving the opposite of what it claims. Still helpful since the legality of the behavior is not the issue here and the remedies that the video suggests rely upon interpersonal skills rather than litigation.
Proactive Management and Sexual Harassment: Recognition, Intervention, Prevention (1992)	AIMS	22:00	$395	Managers	Good idea but not as thorough as it could be. Some helpful suggestions about recognizing warning signs of harassment. Sections on what to do, however, are not as well organized or reinforced.

Table 6-1 (*continued*)

TITLE	DIST.	LENGTH	COST	AUDIENCE	COMMENTS
Sexual Harassment from 9 to 5 (1986)	Films for the Humanities	26:00	$450	Managers	Television segment produced by public station in New York. Opening section that profiles case history is interesting but 10-minute discussion with experts lead nowhere and doesn't provide us with much.
Sexual Harassment: Prevention, Recognition and Correction (1993)	BBP	26:00	$495	Managers	Short scenarios and courtroom lawyers describe the three phases of dealing with harassment. Program is strong in correction segment, delineating specific steps. First two parts are a bit random and need more detail.
Sexual Harassment--Walking the Corporate Fine Line	Salenger	22:00	$495	Managers	Good detailed information about why and how companies should develop a sexual harassment policy. Very direct and straightforward with good reinforcement. Program marred by mediocre production quality.
Not Recommended					
Intent vs. Impact (1988)	BNA	41:00 26:00	$1495	Managers Employees	On-camera narrator and taped seminar make up the bulk of these two programs. Mostly consists of tedious rendering of lists of information. Short acted sequences don't help much and a few are poorly executed.
Sexual Harassment on the Job	Films for the Humanities	28:00	$450	All levels	Old Phil Donahue Show from when he broadcast from Chicago. Program is very dated and format won't work well for corporate audiences.
Sexual Harassment: Shades of Gray (1989)	United Training Media	various	$1495	All levels	Series of five programs that thoroughly covers all aspects of issue. Though on-camera Susan Webb is good at presenting information, the tapes are all talk and wear thin after a while. She tells some good stories but we want to see much more.

Readers should verify cost with distributors as this information is subject to change.

The Role of the EEO Complaint Handler[2]

In every organization the role and responsibilities of the Equal Employment Opportunity (EEO) complaint handler will vary. Several factors may account for these variations. The factors can be categorized into three levels: organization, interpersonal, and procedural. While considering all of these factors, the overall goal should be to establish a role for the complaint handler that is realistic in your organization and will enable the system to work. This material regarding the role of the complaint handler can be used to train those who have been selected, and should refer to the complaint handler's model described in **Chapter 3.**

Organizational

The role of the EEO complaint handlers needs to be looked at in the context of the organization. This includes considering:

- whether there is management support behind the internal complaint procedure
- what organizational resources are available to the interal complaint procedure
- whether the procedure is easily accessible
- whether the process is seen as fair

Personal

At the interpersonal level, there are a number of factors which may influence the selection of a complaint handler. The complaint handler should have:

- some content knowledge of the legal area
- an understanding of the organization
- the ability to do a thorough job
- a willingness to be involved in the process
- the ability to be fair

On a procedural level, there are many factors to consider in determining who should be a part of the various stages in the complaint process. At each stage the role of the complaint handler must be examined.

1. Intake stage. As a result of court cases and recommendations from the EEOC and other federal, state, and local agencies, the complaint procedure should provide for a choice of people available for the intake stage.

---

[2] © 1992. Susan W. Brecker/Cornell University, Inc. All rights reserved. Reprinted with permission.

The practice of having multiple persons available for intake ensures that employees do not have to complaint to the person who may have committed the alleged offense. This practice recognized that employees might use the system more readily if they could select from a number of people the intake person with whom they feel comfortable and trust.

2. Investigation stage.   Sometimes the person who is responsible for intake should not be handling the investigation stage. The person conducting the intake stage may want to consider whether that person is the appropriate person to continue on with conducting the investigation. Similar to determining generally who should handle complaints, the intake person should think about whether he or she:

- has the experience and/or time to handle this investigation
- will be taken seriously and/or have enough authority to effectively investigate this situation
- has the content knowledge, both legally and in some instances an understanding of the technical aspects of the situation

3. Complaint resolution stage.   If it is possible, it is also recommended to have a different person handle the investigation stage than the person who handles the complaint resolution stage. This would be especially true where disciplinary action might be necessary, because separating the two persons handling those stages allows for some distance on the part of the "decision maker" in the complaint resolution stage. The "decision maker" stage appears more neutral and less directly involved in the situation. The investigator might also be able to approach the investigator more objectively since he or she will not be responsible for making the final decisions. If one person must handle both stages then that person should try to discuss the conclusions and recommendations with another manager before actually implementing anything.

Training

Finally once you have determined the role of the complaint handler in your organization, who the complaint handlers will be, and the complaint handlers' responsibilities, then to try to assure achieving your overall goal of making the system work, training is a necessity. Each complaint handler should receive training on how to implement his or her respective responsibilities and how to understand the process as a whole.

In addition, it is a good idea to give complaint handlers an opportunity to conduct mock interviews with each other in a training session so that they can benefit from feedback in the relative safety of the role-playing exercises rather than having their first experience with the real thing. They should role play interviewing the complainant, the alleged perpetrator, and both cooperative and uncooperative witnesses. The training video used by Georgia-Pacific Corp. and available through the Equal Employment Advisory Council in Washington, D.C., offers a useful presentation of a mock interview. It presents strategies such as using open-ended questions when interviewing an alleged harasser, seeking cooperation by using specfic statements such as "You can be of great help to us in getting at the facts," advice about reactions to expect such as transference of the complainant's anger at the accused to the investigator, and the importance of following up on answers given to pin the witness down on the details.

Management's and co-workers' roles in coaching and counseling is covered well in PeopleTech's training video and leader's guide. The program, *Person to Person: Creating Respectful Workplaces,* emphasizes what each person's responsibility is in dealing with sexual harassment. A portion of the leader's guide follows:

What Can I Do? What Can't I Do?[3]

If you experience, observe, or are responsible for managing a sexual harassment problem:

There is only one thing you can't do.

You can't ignore it.

Studies show in 75 percent of all cases, harassment will either continue or escalate if it is ignored.

On the other hand, there are many positive things you can do.

These steps will differ somewhat, depending on your role in the situation.

If You Are Harassed

1. Respond promptly and clearly, verbally or in writing, or both.

Tell the offender that the conduct is unwelcome and unacceptable, say what you want instead, for example, "don't call me babe; my name is Kelly" or "don't hug me when you pass me in the hall; a simple 'hello' is fine."

2. Document in writing every incident, with specific details of the offensive behavior and your response.

---

[3] © PeopleTech, Inc. Reprinted with permission.

3. Don't feel guilty. Sexual harassment is not your fault. By clearly voicing your expectations, you force the offender to choose whether to change the unwelcome behavior, or to purposely continue it.
4. If the problem continues, report the situation to your company agent.

If You Observe Someone Being Harassed

1. Offer your personal support to the person who is the target. Let them know they are not alone, not "imagining things."
2. Speak up. Take a stand against potentially offensive behavior. Let the offender know how you (as an impartial observer) viewed the behavior.
3. Support company policies and practices that discourage sexual harassment.

If You Are Responsible for Managing Employees

1. Take every complaint seriously; give it your prompt attention and open-minded consideration.
2. Be supportive and sensitive; people may be embarrassed not only by the harassment, but by the need the discuss a "personal" problem with a "business" supervisor.
3. Listen to the employee. Don't be judgmental, or contradict what they feel they experienced.
4. Maintain confidentiality. This bears repeating: maintain confidentiality. Protect the rights of both the accuser and the accused.
5. Contact your company agent to be sure you understand company policy and procedures—then follow them carefully.

Remember, sexual harassment is against the law; it is a serious matter for both the individuals involved, and the company.

Mutual Respect Is the Key

Federal agencies and courts have shown us countless ways we can go wrong on the issue of sexual harassment. But mutual respect is the one best way to set things right.

*   Where there is mutual respect, individuals feel free to communicate their different viewpoints.
*   Where there is mutual respect, individuals are willing to acknowledge and accept those differences.

- Where there is mutual respect, there is consideration for the other person's dignity.
- Where there is mutual respect, there will be fewer misunderstandings and fewer behaviors that may be interpreted as sexual harassment.

§ 6.5   Sample Training Programs

Some sample training programs and training outlines are included in this section. They are only offered for illustrative purposes and should be used to generate ideas on different training approaches that would fit the unique needs of your organization. The EEOC has also proposed that all employers be required to give sexual harassment training to all supervisory employees.

The advice in the following training program section on "Sexual Harassment Training for Management" is very useful. It suggests ways for securing management's buy-in and in preparing trainers for the barrage of questions they will receive. A very comprehensive list of sample questions is included.

Sexual Harassment Training For Management[4]

Editor's Note: The following section on how to design an effective sexual harassment training program for managers was prepared by a professional trainer. It is to serve as an example of how a professional trainer approaches management. Because corporate management is often reluctant to take the issue seriously, it is necessary to convince them of the seriousness of the issue to the organization and the value of training to mitigate liability and improve productivity. Similar models can Also be developed for use in schools and other arenas because the principles discussed are readily adaptable for many other contexts.

Damn the Icebergs, Full Steam Ahead!

(How to Design Effective Sexual Harassment Training Programs)

Sexual harassment waits silently at night, like an iceberg, for the corporate ship whose captain does not believe in its existence. Then, striking with the suddenness of a torpedo, sexual harassment jars the work place. Work groups, departments, or even divisions collapse, but the ship seldom sinks. Instead, the ship shudders, heaves to one side, and diverts valuable resources to prevent further damage and to salvage what is left. Unreported

---

[4] Reprinted with the permission of the California Commission on the Status of Women.

sexual harassment may slowly rust the ship from within, weakening the corporate image and the teamwork of its male and female employees. In either situation, the damage is real—whether its cause is attributed to sexual harassment or just buried with other employee turnover statistics.

"We don't have a problem with sexual harassment because we have not received any sexual harassment complaints." This retort is management's (primarily male) response when asked if sexual harassment is occurring within their work place. The challenge faced by departments responsible for dealing with sexual harassment is to convince management to support a training program when they do not perceive there is a need for it. Management often does not realize that their employees will not talk with them about the issue because (a) they do not know what their rights are, (b) who to talk with, or (c) do not believe that anything will be done if they do talk. Therefore, because many management personnel don't have the factual information to make decisions about preventing and resolving sexual harassment in their work places, they use misinformation. That misinformation often is influenced by personal beliefs, biases, and stereotypes about men and women in the work place. Employers who train their employees to recognize, prevent and resolve sexual harassment situations will sail more safely.

This section will discuss the following:

- Ideas and training concepts for designing and conducting effective sexual harassment training programs, i.e., participants knowing their legal liabilities/responsibilities, understanding how to determine when behavior crosses the line between friendly and sexually harassing interactions and understanding how to identify and effectively resolve sexual harassment situations.
- How to gain management's support.
  Sample program learning objectives for sexual harassment training programs for:
  a. management personnel
  b. employees
  c. EEO/personnel/industrial relations.
- A list of participant statements and frequently asked questions.

A sexual harassment training program will only be effective for management and non-management males and females if A is unbiased and relevant to their specific work situations. The following ideas/training concepts are suggested as being the foundations for all sexual harassment training programs.

Ideas And Training Concepts

- Top management must support the programs and make attendance mandatory.
- The trainer must be professional at all times and take the issue seriously because he or she is the role model for how sexual harassment is dealt with in the training program.
- The trainer should know the audience, i.e., jargon, history of sexual harassment situations, sexual harassment policy, complaint process, segregated or integrated work places.
- Most men and women agree that, if a supervisor tells an employee to go to bed with him/her or the employee will lose his/her job, or if an employee is assaulted or threatened physically if he/she does not comply, that is sexual harassment. The challenge of the trainer is to close the male/female perception gap concerning other behaviors that constitute sexual harassment, and how often they occur.
- It is counterproductive to accuse all men of being insensitive to the issue, or of being "potential" sexual harasser just as it is to accuse women of being oversensitive, and of bringing on sexual harassment because of their "provocative clothing, mannerisms," etc.
- The majority of sexually harassing behavior occurring today, is comprised of interactions subject to various interpretations. To some persons this behavior is welcome, but to others it is demeaning and, therefore, constitutes sexual harassment. In order for us to understand when the line is crossed from friendly to sexually harassing behavior, it is necessary to separate the intent of our behavior from its impact.
- The employer/supervisor must understand how to create an environment that encourages recipients of unwelcome behavior to talk with the harasser or employer
- The trainer should have positive expectations of the participants' ability to understand the issue, and assume that they don't want to sexually harass other employees. Although many of the participants may joke or laugh about the issue, an *effective* training program will always persuade the multitude of them that it is a serious issue and deserves their support.

An Effective Sexual Harassment Training Program Will

- Encourage recipients to personally or through their employer's complaint process, resolve their sexual harassment situations.
- Provide clarity concerning the specific differences between friendly and sexually harassing behavior.

- Encourage an environment in which sexual harassment is taken seriously, and where males and females are not paranoid about interacting with each other when dealing with the problem.
- Clarify the employer's management's, and employee's responsibilities to create a sexual harassment-free workplace and to take appropriate collective action if a sexual harassment situation occurs.

Sexual harassment surfaces diverse and sometimes volatile emotions in its participants. Participants may not be aware of what they are angry about, or what they are implying when they make a statement. Therefore, the trainer must understand how to deal effectively with the open and hidden agendas. When trainers are sensitive, educated, unbiased, and conduct the program in a professional way, they will encounter less hostility. Additionally, the training program will be much more effective.

How To Gain Management's Support

When trying to convince management to sponsor and support sexual harassment training programs, apply the following ideas:

- Anticipate questions, concerns, fears and objections, and have answers ready for each of them.
- Arm yourself with factual information (e.g., results of an internal sexual harassment survey).
- Practice your approach, questions, and answers. Offer specific options for approaching the issue, all of which you support and which are in the best interest of the employer.
- Emphasize the tangible gains for the employer, management personnel, and employees if the programs are initiated.
- Build a power base by finding male and female management personnel who support the issue.
- Select a time to discuss the issue carefully.
- Be professional.
- Do not personalize management's negative response or insensitivity regarding the issue or initiating training about it.
- Always think about asserting what is in it for the employer and management.

When an employer does not support sexual harassment prevention education, the following responses to management's objections to training can be used to explain why training should be undertaken.

Some of management's concerns, objections and hesitations for starting prevention education training are:

It will encourage sexual harassment complaints.

Response: Sexual harassment situations either do or do not exist in the work place. If sexual harassment is occurring, the employee will now be encouraged to deal with the situation personally, or she/he will now know who to talk with to get assistance in resolving their situation. If they are not occurring before the program, they will even be *less* likely to occur in the future.

Employees will now bring false charges of sexual harassment.

Response: Even if employees have not received training in their work place, they often hear about the issue in the media. Nothing can stop an employee from trying to abuse an employer's grievance/complaint process, but the employer can protect itself from false charges by having trained and informed personnel to deal appropriately with false charges. An uneducated, uninformed employer and management personnel are much more vulnerable to false charges than are educated employers. Ignorance about sexual harassment is not bliss, but expensive. Employers know that it is cost-effective to train their employees to be safe workers. The same is true for preventing sexual harassment.

It will polarize our male and female employees.

Response: There already is a polarization of many male and female employees around the issue of sexual harassment. It just has not been obvious. Instead, women will talk amongst themselves about men to watch out for, which departments do not support female employees, who not to go on a trip with, and who not to get isolated with in the copy room. Men who have heard about the issue, but do not understand it, will not want to work or travel with a woman to protect themselves from charges of sexual harassment. Effective training clarifies what is and is not sexual harassment, responsibilities of each employee, and how to deal with situations effectively and informally. Sexual harassment prevention training closes the male/female perception gap and dramatically decreases misunderstandings about the issue. This enables men and women to work together more effectively and reduces employee turnover.

We have higher priorities, or there is no money budgeted for this issue.

Response: It is the Catch-22 dilemma for trainers. The employer does not perceive that sexual harassment is a problem because of the lack of complaints. Employees will not talk about the issue because they do not know who to talk with, what their rights are, or do not believe that they will be taken seriously. Employers are losing money by waiting until they have had a major sexual harassment situation before they commit themselves to prevention education.

The following approaches may convince top management of the need for a program.

- Do a survey of your employees and use the results to give management feedback on the extent of sexual harassment in their work place.
- Do a small pilot program for select personnel and have them sell the program for you.
- Find male management personnel who are sensitive to the issue and have them support your efforts to establish a training program.
- Focus your efforts on showing management that sexual harassment is not a women's issue but a management issue that affects all employees.

Sample Learning Objectives For Sexual Harassment Training Programs

Outlined below are learning objectives for three different sexual harassment training programs. Learning objectives for each program may be added or deleted to shorten or lengthen each program. The approximate program length is indicated for each program.

Each program should include: question and answer time, small group discussion, practice exercises to apply the techniques discussed in that program, and mini-lectures and scenarios to dramatize and clarify what is and is not sexual harassment.

Management Personnel—Program Length: 2–8 Hours

This program is designed to reduce an employer's potential legal and financial liability by teaching management personnel to prevent, recognize, and take "appropriate corrective action" to resolve sexual harassment situations in their work place.

Objectives

Upon completion, management personnel will be able to:

- Apply their employer's definition of sexual harassment and policy statement to their work place.
- Recognize their own and the employer's legal responsibilities and potential financial liabilities based on current court decisions and state and federal laws.
- Determine how sexual harassment could occur in their work place.
- Identify blatant-to-subtle forms of sexually harassing behavior in their work place.

- Recognize and minimize barriers which discourage victims of sexual harassment from talking to management.
- Recognize the specific effects of sexual harassment on its victims and the work place.
- Identify and apply specific techniques for preventing sexual harassment in their work place.
- Identify and apply specific methods for receiving and resolving sexual harassment complaints at the management level.
- Determine when to take action and what is "appropriate corrective action."

Employee—Program Length: 1–4 Hours

This program is designed to reduce the employer's and employee's potential legal and financial liability by teaching employees to recognize, prevent, and personally, or through their employer's complaint process, resolve sexual harassment situations.

Objectives

Upon completion, employees will be able to:

- Apply their employer's definition of sexual harassment and policy statement to their work place.
- Identify blatant-to-subtle forms of sexually harassing behavior in their work place.
- Recognize the specific effects of sexual harassment on its victims and the work place.
- Recognize their own legal responsibilities and potential financial liabilities based on current court decisions and state and federal laws.
- Identify and apply specific techniques to personally, or by using their employer's complaint process, resolve sexual harassment situations.

EEO Counselors/Personnel—Program Length: 4–16 Hours

This program is designed to reduce the employer's potential legal and financial liability by teaching EEO counselors/personnel to recognize, prevent and to take appropriate corrective action to resolve sexual harassment situations in the employer's work place.

Objectives

Upon completion, EEO counselors/personnel will be able to:

- Apply their employer's definition and policy statement concerning sexual harassment when resolving sexual harassment situations.
- Recognize their employer's legal responsibilities and potential financial liabilities based on current court decisions and sate and federal laws.

- Determine what is the appropriate corrective actions as defined by state and federal laws when resolving sexual harassment situations.
- Recognize blatant-to-subtle forms of sexually harassing behavior in their employer's work place.
- Identify and minimize barriers which discourage sexual harassment victims from giving their employer the opportunity to resolve the situation.
- Recognize the specific effects of sexual harassment on its victims and the work place.
- Identify and apply specific methods for receiving and resolving sexual harassment situations as a third party.

Participants' Frequent Statements And Questions About Sexual Harassment

This list of frequently asked questions and statements made by participants may be used by trainers to prepare themselves for their sexual harassment training program.

- How do you protect yourself from false charges?
- How do you deal with entrapment, i.e., an employee leads another on then yells sexual harassment?
- Asked of a male trainer: What right do you have to talk about this issue? Are you a sexual harasser?
- When does joking, flirting, teasing, hazing, and everyday behavior stop being OK and become sexual harassment?
- Why is an employer liable for the sexually harassing behavior of a manager if unaware of that behavior?
- Asked of a female trainer: Why should I listen to you, you just hate men?
- How can an employer be liable if his/her employee is sexually harassed by a non-employee?
- Is this the sex class? Where they teach you how?
- What is the difference between sexual harassment and sex discrimination?
- What is the legal basis for sexual harassment?
- I'd like to be sexually harassed!
- Why are we having this training?
- I've never seen it, so what's the problem?
- What are the legal trends?
- Can't the sexual harasser be forced to pay punitive damages to the victim? Why? How?

- Isn't this just another here-today, gone-tomorrow feminist issue?
- Under what circumstances can an employee collect unemployment benefits?
- Under what circumstances can an employee collect workers' compensation?
- Can an employer be liable for sexual harassment situations involving their employees which occur after work hours?
- Why do we have to take down pin-up pictures?
- Why do we have to change our behavior just because a "girl" starts working here?
- Do you have to wait until you receive a sexual harassment complaint before you take action? If not, isn't that interfering in people's personal lives?
- Don't you think that women are oversensitive about this issue?
- If she lets some guys hug her and tell her jokes, why is my behavior sexual harassment?
- It's biological. Men are just being men when they see sexy women.
- If she tells sexual jokes, why is my behavior sexual harassment if I tell her sexual jokes?
- What shouldn't I ask a sexual harassment victim when she/he complains?
- What is the best way to deal with a sexual harassment complaint when it is one person's word against another's?
- How do you deal with a sexual harasser who won't take the situation seriously?
- Why is this issue, all of a sudden, being dealt with?
- A man says, "Now I'm afraid to say anything to women!"
- With more women moving into management positions, will there be more cases of women sexually harassing men?
- Why is this issue so one-sided?
- Does this mean we can't have any more fun?
- What is the best way for a supervisor to talk about this issue with his/her employees?
- Is sexual harassment really a problem? Is it a problem in our workplace?
- How do you deal with a situation where a man sexually harasses a man? Woman to woman?
- What do you do if an employee who tells you about being sexually harassed doesn't want you to do anything about her/his complaint?
- If she tells a black man to stop touching her and files a complaint against him when he won't stop, and the male gets disciplined because of his

harassing behavior, does he have a valid race discrimination complaint against (1) the woman because she lets white guys touch her without claiming sexual harassment? (2) his supervisor?
- A woman says: "I don't understand what the problem is, I like men's attention," or, "Sure I dress sexy. Men love it."

It is imperative that the trainer knows how to respond in a non-defensive way to questions, statements and verbal attacks on them. The trainer gains or loses control and the groups' respect according to how he/she responds to questions and statements.

The major differences between the above model programs are that in the first program the participants will:

- have specific guidelines that tell them where the fine line between friendly and sexually harassing behavior is;
- talk more openly and seriously about the issue;
- recognize and change behavior that is, or may be, perceived as, sexual harassment;
- know how and when to take action to prevent or resolve sexual harassment situations.

Effective sexual harassment training programs are not panaceas for the unfair or sexist treatment of employees. They will encourage male and female employees to work together more effectively. This, in turn, has the impact of improving how everyone is treated and the overall quality of the work done.

The employer who has management personnel and employees who are ignorant about this sensitive issue are finding out that ignorance is not bliss, but is becoming very expensive.

- Northern States Power (NSP)'s program's strength is in that it uses an interactive approach with case studies, with case studies based on incidents that really occurred at NSP. (See **Form 6-4.**)
- The City of Bellevue, Washington has done an excellent job in producing a Management Information Manual provided in its entirety in **Form 6-5** and an Employee Manual provided in its entirety in **Form 6-6.**

The Management Information Manual includes the "Shades of Gray Continuum" described in **Chapter 1,** a discussion of awareness issues, what to do about sexual harassment, communication skills, and covers frequently asked questions. As becomes apparent, the main distinction between the two manuals is that the management program places a lot more emphasis on skills relating to prevention, investigation, data gathering, and knowledge of law and policy. The follow-up section helps managers ensure that their efforts and recommendations are acted upon. In addition, the management manual's case studies give managers typical scenarios to work on in trying out their own intervention skills.

- **Form 6-7** presents an outline for a workshop on sexual harassment issues prepared by staff at Harbridge House, Inc.
- **Form 6-8** is material excerpted from Dupont Corporation's training program. The training program is interactive and is facilitated by a mixed gender team with the use of videos.

FORM 6-4
WHAT IS HARASSMENT? NORTHERN STATE POWER COMPANY*

Northern States Power Company

* Reprinted with permission.

January 31, 1992

Dear fellow employee,

You and your fellow employees are the key to our company's strength. We must conduct our business with total integrity in an environment free of discrimination and other inappropriate behaviors.

All of us have the right to be treated fairly, with dignity and respect. Any violation of this right simply will not be tolerated. We will continue to enforce a "Zero Tolerance" approach to all forms of discrimination and harassment. Inappropriate behavior will result in the strict use of our Positive Discipline program with the possibility of termination.

Join me in making this a company that respects men and women of all ages, races, backgrounds, affectional orientations and physical abilities. With your commitment, we will create a diverse workforce that mirrors the communities we serve, enabling us to better serve our customers and keeping our company a great place to work.

Sincerely,

Harassment

Harassment is defined as verbal or physical conduct, which has the intent or effect of unreasonably interfering with an individual's or group's work performance, or which creates an intimidating, hostile, or offensive work environment. **Harassment could be based on gender, age, race, religion, affectional orientation, or national origin. These are the legally protected areas. However, the company policy covers all forms of harassment not just those covered by the laws.**

Sexual Harassment

Sexual harassment is prohibited most clearly by Title VII of the 1964 Civil Rights Act and by the State Human Rights Act. The legal definition is as follows:

Unwelcome sexual advances, requests for sexual favors, and other verbal or physical conduct of a sexual nature constitutes sexual harassment when:

1 Submission to such conduct is made either explicitly or implicitly a term or condition of an individual's employment.

2 Submission to or rejection of such conduct by an individual is used as the basis for employment decisions affecting such individual. **(Some examples of employment decisions are promotions, performance ratings, salary increases, or preferred work assignments.)**

3 Such conduct has the purpose or effect of unreasonably interfering with an individual's work performance or creating an intimidating, hostile, or offensive working environment. **(Physical or verbal advances, remarks, jokes, teasing or posting of sexually explicit pictures are a few examples.)**

Sexual harassment can occur in situations where one person has power over another, but it can also occur between equals. **Both men and women can be sexually harassed, though women are most often victimized.** Sexual harassment can be as blatant as rape or as subtle as a look. Harassment under the third part of the definition often consists of callous insensitivity to the experience of women.

In some Minnesota cases, personal liability has resulted when there has been harassment in the workplace.

Inappropriate Behavior

Behavior may also be viewed as inappropriate if it is not professional or consistent with a good business environment.

Employee conduct of a harassing or inappropriate nature will be dealt with fairly and objectively. The employee will receive an explanation of the inappropriateness of the behavior and the appropriate level of disciplinary action will be taken.

Zero Tolerance

Harassing behavior can seriously reduce employee morale, work quality, and productivity. It can also exact a heavy cost in both dollar terms and damage to NSP's reputation.

NSP will continue to enforce a "Zero Tolerance" approach to inappropriate behavior, including all forms of discrimination and harassment. **A thorough and objective investigation will take place to determine if an employee's behavior was inappropriate. If this behavior is verified, the employee will be subject to the strict use of our Positive Discipline program and the possibility of termination.**

Management Responsibility

Management has the responsibility of being aware of what is happening in their area. **If they observe or are advised of inappropriate behavior by the victim or a third party, they have the responsibility to act promptly.** This action can include the following:

◆ Thoroughly investigating claimed violations in a timely manner with the assistance of the Human Resources Department.

◆ Treating the matter as confidentially as possible to protect the privacy of the concerned employee(s).

◆ Communicating that any retaliation towards the affected individuals will not be tolerated.

◆ Enforcing appropriate disciplinary actions.

Reporting Harassment

NSP's harassment procedure assures you that you will have support in reporting any type of harassment or related inappropriate behavior. **If you experience or witness any type of harassment or inappropriate behavior, the following procedures are available for you to use:**

◆ You should deal with it immediately, advising the person that you feel the behavior is inappropriate and you would like it to stop.

◆ If you prefer not to discuss the matter with the person, or the person fails to respect your request, you should **report the incident to appropriate NSP management.** Your first contact normally should be your immediate supervisor; however, if you prefer, you can speak to any member of management in your organization.

◆ You may also **contact the Diversity Coordinator** at your location.

◆ Another option, is to **contact the Human Resources Department.** You can reach them at 330-2905, 330-7552, or 330-7714.

In all reported instances, a prompt, thorough and fair investigation will take place, giving careful consideration to protect the rights and dignity of all people involved. In addition, appropriate disciplinary action will be taken when it is determined that individuals have violated this policy.

Summary

In summary, it is the belief of NSP Management that most employees conduct themselves in a professional manner. However, if harassment occurs, NSP is confident that the procedure outlined above will assist you in better understanding how to deal with the issue.

About the cover . . .

This cover reflects potential oppression individuals and groups may suffer because of their differences. The icons represent only a fraction of these differences.

FORM 6-5
BELLEVUE, WASHINGTON SEXUAL HARASSMENT MANUAL

SEXUAL HARASSMENT

Management Information

Manual

City of Bellevue, Washington
1992

SEXUAL HARASSMENT

Employee Information Manual

City of Bellevue
March/April 1992

Contents

The Problem of Sexual Harassment

Sexual Harassment Defined

Sexual Harassment is unwelcome sexual advances, requests for sexual favors, and other verbal or physical conduct of a sexual nature:

- When submission to such conduct is made an implicit or explicit condition of employment;

- When submission or rejection of such conduct affects employment opportunities; or

- When the conduct interferes with an employee's work or creates an intimidating, hostile, or offensive work environment.

I believe sexual harassment occurs most often when:

_____

_____

_____

The most frequent kind of sexual harassment is:

_____

_____

_____

I believe that incidents of sexual harassment can be prevented/handled by:

_____

_____

_____

People are afraid to complain about harassment because:

_____

_____

_____

My organization's policy on sexual harassment is:

_____

_____

_____

Legal Definition of Sexual Harassment

Sexual harassment violates both Title VII of the 1964 Civil Rights Act and Chapter 49.60 of the Revised Code of Washington (Law Against Discrimination). These laws are enforced by the Equal Employment Opportunity Commission (EEOC), which is a federal agency, and by the Washington State Human Rights Commission.

Guidelines used by these agencies state that sexual harassment can be either physical or verbal, and always has some relationship to the employment of the victim. If any one of the following three criteria is present, so is sexual harassment.

Unwelcome advances, requests for sexual favors, and other verbal or physical conduct of sexual nature are illegal:

* If submitting to sexual advances is an open or implied condition of employment;

* If the employee's response to sexual advances becomes the basis for employment decisions such as promotion, transfer, or termination; or

* If the unwelcome conduct creates a hostile, intimidating, or offensive environment which interferes with an individual's job performance.

Case law has made it clear that employers will be held liable for the presence of sexual harassment in the workplace.

In addition, under civil law, individuals can be sued on charges of sexual harassment, and the City of Bellevue will not necessarily provide legal services or insurance for the harasser. (See Bellevue City Code, Chapter 3.81, for additional information.) In those cases involving assault, rape or indecent liberties, criminal charges can also be brought against the harasser.

City Policy on Sexual Harassment

It is the City of Bellevue's official policy that sexual harassment of one City employee by another City employee is prohibited. Sexual harassment is a form of unlawful discrimination under the provisions of Title VII of the 1964 Civil Rights Act and the Washington State Law Against Discrimination.

Sexual harassment is defined as unwelcome sexual advances, requests for sexual favors and other verbal or physical conduct of a sexual nature when:

1) Submission to such conduct is made either explicitly or implicitly a term or a condition of the individual's employment;

2) Submission to or rejection of such conduct by an individual is used as the basis for employment decisions affecting such individual; or

3) Such conduct has the purpose or effect of unreasonably interfering with an individual's work performance or creating an intimidating, hostile or offensive working environment.

Sexual harassment negatively affects morale, motivation and job performance. It results in increased absenteeism, turnover, tension and loss of productivity. It is inappropriate, offensive and illegal. Sexual harassment of any employee by any other employee of the City of Bellevue will not be tolerated.

Any employee who believes that she (or he) is encountering sexual harassment, or any employee who observes a situation which may be sexual harassment of another employee, is strongly encouraged to seek immediate assistance from his/her department director and/or the Personnel Department. It is the responsibility of all supervisory employees to report all complaints of sexual harassment or incidents warranting disciplinary action to their departmental management and the Personnel Department immediately so that the situation can be effectively investigated and resolved.

Because of the sensitive nature of the problem for all involved, any report of sexual harassment will be investigated immediately and confidentially, and appropriate action will be taken in order to protect all parties involved from further harassment, retaliation or false accusations. Appropriate disciplinary action will be taken for sexual harassment based on the severity of the offense.

Sources of Bellevue Policy:

* Personnel Policies and Procedures
* Affirmative Action Plan
* Employee Guidebook
* Union contracts
* Disciplinary Procedures
* Direct communication of department heads, managers and supervisors with all employees

A Practical Definition of Sexual Harassment

The legal guidelines used as a basis for Bellevue's policy on sexual harassment are sometimes not easy to apply to real-life situations. In practical terms, sexual harassment may be defined as follows:

Any verbal or non-verbal behavior in the workplace which:

- Focuses on the sexuality of another person or occurs because of the person's gender.

- Is unwanted.

- Is intentional or unintentional.

- Affects a person's employment.

Shades of Gray Continuum

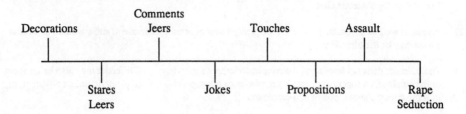

Light Gray   Medium Gray   Dark Gray

Some Important Facts About Sexual Harassment

1) What is sexual harassment to one person in one set of circumstances is not necessarily sexual harassment for someone else.

2) A man as well as a woman may be the recipient/victim of sexual harassment, and a woman as well as a man may be the offender.

3) The offender does not have to be the recipient/victim's supervisor. The offender may also be an agent of the employer, a supervisory employee who does not supervise the recipient/victim, a co-worker, or, in some circumstances, even a non-employee.

4) The recipient/victim does not have to be of the opposite sex from the offender. A male supervisor or co-worker making unwelcome sexual advances to a male employee may also be at fault for sexual harassment.

5) The recipient/victim does not have to be the person at whom the unwelcome sexual advances are directed. For example, sexual advances toward one employee which change the employment conditions of other employees may be harassment of those other employees.

6) The employer may be liable for harassment by a supervisor even if the recipient/victim did not complain to the offender or report the sexual harassment to his/her supervisor or employer. If the offender is a co-worker, the employer is liable if the employer knew or should have known of the harassment.

7) Unlawful sexual harassment does not depend on the recipient/victim's having suffered a concrete economic loss. If the harassment has interfered with the recipient/victim's work performance or has created an offensive environment, sexual harassment has occurred.

8) Retaliation against recipients/victims of harassment by the employer is considered a very serious offense by enforcement agencies.

9) Like rape, there is nothing "sexy" about sexual harassment. Sexual harassment is an abuse of power.

Some Behaviors That Might Be Interpreted as Sexual Harassment

*   Referring to women as "girls" or using other forms of endearment to refer to them at work.

*   Always commenting on the way a person looks; seldom commenting on the quality of his/her work.

*   Interrupting a person who is talking about work with comments about his/her appearance or physical attributes.

*   When working with a person, concentrating more on his/her appearance or sexual attractiveness than on what the person is saying.

*   Eye contact, staring or gazing at a person in a way that implies a sexual message or relationship.

*   Flirting: eye contact, teasing, touching, joking propositions, or comments filled with sexual innuendo or double meanings.

*   Telling jokes with a sexual meaning, tone, or implication.

*   Displaying cartoons, calendars, desk objects, or pin-ups which convey a sexual message, tone, or implication.

Responses to Offensive Behavior

Offensive behavior affects different people differently. Response to harassing conduct can be viewed as a continuum ranging from the minor irritation felt by a "recipient" of less severe behaviors to the extremely painful loss of self-esteem experienced by a "victim".

Based on initial self-confidence, experience, background and many other factors, people start at different points on the continuum. But as harassment is repeated or involves severe or intentional acts, a recipient's response to the situation usually becomes more like that of a victim.

People feeling victimized by sexual harassment do not simply need "assertiveness training" or more "self-confidence". Their feelings are a natural response to an abuse of power by the offender(s) and to being trapped in the situation.

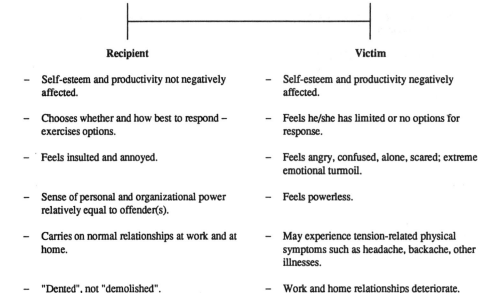

Recipient	Victim
– Self-esteem and productivity not negatively affected.	– Self-esteem and productivity negatively affected.
– Chooses whether and how best to respond – exercises options.	– Feels he/she has limited or no options for response.
– Feels insulted and annoyed.	– Feels angry, confused, alone, scared; extreme emotional turmoil.
– Sense of personal and organizational power relatively equal to offender(s).	– Feels powerless.
– Carries on normal relationships at work and at home.	– May experience tension-related physical symptoms such as headache, backache, other illnesses.
– "Dented", not "demolished".	– Work and home relationships deteriorate.

Understanding the Recipient/Victim and the Harasser

The following discussion of victims and harassers emphasizes the "typical" scenario of the male harasser and a female recipient/victim. <u>No assumption is made that this is the only way sexual harassment happens.</u>

It is true, however, that the greater proportion of harassers are men and the greater proportion of recipients/victims are women, and it has been shown that sexual harassment is a relatively common experience for women. Research studies conducted since 1975 indicate that between 40 to 70 percent of working women have experienced some form of sexual harassment. A major study of 23,000 federal office workers conducted by the Merit Systems Protection Board in 1980 showed that two-thirds of sexual harassment recipients/victims are women, and that women are twice as likely as men to experience more "severe" forms of harassment, such as uninvited touching or "cornering", uninvited pressure for sexual favors, and unwanted telephone calls or mail.

While these statistics indicate the size of the problem, they do not necessarily sensitize us to the **nature** of the problem. Oftentimes it is difficult for people outside the harasser/victim relationship to understand a harassment situation. We may ask ourselves, "Why doesn't Joe stop acting that way around Mary? Why doesn't Mary just tell Joe to bug off?" To understand why these things don't happen requires that we be aware of:

> The basic cultural messages that influence how men and women respond to each other.

> The nature of power and intimidation.

<u>Cultural Messages</u>

Times often change faster than people's values and beliefs. Beneath the modern emphasis on equality for men and women in the workplace, some of us hold deeply ingrained feelings about sexuality which may push us toward the role of harasser or victim. Some opinions about men and women which encourage sexual harassment of working women are:

* Women are sexual objects – they should not be equals or co-workers.

* Women are not as serious about their work and careers as are men.

* Women like sexual attention at work.

* Men need to be pleased and catered to because they are men.

* Men naturally "go as far as they can".

* If a woman doesn't stop a man's advances, it means she wants them to continue.

These messages set the stage for sexual harassment at work because they make it more difficult for men and women to respond to each other on an equal basis.

For example, a woman may feel uncomfortable telling a male co-worker to stop making sexist comments, because she doesn't want to be labeled as one of those "uptight, push" women. The male co-worker, on the other hand, continues to make the comments as a way to reinforce what he believes is his role as a man.

Both the man and woman are acting out cultural messages which have nothing to do with their roles as employees with jobs to get done.

Power Dynamics

One of the strongest cultural messages we have been influenced by is that men are by nature more powerful than women. The effect of this message is magnified many times by the fact that organizations are made up of different levels of power. The relationship of a male supervisor to a female subordinate may involve both a cultural message about men being stronger than women, and an organizational message about one person's job role being more powerful that another's. If the male supervisor makes sexual advances, he is exerting cultural _and_ economic power power.

```
Powerful                                                                          Powerless
   /---------------------------------------------------------------------------------------/
                        Supervisor                    Subordinate
       <----------------                                       ----------------->
                        and Male                       and Female
```

The impact of these combined power relationships on victims of sexual harassment is <u>intimidation</u>. In essence, the victim must choose between three painful courses of action:

* Fight the harassment in the face of 1) an extreme power difference based on both cultural and organizational roles, and 2) fear of retaliation;

* Flee the employment situation by quitting the job;

* Submit to the harassment and compromise personal integrity.

Faced with these choices, victims feel trapped, alone, angry, confused, and scared. <u>Because of the strong cultural and organizational messages about their level of power, victims may experience feelings which block their ability to tell the harasser to stop, especially if the harasser is the victim's supervisor or is someone higher in the organization.</u> They may suffer severe emotional and physical stress, including a loss of self-confidence, the deterioration of family and work relationships, and physical symptoms such as backaches, migraine headaches and signs of nervous tension.

Victims face clear economic, psychological and perhaps physical risks as they choose between confronting the harassment, putting up with it, or avoiding it by leaving the job.

By comparison, the harasser _may_ experience a sense of power over the victim, but in the majority of cases he will feel that he is simply acting out the proper relationship of the sexes within his role as co-worker or supervisor. He may be extraordinarily insensitive to the impact of his behaviors, believing that his actions will be considered desirable by the victim. He probably won't understand why the victim has a hard time telling him to stop. He may not consider the offensive behaviors sexual at all, but simply as signs of personal attention or flattery. When confronted, he may deny that he has harassed anyone and be angry, confused and disappointed. He may engage in open or subtle forms of retaliation against the victim.

Power Relationships

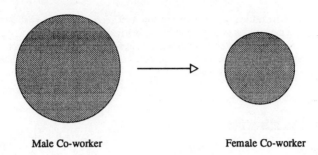

Male Co-worker   Female Co-worker

When a male supervisor makes advances to a female employee, he is exerting both organizational power, based on his position as a supervisor, and cultural power which comes from the traditional societal belief that men are more powerful than ~~men~~. *women*

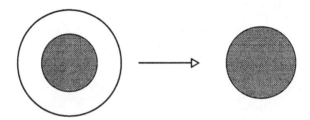

Although two employees may occupy similar jobs for the organization, a male co-worker may still exert organizational power based on seniority, reputation in the work group, technical expertise, or an apparent "'in'" with management. Additionally, he may exert cultural power, and personal power derived from self-confidence, physical size, verbal skills or other sources.

The impact on the recipient/victim in either of the above cases can be devastating.

Why a Person Might Not Say Anything to Stop the Harassment

Sometimes co-workers have difficulty understanding how a recipient/victim of sexual harassment could have a hard time telling the harasser to stop the offensive behaviors. This lack of understanding can lead to less sensitivity to the recipient/victim's situation, and less support for him/her as a person. The opinions and beliefs of co-workers can have a painfully isolating effect, making it even more difficult for the offended person to get the harassment stopped.

Some reasons recipients/victims do not say anything are:

* <u>Repercussions – fear of retaliation</u>

    - Loss of job.
    - Loss of promotional opportunities or other benefits of employment.
    - Loss of respect from co-workers and supervisors; being labeled as a "trouble-maker".
    - Damage to personal reputation through the "rumor mill".
    - Not being considered a "team player".
    - Not being considered someone who has "a sense of humor".

* <u>Low self-esteem</u>

    - Not having the courage to speak out.
    - Having an attitude of "deserving" the harassment.
    - Not knowing the words to use to stop the harassment.

* <u>Not knowing the procedures to use when making a complaint</u>

* <u>Lack of trust in "the system"</u>

The City of Bellevue is committed to preventing sexual harassment and stopping harassment if it occurs. This is a matter of teamwork and mutual support among all employees. Supervisors and co-workers should help a person being harassed not to feel alone or scared. They should help the person get assistance from City resources, such as a department head, anyone in the Personnel Department, or the City Manager's Office.

Possible Indicators That Someone Feels Harassed

Negative changes in the way a person approaches the job are almost always an indication that something is wrong. Although there are many possible explanations for the following behaviors, sexual harassment can also cause such things as:

*   A drop in <u>productivity</u>, in volume or quality of work performed; difficulty with instructions or procedures; repeated mistakes; disinterest in the work; assignments seeming to require more effort than in the past.

*   Persistent <u>attitude or mood shifts</u> with no apparent explanation; evidence of emotional turmoil.

*   <u>Attendance problems</u>, including higher than normal use of sick leave, frequent tardiness , and "on the job" absenteeism through extended coffee breaks, long lunches, frequent trips to the restroom.

*   On-the-job <u>accidents</u>.

*   <u>Alliance building</u> or <u>conflicts</u> with co-workers.

*   Repeated <u>criticism</u> or argumentativeness; making sarcastic, cutting comments.

*   <u>Withdrawal</u> or <u>exclusion</u> by co-workers from work group activities, leading to anger, sensitivity and depression.

*   <u>Negative exchanges</u> with clients of the City.

Other specific behaviors which can be observed in an offended person include – but are not limited to:

*   Overly timid responses to people; low eye contact.

*   Tension, frustration, anger, or depression, expressed through body language and tone of voice.

*   Lack of laughter or smiling, particularly when a potentially offensive joke or comment is made.

*   "Flinching" when coarse language is used.

Management Responsibilities and Skills

Why Sexual Harassment Should be
Taken Seriously by Managers

Taking sexual harassment seriously is a <u>sound management practice</u> which can result in:

* Higher productivity.

* Higher morale.

* Greater time-on-task.

* Clearer standards for employee performance.

* Fewer turnover problems and costs.

Taking sexual harassment seriously is part of <u>compliance with the law</u>, and can result in:

* Reduction of illegal, discriminatory behavior.

* A positive work environment where people are treated fairly and enjoy equal opportunity for hiring, training and promotion.

* Greater understanding of how and why complaints are filed.

* Increased awareness by employees of their legal responsibilities.

Taking sexual harassment seriously is a matter of <u>organization policy</u> which can result in:

* Being able to avoid possible disciplinary action for not doing your job right.

* A decrease in the likelihood of complaints about sexual harassment – which take great time and energy to resolve.

* More confidence in handling complaints if they happen.

* A real contribution to the overall effectiveness of your organization through improvements in productivity, communication, and ethics.

Summary of Management Responsibilities
Related to Sexual Harassment

City of Bellevue managers and supervisors are responsible for maintaining a work environment free of sexual harassment. This means that managers and supervisors must be able to identify sexual harassment, prevent sexual harassment incidents, and respond effectively to sexual harassment if it happens.

Understanding and being able to carry out these responsibilities is a clear expectation for all Bellevue managers and supervisors. **Failure to do so may result in corrective or disciplinary action up to and including termination from City service.**

There are three primary conditions specified by the Equal Employment Opportunity Commission when management, supervisory personnel, or the City will be held accountable for sexual harassment:

1) When the supervisor or manager personally commits acts of sexual harassment.

2) When an employee commits an act of sexual harassment against another employee and a supervisor knew or should have known of the conduct. Unless the supervisor can show that he/she took timely and appropriate action, he/she and/or the City of Bellevue can be held legally responsible.

3) When a non-employee commits an act of sexual harassment against an employee and the supervisor knew or should have known of the conduct and no remedial action was taken.

If a manager or supervisor is in doubt whether one of these conditions applies to a specific situation, he/she should immediately consult with higher management and the Personnel Department.

Responsibilities of Managers and Supervisors

Preventing Sexual Harassment

* Understand federal and state laws, and City policies related to sexual harassment.

* Observe what's going on around you in the workplace. A wide range of behavior can be considered sexual harassment. Supervisors need not define the offensive behavior to a legal certainty, but must recognize conduct that might be construed as sexual harassment and is inappropriate to the workplace. Supervisors must then take steps to eliminate that behavior.

* Model the type of non-offensive behavior you expect from your employees. Do not commit acts of sexual harassment and avoid personal behaviors which could be interpreted as sexual harassment.

* Train your staff in sexual harassment awareness.

Responding Effectively to Sexual Harassment Incidents and Complaints Between Employees

Management staff are expected to immediately intervene in any situation which may be sexual harassment, and to stop further harassment from occurring.

Notify the department head and the Personnel Department (or the City Manager's Office) immediately of any complaint, or of any observed incident which warrants a formal oral warning or more severe disciplinary action.

* Move quickly to work with the possible harassment situation.

* With assistance from appropriate management and personnel staff, **thoroughly** and **confidentially** investigate the situation.

* If someone in your organization is the recipient/victim of sexual harassment, let that person know that you see what is happening and what you intend to do in regard to the harassment. Listen attentively to the recipient/victim. Encourage him or her to be assertive wit the offender. If necessary, work with the recipient/victim to develop a set of strategies which will prevent the offender from continuing the offensive behavior. Be sure to let the victim know about resources which are available to provide additional support.

* Do not be tempted to "let this one go", even if the recipient/victim would like you to, unless the infraction is minor and unrepeated. Managers and supervisors are **obligated** under the law to act if they know of a sexual harassment situation. If unsure as to what constitutes "minor and unrepeated", consult immediately with higher management and the Personnel Department.

* Take appropriate problem-solving and corrective action with the offender. Confront him or her in regard to the offensive behavior and discuss ways to eliminate it. Do not hesitate to discipline the offender if it is warranted. Make sure the offender knows why he/she is being disciplined and what the standards are for appropriate conduct. Carefully monitor the offender's behavior to ensure that further instances of harassment do not occur. Be sure to let the offender know about resources which are available to provide assistance.

* Follow-up with the recipient/victim, offender and observers of the situation. The problem has not been truly resolved until the side-effects of the situation have been addressed. If appropriate, recommend use of the City's Where to Turn Employee Assistance Program to help those involved cope with side-effects of the harassment experience and complaint.

Responding to Sexual Harassment between City Clients and Employees

* In situations involving harassment of a City employee in the workplace by a client of City services, notify your department head and the Personnel Director (or City Manager's Office) immediately.

The department head or other designated manager will investigate the situation, obtaining a written statement from the recipient/victim covering the details of the incident. The manager will then contact the client (if possible) to discuss the complaint, explain City policies prohibiting harassment and obtain the client's cooperation in ceasing the problem behaviors. This discussion should be documented and shared with the employee.

In the event of continued complaints involving the same client, the manager should send a follow-up letter to the client or see the client to address the issue. The designated Bellevue manager should develop a clear agreement with the client that such behavior is to stop. The agreement should be put in writing, and all related discussions should be documented.

In cases involving potential criminal behavior, the recipient/victim or designated manager should report the incident(s) to the Police Department.

The manager will follow-up with the victim (and any observers) to explain how the situation has been resolved, provide appropriate coaching and support, and help remedy other side-effects of the situation.

Expectations for Bellevue Managers and Supervisors

1. The City of Bellevue fully supports equal opportunity laws and the belief that men and women have equal rights to employment in all areas of City service.

2. Managers and supervisors are fully responsible for what happens in the workplace. That is, they are responsible for managing productivity by ensuring a discrimination-free work environment.

3. This responsibility reflects sound management practice which is not only mandated by federal and State laws, but also by specific Bellevue policies and the City's Organizational Philosophy Statement.

4. Individual managers and supervisors are expected to positively implement these policies and values in their day-to-day activities.

Four Key Managerial Responsibilities

Prevention	Investigation	Intervention	Follow-Up
Model appropriate behavior.	Model appropriate behavior.	Model appropriate behavior.	Model appropriate behavior.
Observe interactions in workplace.	Observe interactions in workplace	Observe interactions in workplace.	Observe interactions in workplace.
Educate co-workers and employees.	Educate co-workers and employees.	Educate co-workers and employees.	Educate co-workers and employees.
	Collect data.	Collect data.	Collect data.
	Analyze data.	Analyze data.	Analyze data.
	Determine appropriate responses.	Determine appropriate responses.	Determine appropriate responses.
		Educate co-workers and employees.	Confront harassers.
		Confront harassers.	Counsel harassers and victims.
		Counsel harassers and victims.	Problem solve with harassers and victims.
		Problem solve with harassers and victims.	Discipline harassers.
		Discipline harassers.	Develop a follow-up plan.
			Monitor interaction of those involved.
			Support the victim.

-19-

Prevention

(Includes ideas from supervisors and managers who participated in the 1988 training and prevention program.)

1. Model Appropriate Behavior

Keep in mind that what you do has a profound effect on those who work for you. Be sensitive to real or perceived effects of your actions. Because of the element of "control" associated with their positions, the actions of supervisors can have a great impact on production, be interpreted as favoritism, inhibit honest expression of discomfort, or have other effects.

Exhibit positive behaviors that demonstrate an understanding of sex discrimination issues. Actively model the behaviors you expect from your subordinates.

Implement policies consistently. Don't play favorites.

Demonstrate a willingness to discuss sexual harassment. Don't sweep this topic under the rug. Let employees know you are available to answer their questions.

Contact higher management or the Personnel Department if you have questions about policies or questionable behaviors you have observed.

Let people know you will take action if a case comes to your attention.

Participate in training.

2. Create and Maintain a Positive, Productive Workplace

Foster upward communication from employees and act on the information they provide; conduct a formal or informal "employee satisfaction survey"; make it safe for employees to speak up.

Establish clear work goals and expectations, including standards for job performance and conduct.

Orient new employees. Help them fell welcome and to succeed.

Maintain high visibility in solving workplace problems of all kinds.

Discuss the meaning of the City's Organizational Philosophy.

Engage in team building activities that include anyone in the work-unit; emphasize group problem-solving and respect for individual contributions.

Give positive rewards for desirable behaviors and achievements.

Distribute positive rewards for desirable behaviors and achievements.

Distribute articles about workplace issues, sexual harassment prevention being one of them.

Address work climate issues directly – deal with counter-productive attitudes and interpersonal conflicts.

Get to know your people through staff meetings, open-door policies and "wandering around" management – let them get to know you.

Assess the psychological work environment – think about the ways each person relates to others on the work team; take action where problems exist.

Establish mutual respect and communications as group "norms".

Concentrate on quality – in services provided and in relationships between people.

3.   Observe Interactions in the Workplace

Be conscious of how your employees relate to one another – pay attention to everyday interactions. Don't take it for granted that sexual harassment does not happen in your work area.

Be sensitive to the way in which those who are more vulnerable may react to the behavior of others.

Watch for the more subtle forms of sexual harassment and how they may negatively affect the work and self-esteem of those in your work environment.

Correct environmental considerations, such as an isolated work station, if this creates a real potential for harassment problems.

4.   Educate Co-Workers and Employees

Conduct training on sexual harassment awareness for those who work for you. For example, make sexual harassment awareness part of a staff meeting agenda.

Train people on related communication skills, such as assertiveness and conflict resolution.

Inform employees that sexual harassment is a violation of the law and be specific about the consequences.

Personally express strong disapproval of sexual harassment.

Encourage employees to say "no" if confronted with a harassment situation.

Initiate formal and informal feedback about the issue. For example, provide information as part of scheduled and day-to-day employee guidance, appraisal, mentoring and career development discussions.

Encourage employees to read and understand Bellevue's sexual harassment policies.

Provide others with information about resources within Bellevue that are available to them if they need assistance in handling a situation involving sexual harassment.

Support employees' right to protest illegal harassment.

Show a willingness to intervene with and counsel employees whose behavior could be interpreted as sexual harassment.

Take action on discrimination issues quickly. Let people know what to expect.

Assure employees that incidents of sexual harassment will be corrected promptly.

Investigation

Before initiating any investigatory procedure, contact the Personnel Department for guidance.

A. **Collect Data**

Investigating a sexual harassment complaint is a sensitive matter. You will need to draw on your best supervisory skills. For this reason and due to the great liabilities associated with sexual harassment situations, you should definitely consult with higher management and the Personnel Department throughout the process.

As with any investigation which could lead to disciplinary action, be sensitive to the rights of all parties, and proceed in a manner which demonstrates objectivity, fairness and a concern for appropriate confidentiality. Find a private place to conduct your interviews. **Be sure to document all aspects of the investigation.**

When Talking with an Alleged Recipient/Victim

Keep in mind that it may be very difficult for a person to talk about a potential or real harassment situation. The person may have very strong emotions about harassment, including anger, frustration, embarrassment and self-doubt.

Speak clearly and calmly with an even, non-judgmental tone in your voice. Approach the interview in a sensitive, supportive manner. Keep good eye contact and remember to paraphrase what the person says if you don't fully understand his/her statements. Listen attentively. Your first goal is to develop a true and accurate account of what happened.

1. Obtain the date/time of all offensive incidents.

2. Answer the questions: who, what, when and where. Find out what specifically happened in each incident.

3. Determine the background of the situation, including the relationship between the parties before the offensive behavior.

4. Record the person's _feelings_ about the offensive behaviors and its impact on his/her work performance.

5. Obtain the names of anyone else who ...

   * Saw or heard the incidents.

   * The person has talked to about the incidents.

   * The person believes has been harassed by the alleged offender.

6. Determine what the person did in response to the offensive behavior.

7. Find out whether the person has documentation or other tangible evidence of the offensive incident.

8. Reassure the person that there will be no retaliation for having come forward.

9. Enlist the person's cooperation in maintaining confidentiality.

With an Alleged Harasser

As with the recipient/victim, you need to approach your interview in a non-judgmental, sensitive manner, with due consideration for the strong feelings which the alleged offender may have, including anger, frustration, embarrassment, fear, and confusion. <u>Keep in mind that a person is innocent until proven at fault.</u> Unreasonable assumptions of guilt before an investigation has been completed can <u>create</u> inappropriate behavior, including retaliation against the alleged recipient/victim.

1. If the alleged offender is a member of a City bargaining unit and asks for union representation, allow it.

2. Present the incidents described by the recipient/victim, or your own observations if you directly saw an incident.

3. Get the alleged offender's side of the story in each case.

4. Investigate with such questions as:

   * Describe your interaction with the recipient/victim.

   * Do you think you might have done anything that might have caused the recipient/victim to feel offended?

   * To what degree have you used sexual language, innuendo, jokes or other mannerisms in the workplace?

   * Did you ever threaten or insult the recipient/victim in any way?

   * What were the business reasons for your interactions with the recipient/victim?

5. Listen attentively as the alleged offender talks.

6. Consider the degree to which the behavior was mutual and reciprocal.

7. Advise the alleged offender to cease all behaviors that could be construed as sexual harassment. If appropriate and possible, ask the person to end all contact with the recipient/victim.

8. Advise the alleged offender of the seriousness of any form of retaliation against the recipient/victim, or any action that might be interpreted as retaliation.

9. Remind the alleged offender to keep the matter confidential.

With Observers or Others in the Workplace

Recognize that observers may also be disturbed by the harassment and have strong emotions. After all, "observers" may also turn out to be recipients/victims. Listen attentively.

1. Investigate with such questions as:

   * What type of interaction have you observed between the recipient/victim and the offender?

   * From your point of view, was the offender bothering the recipient/victim?

   * Are there others who might be able to comment on the interaction of the recipient/victim and offender?

   * Did the recipient/victim ever complain to you about the offender's behavior?

   * Has this person ever done anything to offend you? (If so, refer to the questions shown above for interviewing recipients/victims.)

2. Remind the observer to keep the matter confidential, and that no retaliation is permitted.

B. Analyze Data

Review the law, the practical definition of sexual harassment and Bellevue policies.

Determine the extent to which your investigation suggests that sexual harassment – or some other form of inappropriate conduct – has taken place. The following checklist may be helpful:

[ ] Did the situation involve:

    [ ] Pin-ups, cartoons or other "decorations".
    [ ] Staring at a person's body, "mentally undressing" someone.
    [ ] Sexually oriented conversation, comments, or remarks with double meanings.
    [ ] Sexually oriented jokes; jokes that make fun of a particular person's sexuality.
    [ ] Touching that is personal and inappropriate to the workplace, including unwanted "helpful" grooming of another person or "inadvertent" body contact.
    [ ] Serious or "joking" invitations for dates, or other invitations which have sexual overtones.
    [ ] Serious or "joking" propositions.
    [ ] Assault.
    [ ] Rape.

[ ] Do all of the people involved in the situation enjoy and appreciate the behavior in question?

[ ] Could anyone involved be offended by the behavior? Does the behavior put anyone down?

[ ] Has anyone requested that the behavior stop?

[ ] Has the behavior continued after someone requested that it stop?

[ ]   Has anyone shown signs of discomfort or frustration at the behavior?

[ ]   Has anyone's job performance or career been affected by the behavior, or has the recipient/victim been threatened with any loss of job privileges?

[ ]   Does the behavior suggest a "predisposition to discriminate"?

[ ]   Who is the target of the behavior? How vulnerable is this person? How likely is it that this person would complain?

[ ]   Even if the behavior is not sexual harassment, does it interfere with productivity, damage employee morale, or create an atmosphere of negativity and mistrust in the workplace?

[ ]   Is this a common behavior for the person initiating the behavior in question?

[ ]   Has he/she been disciplined for this type of behavior before?

If you decide that sexual harassment or illegal discrimination does exist, document all your answers to these questions.

C. **Determine Appropriate Responses**

Carefully review the data from your analysis in conjunction with the department head and the Personnel Department.

If it is determined that the sexual harassment or other inappropriate behavior is present, develop a list of possible and appropriate responses which will:

* Correct the offensive/inappropriate behavior.

* Appropriately discipline the harasser.

* Allow the recipient/victim to regain his/her self-confidence.

* Re-establish a positive and productive working environment for the recipient/victim and others involved.

* Maintain City policies and standards for behavior.

Select a course of action which will best meet the needs of the recipient/victim and the City.

Considering the Alleged Recipient/Victim

In making your decision, consider the following:

Are the charges true?

Can the charges be verified?

What steps need to be taken to restore the recipient/victim's position, self-esteem, credibility, or privileges?

Inform the person of your decision.

If any of the charges prove false, take appropriate corrective action.

Document your decision and your justifications for it; document all interactions.

Considering the Alleged Harasser

Before corrective action is determined, carefully consider the following:

1. Is the alleged harasser at fault or innocent?

2. If innocent, what needs to be done to maintain or restore his/her credibility/

3. If at fault, how severe was the harassment as indicated by the impact on the recipient/victim, the organization and harasser?

4. Were other policies, laws, or work rules violated?

5. Was the violation intentional or unintentional?

6. Was the offender aware of the policy and/or should he or she have been?

7. How cooperative/truthful was the offender when confronted?

8. Were others involved as harassers or recipients/victims?

9. What was the involvement or level of knowledge of the immediate manager?

10. Do others need to be consulted on the disposition of the case?

11. What corrective action is appropriate?

12. Have all appropriate levels of management been kept informed and involved?

13. Have all available internal resources been used to resolve the issue?

Inform the harasser/alleged harasser of your decision.

Document your decision and interaction.

Intervention

A. Confronting Harassers

Be direct and specific when confronting a harasser. Describe his/her behavior, how it is offensive of inappropriate, and the impact it has on the recipient/victim and others.

If possible, obtain the harasser's agreement that there is a problem.

Outline your expectations for his/her future behavior.

Describe the consequences of your expectations not being met.

Announce any necessary disciplinary action, following City procedures and guidelines.

Document your discussion.

Three Types of Feedback

When a supervisor observes sexual harassment – **or some type of inappropriate behavior which might indicate sexual harassment** – he or she should intervene. Depending on the situation, the nature of the behaviors, and those involved, the type of intervention will vary. Once it is clear what has happened, the first step is to provide feedback regarding your standards for conduct to the offender. This sort of corrective action will have the most powerful effect when it is descriptive of the inappropriate behavior and is given soon after such behavior has taken place. Examples of such feedback are listed below.

Direct and Immediate

"One more sexist comment like that from you, Jones, and you'll be facing disciplinary action."

"Those kind of jokes are totally out of line. I want them stopped now."

"I want those calendars brought down immediately. They don't have anything to do with getting the job done and could easily offend someone who walks in here."

Delayed and Assertive

"Susan, I've noticed that since Jack has joined our staff, you have starting making derogatory comments about men. Your comments and jokes could be offensive to him and to others. They are definitely offensive to me. I don't want to hear them, or hear of them, again."

"Andy, Bill, you were sent out here to repair a sidewalk, not invite citizen complaints by ogling the passers-by, whistling and making comments. If I ever see that kind of behavior again, you'll be written up."

"Mike, when you talk about women and use words like 'broads' or 'chicks', it really puts women down. There's no reason for that kind of talk in our work group when you know we are all trying to improve communication."

"Ed, I was surprised at you this morning at the staff meeting. When Jane made her presentation, you stopped paying attention and started joking around. It made me think you've got a problem with her in the role of team leader. What was going on with you anyway?"

After-the-Fact and General

"I've noticed the language out there in the shop is getting out of line. Let's clean it up out there."

"Remember, when you're interacting with citizens, you can't assume that they'll appreciate the same kind of humor that you do. Be sensitive to the different people you'll be meeting. What you say to others will have a lot to do with how citizens see the City. You have a direct impact on the City's reputation."

"I've been told by some of the women in this division that they get generally frustrated by men who continually refer to women as 'girls'."

"I don't want to hear any more rumors or negative comments about gay men in this department."

B.   Counseling Recipients/Victims

A supervisor can play an important part in helping the recipient/victim cope with and possibly correct the problem on his/her own.

First, indicate that offensive behavior is not part of the job, is clearly against City policies, is not the person's fault, and that **you**, as the supervisor, are willing to address the issue. It is **not** necessary for an offended person to confront the harasser.

Also, do not let the recipient/victim talk you into "letting it go this time" unless the offense is minor and unrepeated. You have an obligation under law to intervene and prevent sexual harassment.

As part of your counseling you should **encourage** the recipient/victim to talk to the harasser and tell him/her to stop the offensive behavior. This may help the recipient/victim overcome some of the feelings of powerlessness that often go with a sexual harassment situation. Encourage the recipient/victim to describe to the harasser how the offensive behaviors interfere with work. The recipient/victim should say things like:

"Don't touch me. I don't like it. It makes me uncomfortable and then I make mistakes."

"No. I don't want to go out with you. Do do not mix my work and personal life."

"I don't think those kind of jokes are funny. They don't have anything to do with work. Please don't tell them when I am in the room."

"I'd like it a lot better if you'd comment on the quality of my work, rather than the way I look."

My name is _____, not 'Honey'."

If appropriate, ask the recipient/victim to consider how his/her own behavior may be contributing to the problem. A recipient/victim may be unknowingly encouraging harassment by style of dress or communications. Recipients/victims should not encourage harassers by smiling, laughing at their jokes or "flirting back". This type of response can lead the harasser to believe the victim really enjoys the offensive behavior.

Encourage the victim to put her/his objections in writing, sending one copy to the harasser and keeping one copy for her/himself.

Be sure to have the recipient/victim tell you if the offensive behaviors continue.

Ask the recipient/victim to document all sexual harassment incidents or conversations by the incidents. The recipient/victim should record the date, time, place, people involved, exactly what happened, and who said what to whom.

As supervisor, you also should document all your discussions with the recipient/victim, and carefully monitor how the situation proceeds.

Let the person know you respect his/her rights to solve the problem independently, but provide a strict time limit. If the situation has not been corrected at that time, take action to resolve the problem.

C. **Counseling Harassers**

Suggest the following action to harassers:

1. "Pay attention to how others respond to what you do and say."

2. "Don't assume that your co-workers or employees enjoy comments about their appearance, hearing sexually oriented jokes or comments, being touched, stared at, or propositioned."

3. "Think about the impact of what you do and say on others' attitudes toward work, job performance, self-esteem, and the City's reputation."

4. "Talk to your spouse, family members, and close friends about experiences they might have had with sexual harassment. As people describe the vulnerability, powerlessness, or anger they experienced as victims, relate those feelings to experiences you have had."

5. "Do not assume that individuals who work for you will tell you if they are offended –or harassed – by what you say or do. Remember that one of your employees may be smiling on the outside but crying on the inside simply because you are the boss."

6. "Remember that sexual harassment is against the law. Recent court decisions have resulted in both organizations and individuals paying large fines, not to mention the adverse publicity and personal gain which results from a legal action."

<u>If the Harasser is a Supervisor or Manager</u>

Remind the person of his/her clear responsibilities under the law to maintain a workplace free of sexual harassment. Remind the person of the serious consequences of failure to fulfill his obligation. Have the harasser carefully re-read this Management Information Manual.

Document your interactions.

D.   Listening Skills

Paraphrasing

In order to paraphrase something someone has said, simply translate his/her message into your own words. For example:

Someone says to you, "I've done everything I know how to do to get those guys to lighten up – and they still keep hassling me."

You paraphrase by saying, "You've tried hard to get them to stop making comments."

Or, "You sound really frustrated."

Or, "It sounds like you've run out of ideas for how to handle their behavior."

Paraphrases are sentences, not questions. They are extremely effective at "checking out" what the other person has said so that you really understand his/her message before you give your response. Plus, in tense situations, they give you additional time to think of what your best response should be. Ways to begin paraphrasing what someone else has said are:

"It sounds to me like ..."
"You seem ..."
"You ..."
"You want/need/intend ..."
"You appear ..."
"You're saying ..."
"You're telling me that ..."
"In other words ..."
"I hear you saying that ..."

Clarifying Questions

Clarifying questions help you to better understand what another person is saying. They gather information as well as insight – both of which are very important for you to have before you express your thoughts in emotionally charged situations. They are open-ended and give the other person plenty of opportunity to respond in any way he/she chooses. Examples of clarifying questions are listed below.

"What do you think might have caused this behavior?"
"How could you have handled the situation differently?"
"How do you expect others to react whey they hear this?"

"Why do you feel this way?"
"What do you think will happen next?"
"What would you like to have happen now?"

Keep in mind that the tone of how you ask the question is all important. For example, using an accusatory tone when asking "What do you think might have caused this behavior?" could be heard as blaming or punishing a person for a situation. By contrast, a neutral or supportive tone to the same question focuses the discussion on problem-solving.

E. **Sending Messages**

Assertive Statements

Assertive statements are short, direct statements which indicate your interests, desires, or intentions. They are more powerful when delivered looking at the other person straight in the eye' spoken with a firm, strong voice where the last syllable spoken has a lowered voice tone. Assertive statements are best when delivered in a polite, non-judgmental tone of voice. They are neither "nice", nor "mean", they are simply assertive.

Some beginnings for assertive statements are:

"I want ..."
"I intend ..."
"I am asking for ..."
"I will ..."
"I need for you to ..."
"I expect ..."

Examples of assertive statements which can be used in situations involving sexual harassment are listed below.

"I expect you to change your behavior immediately."

"If you bother me again, I intend to go straight to your supervisor with this information."

"I need for you to tel me exactly what happened."

"I will follow-up on our discussion and get back to you by next week."

"I'm asking for your cooperation in this matter. I'm trying to find out exactly what happened between _____ and _____ last Wednesday afternoon."

Problem-Solving with the Recipient/Victim and Harasser

Sometimes the best solution to the problem is not formal discipline, but education.

A harasser may be exhibiting offensive behaviors which he/she feels are complimentary, and may be entirely unconscious of the negative impact of these behaviors. All of us are liable to make mistakes from time to time, and it is unreasonable and unfair to "bring down the axe" when the situation might

-32-

be corrected through a brief, non-judgmental discussion. This does not, of course, mean that you should ignore or fail to address infractions.

It could be desirable to have a problem-solving discussion with the recipient/victim or offender. This may be a helpful way to separate out sex discrimination problems from work-related or personality issues having to do with such things as work roles and assignments, office arrangements (i.e., who got the office by the window), distribution of rewards (i.e., who got a special assignment, who did not), or professional jealousies between the parties. **The offensive behaviors may not be related to sexual harassment, but they may still be offensive and need to be resolved.**

Be careful. This is complex territory. It has a direct relationship to how sensitive you are, as a supervisor, to the subtleties of discrimination. If in doubt, consult higher authority and the Personnel Department for assistance. You do not want to inadvertently escalate the situation by being insensitive to the **perception** of sexual harassment.

When investigating a sexual harassment issue you may learn a few things about how your operation is perceived. There may be some problem-solving you can do on your own which will prevent people from incorrectly interpreting coincidental events or "thoughtless" circumstances to be discrimination issues. For example,

* Do the female professional employees happen to always "catch the phone" when the receptionist is tied up, or is that responsibility shared with males?

* Does the office seating arrangement place vulnerable people in a position to be harassed without others knowing it?

* Is there an "informal organizational chart" that gives one sex in the organization better access to information?

* How are decisions made on who gets to attend training programs or conferences? Do employees understand these criteria?

* **How good are you at giving performance feedback and appraisals?** Are people aware of their performance strengths and weaknesses, or are they left to figure out on their own why their job assignments are as they are, why they did or didn't get promoted, why you allowed one employee to have a "flextime" schedule, but not others in the organization?

Don't sugar-coat your appraisal of any employee, and particularly not he problem employee or marginal performer. Accurate, behaviorally-oriented assessments communicate your real standards for performance and will be useful should you need to justify corrective action later.

If there are problems in the above areas, you leave yourself open to unfounded allegations or discrimination which will take considerable time and effort to resolve. Direct, honest communication about the work-related reasons for your decisions, and accurate job performance feedback may save you hours of trouble and problem-solving with employees who have developed a discrimination theory around your unexplained actions. **After-the-fact problem-solving is very difficult to do.**

Disciplining Harassers

Section 3.79.050 of the Bellevue City Code specifically identifies sexual harassment as a cause for disciplinary action against employees. (In fact, it's the first item on the list of causes for disciplinary action.)

Applying corrective action is never easy, and the complexities of sexual harassment make a supervisor's job even more difficult. The following section summarizes general principles about administering corrective action and then ties that information to disciplining sexual harassers.

To begin with, the intent of discipline is to correct and train offenders, not to punish them. Such action should therefore follow "The Hot Stove Rule". That is, administering discipline ought to mirror the effect of someone placing their hand on a hot stove. Corrective action should be:

*   Immediate. Feedback to the offender should be given as soon after the offense as possible.

*   Impersonal. Discipline is not a personal vendetta, nor is it to be carried out while upset or angry. Announcing a disciplinary measure should occur in a calm manner which simply conveys the fact of the action.

*   Forewarning. Just as a hot stove gives off heat as a forewarning to the person who is about to place a hand on the stove, so organizations need to give advance notice to employees of work rules and obligations.

*   Consistent. No matter who touches the stove, that person will be burned. Accordingly, no favoritism should be shown in taking corrective action. Consistency does not mean, however, that every employee is treated identically. The circumstances of an offense, the number of times it has been repeated, whether the person has recently been warned, and other factors need to be considered when applying the principle of consistency.

*   Progressive. The closer the hand to the stove, the greater the pain. The severity of the offense, and whether it has been repeated should dictate the level of action which needs to be taken. In Bellevue, progressive disciplinary procedures are spelled out in the City's Personnel Policies and Procedures and may union contracts.

Progressive Discipline is divided into four stages:

Oral Warning: This stage is used for relatively minor infractions and first-time offenses of a generally non-serious nature. The offender is called aside and informed of the infraction. He/she is warned of the effects of his/her actions and the consequences of further violations. The supervisor documents this discussion and keeps the documentation in a personal file, not the employee's official Personnel File.

Written Warning: This stage is used for more serious offenses, or for repeated offenses which an oral warning did not stop. The specifics of the offense are described in the written warning and are presented to the offender during a disciplinary conference. The consequences of further offenses, including suspension of discharge are explained. The document is placed in the employee's official Personnel File.

<u>Suspension</u>: Suspensions represent a last effort before termination to correct an employee's behavior. If an infraction is serious enough, a suspension may be given without prior oral or written warnings. This is, in effect, a "final warning" that no further infractions will be tolerated. A suspension also provides an opportunity for the employee to decide weather he/she can abide by the work-rules and policies of the employer. If not, the employee should resign.

<u>Termination</u>: Termination is the most extreme penalty. It occurs when an employee chooses to disregard organization rules, breaks the law (and this has a different bearing on the person's ability to perform the job), commits a very serious work-related offense or fails to correct offensive behavior about which he/she has been repeatedly warned. if an offense is sufficiently serious, no prior warnings or suspension need be given.

In general, determining what corrective action is appropriate for sexual harassers means the supervisor must look <u>both</u> at the "Shades of Gray Continuum" for sexual harassment behaviors (see page ____), and at the progressive discipline sequence.

Progressive Discipline <-------------> Shades of Gray Continuum

1.   For "light gray" first-time offenses such as inappropriate office decorations or inappropriate body watching or stares, educational problem-solving or an oral warning may be the best way to solve the problem. If the behavior does not cease, the sequence of written warning, suspension, and termination would follow, depending on the duration of the problem and the unwillingness of the offender to alter the harassment behaviors.

2.   For "gray" first offenses, such as offensive joking about a particular person's sexuality, unwanted sexually oriented conversation, or inappropriate touching, a lengthy oral warning or written warning which intends to educate the offender as well as establish clear conduct standards for the future may be sufficient. However, this is highly dependent on the nature and circumstances of the offense. For particularly offensive touching, behaviors which clearly intend to intimidate the victim, or certain borderline propositions, suspension or even discharge could be appropriate.

3.   For "medium gray" offenses, such as overt, repeated, non-reciprocal sexual advances and propositions, or open physical intimidation, immediate suspension or discharge is appropriate.

4.   "Dark gray" offenses such as assault or rape, or any threat of discharge if sexual favors are not acceded to, warrant immediate termination.

It should be noted that the above list of corrective action is a guideline only. The specific circumstances of the offense, the offender's past behavior and discipline history, and many other factors should be taken into consideration when determining the appropriate action.

Supervisors and managers are advised to work closely within their chain of command and with the Personnel Department to ensure that any discipline given for sexual harassment is appropriate.

Follow-Up

Follow-up is an extremely important part of dealing with sexual harassment incidents and complaints. The impact on recipient/victim, harasser, observers and others in the workplace may last well beyond the formal resolution of a complaint. Managers and supervisors must be sensitive to long-term side effects which influence morale, productivity and self-esteem.

There is no one right way to proceed. Because of this you should consult with higher management and the Personnel Department in developing your strategy. Each follow-up plan carries its won risks and problems, and depends heavily for success on the specific circumstances, and on the perceptions of the people who are involved.

Don't underestimate the impact of a complaint. For example, in a supervisor/employee harassment situation, co-workers can experience considerable frustration, low morale and anger because of disruption to normal operations, and lack of proper attention and direction from the supervisor.

A.   Develop and Implement a Follow-up Plan

Determine who has been directly affected by the sexual harassment situation. This will include the recipient/victim(s). The offender, observes, people the recipient/victim and harasser talked to about the incident, as well as individuals that work closely with the recipient/victim and/or harasser who knew that "something was going on". Contact with all of these people is necessary to put closure on the incident.

Talk with the recipient/victim about how he/she would like the harassment situation and its resolution to be explained to observers and others who were involved. Develop a strategy which is realistic, sensitive, and protects the self-confidence of the recipient/victim. Review and plan with higher authority and the Personnel Department.

Let the recipient/victim know what you plan to do and when you plan to do it.

Talk with the harasser and obtain his/her support for putting closure on the incident through communication with observers and others involved. Tell the harasser exactly what will be said. Make sure the harasser knows why disciplinary action was taken. If appropriate, warn the harasser that "leaking" other versions of the incident may be considered retaliation against the recipient/victim and will not be tolerated.

If the recipient/victim wishes to maintain confidentiality about the details of the incident, respect this, and let those who were involved know this is the person's desire.

If the recipient/victim desires fuller explanation be made, develop a factual statement describing the harassment situation, and the resolution. Meet directly with those involved and present the statement. In many situations this could be done through group meetings. Follow-up with individual discussions if necessary.

During the meetings, review sexual harassment laws and the policies of the organization, or other work rules used as guidelines for resolving the situation. Encourage people to express their feelings and ask questions. Reiterate the organization's commitment to an environment free of sexual harassment.

Set the record straight. Respond directly to observers' and co-workers' perceptions of the victim and harasser. Be aware of the "rumor mill" and make a point of correcting erroneous information and opinions during these meetings. Be particularly sensitive to the false view that the sexual harassment incident was the recipient/victim's fault, and address it directly.

Get back to both the recipient/victim and the harasser after follow-up discussions have been completed to provide a brief summary of what happened at the meetings.

If investigation of the incidents proved the harassment charges false, follow the above procedure to help the alleged harasser regain credibility and respect.

B.   Monitor Interactions of Those Involved

Over time, watch carefully how people respond to the recipient/victim and the harasser.

Check productivity and morale. Counsel observers or co-workers whose continuing emotions bout the incident have a negative effect on the work group. Let them talk it over with you. If appropriate, suggest the City's Where-to-Turn program or other helping resources.

Help refocus energies on the work of the organization. Continue to provide constructive work-related feedback. Set reasonable performance goals and expect them to be attained.

Listen for subtle or open forms of retaliation against **the recipient/victim or harasser,** and take appropriate corrective action. If needed, set clear limits on acceptable conduct to prevent either party from manipulating the situation.

Watch the harasser's conduct carefully for any signs of additional offensive behavior. Continue to provide counseling and feedback. Recommend Where-to-Turn or other resources. Take **immediate** disciplinary action if there is a recurrence of the problem behaviors.

C.   Support the Recipient/Victim

Recognize the real pain associated with being the recipient/victim of sexual harassment and the strong emotions involved in initiating a complaint. Support the person's level of self-confidence and esteem. Be sensitive to possible continuing feelings of anger, fear, isolation or embarrassment.

Watch for signs of unusual stress or tension, illnesses (such as recurrent headaches or backaches), and ongoing problems in work relationships.

Respect the recipient/victim's right to get on with the job and be treated normally. Counsel others to respect this right as well.

Make sure the recipient/victim knows your door is open. From time to time check with the person to make sure things are going well. Ask if the recipient/victim has observed any events in the work group or interactions which he/she felt might have had some connection to the sexual harassment incident or complaint. If appropriate, follow-up on these observations with the individuals involved and get back to the recipient/victim with additional information.

On a regular basis, check with the recipient/victim to make sure that any contacts with the harasser have not involved offensive behaviors. If they have, take immediate corrective action with the harasser.

Refer the recipient/victim to other internal or external resources, such as the Where-to-Turn program if the recipient/victim asks you for assistance or performance continues to be affected. Consult with higher management or Personnel for additional strategies.

Encourage the recipient/victim to feel good about his/her ability to stop the harassment. Reinforce and congratulate the victim for saying "no".

Case Studies

One day on the set of "Southwest General", the soap's director calls Dorothy "Tootsie" once too often. She whirls on him, irate. "My name is Dorothy!", she snaps. "Not 'Tootsie', not 'Toots', not 'Honey', not 'Sweetie', just Dorothy. Tom is always Tom. Allen is always Allen. I'm Dorothy!"

– Susan Dworkin, "What Dustin Hoffman Learned from
Dorothy Michaels", <u>MS.</u>, March, 1983.

Consider the following two situations. For each, answer these questions:

1.   Is this a case of sexual harassment?

2.   If so, who is liable?

3.   What should you, as the supervisor, do about the situation?

Case 1:   Joke Sessions

You are a first-line supervisor in a large City department. At least 15 minutes is spent at the beginning of each shift with employees "joking around". This seems to elevate spirits generally and get people ready to start work. However, the talk is sometimes sexually oriented (some of the jokes are truly gross), and some employees seem to participate more than others. Both male and female employees are present. No one has complained to you about the joke sessions, although they have been going on for several weeks.

Case 2:   "Seductive" Behavior

You are a supervisor in the City's Finance Department. One of your female employees likes to dress in expensive clothes. She seems overdressed for her position in the accounting division. You would describe some of her outfits as "seductive". When she interacts with you, her manner seems flirtatious. You feel awkward about the situation.

Case 3:   Hey, Sweetie, What Brings You Out Here?

You are an upper level manager responsible for a large section of the Public Works/Utilities Department. Your work location is a rental building not far from City Hall. Over a period of six months, three female administrative staff members from City Hall informally comment to you about the sexist comments they receive when they visit your offices. Finally, the most vocal of the three sends a memo to you, describing a specific incident where some remarks about her appearance and about being female were made. The remarks were apparently made by non-supervisory staff including one temporary employee. How will you handle this situation?

Case 4:   Maybe Hey's Gay

You are a manager in a large City department. In your work section there is male employee – a good worker – who is rumored to be gay. Teasing from co-workers increases to the point that others avoid him and don't want to be associated with him for fear of being labelled homosexual. The male employee goes to his supervisor, one of your direct subordinates, asking for assistance in handling the harassment, with sufficient documentation to show that he is being deliberately cut out of the information flow. His supervisor is unsympathetic and puts him off by telling him he "ought to change his style". The male employee finally quits. As he does, he writes a letter to the Department Head, describing his reasons for leaving with specific reference to the supervisor's comment. The letter is forwarded to you by the Department Head. You are asked to handle the situation. How will you proceed?

Case 5:   <u>She Got it Because She's Female</u>

You are a Department Head for a staff department of the City. The situation involves a high-achieving, hard-working female employee. Given opportunities to improve her skills by male supervisors, she has been promoted to Unit Supervisor through a panel selection process. You are aware of comments that she was promoted because she was female and/or she was sleeping with influential people in your department. You know this is not true and dismiss these jealous comments. She comes to you asking for advice on how to handle similar comments which have been directed to her. She feels that the negative attitudes behind them are causing her problems – that once cooperative male co-workers are now carrying a grudge because she was promoted and they were not. How will you handle this situation?

Case 6:   <u>Jane and Bill</u>

Jane is a Programmer in the Data Processing Department. She is divorced, attractive, in her mid-40's. Jane would not be described as a very confident or assertive person. She is known to have had a personal relationship at one time with one of the section heads in the department, Bill, and to have dated other supervisors in City Hall. Her relationship with Bill ended bout a year ago.

Jane goes to her immediate supervisor (a male, hired about a month ago) with the complaint that the "guys" have started making teasing remarks to her about her social life. One of her female co-workers also told her that there's a rumor going around that she is trying to renew her prior relationship with Bill. This rumor is not true. In fact, Bill has been paying her a lot of attention lately and has twice asked her to go to dinner with him. She made an excuse and refused the first time, but went reluctantly the second because she did not know what to say. During dinner Bill suggested that they start seeing each other again; he implied that because of his greater influence in the department now, he could help her get some good work assignments. When he said this, Jane rather meekly implied that she was very busy and didn't have a lot of time to go out. However, she knows that Bill is persistent. She is afraid that if she refuses to go out with him that he will not only spread rumors about her, but will use his influence to make life more difficult for her at work.

Jane seeks the advice of her first-line supervisor because she doesn't know what to do. She feels like she is being manipulated and hassled, but has not defined what's going on as "sexual harassment". Her first-line supervisor, who reports to you, comes to you with the case and asks for your suggestions on how to handle the situation.

Questions:

1.   Is this a case of sexual harassment?

     Yes   No

2.   If **Yes**, is it a case of sexual harassment because:
     (circle one)

   A.   Jane doesn't like the teasing of her co-workers and feels uncomfortable with the attention she gets from Bill.

   B.   When her relationship with Bill ended, she told him that she just wanted to be friends and didn't want to bother her at work.

C.   Bill's implication of being able to "help" her at work carries the threat that if she doesn't go out with him, Jane will be sorry.

D.   Other: (please describe) _____

3.   If **No**, it is not a case of sexual harassment because:
     (circle one)

A.   Jane's behavior indicates that she really likes the attention and the comments of the men she works with.

B.   Jane has not told Bill that she doesn't want to go out with him now.

C.   Because of Jane's reputation, you believe she is just using this situation to gain some attention from her first-line supervisor.

D.   Other: (please describe) _____

4.   What should you tell Jane's first-line supervisor to do?
     (circle two choices)

A.   Advice Jane to be more assertive when people say things to her that she doesn't like.

B.   Wait and see what happens.

C.   Tell Jane to document the comments and invitations of Bill and her co-workers, and to report back on this documentation within two weeks.

D.   Investigate this complaint by talking with Bill and some of the other men and women who work with Jane.

E.   Call the Personnel Department to get their advice.

F.   Document any discussion or action on this situation.

5.   What should you, in your role as manager, do? (circle two choices)

A.   Make sure that the first-line supervisor knows how to do what you tell him to do. Coach him if necessary.

B.   Call the Personnel Department and talk through the situation for your own information.

C.   Get involved yourself by interviewing Jane and talking to Bill.

D.   Tell the Department Head what's happened and ask for advice.

E.   Seat a reasonable time-line for the first-line supervisor and ask that he report back to you on the situation by a certain date.

F.   Document your discussion with the first-line supervisor.

6. How difficult was it for you to answer these questions?
    (circle one)

    A.   Easy.

    B.   It required some thinking.

    C.   Hard – it's a confusing situation.

    D.   Very difficult.

    Please explain your answer.

    _____

    _____

    _____

    _____

Free Speech

Is this an example of sexual harassment? If so, how? If not, why not?

_____

_____

_____

Who could be held liable for this harassment?

_____

_____

_____

Who is responsible for initiating corrective action?

_____

_____

_____

If you were Glen, what would you do?

_____

_____

_____

What type of disciplinary action would you take? Why?

_____

_____

_____

What should Connie do in this situation?

_____

_____

_____

Day of Decision

Is this sexual harassment? Yes? No? Why?

_____

_____

_____

How should ann evaluate this situation? What should she do now?

_____

_____

_____

How can Ann prove her hiring decision is based on merits rather than sexual grounds?

_____

_____

_____

What should Alex do now?

_____

_____

_____

What are the consequences of corporate romances in an organization? Describe what you think would be appropriate guidelines?

_____

_____

_____

Poor Performance or Sexual Harassment?

Deborah, an employee with the City Planning Commission, has come to you and told you the following:

She is uncomfortable with a situation that has happened with her supervisory, Danny, who is continually asking her out for dinner. She does not want to hurt his feelings, so she has always just said that she is busy or has other plans. Unfortunately, he does not get the hint that she does not want to go out with him and keeps asking.

Deborah tells you that the last time they met in his office to discuss her performance she told him what she had been doing on her assigned project and that she did not believe she would be able to complete it by the end of the month as originally planned. He said that she was "doing just fine" and shouldn't worry about the deadline. He then put his hands on her shoulders and said he was taking her to dinner. She told him that she was busy and asked him what suggestions he had for completing the project. He said, "Just keep doing what you've been doing."

She then got up to leave and he again put his arms around her shoulders and asked if she would have time for dinner with him next week. She said she "did not think that would happen", gave him a friendly hug, and left.

Later, he stopped by her office, apparently just to chat. He seemed friendly until he overheard her make a date for the evening with another co-worker. He then became angry and told her he wanted the project successfully completed by the end of the month. She believes that this is not possible, given the unusual nature of this project.

When she tried to ask him why he had changed his mind, he would not answer and said that if she did not hear what he was saying he would "have a problem" with her. She believes he has changed his performance expectations because she will not go out with him.

1.   Has Deborah been sexually harassed? Why or why not?

2.   How might Danny respond if you confront him?

3.   What, if anything could Deborah have done differently?

4.   If Deborah's story is true, what disciplinary action is appropriate?

Tell Me What Happened

Part One

Is this sexual harassment? Why?

_____

_____

_____

What seems to be Cindy's emotional state?

_____

_____

_____

What should Marty do?

_____

_____

_____

Part Two

What is the problem that arises when Marty tries to investigate the situation? Is this realistic?

_____

_____

_____

What should Marty do now?

_____

_____

_____

What should Cindy say to Jack? What should Jack say to Cindy?

_____

_____

_____

Harassment or Setup?

A dispute occurs between two employees in the City Parks Department as to who should be responsible for certain duties involving heavy lifting. Anne (a caucasian and a member of the bargaining unit) accuses Zach, the lead supervisor (an African American and a member of the bargaining unit) of picking on her. When you interview Anne to find out what happened, she tells you that Zach has been harassing her for some time now and that she is sick and tired of it.

She was just recently separated from her husband and she has shared this fact with Zach, as well as some other facts about her sexual relationship with her husband. She says that Zach is now continually pressing her to go out with him, saying things like "I'll show you what a real man is like", telling her she is in his dreams, etc. She has been giving him the cold shoulder and she thinks he is now trying to get back at her.

She tells you that he has done this same thing to other women in the field and that his manager knows about it because she told him (the manager is a good friend of hers, and in fact, hired her). You go to the manager and he says that he has twice verbally counseled Zach, telling him that he could get in big trouble if he makes the wrong comment to the wrong woman, and warning him that he better keep sexual comments to himself.

You interview the two women identified by Anne. They both say that Zach has made inappropriate inquiries into their personal and sex life, comments about their looks, clothing, or bodies, etc. One woman is afraid to be identified because Zach has given her a ride home and knows where she lives. The other woman does not want to be involved at all. Upon further probing, you find out that she has been seeing a psychiatrist to try to deal with the fact that her father sexually abused her sister when they were children. She is clearly very vulnerable.

You interview two other women who work with Anne and Zach and they both say that they have not been harassed by Zach, and in fact, have a good working relationship with him, although neither reports directly to him.

Now you interview Zach. He is angry and demands to know who has made the complaints. You tell him Anne made the complaint and that it is supported by two other women, but that you cannot share their identities. Zach denies that he has said anything inappropriate, and says he has only responded to the off-color jokes and sexual comments that have been made by the women he works with. Zach then says that Anne is making this up because she is prejudiced against African Americans and is trying to get him fired so he will not have to work with him. He says that Anne and other employees, including the manager, have made racial remarks to him and demands that you do something about it.

1. Is there anything that should have been done differently in the investigation thus far?

2. Is any further investigation warranted at this point?

3. How will you decide what response is inappropriate?

4. Assuming you decide that both Anne and Zach are partially at fault and a reprimand is appropriate, what steps would you take to monitor the work situation after the disciplinary action is completed?

5. While you are still investigating, you learn that rumors are flying around the work group and outside it that are worse than the reality. What steps would you take to quell the rumors?

Information for All Employees

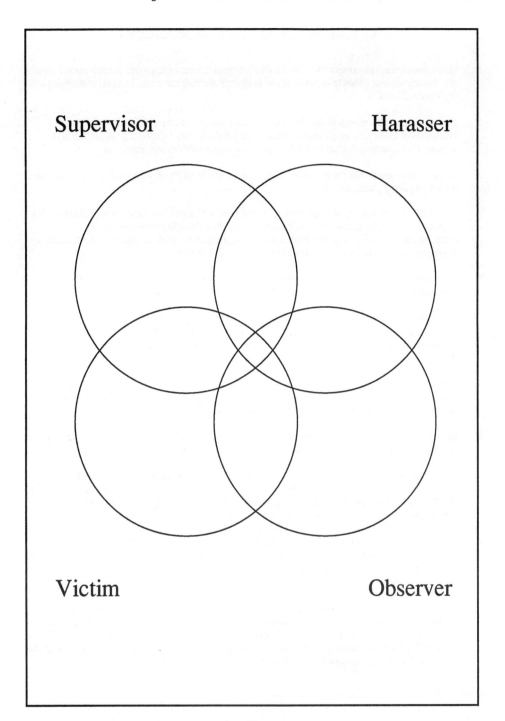

Supervisor

Harasser

Victim

Observer

City Commitments and Expectations

1. Sexual harassment is incompatible with the City's Organizational Philosophy. Employees are asked to treat each other as valuable individuals and to foster teamwork and mutual respect in their day-to-day work activities.

2. This philosophy also applies to the City's service relationship with the community. Sexual harassment of citizens by employees will not be tolerated, not only because it is illegal, but also because of its damaging impact on the City's service responsibilities and reputation.

3. Similarly, City employees are not expected to endure harassment from citizens, clients or contractors. Harassment is not part of the job.

4. Any staff member experiencing harassment from another City employee, contractor or client of City services is encouraged to assertively tell the harasser to stop the offensive behavior. Recipient/victims should seek help from a supervisor, department head, or anyone in the Personnel Department and can be assured their concerns will be taken seriously.

5. Observers of harassment are encouraged to share their observations with those involved in the harassment incident and, if appropriate, with a supervisor or the Personnel Department.

6. Managers and supervisors are expected to intervene immediately, notify the department head and Personnel, and to thoroughly, confidentially, and objectively investigate and resolve harassment situations. They are also expected to take appropriate action to discipline harassers and protect all parties involved from further harassment, retaliation, or false accusations.

7. Employees are expected to positively cooperate in efforts to contain and resolve harassment situations. Those involved in a situation are required to act in a neutral and professional manner during an investigation and after the situation's resolution.

8. Those who choose to violate the City's non-discrimination policies are warned that disciplinary action can and will be used to remedy the situation. The City of Bellevue fully supports federal and state equal opportunity laws, and believes that men and women have equal rights to employment in all areas of City service. These policies are spelled out by specific Bellevue regulations, such as the City's official Personnel Policies and Procedures, Affirmative Action Plan and Employee Guidebook. The disciplinary penalties for harassment are severe, up to and including termination, indicating the seriousness of the City's commitment to equal opportunity.

9. All City employees are expected to review their own behavior to determine the degree to which they contribute to or encourage sexual harassment. Offensive and potentially offensive behaviors are to be eliminated, including making sexist jokes and comments, saying things which openly or through innuendo put others down, as well as all other forms of harassment.

10. Employees are strongly encouraged to develop assertiveness, listening, feedback, and other communication skills which will help eliminate harassment and foster a work environment truly supportive of productivity and individual success. The personal commitment of individual employees to improving communication, openness and trust in the workplace is one of the most important goals of the City's ongoing organizational improvement effort.

What To Do About Sexual Harassment

<u>The Recipient/Victim</u>

1. Recognize sexual harassment when it appears. Understand that it is not your fault and that it does not "come with the job". Remember that sexual harassment is against the law and violates specific Bellevue policies.

2. When you are sexually harassed, talk to the offender. Tell him/her that you find the behavior offensive. Describe how the harassment negatively affects your work. Say things like:

    "Don't touch me. I don't like it. It makes me uncomfortable and then I make mistakes."

    "No. I don't want to go out with you. I do not mix my work and personal life."

    "I don't think those kind of jokes are funny. They don't have anything to do with work. Please don't tell them when I am in the room."

    I'd like it a lot better if you'd comment on the quality of my work, rather than the way I look."

    "My name is _____, not 'Honey'."

    (See the section in this manual, "Giving Someone Else Feedback", for additional examples of what to say.)

3. If verbal feedback doesn't work, put your objections to the harassment in writing, sending a copy to the harasser and keeping one for yourself. If more comfortable for you, present the written statement to the harasser in a meeting between you, the offender and your supervisor.

4. If you can't get the harassment stopped on your own or are having a difficult time confronting the harasser, immediately contact your supervisor, anyone in the Personnel Department, or the City Manager's Office. If your supervisor is the harasser, talk with his/her supervisor or your department head, as well as anyone in Personnel.

5. Document all sexual harassment incidents and conversations about the incidents. Record the date, time, place, people involved, and who said what to whom. Keeping this documentation is very important and will help you and the City investigate and resolve the situation. At some point during an investigation you may be asked to write out a brief, formal statement of all the incidents connected with a harassment situation – your notes and documentation will be extremely helpful to this effort.

6. Consider your own behavior. You may be unknowingly encouraging sexual harassment by the way you dress or communicate. Get feedback from close friends or associates if you feel this might be the case. Never encourage harassers by smiling, laughing at their jokes, or "flirting back". This type of response can lead a harasser to think you really enjoy this type of attention at work.

7. Avoid escalating a harassment situation by trying to "get even" with the harasser. This will only make matters more complicated and make it more difficult to get the harassment stopped quickly and confidentially.

The Harasser

1. If asked to stop a particular behavior, do so immediately. If you think it might help, apologize to the offended person.

2. Think about the impact of what you do and say on another person's attitudes toward work, job performance, and self-esteem.

3. Pay attention to how others respond to what you do and say. Look for indications you might have violated someone else's comfort zone and ask for feedback. (See the sections in this manual devoted to these important skills.)

4. Don't assume that your co-workers or employees enjoy comments about their appearance, hearing sexually oriented jokes or comments, being touched, stared at, or propositioned, even in a teasing or non-serious manner.

5. Understand that it is not how you intend to come across to others so much as their perception of how you actually do come across that is important.

6. Talk to your spouse, family members, or close friends about experiences they might have had with sexual harassment. As people describe the vulnerability, intimidation and anger they have felt as recipients or victims, relate those feelings to experiences you have had.

7. If you have a supervisor, do not assume that individuals who work for you will tell you if they are offended – or harassed – by what you say or do. Remember that one of your employees may be "smiling on the outside, but cringing on the inside" simply because you are the boss. Review your copy of the Management Information Manual on Sexual Harassment, or get a new copy from Personnel.

8. Remember that sexual harassment is against the law. Recent court decisions have resulted in both organizations and individuals paying large judgments and being subject to very negative, long-term publicity. Your personal reputation (and an lot more) is at stake.

9. Keep in mind that the City of Bellevue, through its policies and training programs, has effectively warned all employees that sexual harassment will not be tolerated. This issue is taken very seriously by the City. Those found at fault will be disciplined appropriately.

10. If accused of harassment, even if the charges are false, do not try to "get even" with the recipient/victim or others in the workplace, or do things which could be construed as retaliation. This will greatly complicate matters, and could result in serious discipline should you be found at fault for retaliating. Be patient if an investigation has been initiated. The City's policy is that people are innocent of sexual harassment until proven to be at fault. If unsure how to address your responsibilities or working relationships at any time during or after the investigation, contact your supervisor, department head, or the Personnel Department for advice.

The Observer

1. In many work situations, reporting an incident or a problem that involves other people might be considered evidence you are not a good "team player". However, sexual harassment is a different kind of problem because of the high potential for harm to people, and the significant liability borne by the City. As an observer, you should share your observations with those involved in the harassment situation. If the harasser's behavior is offensive to you or to the recipient/victim, you are encouraged to discuss the matter with your supervisor, your department head and/or the Personnel Department. Help an offended person talk to someone in the chain of command or in Personnel about the situation.

2. Support the offended person's efforts to get the harassment stopped. Let him/her know that you know what's going on. Say things like:

    "You seem to get pretty tense every time _____ comes into the office."

    "I'd really be angry (offended, embarrassed) if he did that sort of thing to me. Do you want to talk about it?"

    "If you get to a point of wanting to complain about _____'s behavior, let me know. I've seen enough to know how _____ interferes with your work."

3. If someone who is being harassed brings concern or complaint to you, help the person not to feel alone, scared, or untrusting of City resources. Help the person get assistance from a supervisor, department head, anyone in the Personnel Department, or the City Manager's Office.

4. Confront harassers by pointing out their behavior and letting them know how the harassment affects the offended individual. Say things like:

    "_____, do you have any idea how much your jokes upset _____? She really has a hard time concentrating on her work because she's embarrassed by the things you say."

    "What makes you think you've got the right to touch her like that? That kind of familiarity is really out of line here."

    "You seem to really enjoy propositioning all the new women who come into our office."

    "If you said that kind of stuff to me, I'd go straight to the boss. Do you have any idea how it feels to hear that sort of thing?"

5. Don't engage in behaviors that could escalate the situation. The goal is to get the harassment stopped, not malign another person or take sides. Keep in mind that most harassers probably are not truly aware of the impact of their behaviors to others. Trying to "get even" with a harasser on someone else's behalf (or retaliate against an individual you believe is making a false charge), will seriously complicate a situation. Falsely and maliciously defaming someone else will lead to disciplinary action against you by the City.

6. During investigation of a situation and after it has been resolved, keep a neutral, professional attitude toward all involved parties. Help contain the situation by avoiding unnecessary discussion. Stay focused on the job and keep the situation confidential. Help others to do the same.

<u>The Supervisor or Manager</u>

(For a more complete discussion of managers' and supervisors' responsibilities, consult the Sexual Harassment Management Information Manual available from the Personnel Department.)

In brief, managers and supervisors are responsible for:

1. Serving as models for appropriate behaviors on the work team.

2. Providing accurate, timely, job-related performance feedback to employees.

3. Taking action on inappropriate behavior in the workplace, whether or not it is related to sexual harassment.

4. Communicating City policies and standards relating to equal opportunity and maintenance of a discrimination-free work environment.

5. Observing interactions on the work team and recognizing those which could be some form of sexual harassment.

6. Intervening with harassers to stop offensive behaviors through education, problem-solving and, when warranted, formal disciplinary action; stopping harassment of staff in the workplace by non-employees.

7. Being available, open-minded and supportive to anyone who feels he/she is experiencing sexual harassment; taking all complaints seriously.

8. Notifying the chain of command and the Personnel Department of any complaints received or serious incidents warranting discipline for a harasser.

9. With guidance from the chain and Personnel, sensitively and confidentially investigating incidents of complaints of sexual harassment.

10. Maintaining confidentiality during investigation of incidents and complaints; intervening with those who intentionally or unintentionally spread rumors.

11. Serving as a continuing resource to the recipient/victim, offender, and observers on how to respond to the harassment situation.

12. Providing support and counsel to recipients and victims of harassment.

13. Following-up to make sure that relationships on the work team have returned to normal and that no further harassment or any form of retaliation has occurred.

Retaliation

Because of the strong negative emotions associated with sexual harassment, retaliation can easily become an element of the situation. Attempts to "get even" or "take sides", however, dramatically complicate sexual harassment problems and at all times are to be avoided. Retaliation usually leads to more harassment, and more serious forms of harassment.

Retaliation can be defined as any action which does not help correct a situation but serves only as a reprisal with the intent of causing pain. There are many ways in which retaliation can occur.

* A harasser retaliates against a recipient/victim for objecting to the harassment or making a complaint.

* A recipient/victim retaliates against an offender for the harassment.

* Observers or co-workers retaliate against the recipient/victim or harasser.

* A supervisor or manager retaliates against the recipient/victim or the harasser because of a complaint.

* Someone falsely accuses another person of sexual harassment in order to "get back at" him/her for some other kind of problem.

Retaliation is no game. It is illegal and strictly prohibited as a matter of the Bellevue policy. Employees found to be retaliating against anyone in a sexual harassment situation are subject to immediate corrective action.

Everybody involved in the investigation and resolution of a sexual harassment complaint – recipient/victim, harasser, observers, managers and supervisors – is expected to exercise self-control, be sensitive to the impact of personal behaviors on others, and to focus energies on the job to be done to the greatest degree possible. If co-workers cannot behave in a positive way toward one another, then at the least they are to behave neutrally. This is an indication of good faith that whatever problem exists can and will be resolved, and supports the basic commitment and trust of people to handle problems in a just and mature manner.

After the resolution of a complaint, all involved should work together to help "make the victim whole" by restoring that person to his/her rightful role in the work team. Falsely accused persons, and those found not to be at fault after an investigation, also need to have their respect and credibility restored to them.

In particular, employees are to avoid such subtle forms of retaliation as:

* Making it tough on someone to get his/her job done by excluding that person from the usual flow of information, work assignments, or work group activities.

* Categorizing someone as a "trouble-maker" or as having mental problems because he or she has spoken up about offensive behavior.

* Suggesting the harassment is really the recipient/victim's fault.

* Taking sides in a harassment situation; spreading rumors, innuendo or gossip about the harasser or recipient/victim.

* Unfair criticism of a person's work or his/her competency as a result of a complaint.

* Suggesting a person's complaint is simply a way to get attention or money.

* Refusing to abide by the principle that a person is innocent until proven at fault.

* If a person has been falsely charged, refusing to acknowledge that the charge is false and that the person is innocent.

* Once a person has been disciplined as a harasser, continuing to persecute that individual.

<u>False Charges of Sexual Harassment</u>

Special note needs to be given to the circumstance in which someone maliciously makes a false charge of sexual harassment in order to defame or discredit someone else. The City does not tolerate this type of harassment by "reverse victimization" and will take disciplinary action up to and including discharge of an employee who falsely, maliciously and without a reasonable basis makes a charge of sexual harassment. <u>Sexual harassment laws and policies are not tools to destroy someone else's reputation</u>. The City considers this form of retaliation as totally inappropriate to the workplace and very serious, and warns all employees that such behavior is expressly prohibited.

**Members
  of the   Incident
Workteam**

**Others in the
Organization**

Retaliation spreads the problem,
affecting more and more people
in the organization,
making it much more difficult to resolve.

Handling Harassment by Non-Employees

Sexual harassment of City employees in the workplace by citizens, vendors, salespeople, repair personnel or any other non-employee is unacceptable. All staff need to understand that sexual harassment is <u>not</u> a part of the job. Those harassed are encouraged to tell the harasser to stop the offensive behavior while maintaining an appropriately polite, business-like manner:

"Mr. Jackson, it makes me uncomfortable when you refer to me as "Sweetie' or 'Honey'. My name is Sara Williams. Please feel free to call me Sara. How can I be of help to you today?"

"Ms. Jones, I consider this to be a business conversation. I would appreciate it if we could keep it at that level, please."

"Please don't stare at me that way. It really interferes with my work. If necessary, I'll have my supervisor speak to you about it."

"I am not 'a dumb girl engineer'. That's the second time in ten minutes you've made a comment like that about me. If you can't address me in a civil manner, I'll be forced to end this phone conversation immediately."

"Don't ever touch me like that again. I'll be reporting this incident to my supervisor."

"No, I'm not interested in going out with you, and I won't put up with being propositioned. If you don't have legitimate business in City Hall, please leave."

A City employee who feels he or she is being sexually harassed on the job by a non-employee is encouraged to discuss the situation with a supervisor, department head, and/or the Personnel Department.

When, for any reason, the employee is unable to stop the harassment on his or her own, the City will designate a manager or supervisor to deal with the situation. That person will investigate the situation, including obtaining a written statement from the recipient/victim covering the details of the incident(s). The manager will then contact the harasser, if possible, and intervene on the employee's behalf in order to get the harassment stopped. <u>Employees facing situations of criminal behavior, such as indecent liberties (sexual touching or self-exposure), assault, or rape should immediately report the incident to the Police Department.</u>

Giving Someone Else Feedback

All of us need to know how to give others feedback, particularly when someone else is behaving in a way that attacks self-esteem.

Good relationships and a strong sense of self-worth <u>thrive</u> on people communicating honestly and effectively about their feelings. If a person is harassing you, the best way you get the harassment stopped is to:

1)   Tell the other person what he/she did to bother you,
2)   How you felt about it, and
3)   The way you would like that person to behave in the future.

Keep in mind that even the most assertive person may not be able to handle every situation alone. Don't hesitate to contact organizational resources, such as your supervisor, a manager in your chain of command, your department head, or anyone in the Personnel Department if you need advice, support or assistance in getting harassment stopped.

Making an assertive statement to someone else is something that can be learned. Assertive statements are simply short, direct statements which indicate your interests, desires, or intentions. They are more powerful when they occur soon after the offensive incident. They should be delivered looking at the other person and making direct eye contact; spoken with a firm, strong voice where the last syllable spoken has a lower voice tone. Assertive statements are best when delivered in a polite, non-judgmental tone of voice. They are neither nice, nor mean. They are sincere, not cutting or demeaning. An assertive statement is a comment on a behavior, not a person, and conveys respect for both yourself and the other person.

Some beginnings for assertive statements are:

"I want ..."
"I intend ..."
"I am asking you ..."
"I need you to ..."
"I expect ..."

Examples of assertive statements which can be used in situations involving sexual harassment are listed below.

"When you come up behind me and put your arm around me, it makes me feel really uncomfortable. I'd like you to stop doing it. If you want to discuss something with me, please just talk to me; don't touch me."

"Mary, it seems like you're spending all your free time around my desk. Even though you might not mean anything by it, it embarrasses me because other people are beginning to think we have something other than a work relationship. I want you to stop flirting. It really irritates me that you seem to enjoy keeping me from my work."

"Don't make jokes like that about gays. You seem to think that nobody could be offended by that type of humor. I would like it a lot better if you told jokes that didn't involve sexual preference.

"Maybe you don't think I notice it, or that I like it when you stare at me, but frankly, it makes me feel like a piece of meat, not a person. When you talk to me, please look at my face, not my body."

"You made several comments today in the lunchroom that sounded like you want to develop a relationship with me. I want you to know how terrible it felt to be propositioned like that in front of my friends. I don't want that kind of relationship with you, and I don't want you to make comments like that again."

"You and I have a super relationship. But there's something you do that makes me feel put down. When you call be 'Babe' or 'Doll' or 'Cutie' it doesn't feel like we are really equals. I know you don't mean to hurt me. I'd like it a lot better if you'd just all me by my first name."

"It seems like you are very much attracted to me, and I want you to know that I'm flattered by that. But I'd prefer that we were friends at work, and didn't get involved. I make it a rule not to mix business and personal relationships."

"I want you to know how angry it made me when you touched me. If you bother me like that again, I intend to go straight to my supervisor with this information."

To a supervisor: "_____ has been staring at me and it makes me very uncomfortable. I'd like your help in getting _____ to stop doing this."

Asking For and Getting Feedback From Others

Being open to new information and asking for feedback from others are two important skills which help people master the changing social environment, particularly the changing roles of men and women in the workplace. The more information a person has about how he/she is coming across to other people, the easier it is for that person to adopt to shifting social standards.

It's important to keep in mind that people do not automatically recognize their impacts on each other. Social research has shown that individuals don't look for reactions they don't want to see in other people, and it is also apparent people do not often directly ask for feedback. Rather, people tend to "live by habit" and be comfortable with familiar behaviors, whether or not these habits support positive interpersonal relationships. Although the following skills would seem to be simple ones, they can truly require some effort and personal development to master.

Being Open to New Information

Being more observant of how others are responding to us is extremely important. What falls in one person's "comfort zone" may not be comfortable for someone else. The rule of thumb is to treat all people as individuals. It's important to not make assumptions about others and to recognize the signs of discomfort. For example:

You told a joke and:

* Some people didn't smile or laugh.
* Nobody else told a similar joke, or when someone did, other people moved away.
* Somebody said the joke bothered him, her, or someone else.
* Somebody took the joke as a put-down.
* Somebody made an angry, sarcastic or cutting comment about you or your joke.

You hugged someone and:

* That person's body became tense.
* The other person pulled away.
* The person didn't return the hug.
* The person didn't smile or look at you.
* The person said he or she didn't like the hug.

You looked at someone or touched someone and:

* The person noticed your stare or touch and gave you a "dirty look".
* The person tried to ignore your stare or pulled away from your touch.
* The person looked tense, uncomfortable or embarrassed but didn't say anything.
* The person told you to stop touching or looking at him/her "that way".

You ask someone for a date and:

* The person said "no" or was reluctant to go out with you.
* The person didn't smile.

* The person couldn't give you an answer.
* The person said "yes" but his/her tone of voice or body language said "no".
* The person looked tense and uncomfortable.
* The person now avoids you.

These are just examples. Any behavior which causes someone else to be tense, not make eye contact, make angry, cutting or sarcastic remarks, get quiet, show frustration, frown, or move away from or avoid you, can be signs that something you are doing, perhaps unintentionally, is bothering that person. Be sensitive to the clues. Someone may be "smiling on the outside, but cringing on the inside".

If there is doubt in your mind that a behavior, such as a joke, a comment, or a touch, might be offensive, it is best to simply avoid that behavior.

<u>Asking for Feedback</u>

Sometimes a person's reactions may not make it clear to you how he or she feels about things you have said or done. Not everyone is assertive or has a desire to give other people direct feedback. This is particularly important if you sense that someone did not appreciate something you did or said.

Some suggestions for asking for feedback are:

1) Be genuine. Asking for feedback in an insincere, teasing, sarcastic, or manipulative way will probably be far more offensive than the behaviors you have a question about.

2) Timing and circumstances are important. Don't embarrass or antagonize someone by asking for feedback at the wrong time or in the wrong place. Be sensitive to the fact that the other person may not really want to talk to you alone or talk to you in a place he/she could feel trapped.

3) Make it comfortable for the other person to tell you how he/she truly feels. Don't be demanding or try to coerce the information from the other person. Always leave the other person the option of <u>not</u> responding.

4) Be comfortable and confident in asking for the feedback. If you approach asking for the information as a sign of personal strength and a display of genuine interest in the feelings and perceptions of others, then the other person is likely to approach your request that way also.

5) Remember, just because someone gives you feedback, you don't need to act. Always, however, use it for your information and as a way to increase your sensitivity about how you affect others.

Use phrases such as:

"Judy, would you give me your opinion of how I'm coming across? You seem to kind of tense up every time we are in a meeting together. If I'm doing something you don't like, I'd sure like to know what it is because I certainly don't want to offend you."

"Bill, I'm not sure I understand what's been happening lately. We don't seem to be working as well together as we used to. Is it something I did or said?"

"Cherie, I know you haven't said anything to me, but I get the impression you're angry with me. If you are willing to tell me, I would sure appreciate understanding what the problem is."

"At shift briefing you blew up at me. What did I do wrong?"

"Did I bother you when I put my hand on your arm? I couldn't tell whether that was okay with you or not and I don't want to make you uncomfortable."

Responding To Feedback

Whether asked for or not, getting feedback from others can be a disconcerting experience. A person discovering that he or she has unintentionally offended someone else can feel the impact on his or her sense of self-esteem. Try to keep in mind that getting feedback is an opportunity to improve the way you relate to other people. Here are some ideas about how to respond.

Do not assume that getting feedback commits you to major personal change.

Ultimately, it is you who determines whether and to what degree you will react on the feedback you are given. Just because someone gives you information of an opinion, it does not automatically mean you must adjust your entire approach to interpersonal relations.

Don't react defensively.

It's a behavior that is the problem, not you as a person. Realize that overreacting with strong emotions is liable to create a greater conflict rather than resolve the situation. Assure the person that you genuinely want to hear what he or she has to say. The most important thing you can do is listen. Be supportive of the other person's interest in giving you feedback and willingness to openly discuss matters with you. Make the exchange as comfortable and low key as possible.

Find out exactly what behavior has bothered the other person.

Help the person tell you what the problem is by focusing your discussion on specific actions and words. Ask questions such as:

"Can you be more specific about what I did (or said)?"

"When was the last time I did something that bothered you?"

"Can you say more about that? I'm not sure I understand what you mean."

"It would help me to have an example."

Place yourself in the other person's shoes – understand the way that person feels and has been affected.

As you talk, try to understand the other person's experience. Don't dismiss that individual's feelings as being unimportant or inappropriate. Recognize that an important part of feedback is how someone else felt about your behaviors. Be sensitive to the fact that how you were intending to come across may not be the same as your actual impact on others.

Before responding to what you believe the other person has said, check out your understanding by paraphrasing the other person's statements and feelings.

Don't try to respond before you are sure you truly understand the other person.

"Paraphrasing" is one good way to do this. To paraphrase means to repeat back the statements and feelings of someone else in a shortened form. Paraphrases are sentences, not questions. They are simply a translation of someone else's message into your terms. Paraphrasing is one of the most effective communication skills anybody can learn.

For example, Susan says to John: "It really bugs me, John, when you start making those kind of joking comments about women."

John paraphrases by saying, "You feel pretty angry about some of the things I say when I'm joking around."

Or, "You sound frustrated by some jokes about women I'm made."

Or, "It sounds like some of my jokes really upset you."

Even if you paraphrase incorrectly because you have missed the person's true message or feelings, it's okay. The other person has a chance to clarify the message. This will help both of you understand what the problem is.

Keep in mind that one of the advantages of paraphrasing is that in a tense situation, it may give you some additional time to consider your response to the other person.

Develop a solution by checking out alternative behaviors.

This state gives you an opportunity to see what kinds of things you need to start or stop doing to resolve the situation. It's very important to be specific, and to give the other person ample opportunity to correct misperceptions about what he/she wants or to comment on additional offensive behaviors. Be sensitive to the other person's reactions. For example, following on the previous exchange:

John: "Joking around is okay as long as I don't make teasing comments about women, is that right?"

Susan: Well, sort of. I personally felt insulted the other day when you made a joke and used the words chick' and 'broad'. Sometimes, even when you're not joking you use those words."

John: "It makes you mad when I use those words and you'd like me to stop using them, whether they are part of a joke or not."

Susan: "Yeah, that's exactly right. Thanks for understanding how I feel about it, John."

Thank the other person for the feedback.

"Susan, I didn't realize those words bothered you. I didn't intend to offend you, but I can see how you feel about them and I really appreciate you giving it to me straight about how they affect you."

"Gary, thanks for telling me about my habit of putting my arm around you. I guess I just didn't think how you might feel about it. I'm glad you talked to me."

I hadn't guessed how embarrassed you felt when I talked about some of my personal relationships. I apologize. And I want you to know how much I appreciate your telling me. I wouldn't want to offend you or anybody else around here by being too familiar."

"I can see how what I thought was a compliment really came off sounding kind of sexist. Maybe what I should have said was simply that I thought you did a great job straightening out that software problem. Thank for telling me how I came across."

Respond from the heart.

You could follow all of the above steps and still not have responded appropriately if you are not truly open to what the other person has to say. You may not agree with the feedback, feel the other person has misinterpreted your actions, or feel that the person has overreacted, but at the very least you have an obligation to listen and to carefully consider that person's message to you. To "respond from the heart" means letting the other person know how important his/her feelings and experience are to you, and demonstrating a personal commitment to a positive relationship with the person.

Act on the feedback/commit to changing offensive behavior.

At this point you are ready to evaluate the feedback and decide whether to make personal changes. Here are some possible steps:

* Carefully reconsider the incidents identified in the feedback to see how you felt at the time – be honest with yourself about your motives and manner, and how they might have been interpreted by others.

* Pay closer attention to the reactions of others in similar situations. Look for a potential "blind spot" in how you see others responding to you.

* Talk to friends, acquaintances and associates to see if their experience of you verifies the feedback you have received. When doing this, don't just talk to people whose values are identical to your own. Pick people who you respect and who will be objective and truthful with you.

* Before acting or speaking, ask yourself whether there is a possibility for others to be offended. If the answer is "yes", refrain from the behavior.

* If you decide to change some potentially offensive habits or behaviors, let others know of the changes you intend to make and ask for their assistance in giving you constructive feedback about your progress.

* Identify and practice alternative non-offensive behaviors that let your true sensitivities and interpersonal skills shine through.

* Reward yourself for having successfully acquired a new skill and for having made an important improvement in your relations with others.

Frequently Asked Questions

What happens if I complain?

The City is committed to getting the harassment stopped. When you make a complaint to a supervisor or manager, several things happen. The department head and the Personnel Department are notified that a complaint has been received. Appropriate people in the departmental chain of command and Personnel staff make a decision about who will be involve din handling the complaint. Then, an impartial, thorough, and confidential investigation is initiated to determine the facts of the situation. You will be asked to describe the specific incident(s) leading to the complaint. You may also be asked to develop a brief written statement of these incidents. The alleged harasser and others who may know of the situation or have seen incidents will be contacted for additional information. Those guiding the investigation will then make a decision on the best course of action to stop all harassment, prevent retaliation of any kind, and appropriately educate and/or discipline the harasser if found to be at fault. Please keep in mind that every situation is unique and the above statements represent only a very general description.

What if I want to handle a situation on my own?

Because Bellevue is legally responsible for sexual harassment in the workplace, once a sexual harassment incident comes to the attention of a supervisor, manager or Personnel Department staff, the department head and Personnel Director are always notified. However, the City will help you handle the situation on your own, so long as the harassing behaviors can be stopped in a reasonably short time period (two to three weeks maximum) and there is no risk that the harassment will be directed at other employees or clients of the City. In this case, your supervisor, a manager, or someone in the Personnel Department will serve as a coach, offering you support and guidance in getting the harassment stopped. If you cannot resolve the situation on your own in the agreed upon timeframe, management will intervene according to the general plan described under the first question.

What if I don't trust my supervisor, the department head or the Personnel Department? Who do I tell I'm being harassed?

Sometimes trusting "the system" is hard to do. The important thing is that you take action to get the harassment stopped. The City prohibits illegal discrimination, believes people should be treated as individuals and is committed to resolving sexual harassment situations in as responsible and confidential a manner as possible. If you do not feel comfortable talking to your department head or people in the Personnel Department, there are other City resources available. Consider:

* The City manager, or staff in the City Manager's Office.

* The Legal Department. Talk to the City Attorney, or any attorney in the Legal Department.

* The Where-To-Turn Counselor. (For more information, get a Where-To-Turn Fact Sheet at the Personnel Department – and note the restriction on maintaining confidentiality of sexual harassment cases.)

* A co-worker who can help you access one of these resources.

What if my supervisor is part of the problem?

You do not need to talk with your supervisor. You may go directly to your department head or someone else in your chain of command, to the Personnel Department, or to any of the resources listed in the previous question. The City prohibits retaliation against people who bring forward a harassment concern or complaint and steps will be taken to correct the situation and protect you from any potential reprisal. Keep in mind that harassment or retaliation by a supervisor is considered extremely serious by the City. You will need to be thoughtful and accurate in describing the specific ways your supervisor has contributed to the problem. If your supervisor is directly harassing you, <u>immediately</u> report this to the department head and/or Personnel.

<u>What if the harassment continues?</u>

The City encourages employees to let someone inside the City know if they are being sexually harassed at worked, and will do everything possible to get the harassment stopped. In the event the City is unresponsive, you may wish to contact private legal counsel or the federal and state agencies which enforce sexual harassment laws. These are the Equal Employment Opportunity Commission and the Washington State Human Rights Commission. It is your legal right to file a complaint with one of these enforcement agencies.

<u>What are my rights as someone accused of harassment?</u>

An individual is not at fault until proven so by the evidence. As an alleged harasser you have the right to an objective, fair and confidential investigation of the facts. Should the facts show that you are not at fault, the City will let those involved in the situation know that you have not done anything wrong and deserve all due respect for your position and reputation. If found at fault, you can expect the City to fairly administer disciplinary action according to the City's policies on discipline. Additionally, since any form of retaliation is forbidden by City policy, the City will also take steps, if necessary, to prevent retaliation against you by the recipient/victim or co-workers.

Employees should keep in mind that individuals as well as the City may be sued under civil law on charges of sexual harassment, and that Bellevue will not necessarily provide legal services or insurance for the harasser. (See Bellevue City Code, Chapter 3.81 for additional information.) In those cases involving indecent liberties, assault or rape, criminal charges can also be brought against the harasser.

<u>Shouldn't the person who is offended tell the harasser first, rather than going to Personnel or my department head right away?</u>

Theoretically, any person who is the recipient/victim of sexual harassment certainly is in a position to tell the harasser to stop. The City actively encourages individuals who feel harassed to assertively approach the offending person. However, victims of sexual harassment can feel very intimidated by the situation and be fearful of reprisals by the harasser or co-workers. For this reason, it's important for victims to feel okay about going to a "higher authority". Moreover, harassment of any kind is a very serious matter which warrants attention by senior management.

<u>Does this Bellevue policy mean we have to talk differently around here?</u>

Is it true that as a result of more information about sexual harassment some things for Bellevue City employees will change, including a whole variety of comments and jokes that may be offensive to people. Creating a truly discrimination-free work environment means all of us have a special obligation to be sensitive to sexist, racist or other offensive language.

What if everybody on the crew (or in the office) enjoys those jokes? They build morale and relieve stress.

It is possible not everyone enjoys the jokes, but that people are unwilling to speak up for fear of being excluded from the group or being labeled as not having a "sense of humor". Keep in mind that sexist behavior, whether considered amusing or not, represents an artificial barrier preventing people from getting to know and treat each other as individuals. What may superficially seem to "build morale and relieve stress" for some employees might actually jeopardize morale and create stress for others.

Does this mean I can't open a door for someone, or touch someone on the arm in friendship?

No. What it means is that we all need to be more sensitive to the "comfort zones" of others. We need to treat people as individuals, rather than simple as a member of some group. Not all people want to have the door opened for them; not everybody likes to be touched on the arm. But some individuals do.

What's wrong with calling someone a "girl"?

For some women, being called a girl is equivalent to calling a black man a "boy". It's not flattery. It can be experienced as an insult because it implies that women are like children and are not equal adults.

Isn't it just that the victim can't take a joke?

The "joke" could really be a put-down that attacks another person's self-esteem. The person feels degraded because it's hard to fight back when everyone else is laughing or taunting. No one deserves that kind of persecution just because of sex or sexual preference.

What about sexual harassment of men?

Men are sexually harassed, too. Perhaps more than we know, since the culture we live in makes it difficult for men to complain about harassment of this kind. Sexual harassment is not a "women's issue". It's a people issue. A man's productivity and self-esteem can be as negatively influenced by harassment as a woman's. It is important to remember, however, that the great majority of harassment is directed at women. Studies have shown that women are at least twice as likely to be harassed as men and twice as likely to experience the more severe forms of harassment, such as unwanted propositions and threats.

Is there such a thing as harassment of gays or lesbians?

Yes. Sexual harassment isn't limited to male/female relationships. If a behavior focuses o sexuality, is unwanted, and is repeated or intentional, it's form of sexual harassment and is illegal. For example, starting a rumor that someone is gay, or attacking someone on the work team because he/she is gay, is also a situation of sexual harassment. People have a legal right to their sexual preference.

However, if a gay supervisor offered a promotion contingent on an employee providing sexual favors to the supervisor, that also would constitute sexual harassment.

What about the unscrupulous person who takes advantage of the law to "get someone" they don't like?

Using the law as a tool, not to secure one's legal rights but simply to maliciously hurt someone else, can be unlawful and violates City standards. Malicious, knowingly false accusations employed to ruin someone's reputation have no place in a responsible business organization. At Bellevue, should it be proven that an employee intended to harm someone else in this manner, that employee will be subject to disciplinary action. The City does not tolerate "game playing" of this kind.

What about office affairs and flirtations?

Sexual attraction is a natural response. To suggest it doesn't or shouldn'T happen between employees is unrealistic. As long as the relationship is mutual and reciprocal, it is not sexual harassment, although it may certainly create other types of problems for the organization. The difficulty with worksite affairs is that if they end, there is the possibility of retaliation by one of the parties using influence to "get" the other person. At that point, the situation may become sexual harassment. Additionally, office affairs can result in "third party" complaints of sexual harassment if the relationship creates favoritism and interferes with the work or promotional opportunities of others in the organization.

What about flirtatious behaviors and dress? Aren't some women just asking for it?

Both men and women may consciously dress in a sexy manner and, if so, are probably asking for some type of sexual comment or response from those with whom they work. In this situation, the person should be reminded of the need to dress in a manner appropriate to the work place. Sometimes a person isn't really aware that his or her apparel is not appropriate, and may simply be trying to dress attractively or wear a current fashion. A few words of guidance from a supervisor would be appropriate.

What do I do if I think I see something that could be sexual harassment?

Talk to the recipient to see how he or she felt about what happened. If the behavior you observed was offensive to you or to the recipient, share your feelings with a supervisor or someone from Personnel. Don't avoid speaking up if it appears people are getting hurt.

FORM 6-6
BELLEVUE, WASHINGTON EMPLOYEE INFORMATION MANUAL

SEXUAL HARASSMENT

Employee Information

Manual

City of Bellevue, Washington
1992

City of
Bellevue   Post Office Box 90012 • Bellevue. Washington • 98009 9012

TO: All City Employees

FROM: Phillip Kushlan, City Manager

SUBJECT: Sexual Harassment Prevention

Every City of Bellevue employee needs to be fully aware of his
or her responsibilities for keeping our organization free of
sexual harassment. This is a matter of compliance with federal
and state law, and City of Bellevue policy, and it also
reflects our commitment to a work environment that fully
credits the rights and the integrity of individual employees.

Please pay close attention to the information provided to you
through this manual on sexual harassment prevention. You will
be held accountable for it. Due to the seriousness of this
issue, any City employee who violates Bellevue policies on
sexual harassment, condones their violation, or chooses to
ignore them, is subject to disciplinary action up to and
including termination.

Sexual harassment hurts good people. It causes exceptional
pain for the victim, disturbs those who see or know of the
harassment, and inevitably results in disciplinary action for
the harasser. All of us--whether we are potential victims,
unconscious harassers, or people who might observe sexual
harassment take place--need more information and awareness
about this complicated subject. It is for this reason that
Bellevue maintains an ongoing prevention program, and this
information is provided to you.

Thanks for your sincere commitment to keeping Bellevue free of
illegal discrimination.

4748i
City of Bellevue offices are located at Main Street and 116th Avenue S.E.

-A-

AWARENESS

One day on the set of "Southwest General", the soap's director calls Dorothy "Tootsie" once too often. She whirls on him, irate. "My name is Dorothy!", she snaps. "Not 'Tootsie', not 'Toots', not 'Honey', not 'Sweetie', just Dorothy. Tom is always Tom. Allen is always Allen. I'm Dorothy!"

– Susan Dworkin, "What Dustin Hoffman Learned from
Dorothy Michaels", MS., March, 1983.

SEXUAL HARASSMENT

Employee Information Manual

Contents

City Policy on Sexual Harassment

"It is the City of Bellevue's official policy that sexual harassment of one City employee by another City employee is prohibited. Sexual harassment is a form of unlawful discrimination under the provisions of Title VII of the 1964 Civil Rights Act and the Washington State Law Against Discrimination.

Sexual harassment is defined as 'unwelcome sexual advances, requests for sexual favors and other verbal or physical conduct of a sexual nature when:

    1)   Submission to such conduct is made either explicitly or implicitly a term or a condition of the individual's employment;

    2)   Submission to or rejection of such conduct by an individual i used as the basis for employment decisions affecting such individual; or

    3)   Such conduct has the purpose or effect of unreasonably interfering with an individual's work performance or creating an intimidating, hostile or offensive working environment.'

Sexual harassment negatively affects morale, motivation and job performance. It results in increased absenteeism, turnover, tension and loss of productivity. It is inappropriate, offensive and illegal. Sexual harassment of any employee by any other employee of the City of Bellevue will not be tolerated.

Any employee who believes that she (or he) is encountering sexual harassment, or any employee who observes a situation which may be sexual harassment of another employee, is strongly encouraged to seek immediate assistance from his/her department director and/or the Personnel Department. It is the responsibility of all supervisory employees to report all cases of observed sexual harassment to their departmental management immediately so that corrective action can be taken.

Because of the sensitive nature of the problem for all involved, any report of sexual harassment will be investigated immediately and confidentially, and appropriate action will be taken in order to protect all parties involved from further harassment, retaliation or false accusations. Appropriate disciplinary action will be taken for sexual harassment based on the severity of the offense."

                                    – City of Bellevue policy established in 1982.

A Practical Definition of Sexual Harassment

The legal guidelines used as a basis for Bellevue's policy on sexual harassment are sometimes not easy to apply to real-life situations. In practical terms, sexual harassment may be defined as follows:

Any verbal or non-verbal behavior in the workplace which:

- – Focuses on the sexuality of another person or occurs because of the person's gender.

- – Is unwanted.

- – Is intentional or unintentional.

- – Affects a person's employment.

*Some incidents would not need to be repeated to be sexual harassment.

Shades of Gray Continuum

Light Gray   Medium Gray   Dark Gray

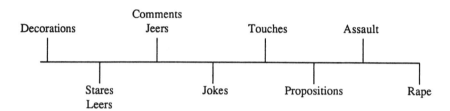

Decorations   Comments Jeers   Touches   Assault

Stares Leers   Jokes   Propositions   Rape

<u>Some Important Facts About Sexual Harassment</u>

* What is sexual harassment to one person in one set of circumstances is not necessarily sexual harassment for someone else.

* A man as well as a woman may be the recipient/victim of sexual harassment, and a woman as well as a a man may be the offender.

* The offender does not have to be the recipient/victim's supervisor. The offender may also be any co-worker or supervisor in the organization, an agent of the employer, or, in some circumstances, even a client of City services or a co-worker.

* The recipient/victim does not have to be of the opposite sex from the harasser. A male supervisor or co-worker making unwelcome sexual advances to a male employee may also be guilty of sexual harassment.

* Like rape, there is nothing "sexy" about sexual harassment. Sexual harassment is like any other form of harassment – it is an abuse of power.

Some Behaviors That Might Be Interpreted as Subtle Forms of Sexual Harassment

*   Referring to women as "girls" or using other forms of endearment to refer to them at work.

*   Always commenting on the way a person looks; seldom commenting on the quality of his/her work.

*   Interrupting a person who is talking about work with comments about his/her appearance or physical attributes.

*   When working with a person, concentrating more on his/her appearance or sexual attractiveness than on what the person is saying.

*   Eye contact, staring or gazing at a person in a way that implies a sexual message or relationship.

*   Flirting: eye contact, teasing, touching, joking propositions, or comments filled with sexual innuendo or double meanings.

*   Telling jokes with a sexual meaning, tone, or implication.

*   Displaying cartoons, calendars, desk objects, or pin-ups which convey a sexual message, tone, or implication.

Responses to Offensive Behavior

Offensive behavior affects different people differently. Response to harassing conduct can be viewed as a continuum ranging from the minor irritation felt by a "recipient" of less severe behaviors to the extremely painful loss of self-esteem experienced by a "victim".

Based on initial self-confidence, experience, background and many other factors, people start at different points on the continuum. But as harassment is repeated or involves severe or intentional acts, a recipient's response to the situation usually becomes more like that of a victim.

People feeling victimized by sexual harassment do not simply need "assertiveness training" or more "self-confidence". Their feelings are a natural response to an abuse of power by the offender(s) and to being trapped in the situation.

Recipient	Victim
– Self-esteem and productivity not negatively affected.	– Self-esteem and productivity negatively affected.
– Chooses whether and how best to respond – exercises options.	– Feels he/she has limited or no options for response.
– Feels insulted and annoyed.	– Feels angry, confused, alone, scared; extreme emotional turmoil.
– Sense of personal and organizational power relatively equal to offender(s).	– Feels powerless.
– Carries on normal relationships at work and at home.	– May experience tension-related physical symptoms such as headache, backache, other illnesses.
– "Dented", not "demolished".	– Work and home relationships deteriorate.

The following discussion of victims and harassers emphasizes the "typical" scenario of the male offender harassing a female employee or co-worker. No assumption is made that this is the only way sexual harassment happens.

To understand the dynamics of the problem, we need to be aware of:

The basic cultural messages that influence how men and women respond to each other.

The nature of power and intimidation.

Cultural Messages

Times often change faster than people's values and beliefs. Beneath the modern emphasis on equality for men and women in the workplace, some of us hold deeply ingrained feelings about sexuality which may push us toward the role of harasser or victim. Some opinions about men and women which encourage sexual harassment of working women are:

* Women are sexual objects – they should not be equals or co-workers.

* Women are not as serious about their work and careers as are men.

* Women like sexual attention at work.

* Men need to be pleased and catered to because they are men.

* Men naturally "go as far as they can".

* If a woman doesn't stop a man's advances, it means she wants them to continue.

These messages set the stage for sexual harassment at work because they make it more difficult for men and women to respond to each other on an equal basis.

Power Dynamics

One of the strongest cultural messages we have been influenced by is that men are by nature more powerful than women. The effect of this message is magnified many times by the fact that organizations are made up of different levels of power. If a male supervisor makes sexual advances, he is exerting cultural and organizational power. Even if the offender is simply a male co-worker, not a supervisor, that person may be seen to have more organizational power than the recipient or victim of the co-worker has more seniority, appears to have an "in" with management, or is a popular member of the work team.

The impact of these combined power relationships may cause people to feel victimized and intimidated. In essence, the victim must choose between three painful courses of action:

* Fight the harassment in the face of 1) an extreme power difference based on both cultural and organizational roles, and 2) fear of retaliation;

* Flee the employment situation by quitting the job;

* Submit tot he harassment and compromise personal integrity.

Faced with these choices, victims feel trapped, alone, angry, confused, and scared. <u>Because of the strong cultural and organizational messages about the level of power, victims may experience feelings which block their ability tot ell the harasser to stop, especially if the harasser is the victim's supervisor or is someone perceived to have more organizational power.</u> They may suffer severe emotional and physical stress, including a loss of self-confidence, the deterioration of family and work relationships, and physical symptoms such as backaches, migraine headaches and signs of nervous tension.

By comparison, the harasser may be very insensitive to the impact of has behaviors, believing that his actions will be considered desirable by the victim. He probably won't understand why the victim has a hard time telling him to stop. When confronted, he may deny that he is a harasser and be angry, confused, embarrassed and disappointed. he may engage in subtle forms of retaliation against the victim.

Why a Person Might Not Say Anything to Stop the Harassment

Sometimes co-workers have difficulty understanding how a recipient/victim of sexual harassment could have a hard time telling the harasser to stop the offensive behaviors. This lack of understanding can lead to less sensitivity to the recipient/victim's situation, and less support for him/her as a person. The opinions and beliefs of co-workers can have a painfully isolating effect, making it even more difficult for the offended person to get the harassment stopped.

Some reasons recipients/victims do not say anything are:

* Repercussions – fear of retaliation

    - Loss of job.
    - Loss of promotional opportunities or other benefits of employment.
    - Loss of respect from co-workers and supervisors; being labeled as a "trouble-maker".
    - Damage to personal reputation through the "rumor mill".
    - Not being considered a "team player".
    - Not being considered someone who has "a sense of humor".

* Low self-esteem

    - Not having the courage to speak out.
    - Having an attitude of "deserving" the harassment.
    - Not knowing the words to use to stop the harassment.

* Not knowing the procedures to use when making a complaint

* Lack of trust in "the system"

The City of Bellevue is committed to preventing sexual harassment and stopping harassment if it occurs. This is a matter of teamwork and mutual support among all employees. Supervisors and co-workers should help a person being harassed not to feel alone or scared. They should help the person get assistance from City resources, such as a department head, anyone in the Personnel Department, or the City Manager's Office.

Possible Indicators That Someone Feels Harassed

Negative changes in the way a person approaches the job are almost always ann indication that something is wrong. Although there are many possible explanations for the following behaviors, sexual harassment can also cause such things as:

* A drop in <u>productivity</u>, in volume or quality of work performed; difficulty with instructions or procedures; repeated mistakes; disinterest in the work; assignments seeming to require more effort than in the past.

* Persistent <u>attitude or mood shifts</u> with no apparent explanation; evidence of emotional turmoil.

* <u>Attendance problems</u>, including higher than normal use of sick leave, frequent tardiness , and "on the job" absenteeism through extended coffee breaks, long lunches, frequent trips to the restroom.

* On-the-job <u>accidents</u>.

* <u>Alliance building</u> or <u>conflicts</u> with co-workers.

* Repeated <u>criticism</u> or argumentativeness; making sarcastic, cutting comments.

* <u>Withdrawal</u> or <u>exclusion</u> by co-workers from work group activities, leading to anger, sensitivity and depression.

* <u>Negative changes</u> with clients of the City.

Other specific behaviors which can be observed in an offended person include – but are not limited to:

* Overly timid responses to people; low eye contact.

* Tension, frustration, anger, or depression, expressed through body language and tone of voice.

* Lack of laughter or smiling, particularly when a potentially offensive joke or comment is made.

* "Flinching" when coarse language is used.

What To Do About Sexual Harassment

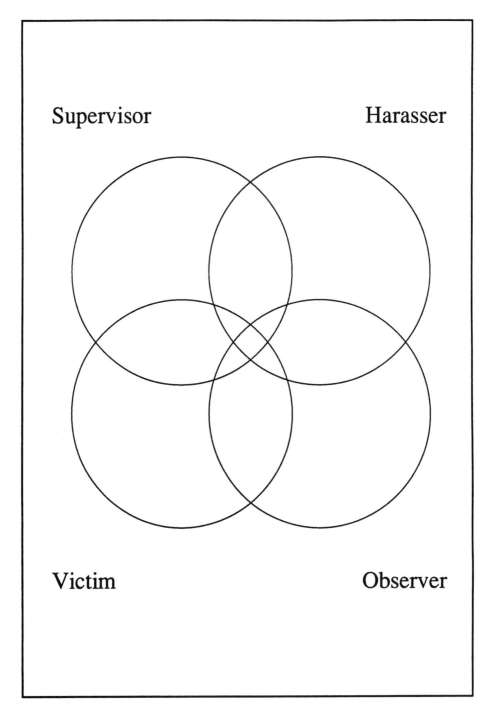

Supervisor

Harasser

Victim

Observer

City Commitments and Expectations

1. Sexual harassment is incompatible with the City's Organizational Philosophy. Employees are asked to treat each other as valuable individuals and to foster teamwork and mutual respect in their day-to-day work activities.

2. This philosophy also applies to the City's service relationship with the community. Sexual harassment of citizens by employees will not be tolerated, not only because it is illegal, but also because of its damaging impact on the City's service responsibilities and reputation.

3. Similarly, City employees are not expected to endure harassment from citizens, clients or contractors. harassment is not part of the job.

4. Any staff member experiencing harassment from another City employee, contractor or client of City services is encouraged to assertively tell the harasser to stop the offensive behavior. Recipient/victims should seek help from a supervisor, department head, or anyone in the Personnel Department and can be assured their concerns will be taken seriously.

5. Observers of harassment are encouraged to share their observations with those involved in the harassment incident and, if appropriate, with a supervisor or the Personnel Department.

6. Managers and supervisors are expected to intervene immediately, notify the department head and personnel, and to thoroughly, confidentially, and objectively investigate and resolve harassment situations. They are also expected to take appropriate action to discipline harassers and protect all parties involved from further harassment, retaliation, or false accusations.

7. Employees are expected to positively cooperate in efforts to contain and resolve harassment situations. Those involved in a situation are required to act in a neutral and professional manner during an investigation and after the situation's resolution.

8. Those who choose to violate the City's non-discrimination policies are warned that disciplinary action can and will be used to remedy the situation. The City of Bellevue fully supports federal and state equal opportunity laws, and believes that men and women have equal rights to employment in all areas of City service. These policies are spelled out by specific Bellevue regulations, such as the City's official Personnel Policies and Procedures, Affirmative Action Plan and Employee Guidebook. The disciplinary penalties for harassment are severe, up to and including termination, indicating the seriousness of the City's commitment to equal opportunity.

9. All City employees are expected to review their own behavior to determine the degree to which they contribute to or encourage sexual harassment. Offensive and potentially offensive behaviors are to be eliminated, including making sexist jokes and comments, saying things which openly or through innuendo put others down, as well as all other forms of harassment.

10. Employees are strongly encouraged to develop assertiveness, listening, feedback, and other communications skills which will help eliminate harassment and foster a work environment truly supportive of productivity and individual success. The personal commitment of individual employees to improving communication, openness and trust in the workplace is one of the most important goals of the City's ongoing organizational improvement effort.

What To Do About Sexual Harassment

The Recipient/Victim

1. Recognize sexual harassment when it appears. Understand that it is not your fault and that it does not "come with the job". Remember that sexual harassment is against the law and violates specific Bellevue policies.

2. When you are sexually harassed, talk to the offender. Tell him/her that you find the behavior offensive. Describe how the harassment negatively affects your work. Say things like:

    "Don't touch me. I don't like it. It makes me uncomfortable and then I make mistakes."

    "No. I don't want to go out with you. Do do not mix my work and personal life."

    "I don't think those kind of jokes are funny. They don't have anything to do with work. Please don't tell them when I am in the room."

    "I'd like it a lot better if you'd comment on the quality of my work, rather than the way I look."

    My name is _____, not 'Honey'."

    (See the section in this manual, "Giving Someone Else Feedback:, for additional examples of what to say.)

3. If verbal feedback doesn't work, put your objections to the harassment in writing, sending a copy to the harasser and keeping one for yourself. If more comfortable for you, present the written statement to the harasser in a meeting between you, the offender and your supervisor.

4. If you can't get the harassment stopped on your own or are having a difficult time confronting the harasser, immediately contact your supervisor, anyone in the Personnel Department, or the City Manager's Office. If your supervisor is the harasser, talk with him/her supervisor or your department head, as well as anyone in Personnel.

5. Document all sexual harassment incidents and conversations about the incidents. Record the date, time, place, people involved, and who said what to whom. Keeping this documentation is very important and will help you and the City investigate and resolve the situation. At some point during an investigation you may be asked to write out a brief, formal statement of all the incidents connected with a harassment situation – your notes and documentation will be extremely helpful to this effort.

6. Consider your own behavior. You may be knowingly encouraging sexual harassment by the way you dress or communicate. Get feedback from close friends or associates if you feel this might be the case. Never encourage harassers by smiling, laughing at their jokes, or "flirting back". This type of response can lead a harasser to think you really enjoy this type of attention at work.

7. Avoid escalating a harassment situation by trying to "get even" with the harasser. This will only make matters more complicated and make it more difficult to get the harassment stopped quickly and confidentially.

The Harasser

1. If asked to stop a particular behavior, do so immediately. If you think it might help, apologize to the offended person.

2. Think about the impact of what you do and say on another person's attitudes toward work, job performance, and self-esteem.

3. Pay attention to how others respond to what you do and say. Look for indications you might have violated someone else's comfort zone and ask for feedback. (See the sections in this manual devoted to these important skills.)

4. Don't assume that your co-workers or employees enjoy comments about their appearance, hearing sexually oriented jokes or comments, being touched, stared at, or propositioned, even in a teasing or non-serious manner.

5. Understand that it is not how you intend to come across to others so much as their perception of how you actually do come across that is important.

6. Talk to your spouse, family members, or close friends about experiences they might have had with sexual harassment. As people describe the vulnerability, intimidation and anger they have felt as recipients or victims, relate those feelings to experiences you have had.

7. If you have a supervisor, do not assume that individuals how work for you will tell you if they are offended – or harassed – by what you say or do. Remember that one of your employees may be "smiling on the outside, but cringing on the inside" simply because you are the boss. Review your copy of the Management Information Manual on Sexual Harassment, or get a new copy from Personnel.

8. Remember that sexual harassment is against the law. Recent court decisions have resulted in both organizations and individual paying large judgments and being subject to very negative, long-term publicity. Your personal reputation (and an lot more) is at stake.

9. Keep in mind that the City of Bellevue, through its policies and training programs, has effectively warned all employees that sexual harassment will not be tolerated. This issue is taken very seriously by the City. Those found at fault will be disciplined appropriately.

10. If accused of harassment, even if the charges are false, do not try to "get even" with the recipient/victim or others in the workplace, or do things which could be construed as retaliation. This will greatly complicate matters, and could result in serious discipline should you be found at fault for retaliating. Be patient if an investigation has been initiated. The City's policy is that people are innocent of sexual harassment until proven to be at fault. If unsure how to address your responsibilities or working relationships at any time during or after the investigation, contact your supervisor, department head, or the Personnel Department for advice.

<u>The Observer</u>

1. In many work situations, reporting an incident or a problem that involves other people might be considered evidence you are not a good "team player". However, sexual harassment is a different kind of problem because of the high potential for harm to people, and the significant liability borne by the City. As an observer, you should share your observations with those involved in the harassment situation. If the harasser's behavior is offensive to you or to the recipient/victim, you are encouraged to discuss the matter with your supervisor, your department head and/or the Personnel Department. Help an offended person talk to someone in the chain of command or in Personnel about the situation.

2. Support the offended person's efforts to get the harassment stopped. Let him/her know that you know what's going on. Say things like:

    "You seem to get pretty tense every time _____ comes into the office."

    "I'd really be angry (offended, embarrassed) if he did that sort of thing to me. Do you want to talk about it?"

    "If you get to a point of wanting to complain about _____'s behavior, let me know. I've seen enough to know how _____ interferes with your work."

3. If someone who is being harassed brings concern or complaint to you, help the person not to feel alone, scared, or untrusting of City resources. Help the person get assistance from a supervisor, department head, anyone in the Personnel Department, or the City Manager's Office.

4. Confront harassers by pointing out their behavior and letting them know how the harassment affects the offended individual. Say things like:

    "_____, do you have any idea how much your jokes upset _____? She really has a hard time concentrating on her work because she's embarrassed by the things you say."

    "What makes you think you've got the right to touch her like that? That kind of familiarity is really out of line here."

    "You seem to really enjoy propositioning all the new women who come into our office."

    "If you said that kind of stuff to me, I'd go straight to the boss. Do you have any idea how it feels to hear that sort of thing?"

5. Don't engage in behaviors that could escalate the situation. The goal is to get the harassment stopped, not malign another person or take sides. Keep in mind that most harassers probably are not truly aware of the impact of their behaviors to others. Trying to "get even" with a harasser on someone else's behalf (or retaliate against an individual you believe is making a false charge), will seriously complicate a situation. Falsely and maliciously defaming someone else will lead to disciplinary action against you by the City.

6. During investigation of a situation and after it has been resolved, keep a neutral, professional attitude toward all involved parties. Help contain the situation by avoiding unnecessary discussion. Stay focused on the job and keep the situation confidential. Help others to do the same.

<u>The Supervisor or Manager</u>

(For a more complete discussion of managers' and supervisors' responsibilities, consult the Sexual Harassment Management Information Manual available from the Personnel Department.)

In brief, managers and supervisors are responsible for:

1. Serving as models for appropriate behaviors on the work team.

2. Providing accurate, timely, job-related performance feedback to employees.

3. Taking action on inappropriate behavior in the workplace, whether or not it is related to sexual harassment.

4. Communicating City policies and standards relating to equal opportunity and maintenance of a discrimination-free work environment.

5. Observing interactions on the work team and recognizing those which could be some form of sexual harassment.

6. Intervening with harassers to stop offensive behaviors through education, problem-solving and, when warranted, formal disciplinary action; stopping harassment of staff in the workplace by non-employees.

7. Being available, open-minded and supportive to anyone who feels he/she is experiencing sexual harassment; taking all complaints seriously.

8. Notifying the chain of command and the Personnel Department of any complaints received or serious incidents warranting discipline for a harasser.

9. With guidance from the chain and Personnel, sensitively and confidentially investigating incidents of complaints of sexual harassment.

10. Maintaining confidentiality during investigation of incidents and complaints; intervening with those who intentionally or unintentionally spread rumors.

11. Serving as a continuing resource to the recipient/victim, offender, and observers on how to respond to the harassment situation.

12. Providing support and counsel to recipients and victims of harassment.

13. Following-up to make sure that relationships on the work team have returned to normal and that no further harassment or any form of retaliation has occurred.

Retaliation

Because of the strong negative emotions associated with sexual harassment, retaliation can easily become an element of the situation. Attempts to "get even" or "take sides", however, dramatically complicate sexual harassment problems and at all times are to be avoided. Retaliation usually leads to more harassment, and more serious forms of harassment.

Retaliation can be defined as any action which does not help correct a situation but serves only as a reprisal with the intent of causing pain. There are many ways in which retaliation can occur.

* A harasser retaliates against a recipient/victim for objecting to the harassment or making a complaint.

* A recipient/victim retaliates against an offender for the harassment.

* Observers or co-workers retaliate against the recipient/victim or harasser.

* A supervisor or manager retaliates against the recipient/victim or the harasser because of a complaint.

* Someone falsely accuses another person of sexual harassment in order to "get back at" him/her for some other kind of problem.

Retaliation is no game. It is illegal and strictly prohibited as a matter of the Bellevue policy. Employees found to be retaliating against anyone in a sexual harassment situation are subject to immediate corrective action.

Everybody involved in the investigation and resolution of a sexual harassment complaint – recipient/victim, harasser, observers, managers and supervisors – is expected to exercise self-control, be sensitive to the impact of personal behaviors on others, and to focus energies on the job to be done to the greatest degree possible. If co-workers cannot behave in a positive way toward one another, then at the least they are to behave neutrally. This is an indication of good faith that whatever problem exists can and will be resolved, and supports the basic commitment and trust of people to handle problems in a just and mature manner.

After the resolution of a complaint, all involved should work together to help "make the victim whole" by restoring that person to his/her rightful role in the work team. Falsely accused persons, and those found not to be at fault after an investigation, also need to have their respect and credibility restored to them.

In particular, employees are to avoid such subtle forms of retaliation as:

* Making it tough on someone to get his/her job done by excluding that person from the usual flow of information, work assignments, or work group activities.

* Categorizing someone as a "trouble-maker" or as having mental problems because he or she has spoken up about offensive behavior.

* Suggesting the harassment is really the recipient/victim's fault.

* Taking sides in a harassment situation; spreading rumors, innuendo or gossip about the harasser or recipient/victim.

* Unfair criticism of a person's work or his/her competency as a result of a complaint.

* Suggesting a person's complaint is simply a way to get attention or money.

* Refusing to abide by the principle that a person is innocent until proven at fault.

* If a person has been falsely charged, refusing to acknowledge that the charge is false and that the person is innocent.

* Once a person has been disciplined as a harasser, continuing to persecute that individual.

False Charges of Sexual Harassment

Special note needs to be given to the circumstance in which someone maliciously makes a false charge of sexual harassment in order to defame or discredit someone else. The City does not tolerate this type of harassment by "reverse victimization" and will take disciplinary action up to and including discharge of an employee who falsely, maliciously and without a reasonable basis makes a charge of sexual harassment. Sexual harassment laws and policies are not tools to destroy someone else's reputation. The City considers this form of retaliation as totally inappropriate to the workplace and very serious, and warns all employees that such behavior is expressly prohibited.

Members
of the   Incident
Workteam

**Others in the
Organization**

Retaliation spreads the problem,
affecting more and more people
in the organization,
making it much more difficult to resolve.

Handling Harassment by Non-Employees

Sexual harassment of City employees in the workplace by citizens, vendors, salespeople, repair personnel or any other non-employee is unacceptable. All staff need to understand that sexual harassment is not a part of the job. Those harassed are encouraged to tell the harasser to stop the offensive behavior while maintaining an appropriately polite, business-like manner:

> "Mr. Jackson, it makes me uncomfortable when you refer to me as "Sweetie' or 'Honey'. My name is Sara Williams. Please feel free to call me Sara. How can I be of help to you today?"

> "Ms. Jones, I consider this to be a business conversation. I would appreciate it if we could keep it at that level, please."

> "Please don't stare at me that way. It really interferes with my work. If necessary, I'll have my supervisor speak to you about it."

> "I am not 'a dumb girl engineer'. That's the second time in ten minutes you've made a comment like that about me. If you can't address me in a civil manner, I'll be forced to end this phone conversation immediately."

> "Don't ever touch me like that again. I'll be reporting this incident to my supervisor."

> "No, I'm not interested in going out with you, and I won't put up with being propositioned. If you don't have legitimate business in City Hall, please leave."

A City employee who feels he or she is being sexually harassed on the job by a non-employee is encouraged to discuss the situation with a supervisor, department head, and/or the Personnel Department.

When, for any reason, the employee is unable to stop the harassment on his or her own, the City will designate a manager or supervisor to deal with the situation. That person will investigate the situation, including obtaining a written statement from the recipient/victim covering the details of the incident(s). The manager will then contact the harasser, if possible, and intervene on the employee's behalf in order to get the harassment stopped. Employees facing situations of criminal behavior, such as indecent liberties (sexual touching or self-exposure), assault, or rape should immediately report the incident to the Police Department.

Some Important Communication Skills

Giving Someone Else Feedback

All of us need to know how to give others feedback, particularly when someone else is behaving in a way that attacks self-esteem.

Good relationships and a strong sense of self-worth <u>thrive</u> on people communicating honestly and effectively about their feelings. If a person is harassing you, the best way you get the harassment stopped is to:

1) Tell the other person what he/she did to bother you,
2) How you felt about it, and
3) The way you would like that person to behave in the future.

Keep in mind that even the most assertive person may not be able to handle every situation alone. Don't hesitate to contact organizational resources, such as your supervisor, a manager in your chain of command, your department head, or anyone in the Personnel Department if you need advice, support or assistance in getting harassment stopped.

Making an assertive statement to someone else is something that can be learned. Assertive statements are simply short, direct statements which indicate your interests, desires, or intentions. They are more powerful when they occur soon after the offensive incident. They should be delivered looking at the other person and making direct eye contact; spoken with a firm, strong voice where the last syllable spoken has a lower voice tone. Assertive statements are best when delivered in a polite, non-judgmental tone of voice. They are neither nice, nor mean, they are sincere, not cutting or demeaning. An assertive statement is a comment on a behavior, not a person, and conveys respect for both yourself and the other person.

Some beginnings for assertive statements are:

"I want ..."
"I intend ..."
"I will ..."
"I need you to ..."
"I expect ..."

Examples of assertive statements which can be used in situations involving sexual harassment are listed below.

"When you come up behind me and put your arm around me, it makes me feel really uncomfortable. I'd like you to stop doing it. If you want to discuss something with me, please just talk to me; don't touch me."

"Mary, it seems like you're spending all your free time around my desk. Even though you might not mean anything by it, it embarrasses me because other people are beginning to think we have something other than a work relationship. I want you to stop flirting. It really irritates me that you seem to enjoy keeping me from my work."

"Don't make jokes like that about gays. You seem to think that nobody could be offended by that type of humor. I would like it a lot better if you told jokes that didn't involve sexual preference.

"Maybe you don't think I notice it, or that I like it when you stare at me, but frankly, it makes me feel like a piece of meat, not a person. When you talk to me, please look at my face, not my body."

"You made several comments today in the lunchroom that sounded like you want to develop a relationship with me. I want you to know how terrible it felt to be propositioned like that in front of my friends. I don't want that kind of relationship with you, and I don't want you to make comments like that again."

"You and I have a super relationship. But there's something you do that makes me feel put down. When you call be 'Babe' or 'Doll' or 'Cutie' it doesn't feel like we are really equals. I know you don't mean to hurt me. I'd like it a lot better if you'd just all me by my first name."

"It seems like you are very much attracted to me, and I want you to know that I'm flattered by that. But I'd prefer that we were friends at work, and didn't get involved. I make it a rule not to mix business and personal relationships."

"I want you to know how angry it made me when you touched me. If you bother me like that again, I intend to go straight to my supervisor with this information."

To a supervisor: "_____ has been staring at me and it makes me very uncomfortable. I'd like your help in getting _____ to stop doing this."

Asking For and Getting Feedback From Others

Being open to new information and asking for feedback from others are two important skills which help people master the changing social environment, particularly the changing roles of men and women in the workplace. The more information a person has about how he/she is coming across to other people, the easier it is for that person to adopt to shifting social standards.

It's important to keep in mind that people do not automatically recognize their impacts on each other. Social research has shown that individuals don't look for reactions they don't want to see in other people, and it is also apparent people do not often directly ask for feedback. Rather, people tend to "live by habit" and be comfortable with familiar behaviors, whether or not these habits support positive interpersonal relationships. Although the following skills would seem to be simple ones, they can truly require some effort and personal development to master.

Being Open to New Information

Being more observant of how others are responding to us is extremely important. What falls in one person's "comfort zone" may not be comfortable for someone else. The rule of thumb is to treat all people as individuals. It's important to not make assumptions about others and to recognize the signs of discomfort. For example:

You told a joke and:

* Some people didn't smile or laugh.
* Nobody else told a similar joke, or when someone did, other people moved away.
* Somebody said the joke bothered him, her, or someone else.
* Somebody took the joke as a put-down.
* Somebody made an angry, sarcastic or cutting comment about you or your joke.

You hugged someone and:

* That person's body became tense.
* The other person pulled away.
* The person didn't return the hug.
* The person didn't smile or look at you.
* The person said he or she didn't like the hug.

You looked at someone or touched someone and:

* The person noticed your stare or touch and gave you a "dirty look".
* The person tried to ignore your stare or pulled away from your touch.
* The person looked tense, uncomfortable or embarrassed but didn't say anything.
* The person told you to stop touching or looking at him/her "that way".

You ask someone for a date and:

* The person said "no" or was reluctant to go out with you.
* The person didn't smile.

* The person couldn't give you an answer.
* The person said "yes" but his/her tone of voice or body language said "no".
* The person looked tense and uncomfortable.
* The person now avoids you.

These are just examples. Any behavior which causes someone else to be tense, not make eye contact, make angry, cutting or sarcastic remarks, get quiet, show frustration, frown, or move away from or avoid you, can be signs that something you are doing, perhaps unintentionally, is bothering that person. Be sensitive to the clues. Someone may be "smiling on the outside, but cringing on the inside".

If there is doubt in your mind that a behavior, such as a joke, a comment, or a touch, might be offensive, it is best to simply avoid that behavior.

<u>Asking for Feedback</u>

Sometimes a person's reactions may not make it clear to you how he or she feels about things you have said or done. Not everyone is assertive or has a desire to give other people direct feedback. This is particularly important if you sense that someone did not appreciate something you did or said.

Some suggestions for asking for feedback are:

1) Be genuine. Asking for feedback in an insincere, teasing, sarcastic, or manipulative way will probably be far more offensive than the behaviors you have a question about.

2) Timing and circumstances are important. Don't embarrass or antagonize someone by asking for feedback at the wrong time or in the wrong place. Be sensitive to the fact that the other person may not really want to talk to you alone or talk to you in a place he/she could feel trapped.

3) Make it uncomfortable for the other person to tell you how he/she truly feels. Don't be demanding or try to coerce the information from the other person. Always leave the other person the option of <u>not</u> responding.

4) Be comfortable and confident in asking for the feedback. If you approach asking for the information as a sign of personal strength and a display of genuine interest in the feelings and perceptions of others, then the other person is likely to approach your request that way also.

5) Remember, just because someone gives you feedback, you don't need to act. Always, however, use it for your information and as a way to increase your sensitivity about how you affect others.

Use phrases such as:

"Judy, would you give me your opinion of how I'm coming across? You seem to kind of tense up every time we are in a meeting together. If I'm doing something you don't like, I'd sure like to know what it is because I certainly don't want to offend you."

"Bill, I'm not sure I understand what's been happening lately. We don't seem to be working as well together as we used to. Is it something I did or said?"

"Cherie, I know you haven't said anything to me, but I get the impression you're angry with me. If you are willing to tell me, I would sure appreciate understanding what the problem is."

"At shift briefing you blew up at me. What did I do wrong?"

"Did I bother you when I put my hand on your arm? I couldn't tell whether that was okay with you or not and I don't want to make you uncomfortable."

Responding To Feedback

Whether asked for or not, getting feedback from others can be a disconcerting experience. A person discovering that he or she has unintentionally offended someone else can feel the impact on his or her sense of self-esteem. Try to keep in mind that getting feedback is an opportunity to improve the way you relate to other people. Here are some ideas about how to respond.

<u>Do not assume that getting feedback commits you to major personal change.</u>

Ultimately, it is you who determines whether and to what degree you will react on the feedback you are given. Just because someone gives you information of an opinion, it does not automatically mean you must adjust your entire approach to interpersonal relations.

<u>Don't react defensively.</u>

It's a behavior that is the problem, not you as a person. Realize that overreacting with strong emotions is liable to create a greater conflict rather than resolve the situation. Assure the person that you genuinely want to hear what he or she has to say. The most important thing you can do is <u>listen</u>. Be supportive of the other person's interest in giving you feedback and willingness to openly discuss matters with you. Make the exchange as comfortable and low key as possible.

<u>Find out exactly what behavior has bothered the other person.</u>

Help the person tell you what the problem is by focusing your discussion on specific actions and words. Ask questions such as:

"Can you be more specific about what I did (or said)?"

"When was the last time I did something that bothered you?"

"Can you say more about that? I'm not sure I understand what you mean."

"It would help me to have an example."

<u>Place yourself in the other person's shoes – understand the way that person feels and has been affected.</u>

As you talk, try to understand the other person's experience. Don't dismiss that individual's feelings as being unimportant or inappropriate. Recognize that an important part of feedback is how someone else felt about your behaviors. Be sensitive to the fact that how you were intending to come across may not be the same as your actual impact on others.

<u>Before responding to what you believe the other person has said, check out your understanding by paraphrasing the other person's statements and feelings.</u>

Don't try to respond before you are sure you truly understand the other person.

"Paraphrasing" is one good way to do this. To paraphrase means to repeat back the statements and feelings of someone else in a shortened form. Paraphrases are sentences, not questions. They are simply a translation of someone else's message into your terms. Paraphrasing is one of the most effective communication skills anybody can learn.

For example, Susan says to John: "It really bugs me, John, when you start making those kind of joking comments about women."

John paraphrases by saying, "You feel pretty angry about some of the things I say when I'm joking around."

Or, "You sound frustrated by some jokes about women I'm made."

Or, "It sounds like some of my jokes really upset you."

Even if you paraphrase incorrectly because you have missed the person's true message or feelings, it's okay. The other person has a chance to clarify the message. This will help both of you understand what the problem is.

Keep in mind that one of the advantages of paraphrasing is that in a tense situation, it may give you some additional time to consider your response to the other person.

Develop a solution by checking out alternative behaviors.

This state gives you an opportunity to see what kinds of things you need to start or stop doing to resolve the situation. It's very important to be specific, and to give the other person ample opportunity to correct misperceptions about what he/she wants or to comment on additional offensive behaviors. Be sensitive to the other person's reactions. For example, following on the previous exchange:

John: "Joking around is okay as long as I don't make teasing comments about women, is that right?"

Susan: Well, sort of. I personally felt insulted the other day when you made a joke and used the words 'chick' and 'broad'. Sometimes, even when you're not joking you use those words."

John: "It makes you mad when I use those words and you'd like me to stop using them, whether they are part of a joke or not."

Susan: "Yeah, that's exactly right. Thanks for understanding how I feel about it, John."

Thank the other person for the feedback.

"Susan, I didn't realize those words bothered you. I didn't intend to offend you, but I can see how you feel about them and I really appreciate you giving it to me straight about how they affect you."

"Gary, thanks for telling me about my habit of putting my arm around you. I guess I just didn't think how you might feel about it. I'm glad you talked to me."

I hadn't guessed how embarrassed you felt when I talked about some of my personal relationships. I apologize. And I want you to know how much I appreciate your telling me. I wouldn't want to offend you or anybody else around here by being too familiar."

"I can see how what I thought was a compliment really came off sounding kind of sexist. Maybe what I should have said was simply that I thought you did a great job straightening out that software problem. Thank for telling me how I came across."

<u>Respond from the heart.</u>

You could follow all of the above steps and still not have responded appropriately if you are not truly open to what the other person has to say. You may not agree with the feedback, feel the other person has misinterpreted your actions, or feel that the person has overreacted, but at the very least you have an obligation to listen and to carefully consider that person's message to you. To "respond from the heart" means letting the other person know how important his/her feelings and experience are to you, and demonstrating a personal commitment to a positive relationship with the person.

<u>Act on the feedback/commit to changing offensive behavior.</u>

At this point you are ready to evaluate the feedback and decide whether to make personal changes. Here are some possible steps:

* Carefully reconsider the incidents identified in the feedback to see how you felt at the time – be honest with yourself about your motives and manner, and how they might have been interpreted by others.

* Pay closer attention to the reactions of others in similar situations. Look for a potential "blind spot" in how you see others responding to you.

* Talk to friends, acquaintances and associates to see if their experience of you verifies the feedback you have received. When doing this, don't just talk to people whose values are identical to your own. Pick people who you respect and who will be objective and truthful with you.

* Before acting or speaking, ask yourself whether there is a possibility for others to be offended. If the answer is "yes", refrain from the behavior.

* If you decide to change some potentially offensive habits or behaviors, let others know of the changes you intend to make and ask for their assistance in giving you constructive feedback about your progress.

* Identify and practice alternative non-offensive behaviors that let your true sensitivities and interpersonal skills shine through.

* Reward yourself for having successfully acquired a new skill and for having made an important improvement in your relations with others.

What happens if I complain?

The City is committed to getting the harassment stopped. When you make a complaint to a supervisor or manager, several things happen. The department head and the Personnel Department are notified that a complaint has been received. Appropriate people in the departmental chain of command and Personnel staff make a decision about who will be involve din handling the complaint. Then, an impartial, thorough, and confidential investigation is initiated to determine the facts of the situation. You will be asked to describe the specific incident(s) leading to the complaint. You may also be asked to develop a brief written statement of these incidents. The alleged harasser and others who may know of the situation or have seen incidents will be contacted for additional information. Those guiding the investigation will then make a decision on the best course of action to stop all harassment, prevent retaliation of any kind, and appropriately educate and/or discipline the harasser if found to be at fault. Please keep in mind that every situation is unique and the above statements represent only a very general description.

What if I want to handle a situation on my own?

Because Bellevue is legally responsible for sexual harassment in the workplace, once a sexual harassment incident comes to the attention of a supervisor, manager or Personnel Department staff, the department head and Personnel Director are always notified. However, if you want to handle the situation on your own, the City will respect your right to do so, so long as the harassing behaviors can be stopped in a reasonably short time period (two to three weeks maximum) and there is no risk that the harassment will be directed at other employees or clients of the City. In this case, your supervisor, a manger, or someone in the Personnel Department might serve as a coach, offering you support and guidance in getting the harassment stopped. If you cannot resolve the situation on your own in the agreed upon timeframe, management will intervene according to the general plan described under the first question.

What if I don't trust my supervisor, the department head or the Personnel Department? Who do I tell I'm being harassed?

Sometimes trusting "the system" is hard to do. The important thing is that you take action to get the harassment stopped. The City prohibits illegal discrimination, believes people should be treated as individuals and is committed to resolving sexual harassment situations in as responsible and confidential a manner as possible. If you do not feel comfortable talking to your department head or people in the Personnel Department, there are other City resources available. Consider:

*   The City manager, or staff in the City Manager's Office.

*   The Legal Department. Talk to the City Attorney, or any attorney in the Legal Department.

*   The Where-To-Turn Counselor. (For more information, get a Where-To-Turn Fact Sheet at the Personnel Department – and note the restriction on maintaining confidentiality of sexual harassment cases.)

*   A co-worker who can help you access one of these resources.

What if my supervisor is part of the problem?

YOu do not need to talk with your supervisor. You may go directly to your department head or someone else in your chain of command, to the Personnel Department, or to any of the resources listed in the previous question. The City prohibits retaliation against people who bring forward a harassment concern or

Frequently Asked Questions

complaint and steps will be taken to correct the situation and protect you from any potential reprisal. Keep in mind that harassment or retaliation by a supervisor is considered extremely serious by the City. You will need to be thoughtful and accurate in describing the specific ways your supervisor has contributed to the problem. If your supervisor is directly harassing you, immediately report this to the department head and/or Personnel.

What if the harassment continue?

The City encourages employees to let someone inside the City know if they are being sexually harassed at worked, and will do everything possible to get the harassment stopped. In the event the City is unresponsive, you may wish to contact private legal counsel or the federal and state agencies which enforce sexual harassment laws. These are the Equal Employment Opportunity Commission and the Washington State Human Rights Commission. It is your legal right to file a complaint with one of these enforcement agencies.

What are my rights as someone accused of harassment?

An individual is not at fault until proven so by the evidence. As an alleged harasser you have the right to an objective, fair and confidential investigation of the facts. Should the facts show that you are not at fault, the City will let those involved in the situation know that you have not done anything wrong and deserve all due respect for your position and reputation. If found at fault, you can expect the City to fairly administer disciplinary action according to the City's policies on discipline. Additionally, since any form of retaliation is forbidden by City policy, the City will also take steps, if necessary, to prevent retaliation against you by the recipient/victim or co-workers.

Employees should keep in mind that individuals as well as the City may be sued under civil law on charges of sexual harassment, and that Bellevue will not necessarily provide legal services or insurance for the harasser. (See Bellevue City Code, Chapter 3.81 for additional information.) In those cases involving indecent liberties, assault or rape, criminal charges can also be brought against the harasser.

Shouldn't the person who is offended tell the harasser first, rather than going to Personnel or my department head right away?

Theoretically, any person who is the recipient/victim of sexual harassment certainly is in a position to tell the harasser to stop. The City actively encourages individuals who feel harassed to assertively approach the offending person. However, victims of sexual harassment can feel very intimidated by the situation and be fearful of reprisals by the harasser or co-workers. For this reason, it's important for victims to feel okay about going to a "higher authority". Moreover, harassment of any kind is a very serious matter which warrants attention by senior management.

Does this Bellevue policy mean we have to talk differently around here?

Is it true that as a result of more information about sexual harassment some things for Bellevue City employees will change, including a whole variety of comments and jokes that may be offensive to people. Creating a truly discrimination-free work environment means all of us have a special obligation to be sensitive to sexist, racist or other offensive language.

What if everybody on the crew (or in the office) enjoys those jokes? They build morale and relieve stress.

It is possible not everyone enjoys the jokes, but that people are unwilling to speak up for fear of being excluded from the group or being labeled as not having a "sense of humor". Keep in mind that sexist behavior, whether considered amusing or not, represents an artificial barrier preventing people from getting to know and treat each other as individuals. What may superficially seem to "build morale and relieve stress" for some employees might actually jeopardize morale and create stress for others.

Does this mean I can't open a door for someone, or touch someone on the arm in friendship?

No. What it means is that we all need to be more sensitive to the "comfort zones" of others. We need to treat people as _individuals_, rather than simple as a member of some group. Not all _people_ want to have the door opened for them; not everybody likes to be touched on the arm. But some individuals do.

What's wrong with calling someone a "girl"?

For some women, being called a girl is equivalent to calling a black man a "boy". It's not flattery. It can be experienced as an insult because it implies that women are like children and are not equal adults.

Isn't it just that the victim can't take a joke?

The "joke" could really be a put-down that attacks another person's self-esteem. The person feels degraded because it's hard to fight back when everyone else is laughing or taunting. No one deserves that kind of persecution just because of sex or sexual preference.

What about sexual harassment of men?

Men are sexually harassed, too. Perhaps more than we know, since the culture we live in makes it difficult for men to complain about harassment of this kind. Sexual harassment is not a "women's issue". It's a people issue. A man's productivity and self-esteem can be as negatively influenced by harassment as a woman's. It is important to remember, however, that the great majority of harassment is directed at women. Studies have shown that women are at least twice as likely to be harassed as men and twice as likely to experience the more severe forms of harassment, such as unwanted propositions and threats.

Is there such a thing as harassment of gays or lesbians?

Yes. Sexual harassment isn't limited to male/female relationships. If a behavior focuses o sexuality, is unwanted, and is repeated or intentional, it's form of sexual harassment and is illegal. For example, starting a rumor that someone is gay, or attacking someone on the work team because he/she is gay, is also a situation of sexual harassment. People have a legal right to their sexual preference.

However, if a gay supervisor offered a promotion contingent on an employee providing sexual favors to the supervisor, that also would constitute sexual harassment.

What about the unscrupulous person who takes advantage of the law to "get someone" they don't like?

Using the law as a tool, not to secure one's legal rights but simply to maliciously hurt someone else, can be unlawful and violates City standards. Malicious, knowingly false accusations employed to ruin someone's reputation have no place in a responsible business organization. At Bellevue, should it be proven that an employee intended to harm someone else in this manner, that employee will be subject to disciplinary action. The City does not tolerate "game playing" of this kind.

What about office affairs and flirtations?

Sexual attraction is a natural response. To suggest it doesn't or shouldn'T happen between employees is unrealistic. As long as the relationship is mutual and reciprocal, it is not sexual harassment, although it may certainly create other types of problems for the organization. The difficulty with worksite affairs is that if they end, there is the possibility of retaliation by one of the parties using influence to "get" the other person. At that point, the situation may become sexual harassment. Additionally, office affairs can result in "third party" complaints of sexual harassment if the relationship creates favoritism and interferes with the work or promotional opportunities of others in the organization.

What about flirtatious behaviors and dress? Aren't some women just asking for it?

Both men and women may consciously dress in a sexy manner and, if so, are probably asking for some type of sexual comment or response from those with whom they work. In this situation, the person should be reminded of the need to dress in a manner appropriate to the work place. Sometimes a person isn't really aware that his or her apparel is not appropriate, and may simply be trying to dress attractively or wear a current fashion. A few words of guidance from a supervisor would be appropriate.

What do I do if I think I see something that could be sexual harassment?

Talk to the recipient to see how he or she felt about what happened. If the behavior you observed was offensive to you or to the recipient, share your feelings with a supervisor or someone from Personnel. Don't avoid speaking up if it appears people are getting hurt.

FORM 6-7
HARBRIDGE HOUSE, INC. WORKSHOP OUTLINE

CREATING A HARASSMENT-FREE ENVIRONMENT:

A Workshop on Issues of Sexual Harassment

2100 Sanders Road, Suite 110
Northbrook, Illinois 60062
(708) 498-9090 Telephone
(708) 498-9630 Fax

Harbridge House, a division of the Coopers & Lybrand Human Resource Advisory Group, is a management education and development firm with a major practice in the area of managing diversity and multiculturalism and specific expertise in workforce gender issues. For further information, contact Muriel Lazar, Managing Director of the firm's Cultural Diversity Practice at (708) 498-9090 or (312) 701-5500.

OBJECTIVES

- To illustrate that sexual harassment can have significant negative effects in the workplace.

- To inform participants of the organization's commitment to eliminate sexual harassment.

- To develop the ability to recognize and deal with sexual harassment proactively.

- To identify managerial actions that create a positive, productive work environment for men and women.

A WORKSHOP ON
SEXUAL HARASSMENT:
ISSUES AND SOLUTIONS

ONE DAY

SUGGESTED AGENDA

I.   What is Sexual Harassment? - Questionnaire

- Personal Definitions
- EEOC Guidelines; Laws
- Court Rulings

II.   Effects/Consequences

- Individual

  — Stress
  — Decreased Job Performance
  — Withdrawal

- Organizational

  — Lawsuits
  — Turnover
  — Lower Productivity
  — Decreased Morale
  — Poor Public Image

III.   Challenges to Traditional Beliefs

- Assumptions of Women in the Workplace

- Case Studies, Video Vignettes, Audio or Written

A WORKSHOP ON
SEXUAL HARASSMENT:
ISSUES AND SOLUTIONS

5 Hours

I.   Introduction to Program

- Senior Manager Statement of Personal Commitment

- Changing Workforce/Behavior Change

- Participant Introductions

- Objectives/Agenda

II.   Changing Demographics of the Workforce:
      Implications for Our Own Business

III. Past Role Stereotypes Vs. Present Expectations

- Four Gender Themes

- Sexism, Sexual Discrimination and Sexual Harassment

- What the law says.

IV.   Identifying Sexual Harassment

V.   Sexual Harassment Issues and Dilemmas

VI.   Handling Sexual Harassment Complaints

- Guidelines for Employees.

- Guidelines for the Managers.

IV.   Remedies - What Can Be Done?

- Personnel Actions

  — Policy
  — Complaint Procedures

- Management Responsibilities

  — EEOC Recommendations
  — Suggestions from Other Companies

- Individual Strategies

V.   Summary/Evaluation

- Evaluation of Workability of Remedies

- Examination of Barriers/Supports to Change

- Suggestions on How to Proceed

FORM 6-8
DUPONT CORPORATION TRAINING MANUAL EXCERPTS

DuPont Corporation
PREVENTION OF SEX DISCRIMINATION AND SEX HARASSMENT
A Matter of Respect
Selected Excerpts

[Excerpts reprinted with permission of DuPont Corporation. These training materials are not intended for use in excerpted form.]

INTRODUCTION

In order to be successful in any organization, it is important to develop and maintain appropriate and productive business relationships.

This publication examines three areas of corporate concern—personal relationships, sexual harassment, and subtle forms of gender discrimination—that can create inequalities in the workplace, suppress initiative, and erode productivity. Because there is often the potential for personal risk and/or liability, it is critical for employees to recognize the issues, become familiar with Company policy, and take appropriate measures to eliminate problems.

The Company seeks to sensitize employees to the issues surrounding sex discrimination—even in its most subtle forms. It is our hope that by working together, we can eliminate sexual discrimination and harassment and facilitate healthy working relationships.

Ultimately, our goal is to promote a business environment of mutual respect where everyone has the ability to achieve his or her very best. It makes good business sense to do so.

MUTUAL ATTRACTIONS AT THE WORKPLACE

As more women enter the work force, especially in areas traditionally held by men, greater opportunity is presented for socialization between the sexes and the onset of new relationships.

In the course of your career, mutual attractions may develop with business associates. We define mutual attraction as a straightforward, natural exchange between two people characterized by mutual consent.

Your personal life is your own business, and the Company does not take a position on your personal involvement with co-workers, customers or vendors. However, if you become romantically involved with a colleague, you are encouraged to examine the relationship to determine if it 1) negatively reflects on you or the Company, 2) affects your feelings on business decisions, and 3) is likely to be disruptive to the effectiveness of the organization.

Here are some examples of relationships which could present a conflict of interest, become disruptive to the workplace, or result in negative consequences for the individuals involved and the Company.

Case in Point:

Larry, manager of a computer operation, has become romantically involved with Barbara, a systems analyst. Barbara is the only female in a group of seven system analysts reporting to Larry.

In this case, it cannot be assumed that Larry can be objective in assigning work, making performance assessments, or making other impartial business decisions which affect Barbara or his other subordinates. Co-workers may claim that the relationship is having a negative influence on their careers and that they are not receiving the same favored treatment. This can result in resentment, anger and loss of productivity.

Going one step further, if Barbara received a special benefit, employment opportunity (perhaps travel to a conference), or promotion, co-workers could argue that she received them because of favoritism based on sex, her submission to Larry's sexual advances, or his requests for sexual favors. In this case, Larry and the Company could be liable for unlawful sex discrimination against other persons who were qualified for, but denied that employment opportunity or benefit.

Another problem stemming from the inequality in rank is Larry's susceptibility to charges of sexual harassment should the relationship sour.

Because this relationship has the potential for disrupting the workplace and damaging the employer, the Company must become involved. One course of action may be to reassign one of the two employees. (This is consistent with the Company's position on nepotism: it is inappropriate for a parent to supervise a son or a daughter, or a spouse to supervise a spouse.)

Summary

Whenever some aspect of DuPont's business could be jeopardized by a personal relationship, the Company should and will become involved in the situation. The Company's interests are limited to altering the work relationship—not interfering with the personal relationship.

SEXUAL HARASSMENT

When one person's repeated conduct toward another is unsolicited, unwelcome and of a sexual nature, that behavior may be considered sexual harassment. Regardless of the relationship of the parties involved, harassment of any type is not tolerated by DuPont. Not only is sexual harassment a clear violation of Company policy, it is a form of sex discrimination and therefore, illegal.

By its very nature, sexual harassment is a difficult subject to address. On the one hand, it may involve personal feelings, perceptions, gestures, and strong emotions; yet, on the other hand, it requires calm, objective logic to appropriately respond. Furthermore, conduct that one employee may find objectionable may not be unwelcomed by another. Instances are so varied, complex and unique that it is difficult to formulate hard and fast rules to prohibit sexual harassment in the workplace.

COMPANY POLICY ON SEXUAL HARASSMENT

Your personal safety and dignity, and your ability to perform your job effectively, without distractions or interference, are of prime concern to DuPont. A comfortable working environment is essential to the well-being of our employees, and it has been a longstanding policy with the Company that harassment of any type will not be tolerated.

In particular, the Company will not tolerate the sexual harassment or abuse of any of our employees—whether the initiator is another DuPont employee or a customer, client or other business associate. Any employee violating this policy, will be subject to disciplinary actions, up to and including discharge.

Case in Point . . . where submission to such conduct is a basis for making business decisions.

John is the only male chemist working in his laboratory.

"At first, I appreciated the special interest my supervisor took in my career. She started out by inviting me to lunch—to discuss our research project. Later, she invited me for drinks after work. That was when I started getting suspicious. I couldn't believe it when one evening she placed her hand on my leg and said, 'John, there's a senior staff position I'm considering you for. I know you've got a lot of talent and drive. Why don't you come home with me and we can discuss the qualifications?' Well, I didn't go home with her. And, maybe you can guess, I didn't get the job."

Case in Point . . . when such conduct creates a hostile, intimidating or offensive environment

Peggy, a machine operator, complained that the men in her section were hostile and intimidating.

"They resented my joining their 'all-male ranks' and told me if I wanted to be treated like one of the guys, I had to act like one of the guys. First, they handed me a uniform about four sizes too small. They laughed when I said I needed a larger one with, 'Gee, we just thought you'd like to show us what you're made of.' They also continued to hang nude pin-up calendars and read sex magazines, despite my objections. If that wasn't enough, they told me I needed to pass the same 'initiation rites' they had—if I wanted to prove myself. I was scared to death.

Resolving the problem

Ignoring sexual harassment will not make it go away. In fact, it may make the situation grow worse. It is always best to stop the problem at its very earliest stage. You can often regain control over the situation by stating your wishes assertively or by saying "NO!" or "STOP THAT!"

You have several options—from developing informal strategies to lodging formal complaints.

- PAY ATTENTION TO CUES or comments indicating harassment. Stay calm and assess the situation as objectively as possible.

- KNOW YOUR RIGHTS. Familiarize yourself with Company policy. Learn to recognize warning signals and try to control the situation before it gets out of hand.

- SPEAK OUT. If a person's behavior offends you or makes you feel uncomfortable, speak up. One approach might be to say "I wish you would cut that out. I find that kind of behavior offensive." Or, you might say, "Please stop. You are making me feel uncomfortable."

In cases where the initiator is generally unaware of the effects of his action, your assertive objection may be enough to resolve the problem. If, however, the behavior continues or escalates, you may wish to take the following steps:

- REPORT IT IMMEDIATELY. It is important to report the problem to someone you trust and who can help. Act immediately, if a blatant incident occurs, or when the behavior has continued once objections were voiced. You may go to your supervisor (if he or she is not the offender), to the offender's supervisor, or to any supervisor with whom you feel comfortable, or to the designated Company resource person. If you wish guidance, you may call the DuPont 24 Hour Confidential Hotline (Tel #).

- KEEP A RECORD of each incident, the date, time and place of the occurrence, and the names of witnesses, if any. Keep any notes or letters received. Also, keep a record of your complaints.
  The supervisor or personnel representative is required to take immediate action. He or she will conduct a quick, thorough and confidential investigation, making every effort to protect your rights as well as the rights of the accused. You will be protected from retaliation or and reprisals.

Where sexual harassment is found, the Company will take appropriate disciplinary action, up to and including the discharge.

If someone comes to you for help

If an employee is a recipient of sexual harassment and comes to you for help, follow these steps:

- LISTEN. Remain calm and objective. Get the facts. Through words and actions, demonstrate your support and concern.

- PROVIDE ASSURANCES. Do your best to help the employee cope with the situation. Make sure that she does not feel ashamed or embarrassed. Assure her that you consider this a serious problem and will act immediately.

- IF YOU ARE THE APPROPRIATE PERSON, CONDUCT A SWIFT AND THOR-OUGH INVESTIGATION. Determine whether there are witnesses who can corroborate the claims or if there are others who have experienced similar behavior. Talk to the alleged offender, politely but firmly requesting his view of what happened. It will be important to protect both the rights of the complainant and the accused and to maintain confidentiality. (Allow access to the report only to persons with a need to know.) Remind the complainant that she is protected from reprisals by both the Company and the law. No one will be fired or punished who has filed a complaint in good faith.

- IF YOU ARE NOT THE APPROPRIATE PERSON, ENCOURAGE THE EM-PLOYEE TO TELL SOMEONE WHO CAN TAKE ACTION.

- TAKE APPROPRIATE ACTION. If the investigation establishes a pattern of repeated, unwelcome sexual conduct, or a single act of blatant sexual harassment, such as assault, take appropriate disciplinary action (as in any other case of serious misconduct), up to, and including, discharge.

NOTICE TO SUPERVISORS: It is a supervisor's responsibility to prevent sexual harassment in the workplace and to act on all complaints. If a complaint goes unanswered and the complainant files a charge with the EEOC, the Company can be held liable. In some cases, there may be personal liability as well.

SUBTLE SEX DISCRIMINATION

While sexual harassment and other forms of sexual discrimination may be readily apparent, visible, and documented, other forms of sex discrimination are more subtle. In this section, we will look at sexually discriminatory biases and covert behaviors which are more difficult to define and document but which have damaging consequences to the recipient, the organization and society at large.

At the workplace, sex biases become apparent when someone is treated negatively or differently—or denied certain rights, opportunities or responsibilities—because of his or gender or sexual orientation.

While the gender bias may be apparent as reflected in certain behaviors, it often goes unnoticed or unchallenged because it is considered acceptable, normal or customary.

Case in Point

Mary has been appointed manager of the department, a job traditionally held by men. A few of her colleagues congratulate her with comments like "This is great . . . but, won't it be difficult for you to get home in time to fix dinner?" and "It's nice to see this Company is meeting its EEOC requirements." Another asks a co-worker, "Didn't anybody else apply for the position?"

These comments—even if intended only in jest—raise questions about Mary's competence, abilities and priorities. Subtly, they are asking if a woman is good enough to handle the job.

These biases also affect Mary at her first management meeting. Her boss introduces her, "I'd like you to join me in welcoming Mary Jones, our most beautiful department manager."

Mary's manager might be applauded for promoting a woman within the organization, but his introduction raises questions about his reasons for promoting her.

When Mary presents her first report—a presentation she spent several days to develop—only a few minutes elapse before various members of the all-male group begin to shuffle papers, doodle on their note pads, and peer out the window. One member of the group gets up to excuse himself. The unspoken message these men send out is "Mary doesn't have anything important to say. I have nothing to learn from her. She was only appointed for her looks."

In each instance, we must ask if the reaction would have been different with a man. If a man had received the promotion, would his colleagues question his abilities or the company's motives? If a man had been introduced, would his looks be considered his primary asset? If the presenter had been a man, would his findings be dismissed so quickly?

CHAPTER 7

HANDLING CHARGES OF SEXUAL HARASSMENT

§ 7.1   Introduction: Handling External Charges of Sexual Harassment

Current and former employees may bring a charge of sexual harassment against your organization. Organizations which do not have an established, credible complaint mechanism for employees to use to informally raise concerns and bring formal complaints are more vulnerable to outside charges of discrimination and, specifically, of sexual harassment. Employees who do not feel safe raising a complaint of sexual harassment in their organization will typically resort to external resources such as government agencies—which are free of charge and will advocate on their behalf.

§ 7.2   Overview of How Agencies Function

In order to handle charges of sexual harassment filed by an employee with a local, state or federal agency such as the Equal Employment Opportunity Commission (EEOC), it is important to understand how agencies function. Some state agency procedures are included at the end of the chapter for illustrative purposes.

The following Questions & Answers cover basic information about how agencies process charges of sexual harassment:

What Are the Federal, State, and Local Agencies That Handle Discrimination Cases?

Individuals file charges of discrimination with the federal agencies such as the Equal Employment Opportunity Commission (EEOC) or the Office of Federal Contract Compliance Programs (OFCCP), a state agency, commonly referred to a State Division or Commission of Human Rights or Civil Rights, or an equivalent local/municipal agency. Generally, individuals bringing a complaint are referred to as the "Charging Party" and their complaints are referred to as "Charges." The organization against which charges are filed is referred to as the "Respondent." Employees typically complete a charge form indicating the factual and legal bases for their complaint of sexual harassment. Unless the employee is relatively sophisticated in legal matters, an agency representative or an attorney will assist her in completing the form.

The agencies are established by the government to enforce fair employment laws, including laws prohibiting sex discrimination in employment, of which sexual harassment is one type (pregnancy discrimination is another example). The agencies receive charges, investigate them, make findings on the merits of the charges (sometimes referred to as "probable cause" determinations), and fashion remedies as they deem appropriate to enforce the nondiscrimination laws. Remedies can include fines, a mandated sexual harassment policy and education of the work force, and monetary and other relief, including reinstatement, designed to make Charging Parties "whole," that is, restoring them to the same positions they would have been in had there been no discrimination.

Which Laws Are Enforced by These Agencies?

The laws enforced by these agencies that are relevant to sexual harassment include: Title VII of the Civil Rights Act of 1964 and Executive Order 11246 (federal law), and State and Municipal Human (Civil) Rights laws.

There are four principal theories of discrimination:

1. intentional disparate treatment of individuals on the basis of protected characteristics like race, sex (including sexual harassment), age or religion
2. policies or practices that perpetuate in the present the effects of past discrimination
3. policies or practices that have an adverse impact on protected groups but are not justified by business necessity
4. failure to make a reasonable accommodation to an employee's known religious observance or practice or an employee's known disability where such disability can be accommodated without undue burden to the employer

Under Title VII of the Civil Rights Act of 1964 (or the applicable state or municipal law), it is an unlawful employment practice for an employer, employment agency, or labor organization to discriminate against an individual employee on the basis of sex (including sexual harassment), with respect to hiring, discharge, compensation, and all terms, conditions or privileges of employment, when a causal connection exists between these areas and the practices of the employer.

What Filing Deadlines Apply to Charging Parties?

Charges must generally be filed with the EEOC within 180 days of the alleged discrimination, and with many of the state and municipal agencies within one year of the discrimination. *Note*: time limits for filing charges vary from state to state and city to city.

What Do the Agencies Request of Employers?

Agencies generally have broad enforcement powers, including the authority to request:

1. documents relating to the Charging Party and members of his or her work group or department, including salary and bonus information, performance reviews, job descriptions
2. interviews with employees
3. statements made by employees relating to the charge
4. personnel files/supervisors' files/medical files
5. company handbooks/policy manuals
6. statistical data on employee composition

7. organization charts
8. on-site inspections
9. fact-finding conferences
10. remedial action/injunctions to cease and desist prohibited conduct

Most agencies have full subpoena power to compel employers to turn over requested documentation or produce requested witnesses. Employers must challenge this process in court if they feel it is being abused by the agency.

How Do the Agencies Handle Charges

While the procedures of agencies vary, the following outlines a typical agency process:

- The agency receives a charge from a Charging Party (See samples at the end of the chapter).
- A copy of the charge, along with a cover memo indicating time limits for responding, is forwarded to the employer at the address on record at the agency or that provided by the Charging Party.
- The agency reviews the charge and the employer's response once they are received and determines what documentation and additional information it needs to investigate the charge, sometimes referred to as "fact-finding." At this early stage, the agency may also consider whether the charge should be dismissed for lack of any conceivable merit or jurisdictional basis (such as where the charge alleges violation of a law not enforced by the agency) and/or whether an early settlement can be negotiated between the parties.
- The agency conducts a formal investigation and reviews all the evidence obtained.
- At the conclusion of the investigation, the agency makes a determination as to whether the allegation(s) of discrimination is(are) supported by the evidence ("Probable Cause" or "No Probable Cause").
- Most agencies propose a conciliation of the charge prior to either dismissing it or issuing a formal complaint on behalf of a Charging Party.
- A public hearing usually follows, with each party examining witnesses and presenting evidence to support its position, at the conclusion of which the agency makes its finding.
- The agency finding is subject to judicial review, in state or federal district court, and a Charging Party generally can bring a lawsuit in court even if the charge was dismissed by an agency.

What Is the Significance of Agency Findings?

In most cases, agencies find no probable cause for believing that unlawful discrimination took place. However, whatever the finding, it may be influential to a judge or jury in a lawsuit. (Courts vary in the degree to which they allow the results of agency fact-finding or agency determinations to be introduced or considered in a trial of the same claims.)

Therefore, employers have an incentive to apply themselves in the agency process. An additional incentive is that it is much harder for individuals whose charges were found to have no probable cause to find an attorney to represent them in bringing a lawsuit, especially on a contingency basis.

§ 7.3   The Charge Process

The charge process begins with the organization's receipt of the charge. It may be received by a member of the Charging Party's department, an in-house law department, a human resources department, or some other designated office. If the organization has a preference on whom should receive agency charges, it is best to inform the agencies of the designated contact to prevent delays and misplaced paperwork that can result in possible adverse decisions based on the organizations failure to respond.

The organization should contact the agency by telephone upon receipt of the charge to establish whom the contact is for that charge. Once the charge is received, a separate charge file should be opened. If the organization has a law department or outside counsel, it should be informed of the charge immediately. Assuming that it does not handle the charges, legal counsel should be consulted throughout the charge process. When the charge is handled and the investigation undertaken upon the instruction of counsel, this may help to ensure, though it will not guarantee, that the charge file and notes will not have to be turned over to the agency without a subpoena or a court order, thereby protecting the organization's own impressions and findings regarding the claims made.

Once a charge has been filed with the agency, an investigator of the agency is assigned to the file (usually based on a "rolling" schedule). The investigator reviews the charge, determines what information is needed from the Charging Party and the Respondent and makes such requests of the parties. The agency may request some or all of the following:

1. any and all documents concerning the Charging Party or any other employees relating to pay, performance, job history, discipline, their race, sex or any other characteristic

2. interviews with current or former employees. The Respondent has a right to be present at management-level employee interviews. When the EEOC or another agency sets up an interview of a non-management-level employee, while the Respondent has no absolute right to be present, it should request the opportunity to have a representative present during the interview

3. employee statements relating to the charge

4. personnel files, including a supervisor's personal or executive files, whether in hard copy or stored on electronic media

5. salary and promotional data for the department and/or the organization

6. employee and supervisory handbooks/policies

7. statistical data regarding sex, race, and/or age of employees in the Charging Party's department or in the entire workforce

8. organization charts

9. on-site inspections

The department representing the Respondent plays a critical role in securing documents and information requested by the agency and providing them in a timely manner. Any questions concerning whether an agency is entitled to a particular document or piece of information requested should be discussed with counsel, if available, and considered carefully prior to complying with the request. The following items, though sometimes requested, have routinely been denied to agencies:

1. a breakdown by sex or race of all [organization] employees

2. statistical data that is not available through current resources, for example, listings of employees by national origin or age that would have to be created specifically for the request at great time and expense

3. internal notes, memos, logs, or correspondence prepared at the request of counsel in conducting the investigation

4. personnel files of all employees in the Charging Party's department, without a request for specific documentation

While it is important to comply with reasonable agency requests, some investigators will go on fishing expeditions hoping to find a "smoking gun." The Respondent must keep the investigation focused on the specific issues raised in the charge. Therefore, any requests that are too vague or general or that are not within the reasonable scope of the charge, should be refused, with a request for greater specificity.

Time limits for responding to charges must be adhered to. Any extensions granted by the agency over established time frames should be documented in writing in a charge log sheet. The first deadline will be for responding to the charge. Generally, agencies give employers three to four weeks to respond. In the event that additional time is needed for good cause, agencies are usually willing to grant an extension of a week or two. Extensions should be sought sparingly. In this way, they are more likely to be granted when truly needed. When an extension is granted, a letter should be sent to the agency confirming the extension with a copy to the file.

Once the position statement is filed, the agency will often follow up with a request for additional documents and/or information. Again, deadlines are tight so the request should be promptly reviewed and responded to. Failure to respond in a timely manner can result in an unfavorable determination and destroy the organization's credibility with the agency.

Based upon the evidence it gathers, the agency will have some time limit in which to determine if it has jurisdiction over the charge (for example, was the charge filed in a timely manner, does it allege a violation of fair employment practice laws), to investigate the charge, to attempt to conciliate, and to make a final determination on the charge.

If the agency is unable to stick to this timetable, as is often the case, it can take an additional period of time to process the charge after giving notice of the delay to the Charging Party. Data from the EEOC shows that the time it took EEOC to resolve a charge "reached a five-year low of 254 days" in 1991. If the charge has still not been resolved within the additional time, the Charging Party is free to bring an action in court regardless of the agency finding.

The agency will at some point request the Respondent's position on conciliation. This can happen at the outset of the process. It is generally a good policy to not settle charges that are perceived to be frivolous or that are likely to lead to a no probable cause finding. Only on such matters when the Respondent may have some legal exposure, or when the costs would seem to outweigh the benefits of defending against the charge, should conciliation at the outset be considered. Organizations should be careful to foster a reputation with employees and agencies that it never settles cases under anything but the most exceptional circumstances. Word gets around among agencies and employees as to which employers readily settle charges against them.

After the agency completes its investigation, it may seek to settle the charge and arrive at a resolution before making its finding. If the charge is settled, the agency will not make a finding and the charge generally will be dismissed. If the agency finds that there is no probable cause to believe that the Respondent violated sex discrimination law, then the charge will be dismissed and the Charging Party is advised of the right to bring a cause of action in court. As is evidenced by the figures on agency findings, more than 80 percent of the time, agencies will find no probable cause.

If a settlement is not reached and the agency has a reasonable belief that the Respondent did engage in unlawful sexual harassment, the agency typically will pursue a resolution through formal conciliation. If conciliation is unsuccessful and a finding of probable cause ensues, the agency has the option to bring suit on behalf of the Charging Party.

§ 7.4 Tips for Handling Charges and Dealing with Agencies

An agency charge represents additional work that most organizations are not regularly staffed to handle. Charges generally are the responsibility of the line of business or unit manager, or the corresponding human resources generalist, and creates work above and beyond day-to-day duties. The following suggestions are intended to help organizations administer the charge process in as effective and efficient a manner as possible, while maximizing the outcome.

1. Establish procedures in advance for investigating charges of discrimination and provide reference materials/training to those who are involved in handling charges. The organization's approach should be consistent from charge to charge, and each new organization representative should not have to reinvent the wheel. Maintain a position statement form bank with samples that can be referred to as needed.

2. Set policy on reasonable limits for agency requests for information, for example, the [organization's] policy is to disclose only as much information as is necessary to comply with each request for information. Unreasonable or unduly burdensome requests will be reviewed with an eye to reducing them to more manageable scope while still providing the agency with what it legitimately needs to make a factual determination.

3. Establish a policy on settlement of charges and consistently enforce it, for example, the [organization's] policy is to not settle charges that are without merit or have a low probability of a probable cause finding. Conciliation may be considered for matters where the [organization] deems it has some risk of liability or negative publicity. Determine who is responsible for paying any settlement or damages award, that is, will the business group or organizational unit be charged back for all or part of the cost; will the individual directly responsible have to pay some or all of the cost out of the individual's

own pocket; will bonuses and/or salary increases be reduced by the cost, and so forth.

4. Maintain confidentiality by appropriately safeguarding investigative files and limiting the dissemination of information to those who have a need-to-know. Reputations can be damaged easily by a charge, even if it turns out to be unsubstantiated.

5. Disseminate and enforce a policy of non-retaliation to protect employees who bring charges and cooperate with an investigation of a charge. (See also **Chapters 1** and **2** for policy language and rationale.)

6. Retain all documents gathered in the investigation at least until the outcome of the charge process (it might be wise to retain documents longer in the event that litigation ensues).

7. Establish and maintain a positive working relationship with agencies, that is, cooperating with all reasonable requests, participating in fact-finding conferences, being forthright, respectful, and prompt in all dealings. Agencies have substantial discretion in how they treat employers and often will extend greater courtesies to employers who cooperate with them than to those who appear to undermine their processes.

8. Minimize the disruption to the workplace by acting with utmost discretion and squelching rumors as they arise. This can also prevent claims of defamation of character should charge turn out to be false or without merit.

9. Counsel employees on their rights and responsibilities, for example, employees' obligation to cooperate with investigations; to be forthright in all statements given; to disclose all knowledge that may be salient to the charge; and to refrain from unnecessary discussion of the matter.

Some sample language for an investigator's manual could include:

1. Nonretaliation:

Retaliation against current and former employees for bringing a charge or complaint of discrimination, for participating in an investigation of discrimination or for testifying or acting as a witness in a discrimination charge is prohibited by [organization] policy and by law.

2. Document Retention:

By law, all documents connected with the charge and the Charging Party must be retained for the duration of the investigation. This includes all documents relating to other employees named in the charge or identified by the agency.

3. File Maintenance:

Investigative files should be maintained separately from other personnel files. Establish a separate case file for each charge received upon receipt of the charge. It is essential that information and documentation gathered pursuant to an investigation remain confidential and be accessible on a need-to-know basis only. These safeguards help to preserve the following interests.

- Attorney-client Privilege and Attorney Work Product protects the notes and files gathered in the course of the investigation. All documentation, notes and memos, should be created and maintained accordingly. A good rule of thumb is to not put anything in writing that would not be stated orally in an agency hearing or a court of law.

- Due to a rise in the number of individuals bringing suit for injury to reputation, it is critical that the complaint and the investigative information surrounding it not be unnecessarily disseminated. The assumption may be made that disclosure beyond those who have a need to know shows ill will or intent to harm the reputation of an individual.

- Some of the documentation gathered and reviewed pursuant to an investigation is of a highly-sensitive nature. For instance, where a charge of disability discrimination is concerned, medical records may be reviewed. Pursuant to the Americans with Disabilities Act, information obtained during a medical examination must be treated as a confidential medical record and is governed by strict limits on disclosure.

4. Working with Agencies:

It is to [organization]'s advantage to maintain a good working relationship with outside agencies. Organization representatives are to be consistent in their approach to charges and responsive to agency representatives and their requests.

§ 7.5 Drafting the Position Statement: The Most Important Part of the Process

The responding organization prepares and submits a position statement, stating its "side of the story," in response to the charge. The Respondent's practice should be to take all charges seriously and prepare a vigorous defense against all charges. This includes conducting a thorough investigation, preparing a well-supported position statement and garnering all its resources in order to prevail at the charge stage. This practice results in a high proportion of no probable cause findings, a track record that organizations should strive for.

Further, a strong position statement can have a deterrent effect, dissuading the Charging Party and/or his or her lawyer from subsequently pursuing the complaint through litigation. If the organization has reason to believe that the employee may be able to substantiate a charge of sexual harassment, it should take advantage of most agencies' opportunity for an early conciliation agreement to settle the matter.

This could include an agreement to perform any or all of the following:

1. reinstate the Charging Party with any lost pay and full benefits
2. discipline the harasser, up to termination, if appropriate
3. training of employees on sexual harassment in the workplace
4. the development and dissemination of a sexual harassment policy and complaint procedure if none exists currently

Reviewing the Charge

1. Establish whether the charge is properly before the agency and whether it was timely-filed.
2. Identify the issues raised in the charge and establish key facts. This includes covering the following areas:
   a. What is (are) the action(s) complained of; for example, failure to promote, termination, transfer, demotion, harassment, denial of salary increase, and so forth.
   b. What is the articulated legal basis for the charge, for example, discrimination based on sex, race, age, harassment, and so forth.
   c. What information is needed to assess the charge? Consider the parties involved: their employment history (years of service, performance, position and salary history, and so forth).
3. What documentation will be needed.
4. Who should be informed of the charge.
5. Who are the potential witnesses.
6. Who are similarly-situated employees.
7. Which company policies, law/regulations are relevant to the charge.
8. What are the organization's potential vulnerabilities.
9. What is the timetable for completing the investigation.

Gather Documents

The second step is to gather and review all documents relating to the charge, including as much documentation as possible about the Charging

Party, any employees named in the charge, the work area, and the alleged discriminatory practices, including:

1. Personnel files for the Charging Party and others in his or her department
2. All performance reviews, salary increases, bonuses for the Charging Party and others in her Department
3. Attendance cards and time sheets for the Department
4. Promotional activity in the Department
5. Job descriptions
6. Demographic data on employees in the Charging Party's department, including breakdowns by gender and length of service
7. Documents supporting the organization's position should be offered at this stage as an Exhibit to the position statement.

Interviewing the Parties and Witnesses

The individuals to be interviewed.   Schedule separate meetings with the parties to the charge and each witness. Interview the alleged victim and harasser first. The other individuals to interview include:

1. Charging Party's supervisor and area manager
2. All other individuals complained about in the charge
3. Any witnesses to the conduct complained of
4. Individuals identified by the alleged victim and/or harasser as having knowledge of the violations alleged

Tips on Optimizing Interviews.

1. Conduct interviews in private offices whenever possible. Detailed and accurate notes should be taken and preserved of all interviews conducted and a log maintained with entries of meetings held, actions taken and to be taken, specific timetables, and strategy.
2. Secure witness cooperation. Some of the witnesses and other parties to the investigation, including managers and supervisors, may not be cooperative. The reasons for lack of cooperation from witnesses generally stems from their misunderstanding their role in the process. It is critical that all witnesses be apprised of and understand the following in order for them to feel comfortable sharing information:
   a. the charge does not necessarily mean that any wrongdoing occurred

b. the details of the interview will be kept confidential

c. the witnesses are protected from reprisals by law and by organization policy

d. the witnesses has not been accused of anything and no complaint has been made about them. They do not have to hire an attorney or defend against anything as they have not been charged. (Of course, this will not apply to instances where an individual employee *is* named in the charge as in those cases the named individuals, though generally represented by the organization at the charge stage, should be informed, as appropriate, of their right to counsel.)

e. the witnesses will play an important part in helping the organization to obtain all the facts and hear all sides of the story and that their candor is greatly appreciated

All witnesses interviewed should be notified that they may be called upon at some future time to testify in an agency fact-finding session to the same facts that they are revealing in the investigation.

3. Develop a list of questions in advance that you would like to use with each witness. This should serve as a guide, and should not be followed so closely that valuable opportunities to probe into facts revealed by witnesses or to observe witness demeanor are compromised. Consider the following interviewing approaches:

   a. Ask open-ended questions, avoid putting words into the mouth of the witnesses or coaching their answers.

   b. Probe into vague answers: generalities and inaccuracies can hurt the organization's ability to respond effectively to the charge and maintain credibility.

   c. Apply the 80/20 rule: the witness should do 80 percent of the talking.

   d. Engage in active listening. It is important to take cues from body language and tone of voice in formulating follow-up questions and in assessing credibility.

   e. Take notes inconspicuously. Explain to individuals that they should not be distracted by your note-taking, but that it will be helpful to you to be able to refer back to the notes as needed rather than having to take more of the individuals' time.

4. Develop a chronology. Based upon a review of the charge, documents gathered, and witnesses interviewed, organize the events surrounding the charge in chronological order. Update the chronology as new information is learned as the charge progresses. Note and clarify all conflicting evidence with respect to facts and circumstances.

5. Draft the position statement. The position statement should set forth in precise and succinct terms facts related to the charge. The position statement is designed to state the relevant facts and to advocate the organization's assertion that there was no sexual harassment, for example, that there were legitimate, performance-related reasons for all employment decisions made with respect to the Charging Party, and that the organization took prompt and appropriate action to investigate the Charging Party's complaint and found it to be without merit.

The first argument, if it can be made under the specific circumstances of the case, in any response to a charge is that it is time-barred. This means that the harassment of which the Charging Party complains took place over 180 days or one year (depending on the applicable agency regulation) from the time the charge was filed with the agency. There may be times when some of the alleged harassment took place within the limitations of the charge's filing date and some beyond that time frame. The time-bar argument should be made with respect to those actions that fell outside of the limitations time frame.

Some actions alleged by employees are of a continuing nature. In those cases, it is difficult for the Charging Party and the Respondent to pinpoint when the harassment actually began and which acts might be time-barred. For instance, if an individual charges that she was touched inappropriately by her supervisor over a year ago and the balance of the charge relates incidents of verbal harassment, it would be helpful to the organization to establish that the touching incident, the one giving rise to the greatest exposure, is time-barred, even though the acts following the touching may not be. The statute of limitations, or time limit within which a lawsuit can be brought, on sexual harassment is tolled during the period of time that the charge resides with the agency.

If the time-barred argument is not applicable, the merits of the charge must be addressed. Consider the following order of presentation:

1. Declare the organization's position, for example, "Employee X was not sexually harassed. She was not terminated because she refused to comply with requests for sexual favors, as she alleges, but because she violated a very clearly-stated organizational policy against fraud and misrepresentation to customers."

2. State the relevant facts. Based on the chronology developed in the course of the investigation, pull and restate the facts that best support the organization's position. If the organization's position is that discipline of the Charging Party was justified in light of misconduct, and that sexual harassment had nothing to do with it, the facts should focus on the serious nature of the misconduct and that the manager acted in accordance with organization policy.

3. Justify the organization's position. Explain the circumstances under which the adverse action was taken with respect to the complainant and why the measure taken was justified by a nondiscriminatory reason in accordance with policy of established practice or by business necessity, depending on the nature of the charge.

4. Tell the agency why it should find no probable cause. Persuade the agency why it should find no merit to the charge and dismiss it. The reality is that due to increasing caseloads and tight agency budgets, investigators have every incentive to move cases out quickly. Offer the investigator the evidence and support that is needed to dismiss the charge.

The following are some techniques to help you draft a winning position statement:

1. Remember that you are an advocate. Once employees, whether active or former, take their complaint out of the organization's internal system, the Respondent must advocate for the good of the organization, not the charging party whose position will be advocated by the agency. This means that your arguments must be persuasive, stated firmly and clearly.

2. Keep it brief and simple. While the statement should be thorough and persuasive, employers should not disclose more information or offer more argumentation than is necessary to prevail in the charge. Do not allow plaintiffs to use the charge process as a fishing expedition.

3. The tone of the statement should be decisive. Use action verbs and the active voice, for example, "it is policy to have employees reviewed annually" versus "managers at [organization X] review their employees annually."

4. The use of a conciliatory tone may be effective when addressing a vulnerable point in the argument or when attempting to couch an adverse action in a positive light, for example, "We regret that we were unable to place Jane Doe in another position following the restructuring of the department and the elimination of her position. However, the decision to eliminate Jane's position was in no way related to her sex, and was not in retaliation for the sexual harassment complaint she brought against her supervisor."

As stated earlier, if there is any merit to the charge, it is best to pursue a settlement of the matter at the preliminary stages of the process.

The Position Statement. The completed position statement is to be forwarded first to legal counsel, if available, for review. Once the statement has been approved, it should be sent to the agency. Document all follow-up steps involving the charge on a fact sheet to be retained in the file.

§ 7.6 Auditing the Charge Process

Based upon the above methodology, an audit of the charge process should show:

1. A well-organized and up-to-date investigation file that is maintained separately from all other files.
2. The fact sheet, the position statement, all agency correspondences, all stamped with the date received by Respondent.
3. Documentation on the Charging Party, including work history, salary and bonus history, performance reviews, time cards, attendance sheets, memos to file, disciplinary actions, and so forth.
4. Notes on all witnesses interviewed by telephone and in-person.
5. A complete chronology of the relevant events leading up to and subsequent to the alleged sexual harassment.
6. Notes regarding strategies considered, including alternative remedial action (promotion, pay increase, severance, transfer, settlement with or without waiver, of right to sue, and so forth).
7. Notes regarding and documentation of applicable organization policies, local, state and federal laws.

In the event that a hearing is scheduled on a charge of sexual harassment, the best preparation is a careful review in advance of the hearing of all of the items contained in the well-documented sexual harassment case file. The next section discussing managers' and human resources' role in the litigation process covers many of the same approaches that apply to agency hearings.

§ 7.7 Court Actions

The goal of this section is not to make lawyers out of managers. Rather, there are some basic elements of the legal process that are useful even to the nonlawyer in an organization. These include:

1. How lawsuits are commenced
2. Who is involved in litigation and what role do they play

3. Discovery, including depositions

4. Trials or hearings

Sexual Harassment Lawsuits

Individuals can sue their employer after attempting to resolve their complaints through an agency, and in most cases, while or after pursuing a grievance or arbitration. Under most state and federal anti-discrimination laws such as Title VII, individuals must first file an agency charge before bringing an action in court. They typically have a short period of time, such as 90 days, from the date their case was dismissed by the agency to file a court action. (Time frames vary, and must be checked with each agency.)

However, under some state anti-discrimination laws, individuals can bring a complaint directly in court without first filing an agency charge.

Lawsuits are commenced by filing and/or serving a Complaint. (In some federal and state courts, actions are commenced when the Defendant is "served" with the Complaint, that is, the Complaint is legally delivered the Defendant. The individual filing the Complaint is designated the Plaintiff. The employer responding to the Complaint is designated the Defendant.

All lawsuits brought by current or former employees should be referred to the organization's law department or to outside counsel upon receipt.

The Role of Line Managers and Human Resources in Litigation

Line managers and/or human resources representatives are often called upon to assist legal counsel in the litigation, including:

1. to help identify witnesses and secure their cooperation

2. to secure management cooperation

3. to assist legal counsel to learn about the business and work environment in which the Plaintiff works (or worked)

4. to gather documentation relevant to the Complaint

5. to assist with responses to requests for documents and for information

The Discovery Process

Managers and human resources play a substantial part in the discovery process. Attorneys cannot possibly learn about the organization and its players as well as insiders to the organization. They rely heavily on managers and human resource personnel to respond to the following discovery request.

Requests for Production of Documents typically include all of the documents mentioned earlier with respect to agencies such as salary and performance documentation, job descriptions, compilations of race and sex data for a department, a division or an entire workforce, the organization's sexual harassment policy, any documentation of prior complaints or lawsuits for sexual harassment or sex discrimination, and personnel files.

Interrogatories are questions posed about the claims made, such as who made employment decisions impacting the Plaintiff, who might have witnessed the matter alleged to be harassment by the Plaintiff, whether any individuals have ever brought formal or informal complaints of sexual harassment or sex discrimination against the organization, who handles complaints of sexual harassment and how they are brought and resolved, whether any sexual harassment prevention training of employees has taken place, and so forth.

Managers and co-workers directly involved with the Plaintiff are likely to be deposed, that is, questioned under oath by Plaintiff's counsel, during the discovery process. Human resources managers with responsibility for investigating and resolving complaints may also be deposed. Attorneys work closely with managers in preparing for depositions and often spend hours reviewing the facts and circumstances surrounding the claims made by the Plaintiff. Managers not only play a critical role in giving their own testimony; but lawyers for the organization rely on them to help select and prepare other witnesses, to help develop a strategy, point out possible areas of vulnerability in testimony, and to ensure that a credible and consistent defense is mounted.

Going to Trial

Most cases are settled out of court. Key managers are directly involved in all settlement negotiations and decisions. They have a good sense of the risks and benefits of settlement versus trial. The risks of going to trial generally include a damaging piece of information or witness not anticipated, a risk of monetary loss, particularly if punitive damages are awarded, and the risk of damaging the organization's reputation whether or not it ultimately prevails at trial.

The benefits of going to trial are to defend the organization against meritless claims and not to develop the reputation of settling all claims, no matter how frivolous. Beyond that, organizations incur substantial legal fees, fees for expert witness testimony relating to the Plaintiff's claim for damages and her emotional and physical damages, often termed "pain and suffering," and a substantial amount of lost productive time of managers and all employees in the Plaintiff's department.

§ 7.8   Follow-up

The organization should learn from each new charge or lawsuit. Management should make every effort to diagnose what went wrong, why it went wrong, and how it can be fixed so as to prevent its recurrence. It may also be advisable to follow-up a charge or lawsuit by re-issuing communications about the organization's sexual harassment policy and complaint procedure, offering sexual harassment training to a department or to the entire organization, and, if warranted, to discipline employees against whom the organization has substantiated wrongdoing. (See also **Chapter 4** for a discussion of policy administration and compliance monitoring.)

§ 7.9   Sample State Filing Procedures (Nebraska)

SEXUAL HARASSMENT
Filing a Complaint
with
Nebraska Equal Opportunity Commission

Persons who file formal allegations of sexual harassment should be aware of the following:

(1) The initial point of contact with the NEOC is the "Intake Interviewer." The Intake Interviewer will discuss the complaint with the complaining party and will make initial determination of the legal relevance of the charge, that is, whether or not the facts of the charge do allege discrimination.

(2) The NEOC allows 180 days from the date of the occurrence of the alleged sexual harassment for the filing of a charge of discrimination with their agency.

(3) The employee must be the aggrieved party in order to file a charge of sexual harassment with the NEOC. The NEOC cannot accept anonymous complaints of sexual harassment.

(4) If a charge of sexual harassment is accepted for investigation by the NEOC, then a formal charge will be developed, in writing, and the agency/company involved will be notified of the allegation by receiving that written charge.

The employee will also receive a copy of the written charge for her/his records.

(5) Following investigation of the charge of sexual harassment by the NEOC staff, the members of the Nebraska Equal Opportunity Commission will make a determination of "reasonable cause" or "no reasonable cause" upon review of the case.

(6) If the Nebraska Equal Opportunity Commission finds in favor of the respondent (i.e., the alleged perpetrator or perpetrators), then the complainant will receive a 90-day "right-to-sue notice."

(7) The NEOC proceedings may result in a pre-determination settlement in order to arrive at an appropriate and reasonable resolution agreed upon by all affected parties.

(8) If the complainant is retaliated against for filing the charge of sexual harassment against an agency or individual, then the employee may file an additional charge with the NEOC alleging such retaliatory activity.

Policies may suggest that employees who observe another person being subjected to sexual harassment report the incident. A number of policies require reporting by those who believe another employee has been a victim of sexual harassment; other policies state that those who have been told of such an incident are to report it.

Reporting procedures may be different for lawyers and administrative staff. Indeed, the lines of complaint may vary for associates and partners.

In a small firm, the managing partner may be the logical person to receive sexual harassment complaints, unless of course, he or she is the harasser. In that case, the complaint should probably be lodged with the next most senior lawyer. In a large firm, a number of choices are available. It is important that the policy provide the titles and names of those to whom the various categories of workers should report complaints. Alternatives should be provided so that complainants can choose between at least two, and possibly several people.

The policy may also employ language recognizing that the investigatory process will probably necessitate some exceptions to the confidentiality rule, as in the following examples:

> **All reports of sexual harassment shall be kept in confidence, except as is necessary to investigate the complaint and to respond to any legal and/ or administrative proceedings arising out of or relating to the sexual harassment report. (Dorsey & Whitney, Minneapolis)**

> **[T]o the extent practical and appropriate under the circumstances, confidentiality will be maintained. (Levin & Funkhoser, Ltd., Chicago)**

Firm size may affect the need for confidentiality protections. In a small firm, the alleged harasser, the complainant, the person who receives the complaint, and the person who maintains records or files may constitute the whole firm. As a practical matter, what makes sense in one firm might require a different approach in another.

The need for flexibilty to deal with unusual situtations on a case-by-case basis should not prelude a firm from describing in general the procedures it will follow in investigating a complaint. The policy may indicate that the investigation will include questioning all employees who may know of the alleged incident or similar problems, and that the investigative steps and findings will be thoroughly documented. Moreover, the policy should identify the investigators:

§ 7.10   Sample Charge Form (California)

HELP YOURSELF: A Manual for Dealing With Sexual Harassment

STATE OF CALIFORNIA—STATE AND CONSUMER SERVICES AGENCY   GEORGE DEUKMEJIAN, Governor

DEPARTMENT OF FAIR EMPLOYMENT AND HOUSING

PRE-COMPLAINT QUESTIONNAIRE - EMPLOYMENT

> The information requested on this form will help us to help you.
> There is no guarantee that the information submitted will
> constitute a basis for filing a formal complaint. If you need
> assistance in preparing this form, please ask the receptionist.
> When completed, give the form to the receptionist.

FOR OFFICIAL USE ONLY

Name of Interviewer _____   Date ___July 10, 1984___

Date of Interview _____

PLEASE PRINT

Name ___Susan_____B._____Anthony_____
        First   Middle   Last

Address ___926 J Street_____
                Street   Apt. Number

___Sacramento_____Sacramento_____95814___
        City   County   Zip Code

Telephone Number: Work (916) 006-3421 Ext. ____ Home (916) 001-4900
                       Area Code   Area Code

I prefer to be contacted by phone at work___ at home_X_ days _Monday_

Name ___E. Candi Stanton_____   Telephone (916) 001-3002
      (Person to contact if you cannot be reached)   Area Code

I wish to complain against: (Name of employer, city, county, agency, etc.)

Name of Employer ___Chris F. Rubini, John Doe's Pizzeria_____

Address ___3200 H Street_____
                            Street

___Sacramento_____Sacramento_____95814___
        City   County   Zip Code

Telephone Number: (916) 063-4251 _____ Number of Employees _20_
                  Area Code

Others: _____

Address _____
                            Street

_____
        City   County   Zip Code

1. I was discriminated against because of my: (check only those which apply)

___ Race   ___ Color   ___ National Origin/Ancestry
_X_ Sex   ___ Age (over 40)   ___ Physical Handicap
___ Medical Condition ___ Religion   ___ Marital Status

2. How do you feel you were discriminated against?

___ Termination   ___ Denied Employment   ___ Denied Promotion

_X_ Differential treatment (i.e., harassment, unequal pay, etc.)

Other _____
                    (Please Specify)

DFEH-600-03 (5/82)

HELP YOURSELF: A Manual for Dealing With Sexual Harassment

3. **What reasons were given by the employer for the action taken against you?**

   No reasons given, but I learned that my supervisor gave me a poor

   evaluation which may have cuased me not to be promoted.

4. **Date of alleged discrimination:**   July 4, 1984

5. **What remedy are you seeking through DFEH?**

   Counsel/advise my employer in order to end sexual harassment and

   reconsider my application for promotion.

6. **Employment data:**

   A. **Date Hired**   October 7, 1983   **Job Title**   Food Service Worker

   B. **Date of Termination**   July 13, 1984

   C. **Job title at time of discrimination**   same

   D. **Title and salary of position in question**   Manager $ /

   E. **Name of immediate supervisor**   Chris F. Rubini

   F. **Is there a union?**   No   **If so, name the union and local #**

   G. **Have you filed a union grievance?**   **If so, what happened?**

   H. **Have you attempted to resolve your problem by discussing the matter
       with a representative of management?**   **If so, name the parties
       contacted**

   I. **If terminated, have you since been employed? Yes ___ No X**

       Name of company   **Date of hire**

       Job title   **Salary $ /**

7. **What information do you have to indicate that you were treated differently
   because of discrimination?**

   My supervisor, Mr. Rubini, more than once took me to his back room

   and held me close, kissed, and offensively touched my body against my

   will. At other times he touched my breasts, legs, and body against my

   will while on the job. I finally left my employment with John Doe's

   Pizzeria because I felt that Mr. Rubini's conduct interfered with my work

   performance as I felt intimidated of losing my job if I failed to fully

   cooperate with Mr. Rubini's sexual harassment.

(Continued on next page)

-2-

HELP YOURSELF: A Manual for Dealing With Sexual Harassment

_____

_____

_____

_____

_____

_____

8. List the names, job titles and telephone numbers (if possible) of witnesses you feel could provide evidence in your support.

Name	Title	Telephone Numbers Home	Work
Elizabeth C. Stanton	Food Service Worker	916/001-3002	916/001-4003

_____

_____

_____

9. Did you file a complaint with EEOC before coming to this agency? Yes___ No X

10. Complaints other than marital status, medical condition and physical handicap filed with DFEH are often simultaneously filed with the Equal Employment Opportunity Commission of the federal government. (Employer must have 15 or more employees, and alleged act must have occurred within 300 days of filing.) In no way does this delay the complaint being processed by this agency. If your complaint is accepted by DFEH, do you wish a copy forwarded to EEOC? Yes _x_ No ___

11. Have you filed with any other group or agency? If so, name, address, and telephone numbers are requested.

OFCC, 450 Golden Gate Avenue, San Francisco, CA 94102

HR, FHC, 2131 Capitol Avenue, Suite 206, Sacramento, CA 95814   444-6903

Unemployment Insurance Program, Employment Development Department

12. Do you have an attorney? If so, please provide name, address and

telephone number.   Gertrude Stein

31 X Street #10, Sacramento, CA 94321

13. Personal Data: For research purposes, please provide us with the following information:

ETHNIC GROUP: Black____ Hispanic____ Asian____ Filipino____ Anglo _X_

Native American____ Other Minority_____
(Please Specify)

SEX: Female _x_ Male _____

AGE: _44_

14. I learned about the Department of Fair Employment and Housing from:

___ Newspaper ___ Radio ___ TV ___ Bus/BART Ad ___ Poster _x_ Friend

Prior Contact with DFEH ___ Other Government Agency _____
(Specify)

Community Organizations (Specify) _____

Other (Specify) _____

-3-

HELP YOURSELF: A Manual for Dealing With Sexual Harassment

Appendix N

*U.S. GOVERNMENT PRINTING OFFICE: 1981-725-822

(PLEASE PRINT OR TYPE)

| APPROVED BY OMB 3046-0013 Expires 12/31/83 | CHARGE OF DISCRIMINATION IMPORTANT: This form is affected by the Privacy Act of 1974; see Privacy Act Statement on reverse before completing it. | CHARGE NUMBER(S) (AGENCY USE ONLY) ☒ STATE/LOCAL AGENCY ☐ EEOC |

__CA State Department of Fair Employment and Housing__ and Equal Employment Opportunity Commission
(State or Local Agency)

| NAME (Indicate Mr., Ms. or Mrs.) Ms. Susan B. Anthony | HOME TELEPHONE NUMBER (Include area code) |

STREET ADDRESS
926 J Street

| CITY, STATE, AND ZIP CODE Sacramento, CA 95814 | COUNTY |

NAMED IS THE EMPLOYER, LABOR ORGANIZATION, EMPLOYMENT AGENCY, APPRENTICESHIP COMMITTEE, STATE OR LOCAL GOVERNMENT AGENCY WHO DISCRIMINATED AGAINST ME. (If more than one list below).

| NAME John Doe's Pizzeria | TELEPHONE NUMBER (Include area code) 916-063-4251 |

| STREET ADDRESS 3200 H Street | CITY, STATE, AND ZIP CODE Sacramento, CA 95814 |

| NAME | TELEPHONE NUMBER (Include area code) |

| STREET ADDRESS | CITY, STATE, AND ZIP CODE |

CAUSE OF DISCRIMINATION BASED ON MY (Check appropriate box(es).)

☐ RACE   ☐ COLOR   ☒ SEX   ☐ RELIGION   ☐ NATIONAL ORIGIN   ☐ OTHER (Specify)

DATE MOST RECENT OR CONTINUING DISCRIMINATION TOOK PLACE (Month, day, and year)   July 4, 1984

THE PARTICULARS ARE

I.   I started to work for Respondent as a waitress on October 7, 1983. On July 13, 1984, I was forced to quit my job because of Mr. Rubini, my supervisor's, offensive sexual advancements towards me.

II. I feel I was forced to quit my job which I liked except for the conditions I had to work under.

III. For the following reasons I believe that I have been forced to quit my job because of sexual harassment I was subjected to during my employment because of my sex, I am female.

   A. Mr. Rubini, my supervisor, more than once took me to his back room (private) and held me close, kissed, and offensively touched my body against my will.

   B. On many other occasions Mr. Rubini touched my breasts, legs, and body against my will while on the job.

   C. I finally left my employment with John Doe's Pizzeria because I felt that Mr. Rubini's conduct interfered with my work performance as I feared losing my job if I failed to fully cooperate with Mr. Rubini's offensive advances and continuous sexual harassment.

☒ I also want this charge filed with the EEOC.

I will advise the agencies if I change my address or telephone number and I will cooperate fully with them in the processing of my charge in accordance with their procedures.

I declare under penalty of perjury that the foregoing is true and correct.

I swear or affirm that I have read the above charge and that it is true to the best of my knowledge, information and belief

SIGNATURE OF COMPLAINANT

SUBSCRIBED AND SWORN TO BEFORE ME THIS DATE (Day, month, and year)

July 15, 1984

NOTARY -- (When necessary to meet State and Local Requirements)

§ 7.11   Sample Agency Procedure

Figure 7–1 illustrates the procedures for instituting an EEO complaint in California.

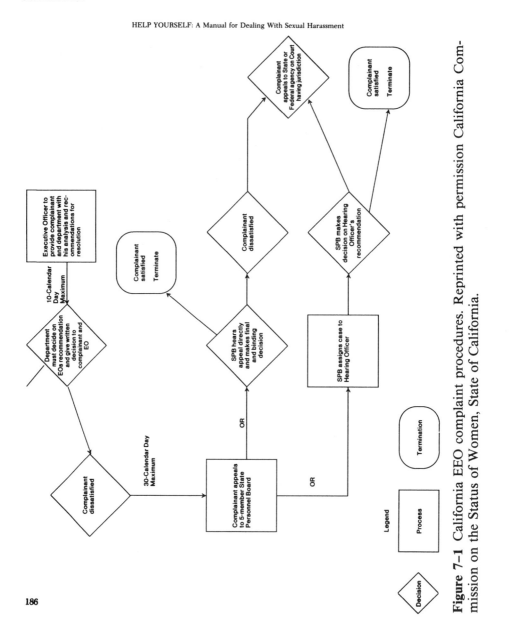

HELP YOURSELF: A Manual for Dealing With Sexual Harassment

Figure 7–1 California EEO complaint procedures. Reprinted with permission California Commission on the Status of Women, State of California.

186

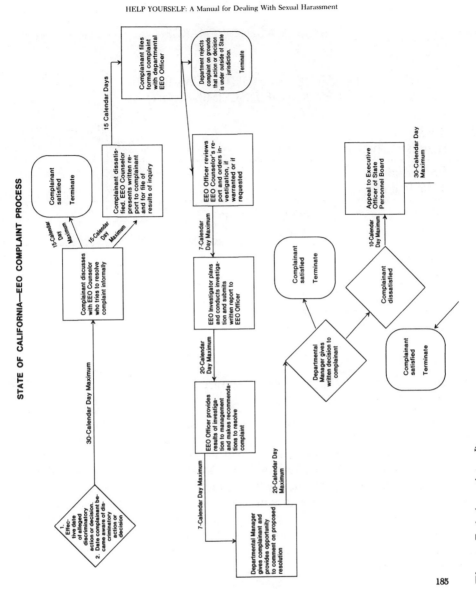

Figure 7–1 *(continued)*.

§ 7.12 Sample Agency Charge

SAMPLE AGENCY CHARGE

STATE OF ALPHA
ALPHA HUMAN RIGHTS COMMISSION
CHARGE OF DISCRIMINATION

(1) Name	Phone Number
Sharon R. Thomas	555-1965

Street Address
8618 Trail Road

City	State	Zip Code
Spring Town	Alpha	71717

(2) _____ Race _____ Color _____ Religion _ X _ Sex
_____ National Origin

(3) Person Alleged to Have Discriminated Against Me:
Name: American Toolworkers of Spring Town
Address: 1008 Words Circle
City: Spring Town   State: Alpha
Zip Code: 71717

(4) Most Recent Date Discrimination Occurred:
August 8, 1993

Explain How You Were Discriminated Against:

I, a White female, have been employed for three (3) years as a Personnel Assistant for American Toolworkers of Spring Town. During this entire period of time, I shared all personnel duties with Mr. Richard Simon, Personnel Manager. These duties included the recruitment, processing, and interviewing of all candidates for either salaried or hourly employment. The only duties performed by Mr. Simon which I did not also perform were related to the company's attendance plan, progressive disciplinary system and the benefits program, which were all handled by Mr. Simon.

On June 7, 1993, Mr. Simon retired. Although I had expressed an interest in being considered for this position on several occasions, the company placed ads in various trade and professional journals for the position. Although I was interviewed on July 22, 1993 and advised by the Vice President that I was the "most likely" candidate (if I would be more intimate and cooperative in our personal relationship), the company hired Roger Brown, a White male, for this position.

Mr. Brown's experience is as a Personnel Manager for a much smaller company in an unrelated industry. I have been advised by Chet Yates, Vice-President of Operations, that I am expected to teach Mr. Brown "the ropes."

I believe that I have been denied this promotion because of my sex for the following reasons:

1. I had already been doing the majority of duties required of the position.

2. The person selected was not knowledgeable about the position and I was requested to train the person who would be my supervisor.

3. The company was always reluctant to allow me to handle any of the personnel responsibilities which would require dealing with the union. I believe that the statement in the job ad that the person selected, "must have experience in employee benefits programs" was designed to restrict by promotability.

4. Although I did not complain to the President, I told the Vice President on July 22, 1993 that our relationship should be professional and not personal, even though he was a very attractive man.

SWORN OR AFFIRMED AND FILED THIS _____ DAY OF

_____, 19_____ .

_____

SIGNATURE

CHAPTER 8

CURRENT DISCOVERY ISSUES IN SEXUAL HARASSMENT CLAIMS*

§ 8.1   Introduction
§ 8.2   Scope of Discovery
§ 8.3   Expert Discovery
§ 8.4   Sexual History
§ 8.5   Sample Written Discovery Requests in a Sexual Harassment Case

§ 8.1   Introduction

The following information is mainly of interest to attorneys representing plaintiffs or defendants in sexual harassment litigation. However, Human Resources professionals and even line managers can benefit from the information to the extent that they may someday find themselves involved in such litigation. The samples below are intended to illustrate the kind of information that is typically requested by plaintiffs. This information is followed by a sample set of defendants' discovery requests.

In *Meritor Savings Bank, FSB v. Vinson,*[1] the Supreme Court clarified that the scope of discovery in sexual harassment claims includes not only data underlying Title VII statistical and economic analyses but also emotional and psychological impacts on the workforce. *Meritor* recognizes the hostile environment theory of sexual harassment as a basis for finding a violation of Title VII and, in the course of doing so, found evidence of "unwelcomeness" of workplace conduct admissible. The determination of what is unwelcome, of course, requires discovery into the effect of the

---

* The author wishes to thank Paul Springer of the Washington D.C. and Minneapolis law firm of Springer & Lang for much of the information contained in this chapter.
[1] 477 U.S. 57 (1986).

harassers' conduct upon the plaintiffs, as well as into plaintiffs' workplace conduct.

Subsequently, *Hopkins v. Price Waterhouse*[2] expanded the scope of discovery even further into the area of sexual stereotyping in the workplace when it found such behavior violative of Title VII. Thus, the Court opened sexual harassment cases even further to psychological and/or psychiatric expert testimony and discovery.

The circuits have also made clear that any workplace fact that could assist the jury in ascertaining the employer's knowledge of and culpability for the harasser's conduct is admissible.[3] If facts are admissible in evidence, they are relevant and thus discoverable.

In spite of the relevance of rulings from the circuits, discovery disputes in the trial courts continue unabated by counsel intent on limiting access to admissible facts. Based on the case law, it is difficult to imagine any proper subject matter limitations on discovery in any events going on in the workplace in a properly plead sexual harassment claim of hostile environment. There are, of course, legitimate bases for geographic and temporal limitations on discovery, largely dependent on the scope of the claims asserted in the complaint. If, for example, the allegation is that only one instance of recent quid pro quo harassment occurred involving two new employees (whose only contact was in the workplace) and excludes any hostile environment claim, it may be reasonable to limit much of the discovery to the period of employment and to the particular facility. Likewise, inquiry into pre-employment sexual history of one or both employees may be properly limited depending on the defenses asserted.

The District Courts struggle with the discovery disputes of counsel with widely diverse results. There is authority for just about any grant or limit on discovery that one can propose. This morass exists primarily because counsel seeking discovery do not clearly articulate to the District Judge or Magistrate Judge the relevance of the discovery sought in their motions to compel.

---

[2] *See* Brown v. Trustees of Boston University, 490 U.S. 228 (1989).

[3] 891 F. 2d 337 (lst Cir. 1989); Malarkey v. Texaco, Inc., 983 F.2d 1204 (2d Cir. 1993); Andrews v. City of Philadelphia, 895 F.2d 1469 (3rd Cir. 1990); E.E.O.C. v. Am. Nat. Bank, 652 F.2d 1176 (4th Cir. 1981); Williams v. General Motors Corp., 656 F.2d 120 (5th Cir. Unit B. 1981), *cert. denied,* 455 U.S. 943, 102 S.Ct. 1621 (1982); Douglass v. Eaton Corp., 956 F.2d 1339 (6th Cir. 1992); Taylor v. Western and Southern Life Ins. Co., 966 F.2d 1188 (7th Cir. 1992); Rush v. McDonald's Corp., 966 F.2d 1104 (7th Cir. 1992); Estes v. Dick Smith Ford, 856 F.2d 1097 (8th Cir. 1988); Burns v. McGregor Electronic Industries, Inc., 955 F.2d 559 (8th Cir. 1992); Penk v. Oregon State Bd. of Higher Educ., 816 F.2d 458 (9th Cir. 1987); Ellison v. Brady, 924 F.2d 872 (9th Cir. 1991); Hicks v. Gates Rubber Co., 833 F.2d 1406 (10th Cir. 1987); Sweat v. Miller Brewing Co., 708 F.2d 655 (llth Cir. 1983); Vinson v. Taylor, 753 F.2d 141 (D.C. Cir. 1985).

While Local Rules on discovery exist, or are proposed, in many jurisdictions, most have no requirement that motions to compel set out the text of the specific request, the response, a concise recitation of why the objection is improper, the relevant authority, and what evidentiary use the response could have at trial. The result is argument and rulings which are not focused but rather read like philosophy texts because they are made in a vacuum.

With or without Local Rules designed to present discovery disputes in a uniform and focused fashion, moving counsel should use the above format. Most importantly, counsel should link up the sought after discovery (for each specific request) to the element of the case for which it will be used as proof at trial. For example, when moving to compel production of other instances of harassment in the form of "internal and external complaints, etc., alleging sexual harassment" it is a simple matter to cite *Vinson v. Taylor* for the proposition that

> [E]vidence tending to show [defendant's] harassment of other women working alongside [plaintiff] is directly relevant to the question whether he created an environment violative of Title VII. Even a woman who was never herself the object of harassment might have a Title VII claim if she were forced to work in an atmosphere in which such harassment was pervasive.

In note 40, the circuit court stated that such evidence is critical because more than an "isolated incident" is needed to prove sexual harassment. This linkage of the sought after discovery to plaintiff's burden of proof at trial is simple to do and logically compelling to the District Court in a discovery dispute over other instances of harassment in the workplace.

Discovery disputes in harassment cases currently center in three areas: (1) the general issue of scope, i.e., whether inquiry can be made beyond the individual plaintiff's employment circumstances; (2) the issue of expert medical, sociological or psychological discovery; and (3) the issue of sexual history of the respective parties outside the workplace. The resolution of these three issues depends primarily upon the nature of the allegations.

§ 8.2 Scope of Discovery

In assessing the issue of scope of discovery beyond the individual plaintiff's facts, both parties should be concerned with two critical areas: workforce statistics and other instances of harassment in the workplace. Statistical discovery of the employer's workforce demographic data, in hostile environment cases, alleging a class or not, is generally allowed as in any other Title VII action on the theory that "any evidence that women are generally treated [by that employer] less favorably in terms of compensation, hiring, and promotions would be supportive of [plaintiff's] claims of a hostile work environment."[4] The same applies to non-hostile environment claims as long as economic losses are alleged. The Plaintiffs' Rule 30(b)(6) Deposition Notice and Document Request in § 8.5 is provided as a sample of what may be used by plaintiffs as part of initial discovery to ascertain the existence and nature of relevant employment data, in both individual and class action cases of sexual harassment. While inadequate responses have been made, courts generally have failed to order a full and complete response, subject to a few limitations on scope. Obviously, the development of statistical proof requires the same techniques as in purely economic Title VII cases.

Discovery of other instances of harassment beyond that which the named plaintiff experienced is generally allowed.[5]

In the course of sexual harassment claims, all management employees who may have direct knowledge of the treatment of the victims involved are identified. They are then either deposed or informally interviewed consistent with the applicable ethical guidelines. The trial testimony resulting from this discovery can be critical, as can be best illustrated in the following excerpt of threatened and actual impeachment based on the prior discovery deposition of a foreman:

Reprinted court transcript from trial in an actual court case

Defense Witness Cross-Examination, Afternoon Session:

Witness, having been first duly sworn, was examined and testified as follows:

By Plaintiff's Counsel:

Q Mr. E., you are currently employed by Manufacturer, Inc.?
A Yes.
Q You have been a foreman at Manufacturer, Inc. from 1977 to the present, correct?
A Yes.
Q And you started as a laborer in 1965?
A Yes.

---

[4] *See* Keller v. Armstrong Industries, Inc., 1988 WL 107374 (S.D. N.Y., July 12, 1988); Best v. State Farm Mutual Automobile Insurance Co., 1990 WL 11043 (D. Kan., Jan. 4, 1990).

[5] *See* Stockett v. Tolin, 791 F.Supp. 1536 (S.D. Fla. 1992) (conduct need not be sexual but includes abusive or demeaning conduct); Sims v. Montgomery County Com'n, 766 F. Supp. 1052 (M.D. Ala. 1990); Cook v. Yellow Freight System, Inc., 112 F.R.D. 548 (E.D. Cal 1990); Broderick v. Ruder, 685 F. Supp. 1269 (D.D.C. 1988).

Q Now, as a foreman at Manufacturer, Inc., you supervised the named plaintiffs in this case from time to time, right?

A Yes.

Q Now based on your observations, they were excellent workers, correct?

A Yes.

Q It's also your opinion, is it not, Sir, that women don't belong working in the mines?

A Yes.

Q It's also your opinion, Sir, that women should not be hired into labor jobs in the pit or in the plant, correct?

A No.

Q Sir, do you recall having your deposition taken on December 6,1989 in this litigation, and being asked this question and giving this answer? That's page 104, line 1.

QUESTION: Do you think because of your beliefs, do you think that when women apply for jobs, they shouldn't be hired?

"ANSWER: Clerical or whatever, yes. Out in the plant or the pit or whatever, I would say no."

Do you recall that sir?

A Yes.

Q It was true then, it's true today, isn't it?

A Could you repeat that, sir?

Q That was your opinion then, that's your opinion today.

A No.

Q You have changed your mind?

A I have changed my mind.

Q When did you change your mind, sir?

A There are certain areas where they should be able to work. I wouldn't let my wife work in the mine.

Q You don't think they should work in the pit.

A No.

Q But you do think they should work in clerical jobs.

A Clerical, lab and labor.

Q But they shouldn't progress beyond entry-level labor?

A Yes. Not to operating jobs.

Q So they shouldn't work in the plant or pit in operating jobs.

A No, I don't think so.

Q Now, you've been around the mines a long time. Based on your observations do you think those are the beliefs also held by management at Manufacturer, Inc.?

Defense Counsel: Objection, foundation, calling for speculation.

The Court: Counsel, are you talking views now or in 1989?

Plaintiff's Counsel: I would ask him his views now. If he couldn't answer that, we'd go back in time.

The Court: I'll overrule the objection to the extent that he has an opinion as to the views of management.

The Witness: There are certain jobs that they can work at, but there are certain jobs that I don't think they should work at.

By Plaintiff's Counsel:

Q   I understand your testimony, sir, on that point. What the Court is permitting you to answer, I think, is whether those same views are held by others in management at Manufacturer, Inc., as you understand it.
A   Others in management?
Q   Yes, sir.
A   Other foremen, it's been discussed.
Q   And they agree with you?
A   They agreed on the same point, more or less what I have said.
Q   Is there anyone in management that doesn't agree with you that you can think of as you sit here today?
A   No.

§ 8.3   Expert Discovery

The second area of discovery disputes in sexual harassment cases concerns expected expert medical, sociological or physiological trial testimony. The Federal Rules of Civil Procedure allow only limited direct discovery of the expected testimony of an expert. Federal Rule of Civil Procedure 26(b)(4) specifically limits "expert interrogatory" responses to those opinions which the party (usually via his attorney) "expects" will be offered, together with the anticipated factual bases. Moreover, a subpoena directed to a designated expert violates Rule 11.[6]

In most Districts, the trial court enforces these limitations absent contrary agreement of the parties, inasmuch as the history and intent of this Rule expressly negate the "open season" concept of the discovery rules generally. Finally, most jurisdictions have medical privilege statutes which can limit disclosure without agreement of counsel.

Even in the absence of agreement, a court may allow discovery of the records of health care providers who treated a party, as opposed to discovery of the opinions of health care providers retained for forensic purposes. It may also order a Rule 35(a) medical examination to the extent

---

[6] *See* Evanka v. Electronic Systems Associations, Inc., 1993 WL 4458 (S.D. N.Y. January 8, 1993).

the Title VII sexual harassment claims are accompanied by personal injury tort claims. No treating health care provider discovery should be permitted where the plaintiff's specific ailments are not put at issue in the Complaint.[7] Moreover, such discovery may be relevant to damages issues but not in the liability phase of a bifurcated trial.[8]

Generally, in Title VII hostile work environment claims, Rule 35 medical examinations of the plaintiff and health care provider discovery should not be allowed since the issue is whether a "reasonable person" would find the environment hostile. Thus, whether the plaintiff was atypical is not material.[9] Such discovery, whether via Rule 35 examination or otherwise, would be relevant at the damages stage of a Title VII bifurcated trial where the specific effect of the environment upon each plaintiff or plaintiff class member may be at issue, depending on the nature of the claims asserted at that stage of the trial. Discovery into the health care history of an alleged harasser may also be discoverable.

A Rule 35 examination may be ordered where the employer asserts a physical or mental problem as a defense. For example, sexual preference, sexual history, lack of control or impotence may be used to defend against the plaintiff's allegations, in which event a medical examination should be allowed.[10] Moreover, such discovery may be allowed where a physical or mental process of a harasser is otherwise put at issue in the case.

One strategy that counsel can take is to suggest a mutual expert: depositions and an exchange of Rule of Evidence 705 "underlying data" in advance of the deposition subject to conditions designed to avoid unnecessary expense and abuse. However, the parties may still want to serve as initial discovery a form of the attached sample First Combined Set of Interrogatories and Requests for Admission and Documents designed to ascertain the identity and expected information as to any expert testimony in the case.

§ 8.4 Sexual History

Finally, both parties in sexual harassment cases should be concerned with discovery of the sexual history of either. Generally, if it happened in the employer's workplace, it is discoverable. However, if it happened outside

---

[7] *See* Broderick v. Shad, 117 F.R.D. 306 (D. D.C. 1987); Jennings v. D.H.L. Airlines, 101 F.R.D. 549 (N.D. Ill. 1984).

[8] *See* Mitchell v. Hutchings, 116 F.R.D. 481 (D. Utah 1987).

[9] *See* Robinson v. Jacksonville Shipyards, Inc., 760 F.Supp. 1486 (M.D. Fla. 1991).

[10] *See* Jones v. Commander, Kansas Army Ammunition Plant, Department of the Army, 1993 WL 70236 (D. Kan. March 1, 1993); Taylor v. National Group of Companies, Inc., 145 F.R.D. 79 (N.D. Ohio 1992).

and is unrelated to the workplace, it should not be discoverable.[11] Conversely, attempts to seal court filed pleadings to suppress the identities of alleged harassers will not be allowed.[12] Generally, any party seeking to compel sexual history discovery should be prepared to overcome a motion for a protective order by demonstrating relevance sufficient to overcome a Rule 403 objection at trial.

§ 8.5 Sample Written Discovery Requests in a Sexual Harassment Case

SAMPLE DISCOVERY REQUESTS

UNITED STATES DISTRICT COURT
DISTRICT OF

Plaintiffs,

　　　　　　　　　　　　　　　PLAINTIFFS' RULE 30(B)(6)
　　　　　　　　　　　　　　　DEPOSITION NOTICE AND
　　　　　　　　　　　　　　　DOCUMENT REQUEST

Defendants.

Please take notice that pursuant to Rule 30 (b)(6) of the Federal Rules of Civil Procedure, plaintiffs, by and through their attorneys, will take the deposition of a witness or witnesses designated by the defendant to testify about the matters described below commencing on DATE at TIME at the law offices of X,Y&Z, ADDRESS, and continuing day to day until completed.

Defendant is requested to produce, at the time and place that the deposition is commenced, all documents identified and described below in No. 1A through 1F as Basic Documents.

The witness(es) designated will be required to testify fully concerning the matters described herein, including a precise identification and reading of all computer and noncomputer readable data files produced in response to this document request, including any coded information. More specifically, the witness or witnesses designated by defendant will be requested to testify about:

---

[11] *See* Kennedy v. Fritsch, 58 E.P.D. 41,493 (Ill. 1991) (discovery of events calculated to humiliate not allowed); Mitchell v. Hutchings, 116 F.R.D. 461 (D. Utah 1987) (discovery of events remote in time and place not allowed when issue is environment as seen by reasonable person); Priest v. Rotary, 98 F.R.D. 755 (N.D. Cal. 1983) (intimidation not allowed as habit, character or motive of victim).

[12] *See* Isaacson v. Keck, Mahin & Cate, 1992 WL 297391 (N.D. Ill. Oct. 8, 1992).

1. The contents of each report and/or summary whether generated manually or by a computer readable system and/or program which contains employment or personnel data or information as identified below:

BASIC DOCUMENTS

A. All tape, disc, or other management systems and/or programs and/or indices of computer readable data systems and/or programs and/or indices of non-computer readable data concerning employment of defendant;
B. Payroll information including, if applicable, all payroll computer readable data systems and/or programs;
C. All employee rosters including, if applicable, employee roster computer readable data-systems and/or programs;
D. All employee information including, if applicable, all exempt and nonexempt salaried and hourly employee computer readable data systems and/or programs;
E. All personnel and/or employee record systems, whether kept manually or in computer readable data systems and/or programs, including all EEO information, qualification inventories, retirement eligibility and/or retirement related materials, discipline records, applicant flow data, applications for employment, including those for hire, transfer or promotion, and all other record systems relating to past, present, or future employees.

2. As to any and all reports, generated either manually or by a system or program in each of the categories referred to in No. 1, the following:

A. When each report was first generated;
B. The frequency of each report;
C. Who currently receives and previously received copies of each report;
D. Where current and noncurrent copies of each report are kept;
E. How long noncurrent copies of each report are kept, where and by whom;
F. What the input data form and format is of each report;
G. Where the input data to each report is kept, for how long and by whom and in what format: e.g., hard copies on file, computer cards, computer tapes, discs, coding forms;
    i.   Whether the input form and procedures for gathering and maintaining said data have changed over time, and if so, how;
    ii. Whether the output procedures for the generation, maintenance, distribution and retention of said data have changed over time and, if so, how;
H. The procedures used to generate such reports, including, if applicable, the form of the programs and/or systems which are used to generate each report, e.g., cards, tape discs, coding forms, and where they are located and stored;
I. For each report which is generated or interpreted by at computer readable data system and/or programs:
    i.   The computer language in which each program and/or system for each report is written: e.g., FORTRAN, COBAL, etc.;

    ii. The file descriptions for each program and/or system which generates each report; and

    iii. The flow charts for each program and/or system which generates each report.

3. All program register(s) or other index identifying in summary form or otherwise one or more of the following aspects of any program(s) and/or system(s) from which the sex of any employees can be ascertained:

A. Identification of program and/or system, including any number or other designation;
B. Data program and/or system description;
C. Name or other reference to programmer that wrote program and/or system;
D. Program and/or system description;
E. Tapes or other file(s) used and/or maintained in program and/or system; and
F. Disc or other file(s) used and/or maintained in program and/or system.

_____, YEAR _____
                         Attorney at Law

SAMPLE COMBINED SET OF INTERROGATORIES, REQUESTS FOR ADMISSIONS AND DOCUMENTS

UNITED STATES DISTRICT COURT
DISTRICT OF
_____

Civil No.

Plaintiffs,

                              FIRST COMBINED SET OF
                              INTERROGATORIES,
                              REQUESTS FOR
                              ADMISSIONS AND
                              DOCUMENTS

    v.

Defendants.

_____

Pursuant to Rules 26, 33, 34, and 36 of the Federal Rules of Civil Procedure, the following interrogatories, requests for production of documents, and requests for admission are propounded by plaintiffs to be answered by defendants fully and separately in writing, under oath, and in accordance with the above cited rules. Defendants are required to serve a copy of their answers to these interrogatories and requests for admission, as well as copies of the documents requested, on plaintiffs' attorney within forty-five (45) days after service of these interrogatories and discovery requests.

Pursuant to Rule 26(e), plaintiffs specifically request supplementation of all discovery requests up through trial.

INSTRUCTIONS

A. In answering these interrogatories, requests for production of documents, and requests for admission (hereinafter referred to collectively as "discovery requests"), the following instructions and definitions apply:

(1) "Defendant" and "you" designates each defendant in this action and any of its or his subsidiaries, agents, representatives, attorneys, etc. "Plaintiffs" designates the named plaintiffs in this action.

(2) "Document" shall be construed in its broadest sense, including any original, reproduction or copy of any kind of written or documentary material, or drafts thereof, including, but not limited to, computer readable data, correspondence, memoranda, inter- or intra-office communications, notes, diaries, calendars, contract documents, publications, calculations, estimates, vouchers, minutes of meetings, invoices, reports, studies, computer tapes, computer disks, computer cards, photographs, negatives, slides, dictation belts, voice tapes, telegrams, notes of telephone conversations and notes of any oral communications.

(3) Any other words used herein shall be defined according to standard American usage, as shown in a dictionary of the English language.

B. You are required to furnish all information which is available to you, including information in the possession of your agents or representatives, or any other person or organization acting on your behalf, and not merely such information known personally to you.

C. If you cannot answer any of the following discovery requests in full, after exercising due diligence to secure the information to do so, so state and answer to the extent possible and state whatever information or knowledge you have concerning the unanswered portions.

D. Each discovery request is intended to and does request that each and every part be answered with the same force and effect as if such part were the subject of and were asked by a separate discovery request.

E. Each discovery request not only calls for information known to defendant, but also for all information available to defendant through reasonable inquiry, including inquiry of defendant's attorneys, representatives, and agents.

F. In each case wherein defendant is asked to identify a person, or where the answer to a discovery request refers to a person, state with respect to each such person:

(1) His or her full name;
(2) His or her last known resident address;
(3) His or her telephone number;
(4) His or her occupation, employer and business address at the date of the event or transaction referred to; and
(5) His or her present occupation, employer and business address.

G. In each case wherein defendant is asked to identify a writing or document, or when the answer to a discovery request refers to a writing or document, state with respect to each such writing or document:

(1) The identity of the person who signed it or over whose name it was issued;
(2) The addressee or addressees;
(3) The nature and substance of the document or writing with sufficient particularity to enable the same to be identified;
(4) The date of the document or writing; and
(5) The identity of each person who has custody of the document or writing or any copies thereof.

H. In each case wherein defendant is asked to identify an oral statement or conversation, or the answer to a discovery request refers to an oral statement or conversation, state with respect to each such oral statement:

(1) The date and place such oral statement or conversation was made or took place;
(2) The identity of each person who made, participated in or heard any part of such oral statement or conversation;
(3) The substance of what was said by each person who made or participated in such oral statement or conversation; and
(4) The identity and present custodian of any writing or any mechanical or electrical recording that recorded, summarized or confirmed such oral conversation, or which refers, relates to or bears upon it.

I. These discovery requests are intended to be continuing in nature so as to require the addition of supplemental information as set forth in Rule 26(e) of the Federal Rules of Civil Procedure.

J. If you contend that you are entitled to refuse to answer any interrogatory or any request for admission, or to withhold from production any or all documents requested herein, on the basis of the attorney-client privilege, the work-product doctrine, or some other ground, state the basis on which you contend you are entitled to refuse to answer or to withhold the document from production and, with respect to each document withheld from production, please describe the nature of the document (e.g., letter, memorandum, computer printout, etc.), state the date of the document, identify the persons who sent and received the original and copies of the document, and state the subject matter of the document.

Admission No. 1

Defendants possess no statistical evidence or non-statistical documentary evidence that would tend to establish that defendants have not discriminated on the basis of sex against any current or former employee (including any plaintiff) with respect to any term or condition of employment.

Interrogatory No. 1

If your answer to Admission No. 1 is anything other than an unqualified admission, identify the statistical or non-statistical documentary evidence that defendants possess that would tend to establish that defendants have not discriminated on the basis of sex against any current or former employee (including any plaintiff) with respect to any term or condition of employment.

Request No. 1

If your answer to Admission No. 1 is anything other than an unqualified admission, produce all statistical evidence and non-statistical documentary evidence that would tend to establish that defendants have not discriminated on the basis of sex against any current or former employee (including any plaintiff) with respect to any term or condition of employment.

Interrogatory No. 2

Identify each person who possesses knowledge and/or information that would tend to establish that defendants have not discriminated on the basis of sex against any current or former employee (including any plaintiff) with respect to any term or condition of employment; identify each such act about which the person possesses knowledge and/or information; and summarize the nature of the person's knowledge or information about defendants' nondiscriminatory conduct.

Interrogatory No. 3

Identify each person, other than a person expected to testify as an expected witness, that defendants intend to call on their behalf at trial, and for each such person state the subject matter about which he/she is expected to testify.

Request No. 2

Produce all documents which defendants may offer at the trial of this case.

<u>Interrogatory No. 4</u>

Identify each person whom defendants expect to call as an expert witness at trial and for each such person state:

(a) The subject matter about which he/she is expected to testify;
(b) The substance of the facts and opinions about which he/she is expected to testify;
(c) A summary of the grounds on which he/she bases those opinions;
(d) The expert witness qualifications;
(e) Whether the person is to be compensated for his or her work and/or testimony in connection with this action, and if so, the rate(s) and terms of such compensation including, but without limitation, whether he or she will receive additional compensation if defendants prevail in this action, the rate(s) and terms of such additional compensation, whether he or she has been paid for his or her efforts to date, and if so, the rate(s) and terms of such compensation, and if not, state the terms of agreement regarding when he or she will be paid.
(f) Whether he or she has a written agreement with defendants with respect to his or her testimony in this matter.

<u>Request No. 3</u>

Produce each written agreement between each expert witness and the defendants or any counsel representative of defendants.

<u>Request No. 4</u>

Produce all documents, including expert reports, which were prepared by each person whom defendants expect to call as an expert witness at trial or in support of any motion or concerning any motion and which contain any opinion, conclusion or inference with respect to any fact or matter about which the expert witness has been retained to testify in this case and/or the facts or data upon which the expert witness bases such conclusion, opinion or inference.

<u>Request No. 5</u>

Produce all documents and correspondence of whatever type authored, sent or received by each expert witness regarding the subject matter of this lawsuit and all notes made by each expert witness of each oral conversation between, the expert witness and defendants' attorney.

<u>Interrogatory No. 5</u>

Identify each of defendants' employees or former employees, which defendants have contacted regarding this case, and for each such employee or former employee state the date and substance of each communication, either oral or written.

Admission No. 2

Defendants do not claim that any person presently or formerly employed by defendants, including plaintiff, has made any statement within the meaning of Federal Rules of Evidence 801 (d) (1) or (2) that defendants claim could be used as evidence in support of defendants' defenses in this action.

Interrogatory No. 6

If your answer to Admission No. 2 is anything other than an unqualified admission, for each prior statement within the meaning of Federal Rules of Evidence 801(d) (1) or (2) that defendants claim could be used as evidence in support of defendants' allegations in this action, please state:

(a) The identity of the person who made it;
(b) The statement that was made;
(c) The date it was made;
(d) The identity of any persons who heard the statement, or saw it if it was reduced to writing; and
(e) The circumstances under which it was made.

Interrogatory No. 7

State whether defendants ever recorded (by tape recorder or otherwise) any conversations (telephonic or otherwise) which included any current or former employee, including any plaintiff. State the approximate date of each conversation, the content of the conversation, whether the conversation was by telephone or otherwise, the reason the conversation was recorded, the address of each party to the conversation, and whether any other individual was present during the conversation.

Request No. 6

Produce all recordings and statements identified in response to Interrogatory Nos. 6 and 7.

Request No. 7

Produce all documents, including affidavits, which memorialize statements made by any person concerning any plaintiff's employment with defendants or relating in any way to this lawsuit.

Interrogatory No. 8

State whether defendants have consulted any physician or therapist concerning any plaintiff as to any matter. If so, state:

(a) The name, address and specialty of each physician or therapist;
(b) The date(s) of consultation;
(c) Describe in detail these discussions or communications; and
(d) Identify any documents relating to these discussions or communications.

Request No. 8

Produce all documents identified in your answer to Interrogatory No. 8.

Interrogatory No. 9

Identify each person who you know or believe has knowledge or information concerning any facts relating to this case, and describe the substance of that person's knowledge or information.

Request No. 9

Produce all documents containing communications between plaintiffs or the defendants and the State Department of Human Rights and/or the Equal Employment Opportunity Commission, regarding charges or complaints of employment discrimination filed by any plaintiff with any federal, state or local agency, including copies of all charges of discrimination.

Request No. 10

Produce all documents relating to any conversations, discussions or meetings of, any plaintiff with any member of defendants' management from January 1, 1975 to date regarding, in whole or part, plaintiff's performance while employed by defendants.

Request No. 11

Produce any documents defendants or its counsel or other representatives obtained from any plaintiff which relate to the allegations in plaintiffs' Complaint or defenses in defendants' Answer.

Interrogatory No. 10

State in detail the basis for the defendants' defense and/or contention that plaintiff has not been damaged by defendants to the extent alleged in plaintiff's Complaint and specify (1) the total amount in dollars which defendants contend each plaintiff may have sustained, if any, and (2) the fringe benefits, if any, defendants contend that each plaintiff may have lost.

Interrogatory No. 11

Describe the manner in which the damage figures contained in the response to Interrogatory No. 10 were calculated, including a breakdown of the dollar amount attributable to each element of the damages.

Request No. 12

Produce all documents relied upon or pertinent to the calculation of any damages, including but not limited to, all documents relied upon in arriving at the answers to Interrogatory Nos. 10 and 11, even though the defendants contend that plaintiffs suffered no damage or, in fact, benefitted from the employment action at issue.

Request No. 13

Produce all personnel files, and other documents concerning, each plaintiff's immediate supervisors at the time he/she was initially hired and all other of his/her supervisors, including all documents relating to the ability, fitness, and qualifications of those persons such as personality tests, employee performance appraisals, and exit interviews.

Interrogatory No. 12

As to each plaintiff, provide the following:

A. Identify all documents which in any way concern any plaintiff's performance or lack of performance and/or the specific reason(s) for termination or any grouping of such specific reasons for termination.

B. Explain in full the circumstances, including the ramifications of the circumstances, concerning each of the specific reasons for any plaintiff's termination that have been set out in writing.

C. Identify each person with any knowledge about each of the written statements identified above. Provide a brief summary of each person's knowledge.

D. If you now contend there are reasons for any plaintiff's termination which have not been reduced to writing, please provide those reasons and identify all persons with knowledge concerning those reasons.

<u>Request No. 14</u>

Produce all documents identified in response to Interrogatory No. 12.

_____, 1993   _____
                                    Attorney for Plaintiff

REQUEST FOR PRODUCTION OF DOCUMENTS

Plaintiff,

                                    Civil No. _____
        vs.   Defendant's First Request for
                                    Production of Documents

Defendant.

_____

1. All documents reflecting any complaints made by or on behalf of the plaintiff, and any other former employee of defendant, to any defendants regarding conduct allegedly constituting sexual harassment.

2. All diaries, logs, communications, documents or other personal notes created by plaintiff during the time period of _____ through _____, reflecting the conduct allegedly constituting sexual harassment.

3. All documents reflecting meetings plaintiff had with defendant held on _____, _____ (dates on which plaintiff complained of unfair treatment).

4. All documents reflecting diagnosis or treatment of the emotional distress and/ or mental anguish allegedly suffered by plaintiff caused by defendant.

5. All documents reflecting the efforts of plaintiff to secure employment following her termination from _____.

6. All documents reflecting plaintiff's earnings from _____ to the present, including, but not limited to, W-2 Forms, 1099 Statements, and K-1 Statements.

7. All documents reflecting communications between the plaintiff and other former employees of defendant for the period of time starting _____ to the present.

APPENDIXES

APPENDIX A

EVELETH MINES SEXUAL HARASSMENT POLICY STATEMENT OF POLICY*

Title VII of the Civil Rights Act of 1964 prohibits employment discrimination on the basis of race, color, sex, age or national origin. *Sexual harassment is included among the prohibitions.*

Sexual harassment, according to the federal Equal Employment Opportunity Commission (EEOC), consists of unwelcome sexual advances, requests for sexual favors or other verbal and physical acts of a sexual or sex-based nature where (1) submission to such conduct is made either explicitly or implicitly a term or condition of an individual's employment; (2) an employment decision is based on an individual's acceptance or rejection of such conduct; or (3) such conduct interferes with an individual's work performance or creates an intimidating, hostile or offensive working environment.

It is also unlawful to retaliate or take reprisal in any way against anyone who has articulated any concern about sexual harassment or discrimination, whether that concern relates to harassment of or discrimination against the individual raising the concern or against another individual.

Examples of conduct that would be considered sexual harassment or related retaliation are set forth in the Statement of Prohibited Conduct which follows. These examples are provided to illustrate the kind of conduct proscribed by this Policy; the list is not exhaustive.

Eveleth Mines and its agents are under a duty to investigate and eradicate any form of sexual harassment or sex discrimination or retaliation. To further that end, Eveleth Mines has issued a procedure for making complaints about conduct in violation of this Policy and schedule for violation of this Policy. Eveleth Mines will appoint a person within the main office to receive complaints and conduct investigations pursuant to this procedure. This person must be approved by counsel for the plaintiffs as a neutral party who is likely to be perceived as a fair

---

* Reprinted with permission of Jane Lang, Sprenger & Lang.

485

and impartial investigator. This person is herein referred to as the Sexual Harassment Officer.

Sexual harassment is unlawful, and such prohibited conduct exposes not only Eveleth Mines, but individuals involved in such conduct, to significant liability under the law. Employees at all times should treat other employees respectfully and with dignity in a manner so as not to offend the sensibilities of a co-worker. Accordingly, Eveleth Mines' management is committed to vigorously enforcing its Sexual Harassment Policy at all levels within the Company.

This Policy applies to all employees of Eveleth Mines including full-time, part-time, hourly, salaried, and temporary employees. This Policy also applies to contractors, vendors, and others doing business with Eveleth Mines while on the Eveleth Mines premises.

STATEMENT OF PROHIBITED CONDUCT

The management of Eveleth Mines considers the following conduct to represent some of the types of acts which violate Eveleth Mines' Sexual Harassment Policy:

A.   <u>Physical assaults of a sexual nature, such as:</u>

   (1)   rape, sexual battery, molestation or attempts to commit these assaults; and

   (2)   intentional physical conduct which is sexual in nature, such as touching, pinching, patting, grabbing, brushing against another employee's body, or poking another employee's body.

B.   <u>Unwanted sexual advances, propositions or other sexual comments, such as:</u>

   (1)   sexually-oriented gestures, noises, remarks, jokes or comments about a person's sexuality or sexual experience directed at or made in the presence of any employee who indicates or has indicated in any way that such conduct in his or her presence is unwelcome;

   (2)   preferential treatment or promise of preferential treatment to an employee for submitting to sexual conduct, including soliciting or attempting to solicit any employee to engage in sexual activity for compensation or reward; and

   (3)   subjecting, or threats of subjecting, an employee to unwelcome sexual attention or conduct or intentionally making performance of that employee's job more difficult because of that employee's sex.

C. Sexual or discriminatory displays or publications anywhere in Eveleth Mines' workplace by Eveleth Mines employees, such as:

   (1) displaying pictures, posters, calendars, graffiti, objects, promotional materials, reading materials, or other materials that are sexually suggestive, sexually demeaning, or pornographic, or bringing into the Eveleth Mines work environment or possessing any such material to read, display or view at work

   (A picture will be presumed to be sexually suggestive if it depicts a person of either sex who is not fully clothed or in clothes that are not suited to or ordinarily accepted for the accomplishment of routine work in and around the mines and who is posed for the obvious purpose of displaying or drawing attention to private portions of his or her body);

   (2) reading or otherwise publicizing in the work environment materials that are in any way sexually revealing, sexually suggestive, sexually demeaning, or pornographic; and

   (3) displaying signs or other materials purporting to segregate an employee by sex in any area of the workplace (other than rest rooms and similar semi-private lockers/changing rooms).

D. Retaliation for sexual harassment complaints, such as:

   (1) disciplining, changing work assignments of, providing inaccurate work information to, or refusing to cooperate or discuss work-related matters with any employee because that employee has complained about or resisted harassment, discrimination, or retaliation; and

   (2) intentionally pressuring, falsely denying, lying about or otherwise covering up or attempting to cover up conduct such as that described in any item above.

E. *Other acts:*

   (1) The above is not to be construed as an all-inclusive list of prohibited acts under this Policy.

   (2) Sexual harassment is unlawful and hurts other employees. Any of the prohibited conduct described here is sexual harassment of anyone at whom it is directed or who is otherwise subjected to it. Each incident of harassment, moreover, contributes to a general atmosphere in which all persons who share the victim's sex suffer the consequences. Sexually-oriented acts or sex-based conduct have no legitimate business purposes; accordingly, the employee who engages in such conduct

should be and will be made to bear the full responsibility for such unlawful conduct.

SCHEDULE OF PENALTIES FOR VIOLATION OF POLICY

The following schedule of penalties applies to all violations of the Eveleth Mines Sexual Harassment Policy, as explained in more detail in the Statement of Prohibited Conduct.

Where progressive discipline is provided for, each instance of conduct violating the policy moves the offending employee through the steps of disciplinary action. In other words, it is not necessary for an employee to repeat the same precise conduct in order to move up the scale of discipline.

A written record of each action taken pursuant to the policy will be placed in the offending employee's personnel file. The record will reflect the conduct, or alleged conduct, and the warning given, or other discipline imposed.

A. Assault

Any employee's first proven offense of assault or threat of assault, including assault of a sexual nature, will result in dismissal.

B. Other acts of harassment by co-workers

An employee's commission of acts of sexual harassment other than assault will result in written warning, suspension, or discharge upon the first proven offense, depending upon the nature or severity of the misconduct, and suspension or discharge upon the second proven offense, depending on the nature or severity of the misconduct.

C. Retaliation

Any form of proven retaliation will result in suspension or discharge upon the first proven offense, depending on the nature and severity of the retaliatory acts, and discharge on the second proven offense.

D. Supervisors

A supervisor's commission of acts of sexual harassment (other than assault) with respect to any other employee under that person's supervision will result in final warning or dismissal for the first offense, depending upon the nature and severity of the misconduct, and discharge for any subsequent offense.

PROCEDURES FOR MAKING, INVESTIGATING AND RESOLVING SEXUAL HARASSMENT AND RETALIATION COMPLAINTS

A. Complaints

These procedures apply to all formal and informal complaints of sexual harassment.

Eveleth Mines will provide its employees with convenient, confidential and reliable mechanisms for reporting incidents of sexual harassment and retaliation. The name, responsibilities, work location, and phone number of the Sexual Harassment Officer will be routinely and continuously posted.

The Sexual Harassment Officer may appoint "designees" to assist him or her in handling sexual harassment complaints. Persons appointed as designees shall not conduct an investigation until they have received training equivalent to that received by the Sexual Harassment Officer. The purpose of having several persons to whom complaints may be made is to avoid a situation in which an employee is faced with complaining to the person, or a close associate of the person, who would be the subject of the complaint.

Complaints of acts of sexual harassment or retaliation that are in violation of the sexual harassment policy will be accepted in writing or orally, and anonymous complaints will be taken seriously and investigated. Anyone who has observed sexual harassment or retaliation should report it to the Sexual Harassment Officer or his or her designee. A complaint need not be limited to someone who was the target of harassment or retaliation.

A complaint that there has been a violation of Eveleth Mines' Policy against Sexual Harassment may be informal or formal. An informal complaint is made verbally to the Sexual Harassment Officer or his or her designees or a superintendent. A formal complaint is a written, signed statement and should be submitted to the Sexual Harassment Officer. An employee may decide to file a formal complaint without first proceeding on an informal level.

Only those who have an immediate need to know, including the Sexual Harassment Officer and/or his/her designee, the complainant, the alleged harasser(s) or retaliator(s) and any witnesses will or may find out the identity of the complainant. All parties contacted in the course of an investigation will be advised that all parties involved in a charge are entitled to respect and that any retaliation or reprisal against an individual who is an alleged target of harassment or retaliation, who has made a complaint, or who has provided evidence in connection with a complaint is a separate actionable offense as provided in the schedule of penalties. This complaint process will be administered consistent with federal labor law when bargaining unit members are affected.

B. Investigations

The Sexual Harassment Officer will receive thorough training about sexual harassment and the procedures herein and will have the responsibility for investigating complaints or having an appropriately trained and designated Eveleth Mines investigator do so.

If an employee choose to make an informal complaint, the Sexual Harassment Officer shall attempt to reach informal resolution within ten (10) days of receiving the complaint. If an employee submits a formal complaint, the Sexual Harassment Officer shall conduct a formal investigation.

All complaints will be investigated expeditiously by a trained Sexual Harassment Officer or his/her designee in a timely manner. Within five (5) days of a submission of a formal complaint, the Investigative Officer will notify the alleged harasser in writing of the nature of the complaint. In carrying out the investigation, the Investigating Officer shall use procedures in accord with due process and feasible confidentiality to all involved. In any meetings called to investigate complaints of sexual harassment, the affected employees may be represented by union representatives, attorneys or other appropriate representatives. The Investigative Officer is empowered to recommend remedial measures based upon the results of the investigation, and as outlined by the schedule of penalties, Eveleth Mines management will promptly consider and act upon such recommendation.

The Investigative Officer will have the duty of immediately bringing all sexual harassment and retaliation complaints to the confidential attention of the office of the President of Eveleth Mines, and Eveleth Mines' EEO Officer.

C. Appeal

A non-bargaining unit employee who is determined to have violated Eveleth Mines' Policy against sexual harassment shall have a right to appeal that determination to the Equal Employment Opportunity Officer of Oglebay Norton Taconite Company.

A bargaining unit employee may appeal through the grievance provisions of the Bargaining Agreement.

D. Cooperation

An effective sexual harassment policy requires the support and example of company personnel in positions of authority. Eveleth Mines agents or employees who engage in sexual harassment or retaliation or who fail to cooperate with company-sponsored investigations of sexual harassment or retaliation may be severely sanctioned by suspension or dismissal. By the same token, officials who refuse to implement remedial measures, obstruct the remedial efforts of other Eveleth Mines employees, and/or retaliate against sexual harassment complainants or witnesses may be immediately sanctioned by suspension or dismissal.

E. <u>Monitoring</u>

Because Eveleth Mines is under legal obligations imposed by Court order, the plaintiffs, their designated representative, and if one is appointed upon motion and a showing of need, a representative of the U.S. District Court for the District of Minnesota are authorized to monitor the Eveleth Mines workplace, even in the absence of specific complaints, to ensure that the company's policy against sexual harassment is being enforced. Such persons are not ordinarily to be used in lieu of the Eveleth Mines Investigative Officers on investigations of individual matters, but instead are to be available to assess the adequacy of investigations. Any individual dissatisfied with Eveleth Mines' investigation of a complaint may contact such persons in writing or by telephone and request an independent investigation. Such persons' addresses and telephone numbers will be posted and circulated with those of the Investigative Officers. Such persons will be given reasonable access by Eveleth Mines to inspect for compliance.

PROCEDURES AND RULES FOR EDUCATION AND TRAINING

Education and training for employees at each level of the work force are critical to the success of Eveleth Mines' Policy against sexual harassment. The following documents address such issues: the letter to be sent to all employees from Eveleth Mines' Chief Executive Officer/President, the Sexual Harassment Policy, Statement of Prohibited Conduct, the Schedule of Penalties for Misconduct, and Procedures for Making, Investigating, and Resolving Sexual Harassment and Retaliation Complaints. These documents will be conspicuously posted throughout the workplace at each division of Eveleth Mines, on each company bulletin board, in all central gathering areas, and in every locker room. The statements must be clearly legible and displayed continuously. The Sexual Harassment Policy under a cover letter from Eveleth Mines' President will be sent to all employees. The letter will indicate that copies are available at no cost and how they can be obtained.

Eveleth Mines' Sexual Harassment Policy statement will also be included in the Safety Instruction and General Company Rules, which are issued in booklet form to each Eveleth Mines employee. Educational posters using concise messages conveying Eveleth Mines' opposition to workplace sexual harassment will reinforce the company's policy statement; these posters should be simple, eye-catching and graffiti-resistant.

Education and training include the following components:

1. <u>For all Eveleth Mines employees:</u> As part of general orientation, each recently hired employee will be given a copy of the letter from Eveleth Mines' Chief Executive Officer/President and requested to read and sign a receipt for the company's policy statement on sexual harassment so that they are on notice of the standards of behavior expected. All employees will participate on company time in annual seminars, of at least 2 hours in length that teach strategies for resisting and preventing sexual harassment. These seminars will be conducted by one or more experienced sexual harassment educators, including one instructor with work experience in the trades.

2. <u>For all employees with supervisory authority over other employees, including step-up foremen, foremen, superintendents, and all employees working in a managerial capacity:</u> All supervisory personnel will participate in an annual, half-day-long training session on sex discrimination. At least one-third of each session (of no less than one and one-half hours) will be devoted to education about workplace sexual harassment, including training (with demonstrative evidence) as to exactly what types of remarks, behavior, and pictures will not be tolerated in the Eveleth Mines workplace. The President of Eveleth Taconite Company will attend the training sessions in one central location with all company supervisory employees. The President will introduce the seminar with remarks stressing the potential liability of Eveleth Mines and individual supervisors for sexual harassment and the need to eliminate harassment. Each participant will be informed that they are responsible for knowing the contents of Eveleth Mines' Sexual Harassment Policy and for giving similar presentations of safety meetings to employees.

3. <u>For all Investigative Officers:</u> The Sexual Harassment Officer and his or her designees, if any, will attend annual full-day training seminars conducted by experienced sexual harassment educators and/or investigators to educate them about the problems of sexual harassment in the workplace and techniques for investigating and stopping it.

    The training sessions will be conducted by an experienced sexual harassment educator chosen jointly by Eveleth Mines and the plaintiffs' counsel after receiving bids. In the event of a disagreement between the parties, the parties will refer the matter to an arbitrator chosen by the parties.

BILL TO BE INTRODUCED BY THE EEOC TO PROHIBIT HARASSMENT ON THE BASIS OF ALL PROTECTED CHARACTERISTICS

§ 1609.1 Harassment

(a) Harassment on the basis of race, color, religion, gender, national origin, age, or disability constitutes discrimination in the terms, conditions, and privileges of employment and, as such, violates Title VII of the Civil Rights Act of 1964, *as amended,* 42 U.S.C. § 2000e *et seq.* (Title VII); the Age Discrimination in Employment Act, *as amended,* 29 U.S.C. § 621 *et seq.* (ADEA); the Americans with Disabilities Act, 42 U.S.C. § 12101 *et seq.* (ADA); or the Rehabilitation Act of 1973, *as amended,* 29 U.S.C. § 701 *et seq.,* as applicable.

(b) Harassment is verbal or physical conduct that denigrates or shows hostility or aversion toward an individual because of his/her race, color, religion, gender, national origin, age, or disability, or that of his/her relatives, friends, or associates, and that: (i) has the purpose or effect of creating an intimidating, hostile, or offensive work environment; (ii) has the purpose or effect of unreasonably interfering with an individual's work performance; or (iii) otherwise adversely affects an individual's employment opportunities.

Harassing conduct includes, but is not limited to, the following: (i) epithets, slurs, negative stereotyping, or threatening, intimidating, or hostile acts, that relate to race, color, religion, gender, national origin, age or disability; and (ii) written or graphic material that denigrates or shows hostility or aversion toward an individual or group because of race, color, religion, gender, national origin, age, or disability and that is placed on walls, bulletin boards, or elsewhere on the employer's premises, or circulated in the workplace.

(c) The standard for determining whether verbal or physical conduct relating to race, color, religion, gender, national origin, age or disability is sufficiently severe

493

or pervasive to create a hostile or abusive work environment is whether a reasonable person in the same or similar circumstances would find the conduct intimidating, hostile, or abusive. The "reasonable person" standard includes consideration of the perspective of persons of the alleged victim's race, color, religion, gender, national origin, age, or disability. It is not necessary to make an additional showing of psychological harm.

(d) An employer, employment agency, joint apprenticeship committee, or labor organization (hereinafter collectively referred to as "employer") has an affirmative duty to maintain a working environment free of harassment on any of these bases. Harassing conduct may be challenged even if the complaining employee(s) are not specifically intended targets of the conduct.

(e) In determining whether the alleged conduct constitutes harassment, the Commission will look at the record as a whole and at the totality of the circumstances, including the nature of the conduct and the context in which it occurred. The determination of the legality of a particular action will be made from the facts, on a case-by-case basis.

§ 1690.2 Employer Liability for Harassment

(a) An employer is liable for its conduct and that of its agents and supervisory employees with respect to workplace harassment on the basis of race, color, religion, gender, national origin, age, or disability: (i) where the employer knew or should have known of the conduct and failed to take immediate and appropriate corrective action; or (ii) regardless of whether the employer knew or should have known of the conduct, where the harassing supervisory employee is acting in an "agency capacity." To determine whether the harassing individual is acting in an "agency capacity," the circumstances of the particular employment relationship and the job functions performed by the harassing individual should be examined. "Apparent authority" to act on the employer's behalf shall be established where the employer fails to institute an explicit policy against harassment that is clearly and regularly communicated to employees, or fails to establish a reasonably accessible procedure by which victims of harassment can make their complaints known to appropriate officials who are in a position to act on complaints.

(b) With respect to conduct between co-workers, an employer is responsible for acts of harassment in the workplace that relate to race, color, religion, gender, national origin, age, or disability where the employer or its agents or supervisory employees knew or should have known of the conduct, and the employer failed to take immediate and appropriate corrective action.

(c) An employer may also be responsible for the acts of non-employees with respect to harassment of employees in the workplace related to race, color, religion, gender, national origin, age, or disability where the employer or its agents or supervisory employees knew or should have known of the conduct and failed to take immediate and appropriate corrective action, as feasible. In reviewing these cases, the Commission will consider the extent of the employer's control over non-employees and any other legal responsibility that the employer may have had with respect to the conduct of such non-employees on a case-by-case basis.

(d) Prevention is the best tool for the elimination of harassment. An employer should take all steps necessary to prevent harassment from occurring, including having an explicit policy against harassment that is clearly and regularly communicated to employees, explaining sanctions for harassment, developing methods to sensitize all supervisory and non-supervisory employees on issues of harassment, and informing employees of their right to raise, and the procedures for raising, the issue of harassment under Title VII, the ADEA, the ADA, and the Rehabilitation Act. An employer should provide an effective complaint procedure by which employees can make their complaints known to appropriate officials who are in a position to act on them.

APPENDIX C

SAMPLE CALIFORNIA SEXUAL HARASSMENT POLICY

DEFINITION

Sexual harassment means "any unwelcome sexual advances or requests for sexual favors or any conduct of a sexual nature when:

(1) submission to such conduct is made either explicitly or implicitly a term or condition of an individual's employment,

(2) submission to or rejection of such conduct by an individual is used as the basis for employment decisions affecting such individual, or

(3) such conduct has the purpose or effect of substantially interfering with an individual's work performance or creating an intimidating, hostile or offensive working environment."

EXAMPLES OF SEXUAL HARASSMENT

The following are examples of sexual harassment. These examples do not cover the full range of conduct that can be considered sexual harassment:

- unwelcome sexual advances
- suggestive or lewd remarks
- unwelcome hugs, touching, kisses
- requests for sexual favors
- derogatory or pornographic posters, cartoons or drawings

REMEDIES

Remedies may include, but are not limited to:

- cease and desist orders
- back pay
- compensatory damages
- hiring, promotion or reinstatement
- damages for emotional distress
- fine up to $50,000

In addition, any person against whom a complaint is made and substantiated will be subject to disciplinary action up to and including termination of employment, and may be subject to criminal and civil penalties under federal and state laws.

NON-RETALIATION

California Code of Regulations, Section 7287.8 of Title 2 and Federal law, as well as Employer X policy, prohibit sexual harassment in any form or retaliation against anyone who brings a complaint of sexual harassment or acts as a witness or otherwise participates in an investigation to a complaint of sexual harassment. All employees are expected to cooperate fully when asked to participate in any investigation of alleged sexual harassment.

COMPLAINT PROCEDURE

Employees who believe they are the subject of sexual harassment are responsible for advising management of the incident(s) and cooperating with any investigation that is conducted. Employees should report incidents of sexual harassment to their supervisor or manager, or if the specific circumstances make such reporting inappropriate, then to X Department [address] [Telephone] [Fax]. Employer X will conduct an investigation of all claims and take appropriate corrective action, ensuring confidentiality to the maximum degree possible.

The California Department of Fair Employment and Housing is charged with enforcing the State sexual harassment law. There are offices located in most regions. For information, contact your nearest office.

SAMPLE CONNECTICUT SEXUAL HARASSMENT POLICY

**SEXUAL HARASSMENT IS ILLEGAL
AND IS PROHIBITED
BY
THE CONNECTICUT DISCRIMINATORY EMPLOYMENT PRACTICES ACT
(Section 46a-60(a)(8))
AND
TITLE VII OF THE CIVIL RIGHTS ACT
(42 United States Code, Section 2000e *et seq.*)
AND
Employer X**

DEFINITION

Sexual harassment means "any unwelcome sexual advances or requests for sexual favors or any conduct of a sexual nature when:

(1) submission to such conduct is made either explicitly or implicitly a term or condition of an individual's employment,

(2) submission to or rejection of such conduct by an individual is used as the basis for employment decisions affecting such individual, or

(3) such conduct has the purpose or effect of substantially interfering with an individual's work performance or creating an intimidating, hostile or offensive working environment."

EXAMPLES OF SEXUAL HARASSMENT

The following are examples of sexual harassment. These examples do not cover the full range of conduct that can be considered sexual harassment:

- unwelcome sexual advances

- suggestive or lewd remarks
- unwelcome hugs, touching, kisses
- requests for sexual favors
- derogatory or pornographic posters, cartoons or drawings

REMEDIES

Remedies may include, but are not limited to:

- cease and desist orders
- back pay
- compensatory damages
- hiring, promotion or reinstatement

In addition, any person against whom a complaint is made and substantiated will be subject to disciplinary action up to and including termination of employment, and may be subject to criminal and civil penalties under federal and state laws.

NON-RETALIATION

State and federal law, as well as Employer X policy, prohibit sexual harassment in any form or retaliation against anyone who brings a complaint of sexual harassment or acts as a witness to a complaint of sexual harassment. All employees are expected to cooperate fully when asked to participate in any investigation of alleged sexual harassment.

COMPLAINT PROCEDURE

Employees who believe they are the subject of sexual harassment are responsible for advising management of the incident(s) and cooperating with any investigation that is conducted. Employees should report incidents of sexual harassment to their supervisor or manager, or if the specific circumstances make such reporting inappropriate, then to X Department [address] [Telephone] [Fax]. Employer X will conduct an investigation of all claims and take appropriate corrective action, ensuring confidentiality to the maximum degree possible.

The Connecticut Commission on Human Rights and Opportunities is charged with enforcing the sexual harassment law. Connecticut law requires that a formal written complaint be filed with the Commission within 180 days of the date when the alleged sexual harassment occurred. The Commission is located in Hartford at 90 Washington Street, Hartford, CT 06106, (203) 566-3350 or TDD (203) 566-2301.

APPENDIX E

ILLINOIS MODEL EMPLOYER SEXUAL HARASSMENT POLICY FOR EMPLOYER DOING BUSINESS WITH THE STATE

**ILLINOIS DEPARTMENT OF HUMAN RIGHTS
PUBLIC CONTRACTS UNIT**

**MODEL EMPLOYER SEXUAL HARASSMENT POLICY
JUNE 23, 1993**

NOTE: This Model Employer Sexual Harassment Policy has been prepared by the Department of Human Rights to assist public contractors and eligible bidders in complying with the requirements of Public Act 87-1257, effective July 1, 1993, that each public contractor and eligible bidder develop a written sexual harassment policy. This Model Employer Sexual Harassment Policy has been adapted from a Policy Statement and Model Policy issued December 18, 1992, by Illinois Governor Jim Edgar to all State Departments, Agencies, Boards, and Commissions.

POLICY REGARDING SEXUAL HARASSMENT IN EMPLOYMENT

I. STATEMENT OF COMPANY POLICY

This company is committed to providing a workplace that is free from all forms of discrimination, including sexual harassment. Any employee's behavior that fits the definition of sexual harassment is a form of misconduct which may result in disciplinary action up to and including dismissal. Sexual harassment could also subject this company and, in some cases, an individual to substantial civil penalties.

The company's policy on sexual harassment is part of its overall affirmative action efforts pursuant to state and federal laws prohibiting discrimination based on age, race, color, religion, national origin, citizenship status, unfavorable discharge from the military, marital status, disability, and gender. Specifically, sexual harassment is prohibited by the Civil Rights Act of 1964, as amended in 1991, and the Illinois Human Rights Act.

Each employee of this company bears the responsibility to refrain from sexual harassment in the workplace. No employee—male or female—should be subjected to unsolicited or unwelcome sexual overtures or conduct in the workplace. Furthermore, it is the responsibility of all supervisors to make sure that the work environment is free from sexual harassment. All forms of discrimination and conduct which can be considered harassing, coercive or disruptive, or which create a hostile or offensive environment must be eliminated. Instances of sexual harassment must be investigated in a prompt and effective manner.

All employees of this company, particularly those in a supervisory or management capacity, are expected to become familiar with the contents of this Policy and to abide by the requirements it establishes.

II. DEFINITION OF SEXUAL HARASSMENT

According to the Illinois Human Rights Act, sexual harassment is defined as:

Any unwelcome sexual advances or requests for sexual favors or any conduct of a sexual nature when

1) submission to such conduct is made, either explicitly or implicitly, a term or condition of an individual's employment.

2) submission to or rejection of such conduct by an individual is used as the basis for employment decisions affecting such individual, or

3) such conduct has the purpose or effect of substantially interfering with an individual's work performance or creating an intimidating, hostile, or offensive working environment.

The courts have determined that sexual harassment is a form of discrimination under Title VII of the Civil Rights Act of 1964, as amended in 1991.

One example of sexual harassment is where a qualified individual is denied employment opportunities and benefits that are, instead, awarded to an individual who submits (voluntarily or under coercion) to sexual advances or sexual favors. Another example is where an individual must submit to unwelcome sexual conduct in order to receive an employment opportunity.

Other conduct commonly considered sexual harassment includes:

■ Verbal: sexual innuendos, suggestive comments, insults, humor and jokes about sex, anatomy or gender-specific traits, sexual propositions, threats, repeated requests for dates, or statements about other employees, even outside their presence, of a sexual nature.

■ Non-verbal: suggestive or insulting sounds (whistling), leering, obscene gestures, sexually suggestive bodily gestures, "catcalls", "smacking", or "kissing" noises.

■ Visual: posters, signs, pin-ups or slogans of a sexual nature.

■ Physical: touching, unwelcome hugging or kissing, pinching, brushing the body, coerced sexual intercourse, or actual assault.

Sexual harassment most frequently involves a man harassing a woman. However, it can also involve a woman harassing a man or harassment between members of the same gender.

The most severe and overt forms of sexual harassment are easier to determine. On the other end of the spectrum, some sexual harassment is more subtle and depends to some extent on individual perceptions and interpretation. The trend in the courts is to assess sexual harassment by a standard of what would offend a "reasonable woman" or "reasonable man," depending of the gender of the alleged victim.

An example of the most subtle form of sexual harassment is the use of endearments. The use of terms such as "honey," "darling," and "sweetheart" is objectionable to many women who believe that these terms undermine their authority and their ability to deal with men on an equal and professional level.

Another example is the use of a compliment that could potentially be interpreted as sexual in nature. Below are three statements that might be made about appearance of a woman in the workplace:

"That's an attractive dress you have on."
"That's an attractive dress. It really looks good on you."
"That's an attractive dress. You really fill it out well."

The first statement appears to be simply a compliment. The last is the most likely to be perceived as sexual harassment depending on the perceptions and values of the person to whom it is directed. To avoid the possibility of offending an employee, it is best to follow a course of conduct above reproach, or to err on the side of caution.

III. RESPONSIBILITY OF INDIVIDUAL EMPLOYEES

Each individual employee has the responsibility to refrain from sexual harassment in the workplace. An individual employee who sexually harasses a fellow worker is, of course, liable for his or her individual conduct.

The harassing employee will be subject to disciplinary action up to and including discharge in accord with the company's disciplinary policy and the terms of any collective bargaining agreement.

The company has designated _____ (Name), _____ (Title) to coordinate the company's sexual harassment policy compliance. Mr./ Ms. _____ can be reached at _____ (Address and Telephone). [NOTE: insert the name of the company's EEO Officer, Human Resources Administrator, Personnel Officer, or other person designated by company management to coordinate compliance with this policy.] He/she is available to consult with employees regarding their obligations under this policy.

IV. RESPONSIBILITY OF SUPERVISORY EMPLOYEES

Each supervisor is responsible for maintaining the workplace free from sexual harassment. This is accomplished by promoting a professional environment and by dealing with sexual harassment as with all other forms of employee misconduct.

The courts have found that organizations as well as supervisors can be held liable for damages related to sexual harassment by a manager, supervisor, employee, or third party (an individual who is not an employee but does business with an organization, such as a customer, contractor, sales representative, or repair person).

Liability is either based on an organization's responsibility to maintain a certain level of order and discipline, or on the supervisor's acting as an agent of the organization. As such, supervisors must act quickly and responsibly not only to minimize their own liability but also that of the company.

Specifically, a supervisor must address an observed incident of sexual harassment or a complaint, with seriousness, take prompt action to investigate it, report it, and end it, implement appropriate disciplinary action, and observe strict confidentiality. This also applies to cases where an employee tells the supervisor about behavior that constitutes sexual harassment but does not want to make a formal complaint.

In addition, supervisors must ensure that no retaliation will result against an employee making a sexual harassment complaint.

Supervisors in need of information regarding their obligations under this policy or procedures to follow upon receipt of a complaint of sexual harassment

should contact _____ (Name), _____ (Title) at
_____ (Address and Telephone). [NOTE: insert the name of company EEO Officer, Human Resource Administrator, Personnel Officer, or other person designated by company management].

V. PROCEDURES FOR FILING A COMPLAINT OF SEXUAL HARASSMENT

A. INTERNAL

An employee who either observes or believes herself/himself to be the object of sexual harassment should deal with the incident(s) as directly and firmly as possible by clearly communicating her/his position to the supervisor, EEO Officer*, and to the offending employee. It is not necessary for the sexual harassment to be directed at the person making the complaint.

Each incident of sexual harassment should be documented or recorded. A note should be made of the date, time, place, what was said or done, and by whom. The documentation may be augmented by written records such as letters, notes, memos, and telephone messages.

No one making a complaint of sexual harassment will be retaliated against even in a complaint made in good faith is not substantiated. Any witness to an incident of sexual harassment is also protected from retaliation.

The process for making a complaint about sexual harassment falls into several stages.

1. DIRECT COMMUNICATION. If there is sexually harassing behavior in the workplace, the harassed employee should directly and clearly express her/his objection that the conduct is unwelcome and request that the offending behavior stop. The initial message may be verbal. If subsequent messages are needed, they should be put in writing in a note or memo.

2. CONTACT SUPERVISORY PERSONNEL. At the same time direct communication is undertaken, or in the event an employee feels threatened or intimidated by the situation, the problem must be promptly reported to the immediate supervisor or the EEO Officer. If the harasser is the immediate supervisor, the problem should be reported to the next level of supervision or the EEO Officer.

3. FORMAL WRITTEN COMPLAINT. An employee may also report incidents of sexual harassment directly to the EEO Officer. The EEO Officer will counsel the reporting employee and be available to assist with filing a formal complaint. The Company will fully investigate the complaint, and will advise the complainant and the alleged harasser of the results of the investigation.

The Company hopes that any incident of sexual harassment can be resolved through the internal process outlined above. All employees, however, have the right to file formal charges with the Illinois Department of Human Rights (IDHR) and/or the United States Equal Employment Opportunity Commission (EEOC). A charge with IDHR must be filed within 180 days of the incident of sexual harassment. A charge with EEOC must be filed within 300 days of the incident.

The Illinois Department of Human Rights may be contacted as follows:

CHICAGO   312-814-6200
CHICAGO TDD   312-263-1679

SPRINGFIELD   217-785-5100
SPRINGFIELD TDD   217-785-5125

The United States Equal Employment Opportunity Commission can be contacted as follows:

CHICAGO   312-353-2713
                   800-669-3362
TDD   800-800-3302

An employee who is suddenly transferred to a lower paying job or passed over for promotion after filing a complaint with IDHR or EEOC may file a retaliation charge with either of these agencies. The charges must be filed within 180 (IDHR) or 300 (EEOC) days of the retaliation.

An employee who has been physically harassed or threatened while on the job may also have grounds for criminal charges of assault and battery.

*[NOTE: Each Company should adapt the provisions of this section to the requirements of their existing disciplinary policy and/or terms of any existing collective bargaining agreement. The name of the Company's Human Resources Administrator, Personnel Officer, or other appropriate person should be used if the Company has no EEO Officer].

VI. FALSE AND FRIVOLOUS COMPLAINTS

False and frivolous charges refer to cases where the accuser is using a sexual harassment complaint to accomplish some end other than stopping sexual harassment. It does not refer to charges made in good faith which can not be proven. Given the seriousness of the consequences for the accused, a false and frivolous charge is a severe offense that can itself result in disciplinary action.

ALASKA REQUIRED POSTING FOR SEXUAL HARASSMENT NOTICE

Sec. 23.10.440. Posting of Information on Sexual Harassment

(a) An employer shall post in the workplace a notice prepared by the State Commission for Human Rights that

(1) sets out the federal definition of sexual harassment;

(2) advises employees of the name, address, and telephone number of the state and federal agencies to which inquiries and complaints concerning sexual harassment may be made; and

(3) sets out the deadlines for filing a complaint of sexual harassment with the agencies listed in (2) of this subsection.

(b) The employer shall select prominent and accessible locations for posting the notice that will permit each of the employees of the employer to read the notice during the course of their regular employment duties.

(c) The State Commission for Human Rights shall prepare and make available to employers notices that meet the requirements of this section.[1]

(d) The department may impose a civil fine not to exceed $500 on an employer for violation of this section.

(e) In this section, "employer" means an employer that employs 15 or more employees at one time and includes the state, the University of Alaska, the Alaska Railroad Corporation, and political subdivisions of the state.

---

[1] Author's note: Notices should be available from the state of Alaska as of April 1994.

SAMPLES OF VERMONT SEXUAL HARASSMENT POLICIES

POLICY 1

It is against the policies of Employer X, and illegal under state and federal law, for any employee, male or female, to sexually harass another employee. Employer X is committed to provide a workplace free from this unlawful conduct. It is a violation of this policy for an employee to engage in sexual harassment.

What is sexual harassment?

Sexual harassment is a form of sex discrimination and means unwelcome sexual advances, requests for sexual favors, and other verbal or physical conduct of a sexual nature when:

(1) submission to that conduct is made either explicitly or implicitly a term or condition of employment;

(2) submission to or rejection of such conduct by an individual is used as a component of the basis for employment decisions affecting that individual; or

(3) the conduct has the purpose or effect of substantially interfering with an individual's work performance or creating an intimidating, hostile, or offensive working environment.

Examples of sexual harassment include, but are not limited to the following, when such acts or behavior come within one of the above definitions:

■ either explicitly or implicitly conditioning any term of employment (e.g. continued employment, wages evaluation, advancement, assigned duties or shifts) on the provision of sexual favors;

■ touching or grabbing a sexual part of an employee's body;

■ touching or grabbing any part of an employee's body after that person has indicated, or it is known, that such physical contact was unwelcome;

- continuing to ask an employee to socialize on or off-duty when that person has indicated s/he is not interested;
- displaying or transmitting sexually suggestive pictures, objects, cartoons, or posters if it is known or should be known that the behavior is unwelcome;
- continuing to write sexually suggestive notes or letters if it is known or should be known that the person does not welcome such behavior;
- referring to or calling a person a sexualized name if it is known or should be known that the person does not welcome such behavior;
- regularly telling sexual jokes or using sexually vulgar or explicit language in the presence of a person if it is known or should be known that the person does not welcome such behavior;
- retaliation of any kind for having filed or supported a complaint of sexual harassment (e.g. ostracizing the person, pressuring the person to drop or not support the complaint, adversely altering that person's duties or work environment, etc.);
- derogatory or provoking remarks about or relating to an employee's sex or sexual orientation;
- harassing acts or behavior directed against a person on the basis of his or her sex or sexual orientation;
- off-duty conduct which falls within the above definition and affects the work environment.

What this employer will do if it learns of possible sexual harassment

In the event Employer X receives a complaint of sexual harassment, or otherwise has reason to believe that sexual harassment is occurring, it will take all necessary steps to ensure that the matter is promptly investigated and addressed. Employer X is committed, and required by law, to take action if it learns of potential sexual harassment, even if the aggrieved employee does not wish to formally file a complaint. Every supervisor is responsible for promptly responding to, or reporting, any complaint of suspected acts of sexual harassment. Supervisors should report to _____ (who has been designated to receive such complaints or reports), or to _____ (the head of this organization). Failure by supervisor to appropriately report or address such sexual harassment complaints or suspected acts shall be considered to be in violation of this policy.

Care will be taken to protect the identity of the person with the complaint and of the accused party or parties, except as may be reasonably necessary to successfully complete the investigation. It shall be a violation of this policy for any employee who learns of the investigation or complaint to take any retaliatory action which affects the working environment of any person involved in this investigation.

If the allegation of sexual harassment is found to be credible, Employer X will take appropriate corrective action. Employer X will inform the complaining person and the accused person of the results of the investigation and what actions will be taken to ensure that the harassment will cease and that no retaliation will occur. Any employee, supervisor, or agent who has been found by the employer to have harassed another employee will be subject to sanctions appropriate to the circumstances, ranging from a verbal warning up to and including dismissal.

If the allegation is not found to be credible, the person with the complaint and the accused person shall be so informed, with appropriate instruction provided to each, including the right of the complainant to contact any of the state or federal agencies identified in this policy notice.

What you should do if you believe you have been harassed

Any employee who believes that she or he has been the target of sexual harassment, or who believes she or he has been subjected to retaliation for having brought or supported a complaint of harassment, is encouraged to directly inform the offending person or persons that such conduct is offensive and must stop. If the employee does not wish to communicate directly with the alleged harasser or harassers, or if direct communication has been ineffective, then the person with the complaint is encouraged to report the situation as soon as possible to _____ at _____ (who has been designated to receive such complaints or reports), or to her supervisor, or to _____ at _____ (the head of this organization). It is helpful to an investigation if the employee keeps a diary of events and the names of people who witnessed or were told of the harassment, if possible.

If the complainant is dissatisfied with this employer's action, or is otherwise interested in doing so, she or he may file a complaint by writing or calling any of the following state or federal agencies:

1. **Vermont Attorney General's office,** Civil Rights Unit, 109 State Street, Montpelier, VT 05602, tel: (802) 828-3171 (voice/TDD). Complaints should be filed within 300 days of the adverse action.
2. **Equal Employment Opportunity Commission,** 1 Congress Street, Boston, MA 02114, tel: (617) 565-3200 (voice), (617) 565-3204 (TDD). Complaints must be filed within 300 days of the adverse action.
3. **Vermont Human Rights Commission,** 133 State Street, Montpelier, VT 05633-6301, tel: (802) 828-2480 (voice/TDD). (Only if you are employed by a Vermont state agency.) Complaints must be filed within 360 days of the adverse action.

Each of these agencies can conduct impartial investigations, facilitate conciliation, and if it finds that there is probable cause or reasonable grounds to believe sexual harassment occurred, it may take the case to court. Although employees are encouraged to file their complaint of sexual harassment through this employer's complaint procedure, an employee is not required to do so before filing a charge with these agencies.

In addition, a complainant also has the right to hire a private attorney, and to pursue a private legal action in state court within 3 or 6 years, depending on the type of claims raised.

Where can I get copies of this policy?

A copy of this policy will be provided to every employee, and extra copies will be available in the following office: _____.

Reasonable accommodations will be provided for persons with disabilities who need assistance in filing or pursuing a complaint of harassment, upon advance request.

SAMPLE SEXUAL HARASSMENT POLICY 2

DRAFT ONLY

SEXUAL HARASSMENT IS ILLEGAL

AND IS PROHIBITED
BY
THE VERMONT FAIR EMPLOYMENT PRACTICES ACT
(Subchapter 6 of Title 21 of the Vermont Statutes)
AND
TITLE VII OF THE CIVIL RIGHTS ACT
(42 United States Code, Section 2000e *et seq.*)
AND
EMPLOYER X

DEFINITION

"Sexual harassment" is a form of sex discrimination and means unwelcome sexual advances or requests for sexual favors or any conduct of a sexual nature when:

(1) submission to such conduct is made either explicitly or implicitly a term or condition of an individual's employment,

(2) submission to or rejection of such conduct by an individual is used as the basis for employment decisions affecting such individual, or

(3) such conduct has the purpose or effect of substantially interfering with an individual's work performance or creating an intimidating, hostile or offensive working environment.

It is unlawful to retaliate against an employee for filing a complaint of sexual harassment or for cooperating in an investigation of sexual harassment.

EXAMPLES OF SEXUAL HARASSMENT

Examples of sexual harassment include:

- unwelcome sexual advances
- suggestive or lewd remarks
- unwelcome hugs, touching, kisses
- requests for sexual favors
- derogatory or pornographic posters, cartoons or drawings
- unwelcome sexual jokes and banter
- retaliating for complaining against sexual harassment

All forms of sexual harassment are prohibited by Employer X.

REMEDIES

Consequences for committing sexual harassment may include:

- disciplinary action, from a verbal warning to dismissal
- damages and other relief to the victim
- civil penalties up to $10,000 per violation
- criminal penalties

In addition, any person against whom a complaint is made and substantiated may be subject to disciplinary action up to and including termination of employment, and criminal and civil penalties under federal and state laws.

COMPLAINT PROCEDURE

It is against the policy of Employer X for any employee, male or female, to sexually harass another employee. Every supervisor is responsible for promptly responding to or reporting any complaint or suspected acts of sexual harassment.

Any employee who believes that she or he has been sexually harassed or retaliated against for complaining of it is encouraged to report the situation as soon as possible to

(a) his or her supervisor, and/or
(b) _____, the Head of Employer X, and/or
(c) this person, who is designated to receive such complaints and reports:

_____
Name and Title

_____
Address and Telephone Number

EMPLOYER X WILL PROMPTLY INVESTIGATE AND RESPOND TO ALL
REPORTS AND KNOWLEDGE OF SEXUAL HARASSMENT

You may also contact the STATE OF VERMONT ATTORNEY GENERAL'S OFFICE, 109 State Street, Montpelier, VT 05602. (802-828-3171 voice/TDD); and/or, if you work for an employer with at least 15 employees, the EQUAL EMPLOYMENT OPPORTUNITY COMMISSION, 1 Congress Street, Boston, MA 02114 (617-565-3200 voice, 617-565-3204 TDD); or, if you work for a Vermont State agency, the Human Rights Commission, 133 State Street, Montpelier, VT 05633-6301 (802-828-2480 voice/TDD).

SEXUAL HARASSMENT POLICY OF BONNEVILLE POWER ADMINISTRATION: BEYOND THE "REASONABLE WOMAN"*

The Most Successful Employers in the 1990s
Will Measure Reasonableness With The
Employee's Calipers

The Reasonable _____*_____ Standard
(* You Fill in the Blank)

What does this reasonable woman want?

In a word, "respect."

What do all reasonable employees want?

I am the Chief Operating Officer of an enterprise that intends to compete for the best and the brightest in an increasingly tight labor market in the 1990s. I am little concerned with feminist legal theories and definitions of human rights. Rather, I am concerned with creating and sustaining an environment in which my employees will be able to contribute maximally to the accomplishment of my agency's mission. Employees who are threatened, intimidated, or otherwise distressed by aspects of their workplace environment do not contribute to the full extent of their capabilities.

Individual employees perceive signals in individual ways. It is up to each supervisor to understand as best (s)he can how the world appears through the eyes and ears of each employee in the supervisor's unit, and to respect and to work

---

* Reprinted with the permission of Steven G. Hickok, Administrator, Bonneville Power Administration.

with the differences. This task is becoming quite daunting in the increasingly diverse workforce of the 1990s.

The challenge for management is quite clear. Long before an employment situation can trip the civil rights laws, long before the employer can be ushered into the Ninth U.S. Circuit Court of Appeals to argue the finer points of discrimination theory, the manager of the most productive, cost-effective, and dedicated workforce will stand in the shoes of every one of its employees, understand their needs—the keys to their development and success—and provide for them.

What this reasonable woman wants is what works for her. It may or may not be what works for the next woman or man who occupies her position in the enterprise. To describe it as a standard is probably to call it simply "respect."

To respect any reasonable employee is to make reasonable accommodation for her/his individual differences—differences in experience, perception, style, needs. In this sense—the only sense that makes sense for business—my job is to enable the employee to succeed to the full measure of his/her capabilities. This is the essence of "equal opportunity" employment. This is the foundation for "diversity management." This is the key to release of the energy potential of high-performing organizations.

This is the 1990s. The Ninth Circuit, as progressive as they [sic] might seem, are in the 1960s. The attached policy of the Bonneville Power Administration for a harassment-free workplace moves well beyond the Civil Rights Act's Title VII.

BPA Harassment-Free Workplace Policy
BONNEVILLE POWER ADMINISTRATION POLICY:
HARASSMENT-FREE WORKPLACE

POLICY: The Bonneville Power Administration's (BPA) policy is to have a harassment-free work environment where people treat one another with respect. BPA's and our contractors' managers and supervisors have the primary responsibility for creating and sustaining this harassment-free environment (by example, by joint supervision, by coaching, by training, by contract enforcement, and by other means). But all employees, contractor personnel, and visitors must take personal responsibility for maintaining conduct that is professional and supportive of this environment.

ACTION   Managers and supervisors must take immediate action to stop
REQUIRED: harassment, to protect the people targeted by harassers, and to take all reasonable steps to ensure that no further harassment or retaliation occurs.

LOCATIONS
COVERED:
The BPA work environment includes areas in and around BPA buildings, facilities, fitness centers, vehicles, food service areas, and break locations, and any other areas or conveyances where BPA employees work or where work-related activities occur, including travel.

DEFINITION:
BPA defines harassment as any unwelcome, inappropriate conduct, including retaliation, that causes a BPA or contractor employee or visitor to feel threatened, intimidated, or distressed in the BPA work environment. Examples of harassment include, but are not limited to, the following:

EXAMPLES:
Physical conduct: Unwelcome touching; standing too close; inappropriate or threatening staring or glaring; obscene, threatening, or offensive gestures.

Verbal or written conduct: Inappropriate references to body parts; derogatory or demeaning comments, jokes, or personal questions; sexual innuendos; offensive remarks about race, gender, religion, age, ethnicity, sexual orientation, political beliefs, marital status, or disability; obscene letters or telephone calls; catcalls; whistles; sexually suggestive sounds; loud, aggressive, inappropriate comments or other vocal abuse.

Visual or symbolic conduct: Display of pictures of nude, scantily clad, or offensively clad people; display of intimidating or offensive religious, political, or other symbols; display of offensive, threatening, demeaning, or derogatory drawings, cartoons, or other graphics; offensive T-shirts, coffee mugs, bumper stickers, or other articles.

OPTIONS:
Individuals who believe they are being harassed or retaliated against should exercise any one or more of the following options as soon as possible:

Tell the harasser how you feel and ask the person to stop the offensive conduct; and/or

Tell a manager or supervisor about the conduct and how you feel about it; and/or

Contact the confidential Harassment Hotline for alternatives on how to deal with the situation.

INTERNAL:
In addition, if you are a BPA employee, you may seek help from your administrative officer, an Equal Employment Opportunity

(EEO) counselor, the EEO office, the Employee Assistance Program, Employee/Labor Relations office, your union steward, or the security office.

PENALTIES: BPA staff who engage in harassment will face consequences ranging from verbal warnings and letters of reprimand up to and including termination from BPA employment, depending upon the seriousness of the misconduct. BPA managers and supervisors who do not take action when they know or suspect that harassment is occurring will face the same range of consequences. Contractor staff who engage in harassment may be subject to comparable penalties from their employers, and a contractor who fails to enforce this policy may have its contract with BPA terminated. Visitors who harass may be removed from any BPA workplace and prevented from returning.

A SUMMARY OF POTENTIAL ADMINISTRATIVE/LEGAL ACTIONS AVAILABLE IN RESOLVING HARASSMENT IN VARIOUS ENVIRONMENTS*

* Reprinted with the Permission of the Status of Women, State of California.

A SUMMARY OF POTENTIAL ADMINISTRATIVE/LEGAL ACTIONS AVAILABLE IN RESOLVING HARASSMENT IN VARIOUS ENVIRONMENTS[1]

THE SEXUAL HARASSMENT ENVIRONMENT

POTENTIAL ACTION AND/OR REMEDY[a]	EMPLOYMENT CONTEXT					EDUCATION CONTEXT		Housing Context	Prison Context	Business Establishment and Public Accommodations	Military Context	Recipients of Government Benefits
	Private Employee or Applicant	Employee of Federal Contractor	Federal Employee	State Civil Service	Other Public Employees	Student	Teachers/ Professors					
FEDERAL												
TITLE VII (42 U.S.C. Section 2000e (et seq.) File with EEOC within 300 days in CA[a] If you work for an employer with at least 15 employees.	X	X		X	X		X					
TITLE VIII of the Fair Housing Act (42 U.S.C. Section 3601-3619). File with HUD within 180 days of harassment incident.								X				
EXECUTIVE ORDER 11246 as amended. File with DOL OFCCP within 180 days of last incident of sexual harassment in employment by a federal contractor with atleast 50 employees and at least a $50,000.00 contract.		X										
TITLE IX (20 U.S.C. Section 1681). File with OCR within 180 days of sexual harassment incident or within 60 days of completion of grievance procedure.						X	X					
42 U.S.C. SECTION 1983 ACTION. A cause of action for sexual harassment by any person acting under government authority. (Note, attorney's fees may be recovered for a Section 1983 action under the authority of Section 1988.)			X	X	X							
EXTRAORDINARY WRIT OF HABEAS CORPUS File to obtain a declaration and the enforcement of a prisoner's right to be free from sexual harassment.									X			
UNITED STATES CONSTITUTION[a] First Amendment Right to Privacy	X	X	X	X	X				X			
Fourth Amendment Right to be Free From Unreasonable Searches and Seizures									X			
Fifth and Fourteenth Amendment Rights to Equal Protection			X	X	X				X			
Eighth Amendment Right To Be Free From Cruel and Unusual Punishment									X			
NLRB UNFAIR LABOR PRACTICE CHARGE Action by Union Member for violation of Labor Management Relations Act (29 U.S.C. Section 141 et seq.) File with NLRB within six months of unfair labor practice												
Against Employer	X	X					X					
Against Union	X	X					X					

THE SEXUAL HARASSMENT ENVIRONMENT

	1	2	3	4	5	6	7	8	9	10	11
FEDERAL EMPLOYMENT INTERNAL COMPLAINT PROCESS Federal employees file with department or agency EEO Counselor within 30 days of sexual harassment incident or consequence.		X									
FEDERAL EMPLOYEES • COMPENSATION ACT (5 U.S.C. Sections 7902, 8101 et seq.; 18 U.S.C. Sections 292, 1920 et seq. See also 41 U.S.C. Section 351 for coverage of service contract employees.) Provide written notice of injury to immediate supervisor within 30 days of injury (see Section 8119). File claim for compensation in writing to Secretary of Labor or designate within three years of injury.		X									X
FEDERAL TORT CLAIMS ACT (28 U.S.C. Sections 2671 et seq. and 1346b.) Claims against a federal agency, and employee of the federal government (including the military), who harasses a person while acting within the scope of his/her office or employment.		X				X				X	
STATE											
STATE CIVIL OR HUMAN RIGHTS LAWS Check State government offices and usually file with State agency.	X										
LOCAL CIVIL OR HUMAN RIGHTS ORDINANCES Check city or county government offices for relevant ordinances or charter provisions and usually file with local enforcement office.	X	X	X		X	X			X		X
CIVIL LAWSUITS											
CONTRACT *file in CA within two years for oral contract or four years for written contract):											
BREACH OF CONTRACT	X	X	X		X	X					X
VIOLATION OF NON-DISCRIMINATION PROHIBITIONS											
BREACH OF UNIONS'S DUTY OF FAIR REPRESENTATION. Action against union for failure to represent a harassed member.	X	X	N	X	X	X			X		X
TORT (You may have to file within one year): ASSAULT AND/OR BATTERY FALSE IMPRISONMENT INTENTIONAL OR NEGLIGENT INFLICTION OF EMOTIONAL DISTRESS BREACH OF IMPLIED COVENANT OF GOOD FAITH AND FAIR DEALING INTENTIONAL INTERFERENCE WITH ECONOMIC ADVANTAGE INTENTIONAL INTERFERENCE WITH CONTRACTUAL RELATIONS											
WRONGRUL TERMINATION (Even if fired or had to leave because of harassment) FRAUD OR MISREPRESENTATION OF TERMS AND CONDITIONS OF EMPLOYMENT	X	X	X		X	X			X		
DEFAMATION: SLANDER (speech) or LIBEL (writings)	X	X	X	X	X	X			X		X
INVASION OF PRIVACY	X	X	X	X	X	X	X		X	X	X

	X		X		X	X	X	X	X		X	X
CRIMINAL CHARGES (The actual crime or attempt).** RAPE (CA Penal Code Section 261) UNLAWFUL SEXUAL INTERCOURSE - Statutory Rape (Penal Code Section 261.5) RAPE of SPOUSE (Penal Code Section 262) SEXUAL BATTERY (Penal Code Section 243.4) BATTERY (Penal Code Section 242) ASSAULT (Penal Code Section 240) FALSE IMPRISONMENT (Penal Code Section 236) FORCED SEXUAL ASSAULT INCLUDING SODOMY (Penal Code Section 286) ORAL COPULATION (Penal Code Section 288) ASSAULT WITH INTENT TO COMMIT RAPE, SODOMY OR ORAL COPULATION (Penal Code Section 220)	X		X		X	X	X	X	X		X	X
VICTIMS OF VIOLENT CRIMES ASSISTANCE PROGRAM: VICTIM WITNESS ASSISTANCE PROGRAMS through the local Officers of the District Attorney as the criminal case is proceeding.	X		X		X	X	X	X	X		X	X
VICTIMS OF VIOLENT CRIMES REIMBURSEMENT PROTRAM - AID TO VICTIMS OF VIOLENT CRIMES (Gov. Code Sections 13959 et seq. and 911.2). File claim with BOC within one year of date of injury or death.	X		X		X	X	X	X	X		X	X

WORKPLACE ANTI-SEXUAL HARASSMENT PROFILE*

Introduction

Complaints of sexual harassment in the workplace have exploded in recent years. The United States Supreme Court's decision in the *Meritor Savings Bank* case officially recognized sexual harassment as a form of sex discrimination prohibited under Title VII of the Civil Rights Act of 1964. In its unanimous decision, the Supreme Court held that victims of a "sexually hostile environment" may state a claim of unlawful sex discrimination. The Court further held that employers may be held liable, even where they did not know of the harassment. Since then, the EEOC and federal and state courts have been flooded with complaints alleging a variety of improper conduct on the part of not only management officials, but also fellow employees and other third parties.

In 1990 alone, more than 56,000 sexual harassment charges were filed with the EEOC. Moreover, it is estimated that only 15 of every 10,000 women who experience harassment ever file charges. Indeed, publicity surrounding the confirmation hearing of Clarence Thomas after his nomination to the Supreme Court should serve to escalate these numbers even further. The Civil Rights Act of 1991 has likewise increased the potential for litigation since, in addition to the normal back pay award, sexual harassment charges can now lead to awards of compensatory and punitive damages ranging from $50,000 to $300,000 depending on the size of the employer's work force.

The Equal Employment Opportunity Commission's guidelines define sexual harassment as "[u]nwelcome sexual advances, requests for sexual favors, and other verbal or physical conduct of a sexual nature" where submission is made a term or condition of employment, is used for making

---

* ©Laurdan & Associates, Employment and Labor Law Audit. All rights reserved. Reprinted with permission.

an employment decision, or the conduct creates a hostile working environment or interferes with the employee's job performance.

Thus, sexual harassment, as defined by the EEOC, is a broad term encompassing a wide range of illegal conduct. As the guidelines make clear, the term sexual harassment includes far more than the classic "quid pro quo" conduct involving sexual favors in return for promotion, advancement, or job security. Therefore, you need to be concerned about a wide range of supervisor/employee conduct; conduct that can create Title VII liability.

In October 1988, the EEOC issued additional guidelines that were aimed at assisting employers in the identification of sexual harassment in the workplace, in the implementation of affirmative programs to prevent its occurrence, and in the use of effective remedial action once complaints are raised. As any employer who has been confronted with a claim of sexual harassment in the workplace knows, investigating claims of this nature requires considerable tact and sensitivity. The livelihood and reputations of all involved, both the complainant and alleged perpetrator, are at stake. Accordingly, such investigations must be conduced discreetly with a full awareness of the serious impact that such allegations could potentially have on all concerned.

The following *Questionnaire* and *Analysis* are designed to monitor the scope of your anti-sexual harassment policy and to determine if your educational programs, internal complaint procedures, and remedial action measures are sufficient to help you create a positive working environment for all employees and help you limit your exposure to this workplace liability.

WORKPLACE ANTI-SEXUAL HARASSMENT PROFILE

Questionnaire
(some questions may have more than one answer)

	YES	NO

Policy Considerations

1. Does your firm state specifically and emphatically in its employment handbook or other policy notices that it is committed to creating and maintaining a workplace free of sexual harassment? ____ ____

2. Does your policy define as "prohibited acts" such actions as: improper suggestions, pornographic objects or pictures, graphic or descriptive comments or discussions about an individual's body or physical appearance, degrading verbal comments, and offensive sexual flirtations? ____ ____

3. Have you made all employees fully aware of your company's policy and procedures dealing with sexual harassment? _____ _____

4. Have you established and promulgated a policy concerning disciplinary actions that may be taken against policy violators? _____ _____

5. Has your firm established a separate and specific grievance or complaint procedure for employees victimized by sexual harassment? _____ _____

6. Is someone other than an employee's supervisor available to receive and investigate sexual harassment complaints? _____ _____

7. Has your policy been reviewed by your labor counsel? _____ _____

8. Does your policy make clear that sexual harassment investigations will be conducted on a confidential basis? _____ _____

9. Does your policy make clear that a sexual harassment complainant will not be retaliated against for filing a complaint? _____ _____

Education and Training

10. Do you hold routine training programs for supervisors, managers, and employees on sexual harassment and your firm's policies? _____ _____

11. Do you record the dates on which these training session take place and keep attendance records? _____ _____

12. Have you surveyed your employees to learn of their concerns about sexual harassment; to discuss their perceptions, experiences, and problems; and to obtain their thoughts on developing, implementing, and maintaining a sexual harassment-free environment? _____ _____

Investigating Process

13. Which individuals are interviewed during the investigation process?

    a. the individual harassed? _____ _____

b.　the alleged harasser? ＿＿＿＿　＿＿＿＿

c.　witnesses? ＿＿＿＿　＿＿＿＿

d.　other victims? ＿＿＿＿　＿＿＿＿

14.　Who in your organization normally conducts the investigation?

a.　personnel? ＿＿＿＿　＿＿＿＿

b.　the employee's supervisor? ＿＿＿＿　＿＿＿＿

c.　top management? ＿＿＿＿　＿＿＿＿

d.　an external or independent investigator? ＿＿＿＿　＿＿＿＿

15.　To whom are the results of the investigation communicated?

a.　the complainant? ＿＿＿＿　＿＿＿＿

b.　the alleged harasser? ＿＿＿＿　＿＿＿＿

c.　personnel? ＿＿＿＿　＿＿＿＿

d.　other employees and supervisors? ＿＿＿＿　＿＿＿＿

e.　top management? ＿＿＿＿　＿＿＿＿

f.　the general public? ＿＿＿＿　＿＿＿＿

Remedying Sexual Harassment

16.　Are complaints of sexual harassment acted upon immediately and investigated fully? ＿＿＿＿　＿＿＿＿

17.　How are violators of your sexual harassment policy disciplined:

a.　counselled? ＿＿＿＿　＿＿＿＿

b.　transferred? ＿＿＿＿　＿＿＿＿

c.　suspended? ＿＿＿＿　＿＿＿＿

d.　demoted? ＿＿＿＿　＿＿＿＿

e. terminated? ____ ____

f. no action is taken? ____ ____

18. What factors influence the type of discipline that is administered?

a. weight of evidence? ____ ____

b. nature of the sexual harassment? ____ ____

c. position of the individual harassed? ____ ____

d. position of the harasser? ____ ____

e. whether or not the complainant has an attorney? ____ ____

f. whether or not the complainant has notified the EEOC? ____ ____

g. whether or not the complainant has notified the press? ____ ____

h. other factors? ____ ____

Lawsuits and Other Claims of Sexual Harassment

19. Has your company experienced one or more sexual harassment-related claims, EEO charges, or lawsuits in the last two years? ____ ____

20. Have you calculated the cost to your organization of sexual harassment in terms of:

a. awards and settlement? ____ ____

b. legal fees? ____ ____

c. administrative costs? ____ ____

d. public relations costs? ____ ____

e. turnover? ____ ____

f. sick leave and personal time off? ____ ____

g. absenteeism and tardiness?   _____   _____

h. lower productivity?   _____   _____

Standards of Workplace Conduct

21. Do you allow employees to display lewd or indecent
     pictures or other materials depicting men or women
     as sex objects?   _____   _____

22. Do you require uniforms to be worn that are sexually
     provocative?   _____   _____

23. Do you allow sexually connotative remarks, sex re-
     lated jokes, or "off color" stories to be routinely told
     in front of mixed audiences?   _____   _____

24. Do you allow a sexually charged atmosphere to per-
     meate the workplace environment?   _____   _____

Workplace Anti-sexual Harassment Profile

Analysis

Questions 1 and 2

One of the first items that an EEO investigator will examine as part of
a sexual harassment investigation is your sexual harassment policy. As
the recent EEOC guidelines make clear, investigators will look for a separate policy specifically setting forth your commitment to a workplace free
from any traces of sexual harassment or a sexually-charged environment.
Simply having a general EEO, non-discrimination policy is not sufficient.
As the guidelines clearly state, a policy tailored specifically to defining,
prohibiting, investigating, and remedying sexual harassment is required.
Although the absence of such a policy is not a "per se" violation, you will
be in a better position to defend a sexual harassment charge if a formal
policy has been implemented.

Any written policy regarding sexual harassment should be broadly
drafted to insure that the full scope of prohibited sexual harassment activity is included.

Question 3

The EEOC's guidelines emphasize the need to communicate your sexual harassment policy to all supervisors and all employees. These communications may include supervisory and employee meetings or the distribution of your sexual harassment policy, either separately or as part of the employee handbook, or as a poster placed in common areas of the workplace. Because management officials, from the president to front line supervisors, are responsible for communicating, administering, enforcing, and adhering to the policy, separate meetings should be held for your management team. Records should be kept documenting when and where these educational sessions were conducted, who was present, and what was discussed. Maintaining these records will go a long way toward defending your position should a sexual harassment complaint be filed against your company. The EEOC will look at your commitment to implementing and enforcing your policy in this area.

Question 4

Employees should be informed that violations of the company's sexual harassment policy will be considered a serious violation of company rules and will be dealt with accordingly. Although there is no requirement that certain violations automatically give rise to specific forms of disciplinary action, you must emphasize that all violations will be dealt with swiftly. The punishment should be tailored to the offense, after consideration of all relevant factors. Questions 17 and 18 identify some disciplinary options, and some of the factors used in meting out discipline.

Questions 5 to 7

An internal system to facilitate employee complaints of sexual harassment should be established. The existence of this complaint procedure should be set forth in your sexual harassment policy and employees should be encouraged to utilize it if the occasion demands. The complaint procedure should give an employee the option of bypassing his or her immediate supervisor, or any other member of management, if that supervisor or manager is the subject of the complaint or is involved in any way with the complainant's difficulty. Remember, employees should be encouraged to resolve their problems internally, rather than seeking outside intervention. Indeed, it is far less costly and time consuming to handle employee problems of this nature "in house," than it is if the EEOC or local civil rights agency gets involved. In many instances, the complaining party will also be better served by a quick and effective resolution of the matter through informal channels. Once developed, you should have your policy reviewed by labor counsel to ensure that the policy conforms as closely as possible to the EEOC guidelines.

Questions 8 and 9

Once a complaint is brought to your attention, you have a duty to investigate the matter thoroughly and expeditiously. Such an investigation naturally requires tact, sensitivity, and an appreciation of the seriousness of the allegations for all concerned. Therefore, any investigation must be limited to designated individuals who have had some training in performing this function. Interviews should be handled privately and confidentially. Reports dealing with the investigation should be revealed only to those with a need to know. The investigation should also be limited to individuals designated as part of the investigation team. All information obtained as a result of the investigation should be dealt with in the strictest confidence. All parties to the investigation should be assured that their participation is appreciated, and that they will not be retaliated against in any way because of their participation and cooperation in the investigation. (For a fuller treatment of these considerations, see the discussion pertaining to questions 13–15).

Questions 10 to 12

The threat of sexual harassment in the workplace is a constant one. Therefore, you must alert supervisors to watch for signs of sexual harassment and remind them of the importance of their role in maintaining a harassment-free workplace. In addition to conducting regular training sessions, you should record the dates of these sessions and list those in attendance, so that this information is available in the event of an EEOC investigation.

It is untrue that the less said about sexual harassment the better. The causes, forms of harassment, and injury caused by sexual harassment need to be discussed. When everyone in your organization is aware of the illegality of sexual harassment, the harm caused by it, and your strong policy against it, it is less likely to flourish.

Questions 13 to 15

An important step in implementing an effective sexual harassment policy is conducting a thorough, confidential investigation of all claims. You will be better able to protect your interests and that of your employees if an incident of sexual harassment is thoroughly and immediately investigated rather than ignored. All supervisory and managerial employees, in addition to the parties involved, should be interviewed to determine if they have any knowledge of the alleged harassment. Although there are seldom witnesses to sexual harassment, other employees may have noticed a change in the victim's behavior following the incident, or the victim may have discussed the harassment with other employees. In addition, a thorough investigation is also a good source for discovering if other employees have experienced sexual harassment.

An investigation is also important in determining if the alleged conduct was unwelcome. Your company's liability is generally limited to unwelcome advances or conduct. Thus, even if the employee consented to the activity, you may still be liable if the employee demonstrated in other ways that the advance or conduct was unwelcome. An investigation may reveal whether the employee had ever manifested any objections to the activity.

The person chosen to conduct the investigation should demonstrate that you wish to encourage victims of sexual harassment to come forward. The investigator should be capable of acting impartially and you should stress in your sexual harassment policy that employees will not be subject to retaliation for filing a complaint or for cooperating in an investigation. The investigator should also have the authority to remedy any violations that he or she discovers. If the employee's supervisor normally conducts the investigation, the employee should be given the name of an alternative person to contact if the complaint involves the supervisor. If the results of the investigation are disclosed, the identity of the parties should not be revealed in order to preserve their confidentiality.

A prompt investigation followed by corrective action will greatly reduce the likelihood of you being held liable for the sexual harassment. If the sexual harassment relates to the work environment, a prompt investigation will also reduce the chance that knowledge of the harassment will be imputed to you. If the sexual harassment resulted in the loss of a promotion, discharge, or otherwise affects the victim's employment status, you can reduce your liability and promote positive employee relations by investigating the incident and remedying the problem.

Questions 16 to 18

Under Title VII of the Civil Rights Act, an employee is guaranteed the right to a work environment free of hostile or offensive behavior. You should implement a separate, preventive program to discourage sexual harassment, and the policy should be clearly and regularly communicated to employees. If sexual harassment does occur, you should take prompt corrective action and ensure that your disciplinary policy is strictly enforced. Your failure to act promptly once you know or should have known that sexual harassment exists may be interpreted as approval of the harassing employee's illegal actions. If, however, you act quickly to remedy the incident, you will generally not be held liable.

The remedy should include whatever actions are necessary to end the harassment and restore lost benefits or opportunities to the victim. The proper disciplinary action will vary from a reprimand to discharge based on the severity of the misconduct. Disciplinary measures should be strictly and consistently enforced against all employees. You should also check with the harassed employee after the matter is resolved to ensure that the harassment has not reoccurred, and that he/she has not suffered any retaliation. Although a victim is not required to exhaust the internal grievance procedure available to him or her before filing a complaint with the EEOC, the commission will normally close any charges if the matter has been satisfactorily resolved. In addition, an employee is less likely to resort to the EEOC or a state agency, which is ultimately more expensive for the employer, if the internal grievance policy is considered fair and effective.

Questions 19 and 20

An employee may use other instances of sexual harassment, especially other incidents involving the person accused of sexual harassment, to corroborate his or her complaint. If the complaint charges a hostile work environment, an employee may also use evidence of other claims against you to establish that sexual harassment was so pervasive in the workplace that you must have had knowledge of it. Thus a poor "track record" can increase the likelihood that you will incur liability in the future.

The lack of an effective sexual harassment policy can be expensive. Costly settlements and legal fees are only some of the possible financial repercussions. Sexual harassment also results in many other hidden costs, including lost productivity. NOTE: Some experts assert that most employers do not know the real cost of sexual harassment. As a result, total management commitment is lacking. The better able you are to show your management team the P & L impact of sexual harassment, the greater the commitment you will receive from them in ensuring compliance. Thus, establishing a strategy that emphasizes prevention, calculates and promulgates the real cost of sexual harassment, and implements a grievance procedure that produces fair results is the most cost-effective method of dealing with sexual harassment.

Questions 21 to 24

Even if an employee does not experience any detriment to his or her job from sexual harassment, you may still be liable if the work environment is hostile or offensive. Title VII protects an employee from having to endure an offensive environment in order to earn a living. However, you will not be liable simply because one employee is more sensitive to certain behavior than another. Instead, you will be liable if a reasonable person in similar circumstances finds the work environment offensive and abusive.

An offensive and abusive working environment is one that unreasonably interferes with the employee's ability to do his or her job. Single incidents are normally not sufficient to establish a hostile environment, although a particularly abusive incident may be sufficient to establish a violation. If the harassment consists solely of verbal conduct, the abusiveness of the work environment will depend upon the nature, frequency, context, and the intended target of the comments. In some instances, the requirement to wear revealing uniforms or other similar employment practices may be enough to constitute an abusive working environment. In workplaces where some vulgar language or actions has traditionally been tolerated, the totality of the circumstances will be considered in determining whether the environment exceeds acceptable, non-hostile levels of behavior.

EMPLOYMENT-LABOR
LAW AUDIT (ELLA)

Second Edition,
Revised

Laurdan Associates, Inc.
Potomac, Maryland
1993

Copyright 1990, 1991, 1992, 1993
by
Laurdan Associates, Inc.
10220 River Road
Potomac, Maryland 20854

This publication is designed to provide general information on a variety of employment and labor relations subjects. It covers most federal labor and employment relations and discrimination laws, but excludes ERISA and some aspects of laws relating to government and defense contracting. Likewise, ELLA concentrates on applicable federal labor and employment-related laws in effect as of the date of this publication, but does not address the specific requirements of state and local labor and employment laws.

In order to ensure that all legal obligations are fully addressed, the reader is directed to seek the advice of competent employment law counsel. Statements made in this publication have neither the effect of law or regulation nor constitute the rendering of legal, accounting, or other professional services by the authors or publisher.

As with the results of any survey or audit procedure, the reader is cautioned on the necessity of addressing any legal deficiencies uncovered by the audit review procedure. The results of your internal audit may be subject to discovery in any legal proceedings involving labor and employment relations practices and procedures. Therefore, it is strongly suggested that, if the audit reveals possible legal deficiencies, you seek the advice of competent legal counsel in bringing your practices and procedures into compliance with the federal laws addressed in this manual, as well as the state and local labor and employment relations laws which apply in your jurisdiction.

INDEX